Critical Survey of Long Fiction

Satirical Novelists

Editor

Carl Rollyson

Baruch College, City University of New York

Salem Press

Ipswich, Massachusetts • Hackensack, New Jersey

Cover photo:
Joseph Heller (© Deborah Feingold/Corbis)

978-1-4298-3685-2

CONTENTS

CONTRIBUTORS

Andrew J. Angyal
Elon University

Margaret Boe Birns
New York University

B. Diane Blackwood
International Press Club of Chicago

Henry L. Carrigan, Jr.
Northwestern University

John R. Clark
Original Contributor

Richard Hauer Costa
Texas A&M University

J. Madison Davis
Original Contributor

Lillian Doherty
Original Contributor

Grace Eckley
Original Contributor

Nettie Farris
University of Louisville

Richard A. Fine
Original Contributor

June M. Frazer
Original Contributor

John L. Grigsby
Appalachian Research and Defense Fund of Kentucky

Melanie Hawthorne
Original Contributor

Gregory D. Horn
Southwest Virginia Community College

Irma M. Kashuba
Original Contributor

John V. Knapp
Original Contributor

Rebecca Kuzins
Pasadena, California

Lawrence F. Laban
Original Contributor

Avril S. Lewis
Original Contributor

Leon Lewis
Appalachian State University

James J. Lynch
Original Contributor

Richard D. McGhee
Arkansas State University

Charles E. May
California State University, Long Beach

Laurence W. Mazzeno
Alvernia College

Martha Nochimson
Original Contributor

Jim O'Loughlin
Penn State Erie, The Behrend College

Donald Palumbo
Original Contributor

Karen Priest
Original Contributor

Rosemary M. Canfield Reisman
Charleston Southern University

Joseph Rosenblum
Original Contributor

Elizabeth D. Schafer
Loachapoka, Alabama

Millicent Sharma
Original Contributor

George Soule
Carleton College

Brian Stableford
Reading, England

Judith K. Taylor
Erlanger, Kentucky

Shawncey Webb
Taylor University

Michael Witkoski
Columbia, South Carolina

Gay Pitman Zieger
Santa Fe College

Satirical Novelists

The Critical Survey series provides students and general readers with in-depth profiles of major authors in one of the major literary genres or forms—in this case, long fiction. While the profiled authors may have written in other genres as well, sometimes to great acclaim, the focus of this volume is on their most important works as they relate to fiction.

Satire is the use of ridicule, hyperbole, absurdity, irony, or similar rhetorical devices in order to expose a problem, weakness, or vice of an individual, group of people, or aspect of society or culture. It is primarily found in literature, and dates back to the beginning of human writing. Examples of what we might consider satire can be found in ancient Egyptian and Greek texts, although the specific designation of the form did not come into use until Latin language texts in the Common Era. The Roman poet Juvenal wrote virulent Satires directed at the corruption and incompetence in his society; these in turn strongly influenced the modern prose form of social satire characterized by the writings of eighteenth-century Irish author Jonathan Swift.

This volume of the Critical Survey series is designed to provide readers with an extensive overview of satirical novels and novelists in the Western tradition of prose writing. The essays included here represent the most influential authors and works starting from the sixteenth century with French author François Rabelais to contemporary writers like Colson Whitehead and Tom Wolfe. In selecting the material for this volume, an effort has been made to represent a broad range of perspectives from authors of different time periods, cultures, social backgrounds, age, and gender, while focusing on issues that are relevant to today's readers.

Because the nature of satire is based upon voice rather than any one subject, the biographies and analyses in this volume deal with those literary texts that are innovative in their own right, but that have had a profound impact on modern literature, shaping the Western culture and society of the last century. Included are writers such as H.G. Wells, whose novella *The Invisible Man* aimed a critical eye at the structure of society, political values, and the importance of science, but has also influenced contemporary popular culture. Other writers like Laurence Sterne, French author Voltaire, and English novelist Henry Fielding have made a major impact on the developing modern perspective on politics, social and cultural roles, and class. Contemporary authors such as William S. Burroughs, Kurt Vonnegut, Vladimir Nabokov, Gish Jen, and Alison Lurie demonstrate how satire has been treated, developed, and reinvented from its historic roots.

Since its birth in the poetry of the ancient world, satire has become one of the most popular genres of modern Western prose. Skewering religion, science, society, cultural values, race, gender inequality, and the hypocrisy of the common person, the breadth of satire is seemingly limitless. As long as individuals continue to find fault with the individuals and institutions around them and are free to express this dissatisfaction openly, satire will continue to flourish.

WILLIAM S. BURROUGHS

Born: St. Louis, Missouri; February 5, 1914
Died: Lawrence, Kansas; August 2, 1997
Also known as: William Seward Burroughs II; William Lee

PRINCIPAL LONG FICTION

Junkie, 1953
The Naked Lunch, 1959 (republished as *Naked Lunch*, 1962)
The Soft Machine, 1961
The Ticket That Exploded, 1962
Dead Fingers Talk, 1963
Nova Express, 1964
The Wild Boys: A Book of the Dead, 1971
Port of Saints, 1973
Cities of the Red Night, 1981
The Place of Dead Roads, 1983
The Burroughs File, 1984
Queer, 1985
The Western Lands, 1987
Ghost of Chance, 1995
My Education: A Book of Dreams, 1995

OTHER LITERARY FORMS

Because of their experimental techniques, the works of William S. Burroughs (BUR-ohz) are especially difficult to classify within established literary forms. *Exterminator!* (1973), for example, although published as a "novel," is actually a collection of previously published poems, short stories, and essays. Other unclassifiable works are book-length experiments, often written in collaboration and in the "cut-up, fold-in" technique pioneered by Burroughs, which might be considered novels by some. The "cut-up, fold-in" technique is similar to the picture art of collage in that text from other authors, news stories, or other works is randomly inserted and then reedited to go with the general text by the author. Examples among Burroughs's works are *Minutes to Go* (1960), written in collaboration with Sinclair Beiles, Gregory Corso, and Brion Gysin; *The Exterminator* (1960), written with Gysin; *Time* (1965), which contains drawings by Gysin; and *Œuvre Croisée* (1976), written in collaboration with Gysin and reissued as *The Third Mind* in 1978. *White Subway* (1965), *Apomorphine* (1969), and *The Job: Interviews with William S. Burroughs* (1970), written in collaboration with Daniel Odier, are additional short-story and essay collections. *The Dead Star* (1969) is a journalistic essay that contains photo-collage inserts, *APO-33 Bulletin: A Metabolic Regulator* (1966) is a pamphlet, and *Elec-*

tronic Revolution, 1970-71 (1971) is an essay that fantasizes bizarre political and business uses for the cut-up, fold-in technique.

Burroughs also published scores of essays, stories, and articles in numerous journals, periodicals, and short-lived magazines. One of Burroughs's most revealing publications, *The Yage Letters* (1963), collects his correspondence with Allen Ginsberg concerning Burroughs's 1952 expedition to South America in search of yage, a legendary hallucinogen. In these letters, Burroughs is Govinda, the master, to Ginsberg's Siddhartha, the disciple.

ACHIEVEMENTS

William S. Burroughs's best-known novel, *Naked Lunch*, was made notorious by American censorship attempts and consequently became a best seller. Burroughs, who wrote primarily for a cult audience, was essentially a fantasist and satirist (some of his work is also considered science fiction), and he is often misread; in these respects he has been compared accurately to Jonathan Swift. Both writers focus on the faults and evils of humankind and society, employ fantastic satire to ridicule these shortcomings, and hope through this vehicle to effect some positive change in the human condition. Burroughs's works are exceptionally vicious satires, however, "necessarily brutal, obscene and disgusting"—his own description of them—because they must mime the situations from which their recurring images and metaphors (of drug addiction, aberrant sexual practices, and senseless violence) are drawn.

Burroughs's focus on drug addiction and the paranoia and nonlinear thought processes of his characters also make his writing comparable to some of Phillip K. Dick's novels, such as *The Man in the High Castle* (1962) and *A Scanner Darkly* (1977). Burroughs's work *Blade Runner: A Movie* (1979), although unrelated to the 1982 Ridley Scott film *Blade Runner*, which is based on Dick's work *Do Androids Dream of Electric Sheep?* (1968), may have at least been the inspiration for the motion picture's title.

Superficially, Burroughs's satiric attacks are aimed at humanity's "addictions" to pleasure or power in any of the many forms either craving might take. Those who, obeying the dictates of "the algebra of need," will stop at nothing to fulfill their desires have, in the terms of the moral allegory Burroughs creates, "lost their human citizenship" and become nonhuman parasites feeding on the life essences of others. They shamelessly lie, cheat, and manipulate to attain what Burroughs's associative imagery repeatedly equates with perversion, excrement, and death. Burroughs's satire, however, cuts deeper than this. It attacks not only humankind and its addictions but also the structures of the cultures that enable these addictions to flourish and proliferate. It attacks the myths and linguistic formulas that imprison the human race, the stone walls of patriotism and religion. It demands that people first free themselves from these "word and image addictions" before they kick their more obvious habits and regain their humanity, and thus calls for nothing less than a revolution of consciousness.

The Grove Press edition of *Naked Lunch* became a national best seller and was cleared of obscenity charges in Los Angeles in 1965 and in Massachusetts in 1966. Ginsberg and Norman Mailer, who described Burroughs as "the only American novelist living today who may conceivably be possessed by genius," were among those who testified in the book's defense. While it does detail with exceptional brutality the ugly, revolting, and perverse, *Naked Lunch* is at bottom a strikingly moral but darkly comic work that employs irony and allegory, as well as more unconventional techniques, to satirize much that is false and defective in modern American life in particular and human nature in general. Especially effective as a subliminal argument against heroin abuse, the book's successful publication in the United States elevated its then practically unknown author to membership in the literary elite.

Many reviewers—some seemingly oblivious to the irony of Burroughs's works—have not been responsive or sympathetic to his themes and techniques, and none of his novels after *Naked Lunch*, with the exception of *The Wild Boys*, received comparable critical acclaim. Whereas *Naked Lunch* was lauded by Terry Southern, Mary McCarthy, Karl Shapiro, and Marshall McLuhan, as well as by Ginsberg and Mailer, the less successfully realized subsequent novels were considered by some critics, not totally inaccurately, as "language without content" and "the world's greatest put-on." Burroughs himself admitted that "*Naked Lunch* demands silence from the reader. Otherwise he is taking his own pulse."

Burroughs warned that his novels do not present their "content" in the manner the reader ordinarily anticipates. One of the triumphs of his unique style is that he has created a low-content form, a narrative near vacuum, on which unwary readers are tempted to project their own psyches, personal myths, and forgotten dreams. While they do have their own messages to convey, his works also encourage readers to develop or invent their own private fictions and to append them to the skeletal narrative structures provided by the author. Readers are thus invited to create Burroughs's works as they read them. In place of relying on the easily perceived, clearly coherent stories one might have expected, Burroughs's best works keep one reading through the hypnotic fascination of the author's flow of images and incantatory prose.

Biography

William Seward Burroughs II was born on February 5, 1914, in St. Louis, Missouri, to Mortimer Perry Burroughs, son of the industrialist William Seward Burroughs I, who founded the Burroughs Adding Machine company. His mother was Laura Hammond Lee, whose family claimed direct descent from Robert E. Lee, Civil War general and commander in chief of the Confederate army. Dominated by his mother's obsessive Victorian prudery and haunted by vivid nightmares and hallucinations, Burroughs led a restless childhood. He was educated in private schools in St. Louis and Los Alamos, New Mexico, where he developed seemingly disparate fascinations with literature and crime. He later studied ethnology and archaeology at Harvard University, where he encountered a group of wealthy gay men. He graduated with an A.B. in 1936, and upon his graduation, his parents bestowed on him a monthly trust of two hundred dollars that allowed Burroughs a great deal of freedom from daily concerns.

Subsequently, Burroughs traveled to Europe. He briefly studied medicine at the University of Vienna, where he met Ilse Klapper, whom he married so that she—a Jewish woman fleeing Nazi Germany—could obtain an American visa. They remained friends, but Ilse divorced Burroughs nine years later, in 1946. Burroughs returned to the United States and Harvard to resume his anthropological studies, which he soon abandoned because of his conviction that academic life is little more than a series of intrigues broken by teas. Although he attempted to use family connections to obtain a position with the Office of Strategic Services, Burroughs was rejected after he deliberately cut off the first joint of his left little finger in a Vincent van Gogh-like attempt to impress a male friend. Moving to New York City, he worked as a bartender and in an advertising agency for a year and underwent psychoanalysis. Burroughs entered the U.S. Army in 1942 as a glider pilot trainee, engineered his discharge for psychological reasons six months later, and then moved to Chicago, where he easily found work as an exterminator and a private detective, among other odd jobs.

In 1943, Burroughs returned to New York City and met Joan Vollmer, a student at Columbia University; they married on January 17, 1945. Because Burroughs's divorce from Ilse was not yet final, several sources describe Joan as his common-law wife. She introduced Burroughs to Jack Kerouac, who in turn introduced him to Ginsberg. The Beat generation was born in Burroughs's 115th Street apartment after Burroughs acquainted Kerouac and Ginsberg with the writings of William Blake, Arthur Rimbaud, and others; the three friends soon emerged as leaders of the movement. Late in 1944, Herbert Huncke, a Times Square hustler involved in criminal activity to support his drug habit, introduced Burroughs to the use of morphine and its derivatives. Burroughs was for most of the next thirteen years a heroin addict who frequently altered his place of residence to evade the police.

In 1946, Burroughs moved to Waverly, Texas, where he tried farming; he and his wife had a son, William, Jr., in 1947. Burroughs voluntarily entered a drug rehabilitation center at Lexington, Kentucky, in 1948. Returning to Waverly and already back on drugs, Burroughs was hounded by the police until he moved to Algiers, Louisiana, later that same year. To avoid prosecution for illegal possession of drugs and firearms after a 1949 raid on his Algiers farm, Burroughs relocated to Mexico City in 1950, where he began writing *Junkie*. He continued his archaeological studies at Mexico City University, pursuing an interest in the Mayan codices. On September 7, 1951, Burroughs accidentally killed his wife, Joan, while allegedly attempting to shoot a drinking glass off her head while playing "William Tell." Although Mexican authorities let the matter drop, Burroughs soon left Mexico for the jungles of Colombia.

He returned again to New York City in 1953, the year *Junkie* was published, lived for a while with Ginsberg, and then settled in Tangier, Morocco, where from 1955 to 1958 he was frequently visited by other Beat writers and worked on the manuscript that would develop into his quartet of science-fiction-like novels: *Naked Lunch*, *The Soft Machine*, *Nova Express*, and *The Ticket That Exploded*. In 1957, Burroughs again sought treatment for his heroin addiction. This time he placed himself in the care of John Yerby Dent, an English physician who treated drug addicts with apomorphine—a crystalline alkaloid derivative of morphine—a drug Burroughs praises and mythologizes in his writings. The following year, cured of his addiction, Burroughs moved to Paris, where *The Naked Lunch* was published in 1959.

In 1960, Gysin, who had helped Burroughs select the Paris edition of *The Naked Lunch* from a suitcase full of manuscript pages, introduced his experimental "cut-up" technique to Burroughs and collaborated with him on *The Exterminator* and *Minutes to Go*. Burroughs's literary reputation was firmly established with the American publication of *Naked Lunch* in 1962, and by the mid-1960's Burroughs had settled in London. He returned to St. Louis for a visit in 1965, covered the Democratic National Convention for *Esquire* in 1968, and moved again to New York to teach writing at City College of New York in 1974. In 1975, he embarked on a reading tour of the United States and conducted a writers' workshop in Denver, Colorado. After returning to London briefly, Burroughs settled in New York. In 1983, he was inducted into the American Academy and Institute of Arts and Letters.

In the late 1980's and early 1990's Burroughs did cameo roles, voice work, and writing for several movies and television shows and consulted on the film version of his book *Naked Lunch*, which was written and directed by David Cronenberg and released in late 1991. Burroughs published a number of novels and collections throughout the 1980's and 1990's, including 1987's *The Western Lands*, the last novel in the trilogy that includes *Cities of the Red Night* and *The Place of Dead Roads*. Shortly after the publication of this novel, Burroughs moved to rural Kansas, where he died in 1997.

ANALYSIS

William S. Burroughs did not begin writing seriously until 1950, although he had unsuccessfully submitted a story titled "Twilight's Last Gleaming" to *Esquire* in 1938. His first novelistic effort, *Queer*, which deals with homosexuality, was not published until 1985. Allen Ginsberg finally persuaded Ace Books to publish Burroughs's first novel, *Junkie*, which originally appeared under the pseudonym William Lee as half of an Ace double paperback; it was bound with Maurice Helbront's *Narcotic Agent*. While strictly conventional in style, *Junkie* is a luridly hyperbolic, quasi-autobiographical first-person account of the horrors of drug addiction. Of little literary merit in itself, this first novel is interesting in that it introduces not only the main character, Lee, but also several of the major motifs that appear in Burroughs's subsequent works: the central metaphor of drug addiction, the related image of man reduced to a subhuman form (usually an insectlike creature) by his drug and other lusts, and the suggestion of concomitant and pervasive sexual aberration.

In *Naked Lunch* and its three less celebrated sequels, *The Soft Machine*, *Nova Express*, and *The Ticket That Exploded*, Burroughs weaves an intricate and horrible allegory of human greed, corruption, and debasement. Like Aldous Huxley's *Brave New World* (1932) and George Orwell's *Nineteen Eighty-Four* (1949), these four works seize on the evils—or the tendencies toward a certain type of evil—that the author sees as particularly malignant in the contemporary world and project them into a dystopian future, where, magnified, they grow monstrous and take on an exaggerated and fantastic shape.

While progressively clarifying and developing Burroughs's thought, these novels share themes, metaphorical images, characters, and stylistic mannerisms. In them, Burroughs utilizes the "cut-up, fold-in" technique, which has its closest analogue in the cinematic technique of montage. He juxtaposes one scene with another without regard to plot, character, or, in the short view, theme, to promote an association of the reader's negative emotional reaction to the content of certain scenes (sexual perversion, drug abuse, senseless violence) with the implied allegorical content of others (examples of "addictions" to drugs, money, sex, power). The theory is that if such juxtapositions recur often enough, the feeling of revulsion strategically created by the first set of images will form the reader's negative attitude toward the second set of examples.

In these novels, Burroughs develops a science-fiction-like, paranoid fantasy wherein, on a literal level, Earth and its human inhabitants have been taken over by the Nova Mob, an assortment of extraterrestrial, non-three-dimensional entities who live parasitically on the reality of other organisms. Exploitation of Earth has reached such proportions that the intergalactic Nova Police have been alerted. The Nova Police are attempting to thwart the Nova Mob without so alarming them that they will detonate the planet in an attempt to destroy the evidence (and thus escape prosecution in the biologic courts) while trying to make what escape they can. The most direct form of Nova control, control that enables the Nova Mob to carry on its viruslike metaphysical vampirism with impunity, is thought control of the human population through control of the mass-communication media. Nova Mob concepts and perspectives attach themselves to and are replicated by the terrestrial host media much as a virus invades and reproduces through a host organism, a thought-control process analogous to the "cut-up, fold-in" technique itself. By the middle of *Nova Express*, the reader is caught up in a war of images in which the weapons are cameras and tape recorders. The Nova Police and the inhabitants of Earth have discovered how to combat the Nova Mob with their own techniques (of which these novels are examples) and are engaged in a guerrilla war with the Nova Criminals, who are desperately trying to cut and run. The ending of *The Ticket That Exploded* is optimistic for Earth but inconclusive, leaving the reader to wonder if Earth will be rid of the Nova Mob or destroyed by it.

NAKED LUNCH

A vividly and relentlessly tasteless fantasy-satire that portrays humankind's innate greed and lack of compassion in general and contemporary American institutions and values in particular, *Naked Lunch* immerses the reader in the impressions and sensations of William Lee (Burroughs's pseudonym in *Junkie*). Lee is an agent of the Nova Police who has assumed the cover of a gay heroin addict because with such a cover he is most likely to encounter Nova Criminals, who are all addicts of one sort or another and thus prefer to operate through human addict collaborators. Nothing of importance seems to occur in the novel, and little of what does happen is explained. Only toward the conclusion does the reader even suspect that Lee is some sort of agent "clawing at a not-yet of Telepathic Bureaucracies, Time Monopolies, Control Drugs, Heavy Fluid Addicts." The "naked lunch" of the title is that reality seen by Lee, that "frozen moment when everyone sees what is on the end of every fork." The random scenes of mutilation and depravity, bleak homosexual encounters, and desperate scrambles for drug connections into which the book plunges yield its two key concepts: the idea of addiction, the central conceit that human beings become hooked on power, pleasure, illusions, and so on much as junkies do on heroin, and that of "the algebra of need," which states simply that an addict faced with absolute need (as a junkie is) will do anything to satisfy that need.

The Nova Criminals are nonhuman personifications of various addictions. The Uranians, addicted to Heavy Metal Fluid, are types of drug addicts. Dr. Benway, Mr. Bradley Mr. Martin (a single character), and the insect people of Minraud—all control addicts—are types of the human addiction to power. The green boy-girls of Venus, addicted to Venusian sexual practices, are types of the human addiction to sensual pleasure. The Death Dwarf, addicted to concentrated words and images, is the analogue of the human addiction to various cultural myths and beliefs; he is perhaps the most pathetic of these depraved creatures. Burroughs explains: "Junk yields a basic formula of 'evil' virus: the face of evil is always the face of total need. A dope fiend is a man in total need of dope. Beyond a certain frequency need knows absolutely no limit or control." As poet and literary critic John Ciardi noted, "Only after the first shock does one realize that what Burroughs is writing about is not only the destruction of depraved men by their drug lust, but the destruction of all men by their consuming addictions, whether the addiction be drugs or over-righteous propriety or sixteen-year-old girls."

THE SOFT MACHINE

Burroughs viewed *The Soft Machine* as "a sequel to *Naked Lunch*, a mathematical extension of the Algebra of Need beyond the Junk virus." Here, the consuming addiction, displayed again in juxtaposition with scenes of drug abuse and sexual perversion, and through a number of shifting narrators, is the addiction to power over others. The central episode is the destruction by a time-traveling agent of the control apparatus of the ancient Mayan theocracy (Burroughs's primary archaeological interest), which exercises its control through the manipulation of myths; this is a clear analogue of the present-day struggle between the Nova Police and the Nova Mob that breaks into the open in the subsequent two novels.

The time traveler uses the same technique to prepare himself for time travel as Burroughs does in writing his novels, a type of "cut-up, fold-in" montage: "I started my trip in the morgue with old newspapers, folding in today with yesterday and typing out composites." Because words tie people to time, the time traveler is given apomorphine (used to cure Burroughs of his heroin addiction) to break this connection.

The "soft machine" is both the "wounded galaxy," the Milky Way seen as a biological organism diseased by the viruslike Nova Mob, and the human body, riddled with parasites and addictions and programmed with the "ticket," obsolete myths and dreams, written on the "soft typewriter" of culture and civilization. Burroughs contends that any addiction dehumanizes its victims. The Mayan priests, for example, tend to become half-man, half-crab creatures who eventually metamorphose into giant centipedes and exude an erogenous green slime. Such hideous transformations also strike Lee, a heroin addict, and other homosexuals. Bradley the Buyer, who reappears as Mr. Bradley Mr. Martin, Mr. and Mrs. D., and the Ugly Spirit, has a farcical habit of turning into a bloblike creature who is addicted to and absorbs drug addicts.

NOVA EXPRESS *and* THE TICKET THAT EXPLODED

Instances of metamorphosis are almost innumerable in *Nova Express* and *The Ticket That Exploded*. These novels most clearly reveal the quartet's plot and explore the Nova Mob's exploitation of media. Here addiction to language is investigated. As Stephen Koch has argued: "Burroughs's ideology . . . is based on an image of consciousness in bondage to the organism: better, of consciousness as an organism, gripped by the tropisms of need. Consciousness is addicted—it is here the drug metaphor enters—to what sustains it and gives it definition: in particular, it is addicted to the word, the structures of language that define meaning and thus reality itself." Thus, while in *The Soft Machine* the time traveler is sent to Trak News Agency (the motto of which is "We don't report the news—we write it") to learn how to defeat the Mayan theocracy by first learning "how this writing the news before it happens is done," in *The Ticket That Exploded* it is axiomatic that "you can run a government without police if your conditioning program is tight enough but you can't run a government without [nonsense and deception]."

Contemporary existence is seen ultimately as a film that is rerun again and again, trapping the human soul like an insect imprisoned in amber, negating any possibility of choice or freedom. In these last two novels of the quartet, Burroughs issues a call for revolt against humanity's imprisoning addiction to language. In *Nova Express*, he notes that "their garden of delights is a terminal sewer" and demands that everyone heed the last words of Hassan I Sabbah (cribbed out of context from Fyodor Dostoevski's Ivan Karamazov): "Nothing is True—Everything is Permitted." In *The Ticket That Exploded*,

Burroughs rages, "Better than the 'real thing'?—There is no real thing—Maya—Maya—It's all show business."

The Wild Boys

Burroughs's other notably science-fiction-like novel, *The Wild Boys*, is also composed of scenes linked more by associated images than by any clearly linear narrative framework. Here the author posits a bizarre alternative to the problematic apocalypse-in-progress depicted in his earlier quartet. In a world wrecked by famine and controlled by police, the wild boys, a homosexual tribe of hashish smokers, have withdrawn themselves from space and time through indifference and have developed into a counterculture complete with its own language, rituals, and economy. The existence of this counterculture poses a threat to those who create the false images on which the larger, repressive, external society is based, but the wild boys cannot be tamed because their cold indifference to the mass culture entails a savagery that refuses to submit to control. Although Burroughs's thinking clearly becomes more political in *The Wild Boys* and in the book that followed it, *Exterminator!*, a collection of short stories and poems that revolve around the common theme of death through sinister forces, his primary concern for freedom from the controllers and manipulators—chemical, political, sexual, and cultural—remains constant from the beginning of his literary career.

Cities of the Red Night

Continuing the utopian vision of *The Wild Boys*, but encompassing it into a larger, more anthropological context, Burroughs's next three works form a trilogy to expand his vision of society and its place in the natural order. The first book in the series, *Cities of the Red Night*, continues the twin themes of freedom from control and the power of mythmaking, but does so on a much larger scale. One of Burroughs's longest works, *Cities of the Red Night* is unique in that in it he sustains a rather conventional narrative voice, utilizing conventional popular genre, to achieve a re-creation of history through fantasy and myth.

The novel begins with three distinct plots that seem at first to be only tenuously related. One plot concerns a retroactive utopia founded by eighteenth century pirates, which Burroughs uses as a foundation for social criticism. A second plot, from which the title comes, depicts mythical "cities of the red night," which existed in prehistoric time and function as a dystopia through which the reader views present culture. A third plot involves a present-day investigator who traces the mystery of a deadly virus known as B-23 to its historical origins in the "cities of the red night." Each plot employs conventions from one popular genre or another: The story of the utopian pirates' colony reads very much like a boys' adventure story, the story of the advanced prehistoric cities takes its structure from science fiction, and the story of the investigation of the virus lends itself to the conventions of the hard-boiled detective story.

THE PLACE OF DEAD ROADS

In the second book of the trilogy, *The Place of Dead Roads*, Burroughs continues the process of mythmaking. His protagonist is Kim Carsons, a late nineteenth century gunslinger who utilizes a sort of "hole in time," a phenomenon introduced in *Cities of the Red Night*. Through this hole, Carsons becomes a time traveler, moving precariously across time and space, encountering different cultures and time periods in an effort to forge some sense of the whole, some sense of control over his own destiny. He seeks fulfillment in disparate, almost lonely, gay-sex encounters; in drugs; and in the sense of power he feels by manipulating others.

The story begins with a clipping from a Boulder, Colorado, newspaper that tells the reader that William Seward Hall, who writes Western novels under the pen name Kim Carsons, was shot in a gunfight in the year 1899. The story then introduces the character Carsons and, after a disjointed series of adventures and misadventures, returns the reader to that same date when Carsons loses his life, as if to say that destiny will not be averted in the end. The similarity of Carsons's true name to Burroughs's is striking here because, like Hall, Burroughs tends to fictionalize himself as author, as though authors can reach their true potential only through the lives of their characters—perhaps another way of understanding Burroughs's fascination with somehow circumventing destiny through manipulation.

THE WESTERN LANDS

In the third book of the trilogy, *The Western Lands*, the reader learns that Carsons was not shot by his opponent, Mike Chase, but by a killer from the Land of the Dead named Joe, described as a NO (Natural Outlaw), whose job it is to break natural laws. The Western land itself is a mythical place, a utopian vision of a place beyond one's images of Earth and Heaven—a land where natural law, religious law, and human law have no meaning. It is a paradise, but a paradise difficult to reach.

The intent of Burroughs's trilogy is first to create a science-fiction myth that explains all of human history, then to reveal the power of fantasy and myth to offer alternative histories, and finally, by realizing these alternative histories, to explore alternative anthropological patterns by which to organize society. The three separate plots interrelate and merge at various points throughout the trilogy, but eventually each is abandoned before completion—a technique that, Burroughs claimed, allows readers to create their own stories, to engage their own sense of mythmaking. Readers are encouraged to play a kind of "what if" game along with Burroughs: What if the Spanish had not defeated the New World into submission? What if the true foundations of liberty and individual freedom had taken hold in the Third World? What if all of our assumptions, whether religious, historical, or psychological, are wrong? This process of mythmaking in Burroughs is not a means to an end; rather, it is the object of the struggle—the great creative process of defining and redefining ourselves, which is our ultimate defense against those who would manipulate us.

Queer

Set in Mexico and South America during the 1940's, *Queer* details in fictional guise both the author's homosexual longing and his drug addiction. Burroughs wrote, "While it was I who wrote *Junky* [*sic*], I feel that I was being written in *Queer*." Although it was not published until 1985 because of its homosexual content, *Queer* was Burroughs's first attempt at novel writing. It is the most linear and perhaps most coherent of Burroughs's novels.

William Lee is the story's protagonist, and, though not told in first person, the novel looks at the world through his eyes. Lee shares much in common with Burroughs, as explained in the novel's introduction. Lee is a heroin addict mostly trying to kick the habit. He lusts for boys and young men, and he has an obsession with Eugene Allerton, a younger bisexual man who tolerates Lee until better circumstances happen along. Part of the story involves Lee's search, with Allerton in tow, for a plant-based hallucinogen called yage that is purported to enhance telepathic powers. In *The Yage Letters*, Burroughs's letters regarding his real-life search for yage are collected.

Queer is a short novel—only 134 pages—prefaced by a 23-page introduction by Burroughs in which he further explains Lee's motivations and actions along with some of his own. Lee is looking for an audience, a distraction from the drug addiction, and, like many addicts, becomes obsessive about a sex object in replacement. Allerton is that object, and, in order to keep his audience interested, Lee develops what he calls "Routines": entertaining, shocking, or outrageous stories to amuse and draw attention. These stories, interwoven into the love-story travelogue, provide flashes of humor that are sometimes perverse, such as the recipe for pig served cooked on the outside but still living on the inside or the story of "Corn Hole Gus' Used-Slave Lot."

Burroughs's Mexico of the 1940's is seedy and primitive. Many of the characters in the book are fellow American expatriates, and the highlight of their day is to stop in at the local bars to share the latest gossip. In the twenty-first century world of television, video games, and cell phones, younger readers may find the place descriptions more like nightmares than like historic information—especially as the switches among inner musings, location descriptions, and "Routines" are not always clearly demarcated. William Lee continues his adventures in *Naked Lunch*.

Although Burroughs's innovative, highly unconventional fiction style and often abrasive thematic preoccupations are not without their detractors, by the end of his career Burroughs had firmly established his place as one of late twentieth century fiction's most significant innovators. In fact, his "cut-up" technique has reached beyond the bounds of obscure cult fiction to influence both mainstream cinema and popular music. Burroughs played a semiautobiographical role as Tom the Priest in Gus Van Sant's 1989 film about drug addiction, *Drugstore Cowboy*; in 1991, acclaimed director David Cronenberg adapted *Naked Lunch* to the screen. In her introduction to his unprecedented reading on the popular American television show *Saturday Night Live* in 1981, actor Lauren Hutton lauded Burroughs as "America's greatest living writer," and rock music icons Lou Reed and David Bowie have both recognized Burroughs's disjointed and surreal but surprisingly moralistic approach to writing as enormously influential on their own work. The heavy metal genre of rock-and-roll music takes its name from a phrase in Burroughs's *Naked Lunch*, and the name of the popular band Steely Dan is also borrowed from his writing.

Upon his death in 1997 at age eighty-three, Burroughs was eulogized as everything from the "most dangerous" of Beat writers to the undisputed patriarch of this important movement in twentieth century American writing. Although Burroughs's lifelong penchant for the cutting edge of fiction continues to intimidate some scholars and critics, none can dispute his role as a significant innovator and catalyst for change in twentieth century fiction and popular culture.

Donald Palumbo; Gregory D. Horn
Updated by B. Diane Blackwood

OTHER MAJOR WORKS

NONFICTION: *The Yage Letters*, 1963 (with Allen Ginsberg); *APO-33 Bulletin: A Metabolic Regulator*, 1966; *The Job: Interviews with William S. Burroughs*, 1970 (with Daniel Odier); *Electronic Revolution, 1970-71*, 1971; *Letters to Allen Ginsberg, 1953-1957*, 1983; *The Adding Machine: Collected Essays*, 1985; *The Cat Inside*, 1992; *The Letters of William S. Burroughs, 1945-1959*, 1993 (Oliver Harris, editor); *Conversations with William S. Burroughs*, 1999 (Allen Hibbard, editor); *Last Words: The Final Journals of William S. Burroughs*, 2000; *Everything Lost: The Latin American Notebook of William S. Burroughs*, 2008 (Oliver Harris, editor).

MISCELLANEOUS: *The Exterminator*, 1960 (with Brion Gysin); *Minutes to Go*, 1960 (with Sinclair Beiles, Gregory Corso, and Gysin); *Time*, 1965 (drawings by Gysin); *White Subway*, 1965; *Apomorphine*, 1969; *The Dead Star*, 1969; *The Last Words of Dutch Schultz*, 1970; *Exterminator!*, 1973; *The Book of Breeething*, 1974; *Œuvre Croisée*, 1976 (with Gysin; also known as *The Third Mind*, 1978); *Blade Runner: A Movie*, 1979; *Interzone*, 1989; *Word Virus: The William S. Burroughs Reader*, 1998 (James Grauerholz and Ira Silverberg, editors).

BIBLIOGRAPHY

Burroughs, William S. *Burroughs Live*. Cambridge, Mass.: MIT Press, 2002. Collection of interviews is informative for readers hoping for a personal glimpse of the novelist. Burroughs, however, was notorious with interviewers for being a difficult subject to draw out.

Caveney, Graham. *Gentleman Junkie: The Life and Legacy of William S. Burroughs*. Boston: Little, Brown, 1998. Unconventional biography features an imaginative visual presentation that superimposes the text on reproductions of photographs, newspaper clippings, and other visual elements, all printed on multicolored pages. Considers the myths and legends surrounding Burroughs as well as his life and influence on later generations of musicians, writers, and artists.

Goodman, Michael Barry. *Contemporary Literary Censorship: The Case History of Burroughs's "Naked Lunch."* Metuchen, N.J.: Scarecrow Press, 1981. Offers a narrative history of the writing, publication, critical reception, and subsequent censorship of *Naked Lunch* in the United States. Provides much previously unpublished Burroughs material.

Harris, Oliver. *William Burroughs and the Secret of Fascination.* Carbondale: Southern Illinois University Press, 2003. Focuses on the novels *Junkie*, *Queer*, and *Naked Lunch*, as well as *The Yage Letters*, to trace Burroughs's creative history during the 1950's.

Hibbard, Allen, ed. *Conversations with William S. Burroughs.* Jackson: University Press of Mississippi, 1999. Collection of previously published interviews with the author spans thirty-five years (1961-1996). Includes chronology and index.

Johnson, Rob. *The Lost Years of William S. Burroughs: Beats in South Texas.* College Station: Texas A&M University Press, 2006. Discusses Burroughs's experiences during a period in his life (1946-1949) before he began publishing, when he farmed cotton (as well as marijuana and opium poppies) and socialized with Beat writers such as Allen Ginsberg and Neal Cassady. Sheds some light on Burroughs's early work. Includes illustrations and index.

Lardas, John. *The Bop Apocalypse: The Religious Visions of Kerouac, Ginsberg, and Burroughs.* Urbana: University of Illinois Press, 2001. Combines cultural history, biography, and literary criticism in examining the spiritualism and religious concerns of the three Beat writers.

Morgan, Ted. *Literary Outlaw: The Life and Times of William S. Burroughs.* New York: Holt, 1988. Standard biography remains an important source of information on Burroughs. Examines his life and career, with particular emphasis on the influence of other Beat writers on his work.

Skerl, Jennie. *William S. Burroughs.* Boston: Twayne, 1985. Attempts to provide an overview of contemporary thought on Burroughs's art and life for the general reader and literary historian. Also provides a concise analysis section.

CYRANO DE BERGERAC

Born: Paris, France; March 6, 1619
Died: Paris, France; July 28, 1655
Also known as: Hector Savinien de Cyrano

PRINCIPAL LONG FICTION

L'Autre Monde: Ou, Les États et empires de la lune et du soleil, 1656-1662 (*Comical History of the States and Empires of the Worlds of the Moon and Sun*, 1687; also known as *Other Worlds: The Comical History of the States and Empires of the Moon and the Sun*, 1965; includes *Histoire comique des états et empires de la lune*, 1656 [*Comical History of the States and Empires of the Moon*; also known as *The Government of the World in the Moon*, 1659], and *Histoire comique des états et empires du soleil*, 1662 [*Comical History of the States and Empires of the Sun*])

OTHER LITERARY FORMS

In the course of his brief and turbulent life, Cyrano de Bergerac (SEE-rah-noh deh BEHR-zheh-rahk) tried his hand at an array of genres and acquitted himself honorably in all of them. His tragedy *La Mort d'Agrippine* (pr. 1653) compares favorably with the lesser works of Pierre Corneille. Cyrano's one comedy, *Le Pédant joué* (pb. 1954; the pedant outwitted), though never staged in his lifetime, was almost certainly the unacknowledged source of two highly effective scenes in Molière's *Les Fourberies de Scapin* (pr., pb. 1671; *The Cheats of Scapin*, 1701). *Le Pédant joué* is essentially a burlesque of the pedantry and *préciosité* that were rife in Cyrano's day—though Cyrano himself could tap a "precious" vein when he chose.

The same gift for burlesque is evident in Cyrano's satiric poem, or *mazarinade* (attack on Cardinal Mazarin), of 1649, *Le Ministre d'état flambé* (the minister of state goes up in flames), and in the best of his letters. The latter were not genuine correspondence but showpieces designed for publication. They are of several kinds: love letters full of exaggerated compliments and reproaches, set off by far-fetched figures of speech in the worst *précieux* style; elaborate and fanciful descriptions of nature; satiric attacks on real and imagined enemies; and polemic pieces on a variety of political and philosophical issues. The letters "For the Sorcerers" and "Against the Sorcerers" are especially noteworthy for their satiric power and cogency of argument; they also anticipate the attacks on superstition and intolerance in *Other Worlds*, Cyrano's most important work.

ACHIEVEMENTS

It is a great irony of literary history that Cyrano de Bergerac, a minor but talented and aggressively ambitious seventeenth century writer, at last achieved world renown in the

Cyrano de Bergerac
(Library of Congress)

twentieth century—as a fictional character who scarcely resembles his original. To be fair to Edmond Rostand (the playwright whose *Cyrano de Bergerac*, staged in 1897, spread Cyrano's fame), the unexpurgated manuscripts that were to reveal the full extent of his hero's boldness and malice were as yet unpublished when he wrote; yet it took a deal of willful misreading—and, of course, imaginative reworking—to make a noble Platonic lover of the dissolute and misanthropic Cyrano. Whatever his failures as a man, the real Cyrano deserves to be remembered as a competent literary craftsman and an inspired satirist. There is no denying that his libertinism had its sordid side, but its essence was simply "freethinking," a rejection of the Catholic Church's exclusive claim to truth and an espousal of the cause of scientific investigation.

In his best works, the two volumes of *Other Worlds* and the letters for and against sorcerers, Cyrano anticipates the form and some of the major themes of Voltaire's *contes philosophiques* (philosophical tales—a distinct genre). Indeed, Voltaire's *Le Micromégas* (1752; *Micromegas*, 1753), as well as Jonathan Swift's *Gulliver's Travels* (1726), owes a debt of inspiration to Cyrano. Perhaps Cyrano's greatest single achievement was his astonishing vision of cultural pluralism and toleration in an age clouded by superstition and repression.

BIOGRAPHY

For serious readers of his works, the facts of Cyrano de Bergerac's life offer an important corrective to his legend. Though his family laid claim to noble status, the only basis for that claim was their ownership of two "fiefs," or manorial properties—Mauvières and Bergerac—in the valley of the Chevreuse near Paris. The Cyranos were in fact of bourgeois origin; their son was christened Hector Savinien de Cyrano, and he himself added the title "de Bergerac" as a young man (as he occasionally assumed the pretentious given names of Alexandre or Hercule). This was deceptive on two counts, for, aside from smacking of nobility, the title suggests a Gascon origin. Rostand thus portrays his hero as born and bred in Gascony, which the real Cyrano never visited.

Cyrano was born in Paris and christened there on March 6, 1619. Some of his childhood was spent on his father's properties in the Chevreuse valley, where he acquired a love of nature and a hatred of dogmatic authority. The hatred was inspired by a country priest to whom Cyrano was sent for schooling; it was to grow into a lifelong passion, reinforced by his experiences at the Collège de Beauvais in Paris, where he completed his education. (The headmaster of the collège, Jean Grangier—a man of considerable scholarly reputation—is mercilessly satirized in Cyrano's comedy, *Le Pédant joué*, while the country priest is pilloried in *Comical History of the States and Empires of the Sun*.) Once out of school, Cyrano gave free rein to his rebellious streak and joined the circles of *libertins*, or freethinkers—and free livers—who frequented certain Paris cabarets. Among his libertine friends were several pupils of the materialist philosopher Pierre Gassendi, including the avowed atheist Claude-Emmanuel Chapelle and possibly the young Molière. Whether he studied with Gassendi himself, Cyrano was heavily influenced by his ideas, which are discussed at length in *Other Worlds*.

At about this time, Cyrano's father suffered serious financial reverses and was forced to sell his fiefs; it has been suggested that Cyrano's gambling losses may have been a factor. Whatever the reasons, relations between father and son were strained, and they continued to be so until the father's death; according to records left by his lawyers, Abel de Cyrano suspected his two sons of robbing him as he lay on his deathbed. It is worth noting as well that Cyrano includes a bitter tirade against fathers in *Other Worlds* and depicts the sons of the moon people as exercising authority over their old fathers.

His financial straits, as well as the desire to make a name for himself, inspired Cyrano to seek a commission in the Guards, a company made up almost entirely of Gascons, whose reputation for bravado was apparently well deserved. One element of the Cyrano legend that seems to bear up under inspection is his reputation for bravery in the duels for which the Guards were notorious. After being wounded in two battles, however (at the sieges of Mouzon and Arras), he gave up the military life in disgust and turned to a literary career. Frédéric Lachèvre, who produced the first accurate biography of Cyrano in 1920, has suggested that the serious illness from which Cyrano suffered during this period also influenced his decision by forcing him to withdraw from other spheres of activity. The exact nature of the disease is unknown, but several biographers have accepted Lachèvre's suggestion that it may have been syphilis. Illness and poverty combined to reinforce the misanthropic strain in Cyrano's character; during this period, he broke with and reviled many of his former friends.

An opponent of Cardinal Mazarin at the outbreak of the Fronde in 1649, he changed sides—possibly for pay—and wrote a scathing letter, *Contre les Frondeurs* (1651; against the Frondeurs). Jacques Prévot, editor of Cyrano's complete works, suggested that one of the most violent of these ruptures may have had an erotic dimension: Charles d'Assoucy, a satiric poet, was known to be homosexual, and Cyrano seems to have shown little interest in women.

Unfortunately, Cyrano enjoyed no greater success as a writer during his lifetime than he did as a soldier. In an age of censorship, he was too bold for most publishers, and he succeeded in publishing his plays and some letters only after accepting the patronage of the duke of Arpajon, a man of limited intelligence who wished to make a name for himself as a patron of the arts. With his support, Cyrano staged his tragedy, *La Mort d'Agrippine*, but it was closed after a few performances by a group hired to boo his "atheistic" stance (the hirelings, ironically, missed the more daring speeches and booed at a line they simply misunderstood). Shortly thereafter, Cyrano was hit on the head by a log dropped by one of the duke's servants. It seems at least as likely that this was an accident as that someone hired the servant to ambush Cyrano (for fear of facing him in a fair fight, as Rostand would have it): By this time, Cyrano's dueling days were behind him. The incident precipitated a rupture with the duke, however, and forced Cyrano to take to his bed. Fourteen months later, on July 28, 1655, he died at the age of thirty-six.

Lachèvre suggests that the primary cause of death was tertiary syphilis, but a lack of definite evidence has left this surmise in doubt. Cyrano is said to have returned to the faith on his deathbed at the urging of his relative, Mother Marguerite of Jesus, and his oldest friend, Henry Le Bret. Le Bret became Cyrano's literary executor and published a heavily expurgated version of *Other Worlds* in 1657, two years after Cyrano's death.

Analysis: Other Worlds

Erica Harth, in *Cyrano de Bergerac and the Polemics of Modernity* (1970), claims Cyrano de Bergerac to have been "the first of the Moderns," forerunner of a position more clearly formulated later in the seventeenth century in the great Quarrel of the Ancients and

Moderns. Cyrano went beyond his contemporaries the *libertins*, Harth argues, by refusing to settle for a critique of received wisdom; the "destructive spirit" in which he attacks tradition and Church authority "is accompanied by a positive acceptance and propagation of the same scientific and philosophical ideas which, although not directly transmitted by Cyrano, were to have a profound impact on the minds of the eighteenth century *philosophes*."

Cyrano, however, was also undeniably a man of his own time, attracted to as well as repulsed by the excesses of *préciosité*, charmed as well as amused by the arcane theories of thinkers such as Tommaso Campanella, in which allegory and myth are still intertwined with rationalistic investigation. If we can trust the priest's report, Cyrano even returned to the faith in time to die "a good Christian death," and as one critic has shown, it is impossible to deduce a consistent atheistic view even from the unexpurgated manuscripts of *Other Worlds*. However one looks at Cyrano's masterpiece, contradictions emerge. Before examining these contradictions in detail, a brief description of the work is in order.

Although *Comical History of the States and Empires of the Sun* was first published separately from *Comical History of the States and Empires of the Moon*, it seems clear that this division does not reflect any intention of the author; the two works relate voyages of similar scope by a single narrator, and the second of these voyages is said to be motivated by persecution arising from a published account of the first. Combined, the voyages form a continuous narrative—as do, for example, the two parts of Miguel de Cervantes' *Don Quixote de la Mancha* (1605, 1615)—and may be referred to without distortion by the collective title *Other Worlds*. (The French title, literally translated, is "the other world," a phrase that in French as well as English usually refers to the abode of souls after death; Cyrano probably meant it to be taken ironically, for his aim is to suggest that there are "other worlds" in the here and now as well.) This was Cyrano's only work of prose fiction, but it proved to be the most effective vehicle for his fractious talents and libertine perspective. Because of its subject, it has often been classified as a work of utopian fiction, but the genre to which it really belongs is that of the *conte philosophique*, or philosophical tale, as practiced preeminently by Voltaire one hundred years later.

A PHILOSOPHICAL TALE

The essence of the *conte philosophique* is its unique combination of satiric, even farcical, elements with serious philosophical or ideological ones. Consistency or fullness of characterization and cogency of plot tend to be sacrificed to the primary goals of ridiculing an opposing (usually dogmatic) intellectual position and of suggesting more enlightened alternatives. Because of the variety of scientific and philosophical positions, many of them incompatible, that are detailed by different characters of *Other Worlds*, it has been maintained that Cyrano—admittedly a dilettante rather than a true scholar—was himself confused about the ideas he wished to advance. While the confusion may be real, Prévot, in *Cyrano de Bergerac, romancier* (1977), has argued for a subtler reading that qualifies the didactic intent of the work. Insofar as Cyrano has a "message," Prévot suggests, it is one of radical skepticism; Cyrano considers all doctrines, however scientific, inherently suspect, and having rid himself of one set is not at all eager to embrace another.

In addition to fitting Le Bret's description of his old friend's beliefs, this analysis would tally with Cyrano's own warnings, in the second chapter of his fragmentary treatise on physics (never completed but published in Prévot's edition of *Œuvres complètes*, 1977) against taking one's hypotheses for realities. There is, moreover, an anarchic streak in *Other Worlds*, corresponding to its satiric intent; in that respect, Cyrano is a worthy heir of Aristophanes, Lucian, and François Rabelais, from whom he may have borrowed specific motifs but whose satiric vein he made his own.

The narrator of *Other Worlds*, who speaks in the first person, is not named until the opening pages of the second volume; he is there called Drycona, an obvious anagram of Cyrano. On the strength of his anagrammatic name, many critics have assumed that the narrator speaks for the author. While at times it is hard to deny that he does, his own position fluctuates from scene to scene, enabling him to serve as a foil for a variety of interlocutors. Thus, in conversation with an avowed atheist he defends the faith, whereas in conversation with an Old Testament prophet he blasphemes. Nor is he always in opposition: He listens deferentially to speakers of the most disparate opinions. It seems best to admit, with Prévot, that Drycona is primarily a fictional creation—as are the other "real" characters who appear, such as Campanella and René Descartes.

THE VOYAGES

The narrator's first voyage is inspired by a moonlit walk with friends, who try to outdo one another in *précieux* descriptions of the full moon (an attic window on heaven, the sign outside Bacchus's tavern). His friends ridicule the narrator for suggesting that the moon may be "a world like this one, for which our world serves as a moon." On reaching home, however, the narrator finds that a book has mysteriously appeared on his desk and is lying open at the page where the author (Jerome Cardan, a sixteenth century mathematician and astrologer) describes a visit from two men who said they lived on the moon. The narrator, determined to verify his hunch, contrives a first mode of space travel: He covers himself with small flasks of dew, which the sun draws upward. He rises so quickly toward the sun, however, that he is obliged to break most of the flasks, and falls back to the earth—in Canada, at that time New France. There he is entertained by the viceroy, with whom he discusses his belief that the earth travels around the sun (still a heretical proposition in 1648); his own displacement from France to Canada is of course evidence that the earth rotates.

In a second attempt to reach the moon, he builds a flying machine, which at first crashes; while he is tending his bruises, the colonial troops outfit the machine with fireworks, transforming it into a multistage rocket. The narrator manages to jump in before it takes off and, when the last stage falls to earth, finds himself still being drawn to the moon by the beef marrow he had rubbed on his bruises. (It was a popular superstition that the waning moon "sucked up" animal marrow.) As luck would have it, he falls in the Earthly Paradise and strikes against an apple from the Tree of Life, whose juice revivifies and rejuvenates him. The prophet Elias, one of two inhabitants of the Earthly Paradise (the other is Enoch), tells him its history, but the narrator cannot resist the impulse to tell a blasphemous joke, and he is cast out of Paradise.

The rest of the moon is inhabited by a race of giants who resemble human beings but move about on all fours; indeed, they take the narrator for an animal because he walks on two feet, and they exhibit him as a kind of sideshow (an idea borrowed by Swift). He is befriended by a spirit whose native land is the sun but who has visited the earth in various ages and was once the Genius or monitory Voice of Socrates; the spirit speaks Greek with the narrator and arranges to have him brought to the royal court. There he is taken for a female of the same species as a Spaniard who has arrived before him (the Spaniard, Gonsales, was the hero of Francis Godwin's 1638 book *The Man in the Moone: Or, A Discourse of a Voyage Thither*).

In the hope of producing more "animals" of their species, the moon people have them share a bed, where they have long talks on various scientific problems. As the narrator learns the moon language (which is of two kinds, musical notes for the upper classes and physical gestures for the lower), a controversy arises over his status: Is he a man or an animal? The moon priests consider it "a shocking impiety" to call such a "monster" a man, so he is interrogated before the Estates General. He tries to defend the principles of Aristotle's philosophy but is unanimously declared an animal when he refuses—as he was taught in school—to debate the principles themselves. A second trial, occasioned by his claim that "the moon"—that is, our earth—"is a world," leads to acknowledgment of his human status, but he is forced to recant the "heresy" of the claim itself. For the remainder of his stay, he is the guest of a moon family in which—according to custom—the son has authority over the father. In a series of conversations, the young man explains his radical materialist views of the universe; he is defending his atheism when a devil appears to snatch him away. The narrator, who tries to help his host, is thus transported back to earth (presumably because Hell is at its center). Thus ends the first volume.

The second volume opens with a clear reference to the first. Urged by a friend who shares his philosophical and scientific interests, the narrator—hereafter known as Dyrcona—writes an account of his moon voyage. He becomes a local celebrity but is accused of witchcraft by a malevolent country priest, who exploits the people's ignorance and persuades them to arrest the "sorcerer." Drycona escapes from prison by building a new flying machine—this one using the principle of the vacuum—in which he takes off for the sun. Once again, the machine can get him only part of the way there; it is the force of his desire, drawing him to the sun as source of life, that enables him to complete the voyage (which takes twenty-two months). The sun is divided into many regions of differing "opacity" (suggested by the then-recent discovery of sunspots); there is a rough correspondence between the intensity of light and the "enlightenment" of the inhabitants.

One race—that of "spirits," such as the Genius of Socrates—can alter their outward forms as their imagination dictates.

The race of birds, who prevent abuses of power by choosing as king one of their weakest members (a dove), capture Drycona and put him on trial, as had the moon people; this time, however, the charge is simply "being a man"—belonging to a pernicious and destructive species. On the advice of a friendly bird, Drycona claims to be a monkey raised by humans, but he is convicted; he is on the point of being devoured by insects (included among the birds) when a parrot whom he had once freed on earth testifies on his behalf and obtains a pardon for him. After an encounter with a forest of talking trees, who try to convince him of their moral superiority, Drycona witnesses a battle between a Fire-Beast and an Ice-Animal (the latter is defending the trees). The battle is also observed by the philosopher Tommaso Campanella (author of *La città del sole*, 1602; *The City of the Sun*, 1880), who becomes Drycona's guide. Together, they visit the Lake of Sleep and the Streams of the Five Senses, which empty into the Rivers of Memory, Imagination, and Judgment. A couple from the Province of Lovers, on their way to the Province of Philosophers (where the soul of Socrates is to settle a dispute between them), give the two travelers a lift in a basket suspended from a giant bird. Campanella is returning to his province to greet the soul of Descartes, newly arrived (he died in 1650). The narrative of the second volume ends, unfortunately, at the moment that Drycona and Campanella meet Descartes; Cyrano's ill health during the last year of his life prevented him from finishing the manuscript.

Dimensions of the novel

A brief résumé can give only the faintest idea of the inventiveness and satiric verve of *Other Worlds*. Cyrano takes every opportunity to make minor but telling—and often cutting—observations on various aspects of the human condition. The chief defect of his masterpiece, lack of unity, is merely the excess of a virtue: the acknowledgment that there are more things in heaven and on earth than are dreamed of in any one human philosophy. Quick of wit and eye, Cyrano was ever ready to bolt off in new directions. This quality gives his narrative a certain inclusiveness and makes it consistently entertaining, despite long stretches of philosophical argument. It also, however, gives the work a chaotic quality, which seems to reflect both the temperament of the author and the intellectual ferment of his day. (This feature of *Other Worlds* has been aptly contrasted with the unity, in tone and perspective, of Swift's *Gulliver's Travels*.) Perhaps the only way to do justice to the many dimensions of *Other Worlds* is to isolate some of the most important ones and assess them individually. They are, in ascending order of importance, *préciosité*, utopianism, didacticism or popularization, and satire.

Cyrano's use of *préciosité* reveals a deep-seated ambivalence symptomatic of his relationship to his own age. The *préciosité*, or cultivation of extravagantly refined language, that flourished in seventeenth century France grew out of the court mentality fostered by centralization of the monarchy; the salons, where *préciosité* emerged, were miniature "courts" on the model of the royal one and could be stepping-stones to power for those who learned the "art of pleasing." The earliest of Cyrano's letters seem to have been undertaken as exercises in this courtly form of entertainment. That he longed for fame, and for public acceptance of his work, is clear, but it is equally clear that his wit was too sharp for his own good and that, instead of ingratiating, it often alienated his audience. This tendency was not altogether involuntary.

Cyrano was rebellious by nature and could not resist the shock value of a daring bon mot; he was also too intelligent not to see how easily *préciosité* could be turned to ridicule. Yet he had a truly lyric imagination, which lent itself to *précieux* elaboration, as in some descriptive passages of *Other Worlds*. The landscape of the Five Senses recalls Mademoiselle de Scudéry, the *précieuse par excellence*, and it is hard to deny the passage its charm, despite a hint of affectation. At his best, Cyrano manages to walk the fine line between *préciosité* and burlesque. He can indulge in witty definitions of the moon, ascribing them to Drycona's friends, and then allow his hero to deflate them by remarking that they serve only to "tickle the time, to make it go faster." Like Aristophanes, who made his characters trot out old jokes while affecting disdain for them, Cyrano usually manages to have it both ways.

In addition to its occasional *préciosité*, *Other Worlds* also contains a utopian vein, though it scarcely belongs to the utopian genre. This vein is chiefly visible in Cyrano's treatment of machines and practical inventions. The most prominent are, of course, the flying machines, which, though fanciful (and less than fully effective), are all posited on genuine physical principles—the vacuum, magnetism, evaporation. It was doubtless the sheer fluidity and daring of his imagination that enabled Cyrano to anticipate other inventions of whose physical bases he was wholly ignorant; most striking of these inventions is the "talking book," or phonograph. There are also some radical social and political innovations in Cyrano's vision of the "other worlds" his protagonist visits: Battles on the moon can be fought only between armies of perfectly equal numbers, while the most important "battles" are debates between the scholars and wits of the two sides; in the realm of birds, the king is seen as the servant, not the master, of his people. Some of these innovations are transparent wish fulfillments to one familiar with Cyrano's life; the most pointed is the role inversion of fathers and sons, but there are humorous ones as well, such as the use of poetry for money (with value based on quality, not quantity) and the recognition, among the moon people, that a large nose is the infallible sign of a noble and witty nature.

Despite such pleasant surprises, however, Drycona encounters no ideal society: The moon people have their bigoted priests and heresy trials; the sun people, their disputes and unequal "enlightenment." The realm of the birds, which comes closest to a model state, also has the Draconian stamp that makes many utopias (Plato's Republic, Swift's land of the Houyhnhnms) so unpalatable, and Cyrano acknowledges that—as did Swift, perhaps in emulation of Cyrano—human beings may not live there. Despite a certain escapist impulse, then, the book is never more than guardedly optimistic about the realization of ideals. It may be significant that the closest thing to an ideal state of affairs in *Other Worlds* is set in our world: This is Drycona's brief but happy stay with his friends Colignac and Cussan. In a passage reminiscent of Rabelais's Abbey of Thélème (*Gargantua*, 1534; chapter 53), he describes the material comfort and intellectual stimulation of their life together:

> The innocent pleasures of which the body is capable were only the lesser share. Of all those the mind can derive from study and conversation, we lacked none; and our libraries, united like our minds, summoned all the learned into our company.

The idyll is soon threatened, and then shattered, by the malice of a priest and the ignorance of the peasants, but it offers a glimpse of the conditions Cyrano considered most likely to foster human happiness.

The prominence of learning in this vision raises the questions of whether Cyrano had a didactic or pedagogical aim in writing *Other Worlds*. It has been claimed that he was essentially a popularizer, concerned to present the new scientific theories of his contemporaries in a form accessible to the commoner. As with the utopian view, there is clearly some warrant for this interpretation; again, however, it seems less than adequate to account for the work as a whole. Drycona's abortive first flight, which lands him in Canada, is surely designed as a concrete illustration of the Copernican theory; it is appropriately followed by a discussion of the theory, and of various objections to it, in the conversation between Drycona and the viceroy. The sheer amount of space devoted to similar conversations throughout the book is an indication of their importance to Cyrano. At times, as in Drycona's long exchange with the young atheist on the moon, the plot is allowed to atrophy entirely: The focus of interest is on the ideas discussed and on the arguments for or against them. Yet Prévot has done well to point out that in each such discussion personalities are involved; there is no omniscient narrator and no completely reliable speaker.

Moreover, the universe of the book is hardly constrained by any one of the theories it sets forth, and it sometimes operates according to superstitious or supernatural beliefs: A devil can carry a man off for impiety, and the waning moon can "suck" the beef marrow Drycona uses as a salve. It seems particularly striking that on *both* of Drycona's outward voyages, the "scientific" method gets him only halfway there at most; the beef marrow gets him to the moon, while the "strength of his desire" for the source of all life draws him to the sun. The fictional data thus undercut not only specific scientific accounts but also any thoroughgoing rationalistic perspective.

This is not to suggest that the author has no clear-cut attitudes to convey: He does indeed, but his medium is satire rather than exposition. Drycona's motive in leaving the earth may be to explore the heavens, but Cyrano's purpose is to find a radically different perspective from which to observe the human world. The heliocentric theory espoused by the Church is symptomatic of human vanity, which insists that the universe was made for humans and continues, literally and figuratively, to revolve around them. Cyrano's protagonist finds himself in a position from which he is forced to reexamine virtually all of his assumptions—scientific, philosophical, religious, and social. Indeed, he is twice put on trial, not as an individual but as a representative of the human species. Yet each of the extraterrestrial societies he visits displays some of the defects of human societies, so that the lesson is one of cultural relativism, and the necessity for tolerance is made obvious, as in Voltaire's *contes philosophiques*, by the mistreatment of the sympathetic protagonist. The satire of religious abuses is particularly prominent, as befitted an age in which the Church was the chief opponent of free speech and investigation. Yet, as Prévot has shown, Cyrano's quarrel is not with God so much as with his vicars, who abuse their moral authority to indulge their own base motives.

The satiric effectiveness of *Other Worlds* is fueled by a keen sense of the comic. Cyrano's attitude toward his fellow humans was a complex one, compounded of anger, amusement, occasional admiration, and occasional hatred. It is the amusement, however, that tends to predominate. In this respect, Cyrano resembles his compatriots Rabelais and Voltaire (the first of whom he read, and the second of whom read him) more than he resembles his great English emulator, Swift. Between philosophical debates, he finds time to tell how the moon people make sundials of their teeth by pointing their noses toward the sun, how a "hypervegetarian" abstains even from vegetables that have not died a natural death, how a man from the Province of Lovers is forbidden to use hyperbole on pain of death after nearly persuading a young woman to use her own heart as a boat—because it is so "light" (fickle) and can hold so many. As well as an eloquent plea for tolerance and freedom of thought, *Other Worlds* is a consistently entertaining book, whose author clearly deserves to be remembered as an original writer of fiction, not merely as a character in a play by Rostand.

Lillian Doherty

OTHER MAJOR WORKS

PLAYS: *La Mort d'Agrippine*, pr. 1653; *Le Pédant joué*, pb. 1954.

NONFICTION: *Contre les Frondeurs*, 1651; *Lettres*, 1654 (*Satyrical Characters and Handsome Descriptions in Letters*, 1658).

MISCELLANEOUS: *Cyrano de Bergerac: Œuvres complètes*, 1977 (Jacques Prévot, editor).

BIBLIOGRAPHY

Addyman, Ishbel. *Cyrano: Adventures in Space and Time with the Legendary French Hero*. New York: Simon & Schuster, 2008. Presents a precise, balanced, and well-documented study of Cyrano. Includes notes, select bibliography, and index.

Aldington, Richard. *An Introduction to "Voyages to the Moon and the Sun."* New York: Orion, 1962. Aldington, one of England's best critics and a translator of Cyrano's fiction, discusses the legend and life of Cyrano as well as his friends and works.

Alter, Jean. "Figures of Social and Semiotic Dissent." In *A New History of French Literature*, edited by Denis Hollier et al. Cambridge, Mass.: Harvard University Press, 1994. Alter's essay includes information about Cyrano and his contemporaries. It is one of many brief, chronologically arranged essays that in their totality provide a comprehensive survey of French literature.

Campbell, Mary Baine. "A World in the Moon: Celestial Fictions of Francis Godwin and Cyrano de Bergerac." In *Wonder and Science: Imagining Worlds in Early Modern Europe*. Ithaca, N.Y.: Cornell University Press, 1999. Campbell analyzes a number of early modern texts, including fiction by Cyrano and other French and English writers, to demonstrate how people responded with awe to the new geographic and scientific discoveries of the seventeenth century.

Harth, Erica. *Cyrano de Bergerac and the Polemics of Modernity*. New York: Columbia University Press, 1970. Contains a thoughtful analysis of Cyrano's criticism of core Christian beliefs and his development of a mechanistic view of the universe in which God is not necessary, according to Cyrano.

Muratore, Mary Jo. *Mimesis and Metatextuality in the French Neo-Classical Text, Reflexive Readings of La Fontaine, Molière, Racine, Guilleragues, Madame de La Fayette, Scarron, Cyrano de Bergerac, and Perrault*. Geneva: Droz, 1994. Analyzes Cyrano as a science-fiction writer. Muratore makes good use of late twentieth century criticism. In spite of some jargon, this book can be helpful even for beginning students.

Popkin, Richard H. *The History of Scepticism from Erasmus to Descartes*. New York: Humanities Press, 1964. Provides a good description of Cyrano's originality in relation to other European freethinkers of the sixteenth and seventeenth centuries. The one weakness of Popkin's book is that he links atheists, such as Cyrano, to liberal-minded Christians, such as Desiderius Erasmus and René Descartes.

Sankey, Margaret. "From Seventeenth-Century Clandestine Manuscript to Contemporary Edition: *L'Autre Monde* of Cyrano de Bergerac." In *The Editorial Gaze: Mediating Texts in Literature and the Arts*, edited by Paul Eggert and Margaret Sankey. New York: Garland, 1998. Examines Cyrano's novel from a postmodern perspective, analyzing how his work was altered by editing and how editing changed the relationship between the book and its readers.

Van Baelen, Jacqueline. "Reality and Illusion in *L'Autre Monde:* The Narrative Voyage of Cyrano de Bergerac." *Yale French Studies* 49 (1973): 178-184. An excellent literary study, concentrating on the structure of the novel.

PETER DE VRIES

Born: Chicago, Illinois; February 27, 1910
Died: Norwalk, Connecticut; September 28, 1993

PRINCIPAL LONG FICTION

But Who Wakes the Bugler?, 1940
The Handsome Heart, 1943
Angels Can't Do Better, 1944
The Tunnel of Love, 1954
Comfort Me with Apples, 1956
The Mackerel Plaza, 1958
The Tents of Wickedness, 1959
Through the Fields of Clover, 1961
The Blood of the Lamb, 1962
Reuben, Reuben, 1964
Let Me Count the Ways, 1965
The Vale of Laughter, 1967
The Cat's Pajamas and Witch's Milk, 1968
Mrs. Wallop, 1970
Into Your Tent I'll Creep, 1971
Forever Panting, 1973
The Glory of the Hummingbird, 1974
I Hear America Swinging, 1976
Madder Music, 1977
Consenting Adults: Or, The Duchess Will Be Furious, 1980
Sauce for the Goose, 1981
Slouching Towards Kalamazoo, 1983
The Prick of Noon, 1985
Peckham's Marbles, 1986

OTHER LITERARY FORMS

In addition to his work as a novelist, Peter De Vries (duh VREEZ) was a short-story writer of some repute; a number of his stories are collected in *No, but I Saw the Movie* (1952) and *Without a Stitch in Time: A Selection of the Best Humorous Short Pieces* (1972). He also collaborated with Joseph Fields in writing a stage version of one of his novels, *The Tunnel of Love: A Play* (pb. 1957), and wrote the play *Spofford* (pb. 1968). In addition, he published a handful of essays and interviews.

Achievements

In the 1950's, Kingsley Amis called Peter De Vries the "funniest serious writer to be found either side of the Atlantic." De Vries was certainly a clever punster and wit, a master of situation comedy, and a devastating observer of the foibles of suburbia. His droll humor often involves the amorous adventures of the middle-aged suburban male, torn between the sophisticated mores of Connecticut suburbia and his simpler childhood roots, usually in the Dutch Reformed Church or some other equally strict background. De Vries writes knowingly about the same suburban milieu as that of John Updike and John Cheever, but with less overt seriousness and more sheer fun. In fact, he resisted the label of "serious writer" (or, for that matter, "religious writer"), although he dealt extensively with serious topics, including religion, in most of his works. The predominant tone of his writing, with the exception of *The Blood of the Lamb*, is comic and even lighthearted.

De Vries was a prolific novelist, with more than two dozen novels published, along with several collections of short stories reprinted from *The New Yorker.* With so many novels to his credit, there is bound to be some repetitiveness, and De Vries often uses the same basic plot situation—the comic mischances of the lecherous suburban male who is thwarted by his moral scruples, his underlying decency, the vestiges of his past, or simply unlucky circumstances. There is a sameness about so many of his protagonists—particularly in their recollections of their strict religious backgrounds and their ambiguous attempts to "liberate" themselves from middle-class conventionality—that some critics have accused De Vries of being too autobiographical.

What saves his novels from redundancy is the variety of his humor: the puns, witticisms, drollery, repartee, lampoons, parodies, caricatures, and spoofs. De Vries displays the comic instincts of a cartoonist or a comedian, the ability to coin phrases or epigrams so funny that they are almost distracting. His fictional scenes seem to be built around the humorous or witty line, sometimes to the detriment of plot, narrative, or characterization. Given that De Vries repeatedly insisted that his primary purpose as a humorist was to entertain, the loose structure of his work may be judged a necessary evil.

The targets of De Vries' humor are the pretenses and absurdities of modern, affluent suburbia. In an interview, the author once commented, "I'm a regionalist, like Thomas Hardy. And I love those yokels who get off the same bar car at the same time every night and have never swum in anything but a pool in their own backyards. It's really a new provincialism." His "Avalon" and "Decency" are the fictional counterparts of the wealthy, exclusive suburbs, such as Greenwich, Darien, Stamford, and Westport, along Connecticut's "Gold Coast." His characters—or sometimes caricatures—show all the vanities, postures, and affectations of wealth, education, and "good breeding" that might be expected of sophisticated Connecticut suburbanites, yet De Vries is never harsh or satiric, commenting that the purpose of humor, unlike satire, is not to kill one's prey but to bring it back alive to be released. De Vries' humor is thus more charitable than satire; he invites humankind "to laugh at itself."

De Vries is a master of the humorous scene and the comic caricature. Many of his characters are immediately recognizable as "types"—the ultraliberal clergyman, the suave newspaper columnist, the lecherous poet, the hick farmer, the small-town atheist, the unsuccessful artist, and the television game-show host—and they behave in predictable ways. The humor occurs as De Vries builds his scenes toward a hilarious climax—such as the cup of bourbon switched with the teacups at the church ladies' reception in *The Mackerel Plaza* or the social worker's visit to a disorganized family in *The Tunnel of Love*.

Often the comedy takes the form of a continuation of James Thurber's "battle of the sexes," with De Vries' male characters seeking a worldly sophistication and urbanity in which to live out their fantasies, only to be thwarted by the forces of female respectability. Virtually all of De Vries' novels have a male protagonist, and he wrote from a decidedly male perspective on the themes of sex and marriage, explaining once in an interview that bawdy literature is written predominantly by men. His characters *think* they want the freedom and irresponsibility of a carefree bachelor life, with its worldliness and sophistication, but they seem bewildered or disappointed if they get what they seek. The theme of many of his comic novels (and hence the source of their humor) is the shallowness and superficiality of the sophisticated suburban life.

Perhaps the key to De Vries' best work is in the tragicomic tone of his humor—that urge to laugh so as not to cry that marks the grotesque "as a blend of the tragic and comic." Too often in De Vries' novels, however, the comic is present without the tragic, the burlesque and farcical without the serious note that could redeem the work from being merely superficial entertainment. De Vries' inferior works always seem to verge on situation comedy, with their frequently contrived or manufactured scenes, and it is not surprising that he collaborated on a successful Broadway production based on his novel *The Tunnel of Love*. *The Blood of the Lamb* is incomparably De Vries' best novel, with its poignant mixture of humor and pathos; coming at midcareer, it is the touchstone against which the remainder of his novels must be measured. The earlier works in comparison seem to strain after a false sophistication, and the later novels appear increasingly superficial, employing forced gags and contrived situations and depending too heavily on topical humor and burlesque of current trends and fashions.

BIOGRAPHY

Peter De Vries was born in Chicago, Illinois, on February 27, 1910. His parents, Joost and Henrietta De Vries, emigrated from Holland and settled in a closely knit Dutch Calvinist community on Chicago's South Side. De Vries' father was an iceman and furniture mover who started with "a one-horse outfit that he gradually built to a sizeable warehouse business." During De Vries' boyhood, the family lived in a three-room apartment behind his father's business office.

The De Vries family were members of the strict Dutch Reformed Church, and their domestic life was probably much like that described in the autobiographical *The Blood of the*

Lamb: a large, contentious family with parents and in-laws forever arguing about some obscure point of theology or church doctrine. Apparently, such disagreements were commonplace in the Dutch Reformed Church, for in the novel *The Mackerel Plaza*, when someone boasts to the protagonist's father that *his* denomination has not had a schism in the past one hundred years, the father replies, "Rotten wood you can't split." De Vries' parents were also strict about forbidding any form of worldliness: Card playing and watching motion pictures were forbidden, and Bible reading and theological discussions were encouraged. During his adolescence, De Vries rebelled against these strictures, but he later expressed fond memories of the Dutch-language services and hymns of his childhood.

Young De Vries attended the Chicago Christian High School of the Dutch Reformed Church and then entered Calvin College in Grand Rapids, Michigan, a private liberal arts college founded by the same denomination. There he won a Michigan state extemporaneous speaking contest and graduated with a degree in English in 1931. That summer he also studied briefly at Northwestern University. His family had hoped that he would enter the ministry after graduation, but instead he decided to become a writer and embarked on a series of odd jobs in Chicago to support himself. He edited a community newspaper, tended vending machines, peddled candy apples, served as a radio actor, and spoke before women's clubs.

From 1938 to 1944, he served capably as an editor of *Poetry* magazine. There he met his future wife, Katinka Loeser, who was a poetry contributor and later became a short-story writer of some note. They were married on October 16, 1943. During this time, De Vries had published three early novels, *But Who Wakes the Bugler?*, *The Handsome Heart*, and *Angels Can't Do Better*, which earned him some critical notice but met with only limited financial success. In 1943, De Vries invited James Thurber to speak at a Chicago benefit for *Poetry* magazine and Thurber subsequently persuaded De Vries to go east and write for *The New Yorker*. De Vries joined the staff of *The New Yorker* in 1944 and served as a contributor and cartoon editor until his death. At *The New Yorker*, he worked with editor Harold Ross and such famous humorists as E. B. White and Thurber on a staff that had once included Robert Benchley and S. J. Perelman.

De Vries settled with his wife in suburban Westport, Connecticut. They reared three children—Jan, Peter Jon, and Derek. A fourth child, Emily, died of leukemia before adolescence, a deep personal loss registered in De Vries' most serious novel, *The Blood of the Lamb*, in which a similar event occurs. Unlike the zany characters in many of his novels, De Vries was a man of conventional tastes, happily married and devoted to his family.

During his long career, De Vries published more than two dozen novels, along with his collections of short stories. He won wide critical acclaim for his humorous novels, and he received grants from the American Academy of Arts and Letters and the National Institute of Arts and Letters, of which he was a member. He died on September 28, 1993, in Norwalk, Connecticut.

ANALYSIS

"If I spent my time portraying life as it actually is," Peter De Vries once remarked, "I think I would go insane with boredom inside of two weeks." Eschewing the realistic novel, De Vries has instead concentrated on entertaining his readers with witty and humorous works, filled with hilarious but highly improbable incidents. He was satisfied to write a good comic novel without aiming for any higher artistic qualities. This self-acknowledged limitation has been the source of much of the unevenness in De Vries' work, with the overemphasis on humor weakening the structure of his novels—often to the neglect of narrative continuity, consistent point of view, clear transitions, and strong characterizations. In fact, many of his novels are so seriously flawed as scarcely to be considered novels at all; rather, they are loosely constructed narratives that simply provide a framework for the author's comic genius.

Beyond the purpose of sheer entertainment, De Vries was ambiguous about the intent of his humor, minimizing the social commentary and underlying seriousness of his work so that it is difficult to categorize him as a comic novelist of manners or a satirist. Like his mentor, James Thurber, De Vries chose to limit the scope of his humor and to evoke laughter through grotesque or absurd depictions of modern suburban life, but as his later novels suggest, he risked reducing his work to formulaic entertainment or, worse, self-parody. Stylistically, De Vries is not as original as Thurber, but he is perhaps at his best as a parodist of other writers, or as a writer of brilliant puns and epigrams rather than as the creator of a unified and coherent comic vision. His weakness as a comic novelist comes from his failure to unify his material and to offer an implicit corrective vision to the world he ridicules.

THE TUNNEL OF LOVE

De Vries' first three novels are of slight artistic value. His first novel of note, and still perhaps his most popular, is *The Tunnel of Love*. Here one enters the affluent world of Connecticut suburbia as seen through the eyes of the first-person narrator, a New York magazine cartoon editor much like De Vries himself. The focus of the novel, however, is on the comic imbroglios of his next-door neighbors, Augie and Isolde Poole, a young, well-to-do, "artistic" couple who try to adopt a child to save their marriage. The novel alternates between Manhattan and Avalon, Connecticut, through a round of weekend cocktail parties and dinners that provide a backdrop for De Vries' wit and cleverness. De Vries peoples the book with a humorous collage of "artsy" types—would-be actresses and directors, abstract painters, mediocre illustrators, poets manqués, affected snobs, precious aesthetes, and other rarefied types. In short, one finds all the empty worldliness of "Vanity Fair," which De Vries is quick to mimic and satirize, yet one also feels the narrator's attraction to these values, which lends the novel a curiously mixed tone of admiration and ridicule. De Vries is a shrewd observer of suburban language and behavior, with a good ear for nuances of conversation, and he creates a wonderful satire of the pretentious cocktail chitchat about creativity and neuroses that the characters employ to boost their sagging egos and disguise from themselves the truth of their mediocrity.

The protagonist, Augie Poole, is a good gag writer though a poor cartoonist who cannot sell his work, so he turns to profligacy to salve his ego. A self-confessed "rotter," he is never quite as wicked as he pretends to be. Superficially a glib and literate ladies' man, he is basically shallow and conceited, though not beyond eventual redemption through the responsibilities of parenthood. The Pooles ironically adopt the illegitimate child of Augie and his artist mistress, but not before a comic series of mishaps during the adoption process. Augie is forced to compromise his "artistic integrity" and sells his gags without the cartoons to prove himself a responsible prospective parent with a steady income. Much of the humor is generated in the domestic life of the narrator, however, in a genial "battle of the sexes" with his wife and family. In conversations with his wife, the narrator of course defends Augie, while she defends Isolde, with predictable results.

In *The Tunnel of Love*, husbands and wives are torn between the routines of respectable suburban life and the allure of a self-indulgent and liberated "artistic" life, with its glamour and sophistication. De Vries contrasts the romantic myth of personal creativity and self-indulgence with the more staid world of middle-class marriage and commuter life. His characters enjoy all the luxuries of suburban affluence, yet they seem to yearn for a vague "something more"—a vicarious excitement missing from their lives and beckoning from the bohemian life or from the narrator's vicarious dreamworld of "Moot Point," a Hollywood fantasy-world of cinema clichés. The comedy is generated by the clash of illusion and reality as Augie and the narrator slowly learn to accept the world as it is; "Moot Point" is eventually replaced by "Drowsy Dell," the summer cabin on a New Hampshire lake that both families enjoy.

The Mackerel Plaza

After De Vries' commercial success with *The Tunnel of Love*, he adapted the novel for stage and screen, and the play ran for a year on Broadway. His fiction writing continued in the same comic vein with his next three novels, *Comfort Me with Apples*, *The Mackerel Plaza*, and *The Tents of Wickedness*. Once more he took aim at the hollow values and assumptions of modern suburbia, particularly the jargon of psychology and adjustment, though not necessarily to replace them with more traditional values, but simply to show their comic inadequacy. The protagonist of *The Mackerel Plaza* is a pompous, ultraliberal minister, the Reverend Andrew Mackerel, as rigid and narrow in his "advanced thinking" as the fundamentalists he opposes. His People's Liberal Church, a nondenominational congregation, is the "first split-level church in America," with a church clinic and psychiatric facilities designed to meet all the needs of modern humanity. Mackerel preaches short, iconoclastic sermons intended to demolish whatever remains of his parishioners' traditional Christian beliefs, though he is the one who ultimately loses his faith in unbelief. A young widower, he is thwarted in his desire to marry an aspiring actress by the forces of

New England respectability in his congregation and by an elderly parishioner's desire to erect a memorial to his late wife.

None of the characters is really convincing in this book, and De Vries seems to play off orthodox beliefs against liberal Christianity merely for laughs, without either appearing credible. Mackerel loses his actor, Molly Calico, to a Romanian director and ends up marrying his own sister-in-law, Hester, a caricature of New England primness and domesticity. Like Flannery O'Connor, De Vries uses the humor of the grotesque to show the inadequacy of secular humanism and to point to religious concerns, though not with as much intensity, conviction, or originality as the Georgia writer.

THE TENTS OF WICKEDNESS

In *Comfort Me with Apples* and *The Tents of Wickedness*, De Vries introduces Chick Swallow, a suave newspaper columnist who dispenses inept advice to his readers and generally muddles their lives with his well-intentioned but wrongheaded amateur therapy. Chick and his brother-in-law, Nickie Sherman, are self-styled Oscar Wilde types, adept at café repartee and clever rejoinders but unable to manage their lives or marriages. The pair continually confuse literature and life, and Swallow, who narrates *The Tents of Wickedness*, insists on viewing his personal crises through the eyes of famous writers, which allows De Vries to display clever parodies of the styles of Thurber, J. P. Marquand, William Faulkner, Marcel Proust, Ernest Hemingway, Graham Greene, Henry James, Theodore Dreiser, Franz Kafka, James Joyce, and others.

The plot of *The Tents of Wickedness* consists of a series of thinly contrived situations involving Swallow's blundering attempts to mend his brother-in-law's split personality and to advise Sweetie Appleyard, an innocent young poetess whom he urges to take up the bohemian life, with disastrous results. Nickie vacillates between private detective and a Raffles-like jewel thief, while Sweetie is transformed from a Pre-Raphaelite poetaster to a liberated Greenwich Village type who persuades Swallow to father the child she wants in order to fulfill herself as an "emancipated woman." The action alternates between Greenwich Village and Decency, Connecticut, with De Vries predictably contrasting middle-class and beatnik lifestyles. Without De Vries' clever stylistic parodies and his brilliant verbal wit, this would be unlikely material even for a comic novel. *The Tents of Wickedness* strains credulity with its clumsy social satire and wooden characterizations. Unfortunately, De Vries never allows his characters lives of their own; instead, they serve merely as mouthpieces for his humor. These same flaws are evident in *Through the Fields of Clover*, which takes as its occasion a New England family's fortieth wedding anniversary for De Vries' satire of modern notions of family and marriage.

THE BLOOD OF THE LAMB

De Vries' next novel, *The Blood of the Lamb*, marked a sharp departure from the slapstick comedy of his earlier novels. In what is undoubtedly his finest book, he blends comedy and pathos in the story of Don Wanderhope, an obviously autobiographical character who breaks away from Chicago and his strict Dutch Calvinist background and goes east to work in a New York advertising agency. The focus of the novel is on the relationship between the protagonist and his daughter Carol, a graceful and precocious child who is stricken with leukemia. Her illness, suffering, and eventual death test Wanderhope's faith, and, through the example of his daughter's courage, lead him back to grace. *The Blood of the Lamb* contains a depth and seriousness otherwise missing in De Vries' work, since it is based on the author's loss of his own daughter Emily to the same disease. Here De Vries finds a theme that permits him to move beyond cleverness for its own sake and create characters of substance and credibility.

"What people believe is a measure of what they suffer," remarks Don Wanderhope, who is himself tried by a series of misfortunes, including the death of his older brother Louie, his father's insanity, his wife's suicide, and finally his daughter's death. Since De Vries' characters are for the most part unable to accept the consolations of traditional belief, and since they are uneasy with modern, relativistic assumptions, their suffering often seems grotesque, and it is from this quality that De Vries extracts much of his humor. This "gallows humor" is what ultimately saves Wanderhope from despair, as when, in a scene of bitter poignancy after he learns of his daughter's death, he pitches her birthday cake at a statue of the suffering Christ. The theme of the novel seems to be that, contrary to received opinion, suffering does not teach one anything; hence, laughter is the best antidote to despair.

There are some very funny episodes in *The Blood of the Lamb*, such as when Wanderhope and his future wife, Greta, are caught in bed together by Greta's parents in a model home that her parents are showing to a client. The emotional center of the book, however, is Carol, especially after her mother's suicide. Carol is the most compelling and believable character in any of De Vries' books. She is, of course, the "Lamb," and her blood is shed gratuitously to a disease for which there is no cure. "The blood of the Lamb" does not redeem anything (except perhaps the protagonist, though that point remains deliberately ambiguous), and hence her suffering and that of the other children in the leukemia hospital remains meaningless. It recalls King Herod's slaughter of the innocents. One's only defense against such realities is to laugh at the tragic absurdity of life; this tragicomic note is best illustrated by the birthday party in the hospital for the young leukemia patients.

Once Carol's illness has been diagnosed, Wanderhope must race against time to cherish every moment with his daughter while sparing her the truth of her condition. As he observes, in such a case "the greatest experience open to man is the recovery of the commonplace." In another moment of bitter emotional truth, a parent remarks to Wanderhope that grief does not unite people, it separates them. De Vries' personal credo may be reflected in the philosophical statement written by Wanderhope for his alma mater, which is read back to him in a tape recording by his daughter Carol: that man has only "Reason, Courage, and Grace" to see him through.

Later novels

Though De Vries never achieved the same artistic success with any of the novels that followed *The Blood of the Lamb*, he managed in several books to temper the humor with serious themes. In *Reuben, Reuben*, his longest novel, De Vries returned to suburban situation comedy and his burlesque of artsy sophistication. Written in three parts, the novel shifts from Frank Spofford, a shrewd chicken farmer, to Gowen McGland, a crude and dissolute Welsh poet, to Alvin Mopworth, a hapless English journalist, all of whose lives become entangled in a humorous chain of events.

In *Let Me Count the Ways*, agnostic piano mover Stan Waltz is pitted against his fundamentalist wife Elsie. *The Vale of Laughter* finds comedian Joe Sandwich trading witticisms with his humorless rival, Wally Hines, a dull professor of humor; and the novellas *The Cat's Pajamas* and *Witch's Milk* deal with characters dissatisfied with their professions or marriages. *Mrs. Wallop*, another situation comedy, finds a middle-aged woman taking on the forces of modernism.

Following the publication of these novels, De Vries proceeded to lampoon modern art and the sexual revolution in a short-story collection, *Without a Stitch in Time*, and a series of unimpressive novels: *Into Your Tent I'll Creep*, *Forever Panting*, *I Hear American Swinging*, *Madder Music*, and *Consenting Adults*.

One of De Vries' few novels that does not deal with sexual comedy is *The Glory of the Hummingbird*, an account of a likable young couple of Dutch Reformed background who, unable to have a child of their own, decide to adopt a teenage juvenile delinquent in the hope of reforming him. The protagonist, Jim Tickler, gravitates from advertising to television, where he eventually comes to host a rigged game show called the "Little Red Poolroom," where in a variation of the "Fortunate Fall," as one critic points out, he wins his foster son's affection after the show is exposed and Jim and his wife Amy are shown to be fallible.

De Vries' novels of the 1980's continued to play out clever variations of the battle of the sexes in a world of changing social mores. In *Sauce for the Goose*, Daisy Dobbin, a young feminist writer from Terre Haute, Indiana, escapes to New York to take a position at the *Metropole* magazine in order to expose the sexual harassment of women and ends by falling in love with the publisher, Dirk Dolfin, a wealthy Dutch businessman. An unconvincing feminist, Daisy betrays her "cause" in a conflict between head and heart, implying that her feminism is an inadequate substitute "religion." In *Slouching Towards Kalamazoo*, Maggie Doubloon, another liberated heroine, attempts to capitalize on her unwed motherhood by marketing T-shirts emblazoned with a scarlet "A+" after she is impregnated by one of her students. Despite its many puns and literary allusions, the novel teeters between comedy and vulgarity.

The Prick of Noon and *Peckham's Marbles* both involve picaresque rascals who attempt to rise in social class or redeem their failed literary careers by using others. In *The Prick of Noon*, Eddie Teeters, a successful pornographic film director from Backbone, Arkansas, attempts to crash into the genteel country-club society of Merrymount, Connecticut, through his affair with socially prominent Cynthia Pickles. Teeters yearns for a world that he cannot enter. Since marriage with Cynthia is out of the question, Teeters eventually settles for an attractive waitress, Toby Snapper, who shares his modest background. In *Peckham's Marbles*, Earl Peckham, a failed novelist, pursues Nelly DelBelly, the wealthy, overweight owner of the Dappled Shade rest home, and Poppy McCloud, the young author of best-selling romances, in a humorous quest for love and money.

Despite the large number of books he wrote, De Vries was essentially a one-book novelist, with *The Blood of the Lamb* rising above the level of his other works, which remain primarily entertainment. Distracted by his own cleverness, De Vries did not employ his humor in the service of any coherent social vision. Unlike Miguel de Cervantes, William Shakespeare, Mark Twain, or any of the other great comic writers, De Vries did not humanize his readers so much as divert them temporarily from the human condition. Because his characters are for the most part weakly drawn, one does not empathize with them; rather, one merely enjoys a laugh at their expense and then turns away without having gained in any measure. This lack of depth, along with the sameness of so much of his work, marks the failure of De Vries to move beyond wit to an underlying seriousness of purpose in his art.

Andrew J. Angyal

Other major works

SHORT FICTION: *No, but I Saw the Movie*, 1952; *Without a Stitch in Time: A Selection of the Best Humorous Short Pieces*, 1972.

PLAYS: *The Tunnel of Love: A Play*, pb. 1957 (adaptation of his novel; with Joseph Fields); *Spofford*, pb. 1968.

Bibliography

Boston, Richard. *An Anatomy of Laughter.* London: Collins, 1974. Study of laughter includes analysis of De Vries' work. Boston considers De Vries among the best humorists of his generation. Includes bibliography.

Bowden, Edwin T. *Peter De Vries*. Boston: Twayne, 1983. Concise critical biography provides an informative overview of De Vries' life and works. An introductory biographical chapter is followed by discussion of each of the major novels. Includes a chronology, notes, and a selected bibliography of primary and secondary works.

Campion, Dan. *Peter De Vries and Surrealism.* Lewisburg, Pa.: Bucknell University Press, 1995. Discusses De Vries' literary life, his encounter with Surrealism in the 1930's, his novel *But Who Wakes the Bugler?*, and his use of humor. Includes detailed notes and bibliography.

Davies, Robertson. *A Voice from the Attic: Essays on the Art of Reading*. Rev. ed. New York: Penguin Books, 1990. Collection of essays about literature and reading includes discussion of De Vries' fiction. Robertson, a noted Canadian novelist and playwright, lauds De Vries' ear for language and defends his relaxed use of first-person narrators.

De Vries, Peter. "An Interview in New York with Peter De Vries." Interview by Richard B. Sale. *Studies in the Novel* 1 (1969): 364-369. De Vries discusses his writing habits and answers questions about the type of humor in his novels and his view of the world.

_______. "An Interview with Peter De Vries." Interview by Douglas M. David. *College English* 28 (April, 1967): 524-530. De Vries answers some interesting questions about his style of humor in this lively interview. He also discusses his use of suburban settings, his character types, and his humorous attitude toward sexuality.

Frank, Jeffrey. "Riches of Embarrassment." *The New Yorker* 80, no. 13 (May 24, 2004). Presents a detailed examination of De Vries' life and novels. Frank concludes that "few writers have understood literary comedy as well as De Vries, and few comic novelists have had his grasp of tragedy."

Jellema, Roderick. *Peter De Vries: A Critical Essay.* Grand Rapids, Mich.: Wm. B. Eerdmans, 1966. Critical study of De Vries' first eight novels points to the religious issues that are often overlooked in discussions of De Vries as a humorist.

Kort, Wesley A. *Shriven Selves: Religious Problems in Recent American Fiction.* Philadelphia: Fortress Press, 1974. Examines fiction by De Vries and other writers in which the main characters are "shriven" or confessed selves. Kort sees De Vries as someone comfortable neither in the community of faith nor outside it.

Yagoda, Ben. "Being Seriously Funny." *The New York Times Magazine*, June 12, 1983. Feature article presents a portrait of De Vries and an overview of his literary career. Offers a good introduction to the writer and his work.

MARGARET DRABBLE

Born: Sheffield, South Yorkshire, England; June 5, 1939
Also known as: Lady Holroyd

PRINCIPAL LONG FICTION

A Summer Bird-Cage, 1963
The Garrick Year, 1964
The Millstone, 1965 (also known as *Thank You All Very Much*)
Jerusalem the Golden, 1967
The Waterfall, 1969
The Needle's Eye, 1972
The Realms of Gold, 1975
The Ice Age, 1977
The Middle Ground, 1980
The Radiant Way, 1987
A Natural Curiosity, 1989
The Gates of Ivory, 1991
The Witch of Exmoor, 1997
The Peppered Moth, 2000
The Seven Sisters, 2002
The Red Queen, 2004
The Sea Lady: A Late Romance, 2006

OTHER LITERARY FORMS

Margaret Drabble has combined literary scholarship with her career as a novelist. Among other works, she has published a short critical study of William Wordsworth, *Wordsworth: Literature in Perspective* (1966), and has edited a collection of critical essays about Thomas Hardy, *The Genius of Thomas Hardy* (1975). Over the years, she has edited or written introductions for most of Jane Austen's works for various publishers, including *Lady Susan*, *The Watsons*, and *Sanditon*. She has also edited editions of Thomas Hardy's *The Woodlanders* and Emily Brontë's *Wuthering Heights* and *Poems*. In 1989, she published her Gareth Lloyd Evans Shakespeare Lecture at Stratford-Upon-Avon as *Stratford Revisited: A Legacy of the Sixties*. She has also written two major biographies: *Arnold Bennett* (1974) and *Angus Wilson* (1995). Her literary travelogue *A Writer's Britain: Landscape in Literature* was published in 1979, and she is well known for editing the fifth edition of *The Oxford Companion to English Literature* (1985, revised 2000).

In addition, Drabble has had a long-standing connection with drama. Her works include *Bird of Paradise* (pr. 1969), a stage play; *A Touch of Love* (1969), a screenplay based on her novel *The Millstone*; and *Laura* (1964), a play for television. Drabble has also written a fair number of short stories that are as yet uncollected and only partially available to American audiences. In 1978, she published the children's book *For Queen and Country: Britain in the Victorian Age*.

ACHIEVEMENTS

Margaret Drabble's novels charm and delight, but perhaps more significant is that they reward their readers with a distinctively modern woman's narrative voice and an unusual blend of Victorian and modern structures and concerns. Although there seems to be critical consensus that Drabble has, as Bernard Bergonzi has said, "devised a genuinely new character and predicaments," the exact nature of this new voice and situation has not been precisely defined. Bergonzi sees the new character as an original blend of career woman and mother, yet Drabble's career woman begins to appear only in her seventh novel, *The Realms of Gold*. Her earlier, equally freshly portrayed heroines are often not mothers—for example, Sarah in *A Summer Bird-Cage* or Clara in *Jerusalem the Golden*. Most of the mothers who precede Frances Wingate in *The Realms of Gold* can in no way be considered career women. Rose Vassiliou in *The Needle's Eye* does not work; Rosamund Stacey in *Thank You All Very Much* works only sporadically to support her baby, and her job can hardly be considered a career.

Other critics have claimed that the new voice involves an unprecedented acquaintance with the maternal attitude toward children. This is the voice Erica Jong predicted would emerge once motherhood was no longer thought incompatible with literary artistry. In fact, only three Drabble novels can be said to contain this voice—*Thank You All Very Much*, *The Ice Age*, and *The Middle Ground*—yet all the novels seem to present something original in their female point of view.

Female characters have illuminated literature for more than a thousand years, but until relatively recently they have appeared as secondary figures. The female has been present, but her point of view and voice have been lacking. Drabble seems to be able to evoke not only the female point of view but also the cadence of the female voice. Her ear for speech rhythms is exceptional, and each central female character has a distinct speech pattern and cadence. This is, of course, more intensely true in the first-person narratives of Drabble's earlier novels, but it is also true of her later novels in which the heroine's interior life is rendered by an omniscient narrator who mimes her speech in order to discuss her feelings and thoughts. Perhaps Drabble's artistry in portraying the sound of the female voice is among her most significant accomplishments, more simple and more complex than the evocation of a maternal career woman or of the mother-child bond.

Drabble has also begun to experiment with the return of the outspoken omniscient narrator. Drabble's rediscovery of an old literary technique seems timely rather than regressive. She does not embed the characters in the amber of the narrator's point of view, preventing them from dramatizing themselves. Drabble's omniscient narrator gives the reader a sense of place, a sense of location and history, without forcing the characters to bear the burden of carrying all that perception in their minds. It frees the characters to notice only what they perceive within the confines of their personalities, for there is a narrative voice to create the density of the social and physical scene.

The narrator's involvement in place and history has important thematic implications for Drabble's fiction. Drabble departs from the prevalent modern emphasis on the centrality of the individual sensibility, reaching back instead to the tradition of two authors she admires, Arnold Bennett and George Eliot. She explores modern fragmentation as a function, to some extent, of human choice. She explores the consequences of choosing to submit to centrifugal forces as opposed to struggling against them in an effort to be true to one's roots. This original blend of a deep concern for society's conventions and origins and an unusually sensitive evocation of the individual female sensibility gives Drabble's works their particular flavor.

Drabble's novels have won many prizes, including the John Llewelyn Rhys Memorial Award (1966), the James Tait Black Memorial Prize (1968), the Book of the Year Award from the *Yorkshire Post* (1972), and the E. M. Forster Award of the American Academy of Arts and Letters (1973). Drabble has received honorary D.Litt. degrees from many universities, including Sheffield, Manchester, Keele, Bradford, Hull, East Anglia, and York. She was made an honorary fellow of the Sheffield City Polytechnic in 1989. In 1980, she was made a Commander of the Order of the British Empire; in 2008, she was promoted to Dame Commander.

BIOGRAPHY

Margaret Drabble was born into a family that reflects at once the breakup of old patterns and the power of conventions, which may account for her receptiveness to both aspects of modern England. Her parents, John Frederick Drabble and Kathleen Marie (Bloor) Drabble, were the first of their families to attend university. The results of her parents' upward mobility were both creative and destructive. Her father became a barrister and then a judge; her mother suffered the dislocations that attend such rapid social changes. She became an atheist and thus estranged herself from her religious fundamentalist parents. Drabble has stated that her mother was released from the harshness of her religious training when, as a young woman, she read George Bernard Shaw. As she turned the pages she had a revelation that there is no God. "One could say," says Drabble, "that that was a revelation from God not to worry about him because it was going to drive her mad if she did." Drabble's mother struggled against clinical depression until her death.

Margaret Drabble is the second of three daughters. Her sisters are Dr. Helen Langdon, a scholar, and Susan Duffy, a novelist, whose pen name is A. S. Byatt. She also has a brother, Richard J. B. Drabble. She attended a Quaker boarding school in York, The Mount School, and then read English at Newnham College, Cambridge, where she finished among the top of her class. In 1960, in the week that she finished at Cambridge, she married Clive Swift.

Swift was an aspiring actor who worked with the Royal Shakespeare Company. In the early years of their marriage, Drabble spent much of her time having three children, writing novels, and acting in bit parts and understudying for the Royal Shakespeare Company. While she was writing *The Garrick Year*, she understudied Imogen in *Cymbeline*, played a fairy in *A Midsummer Night's Dream*, and had a bit part in *The Taming of the Shrew*. Drabble separated from her husband in 1972; their divorce became final in 1975.

Drabble is a member of the National Book League and served as its chair from 1980 to 1982. During the 1980's she devoted much of her energy to revising *The Oxford Companion to English Literature* for its fifth edition. In 1982, she married the biographer Michael Holroyd. They settled in the Notting Hill district of London and at Porlock Weir, Somerset.

Analysis

Margaret Drabble's novels begin as female arias in the bel canto style, predominantly elaborate embellishments on a simple series of events relative only to the first-person narrator, events that reflect a brief but formative time in the narrator's life. The early novels deal with the lives of rather ordinary middle-class girls and, but for their sensitivity and subtlety of insight, come dangerously close to being considered women's magazine fiction. The later novels are more complex, exploring the delicate webs of social interconnections and covering longer periods of time in which the convergences of many lives on one another effect subtle and not-so-subtle changes. Both the early and later novels express Drabble's concern with finding the legitimate sources of growth and development. Her later novels explore global concerns in addition to the domestic. Throughout the entire canon of Drabble's novels one finds the use of irony and the display of comedic wit, sometimes in the form of black comedy.

A Summer Bird-Cage

Drabble's distinctive narrative voice is clear in her first novel. Sarah Bennett, a recent college graduate, is the protagonist of *A Summer Bird-Cage* but figures mainly as a witness to her sister Louise's marriage. From her older sister's mistakes, Sarah learns about her own attitude toward the future. The novel begins as Sarah returns from Paris to attend Louise's marriage to Stephen Halifax, a boring, trendy, wealthy, satirical novelist. Louise is a stunning and exciting raven-haired beauty, and Sarah cannot understand why she is marrying the bloodless Stephen. Sarah and her friends attempt to puzzle this out through the progress of the novel, especially as it becomes increasingly obvious that Louise has been having an affair with a very attractive actor, John Connell. In the end, Sarah learns directly from Louise what was obvious all the while: Louise married Stephen for his money. Rather than seeming anticlimactic, this knowledge solidifies Sarah's growing understanding of what fidelity and betrayal are about. Despite its socially sanctioned position, the marriage Louise has contracted is in fact adulterous because it is a betrayal of her heart and affections. The technical adultery is an act of faith.

Louise divorces Stephen to take her chances with John, and Sarah ends the novel with a forged bond of affection with Louise. Sarah is thus prepared for the return of her boyfriend, Francis, from America. Having observed Louise, Sarah realizes that fidelity to her vow to marry Francis is not as important as waiting to see if in fact their relationship has its roots in truth. Sarah will only marry if the action follows from an authentic feeling.

JERUSALEM THE GOLDEN

In her fourth novel, *Jerusalem the Golden*, Drabble experimented for the first time with omniscient narration, maintaining an ironic distance from her protagonist. Clara Maugham, a provincial girl from Northam, a small town in the North of England, is that young woman all too familiar in fiction, the woman whose capacities for development are greater than the opportunities presented by her narrow circumstances. In general, such a character is often created by a writer who has escaped the clutches of small minds and tight social structures; an identity of author and character is usually suspected. The character becomes a vehicle through which the author gets back at the tormentors of his or her youth; the character finds dazzling fulfillment in the city.

Clara Maugham, then, comes out of this tradition, but she does not lead the reader into the usual pitfalls. Drabble considers the problems of leaving one's roots for fuller possibilities. As impoverished as one's heritage may be, it provides one with a foothold in reality. Hence the title of the novel is a mocking one—it alludes to the utopian dream that emerges from a hymn to which Clara is attracted as a schoolgirl:

> Jerusalem the Golden
> With Milk and Honey blest
> Beneath thy contemplation
> Sink heart and voice oppressed.
> I know not, oh, I know not
> What social joys are there
> What radiance of glory
> What light beyond compare.

For Clara, the mysteries of ecstasy counterpoint the threadbare, wretched, familiar world. For her there is nothing in between, and she leaves Northam only to find a sham Jerusalem in London.

Clara begins life believing that she is doomed to be as her mother is, a woman without hope who remarks that when she is dead the garbage collector can cart her off. Mrs. Maugham is a jealous, inconsistent woman who verbally snipes at her neighbors behind her lace curtains because of their concern for their proprieties, and then she outdoes them in cheap ostentation. Rejecting such a life, Clara finds hope in literary images. Metaphors provide avenues of escape, as in the hymn; so too does a children's story that makes a deep impression on her, *The Two Weeds*. The story presents the choices of two weeds. One decides on longevity at the cost of a miserly conservation of its resources, growing "low and small and brown"; the other longs for intensity, the spectacular but short life, and puts its efforts into fabulous display. Each weed achieves its goal. The small, plain one survives, as it had hoped. The magnificent, attractive weed is plucked and dies happily at the bosom of a lovely girl. What impresses Clara about this story is the offer of any possibility other than the low road of mere survival. Little by little, Clara chooses the mysteries of ecstasy.

Clara has to make her way to these mysteries by rejecting a more moderate course, thus losing real opportunities to grow and succeed. Her intellect is widely despised by the good people of Northam, although it is valued by some of her teachers, who fight to attach her to their subjects. She is also revered by a boy named Walter Ash, who values culture and comes from a family tradition that stresses intellectual stimulation. Clara is cynical about her teachers' admiration; she does not value their esteem. She allows Walter to go out with her, but she has little regard for him. She ultimately rejects him, thinking, "I shall get further if I'm pulled, I can't waste time going first."

This cryptic remark makes sense only in the light of her choices in London, to which she goes on scholarship to attend Queens College. By chance, she meets Clelia Denham at a poetry reading. This meeting drives her to an instinctual attachment to the girl and subsequently to her family, especially Clelia's brother Gabriel, with whom she has an affair. Although her attachments to the Denhams "pull her," and she does not need to "go first," it is questionable whether they take her anywhere. Indeed, the Denhams provide her the accoutrements of ecstasy. The life she leads with them, however, having torn herself away from her unsatisfactory family, is not one that she builds herself. It is one that envelops her in a "radiance of glory."

The Denhams are rich, and their money is old. Their family house is exquisitely done in tile, with fireplaces, pictures, and mirrors—old, good things. Outside the house is a terraced garden that to Clara is the original Eden. The Denhams themselves are good-looking people who dress well and speak cleverly. Mrs. Denham is a writer known professionally as Candida Grey. Mr. Denham is a lawyer. Magnus, the oldest boy, is a rich capitalist. Gabriel is in television, and Clelia works in a chic art gallery.

To the detached eye, the Denham children seem smothered by this "good life." The oldest child, no longer living in the Denham house, has gone crazy. Clelia is startlingly infantile. She speaks in all situations as if to a close relative, never using tact or discretion. Although twenty-seven years old, she lives at home, seemingly unable to establish herself on her own as wife, mother, or career woman. The job she holds in the gallery is purely decorative, one she obtained through family connections, and on which she could never support herself. Her extremely chic room contains her childhood toys as part of the decor. Clara interprets their presence as part of Clelia's enviable sense of continuity with a happy childhood. Unfortunately for both Clelia and Clara, they are signs of a childhood that has never ended.

Gabriel is married and lives with his wife and children in one of those fashionable sections of London that are emerging from slum conditions. He has a good job with Independent Television and makes a good salary. He and his wife, Phillipa, make stunning personal impressions. When Clara visits the couple, however, she is appalled to find that their home is in a state of chaos. The house is potentially as beautiful as others in the neighborhood that have been renovated, but nothing has been done to it. The floors are pitted and worn, the walls are badly in need of paint, the ancient wallpaper hangs in tatters, and the rooms are poorly lit. The kitchen is a war zone in which the litter of cracking plaster vies with expensive cooking equipment. Phillipa is unable to provide food for her family or any kind of supportive attention to the children. Gabriel is unable to organize a life of his own, so dependent is he on the glorious life of his parents' house. Gabriel becomes obsessively attracted to Clara and dreams of a ménage à trois between them and Clelia.

Magnus is an industrial mogul, a bachelor who becomes parasitically and emotionally attached to Gabriel's women. At first in love with Phillipa, when he senses the affair between Gabriel and Clara he begins an erotic flirtation with Clara. Clara gives herself over emotionally to all the Denhams, and sexually to the brothers Magnus and Gabriel. She feels little for them, or anyone, but the lust for inclusion in a beautiful life. She acts out increasingly more elaborate scenes with them, climaxed by a visit to Paris with Gabriel. During this journey, a flirtation between Clara and Magnus sends Gabriel back to the hotel where he and Clara are staying. Clara outdoes him by leaving him sleeping to miss his plane while she returns to London alone. Once there, she discovers that her mother is dying of cancer.

Clara visits her mother, but there is no feeling between them. Returning to London, her connections to her childhood severed, she finds that the affair with the Denhams is just beginning. Despite the seemingly decisive break in Paris, Clara is now well into Denham games. Her future is to be composed of "Clelia, and Gabriel and she herself in shifting and ideal conjunctions." There is no mention of the development of her intellect or talents.

Clara, at last, contemplates her victory: her triumph over her mother's death, her triumph over her early life, her survival of all of it. "Even the mercy and kindness of destiny she would survive; they would not get her that way, they would not get her at all." These final words are fully ironic: Clara has not triumphed over anything. She is a victim of her own fear of life. Her evasion of a nebulous "them" is a type of paranoid delusion that amounts to a horror of life. Clara has been true to her need to expand but false to what she is. The outcome is not a joyous one. She has achieved a perverse isolation in a bogus, sterile Jerusalem.

THE WATERFALL

The same themes are explored in Drabble's next novel, *The Waterfall*. Though rendered in the first person by the central character, Jane Grey, *The Waterfall* is a highly ironic, fearfully complex exploration of the question that informs *A Summer Bird-Cage* and *Jerusalem the Golden*: To what must one be true? A vast variety of claims are made on one's fidelity, and these claims frequently pull in different directions. Shall one be true to one's family? One's religion? One's friends? One's heart? One's sexuality? One's intellect? Even from the simple personal perspective, Drabble arrives at an impasse from which the protagonist herself cannot reckon her obligations or even the main issue deserving of her attention.

Jane Grey begins her story giving birth, overwhelmed, that is, by her biology, shaped and determined by her gender, her flesh, her sexuality. This is confirmed by her statement to her husband, Malcolm, who has left her before the birth of their second child, "If I were drowning, I couldn't reach out a hand to save myself, so unwilling am I to set myself up against my fate."

Jane Grey is a woman who does not give allegiance to anything that requires conscious choice. She cannot sustain a marriage, a career, or any affiliation that calls for directed will. She is faithful only to what takes her, overwhelms her, leaving her no choice—her sexuality. Thus she can be a mother, but not a wife. She can be a lover, but not a companion. The result is that she becomes the adulterous, almost incestuous lover of James, her cousin Lucy's husband. This comes about in a way that can be seen as nothing less than a betrayal of a number of social norms.

Because Jane has been deserted by Malcolm, Lucy and James alternate visits to assist her. Lucy, who has been like a sister to Jane, initiates these visits without Jane's request. Jane's breaking of her marriage vows and her betrayal of Lucy are not as uncomplicated as Louise's affair with John in *A Summer Bird-Cage*. Louise has violated nothing more than the law; Jane has violated the bonds of her heart, since Lucy has been so close to her, and the bonds of family and morality, as well as the bonds of law and ethics. Nevertheless, there is a fidelity in Jane's choice. She and James, whose name is deliberately the male reflection of hers, are, in being overwhelmed by each other, satisfying the deepest narcissistic sexuality in each other. It is, of course, true that in so doing they create social limbo for their mates and their children, and for themselves.

Their adultery is discovered when they are in an automobile accident. James's car hits a brick, although he is driving carefully, as they begin a weekend outing together with Jane's children. The car turns over; only James is hurt, and he recovers almost fully. Jane and James continue with their ordinary life. Neither Malcolm nor Lucy exacts any payment from them. The lovers meet when they can. The novel ends with their only full weekend together after the accident. Jane and James climb the Goredale Scar, one of England's scenic wonders. They are there because someone described it so enthusiastically to Jane that it became her goal to see it herself. The Scar is the quintessential female sexual symbol, a cavernous cleft in the mountains, flushed by a waterfall and covered by a pubic growth of foliage. Drabble then sends the lovers back to their hotel room to drink Scotch inadvertently dusted by talcum powder, which leaves a bad taste in their mouths. They have been faithful in their own minds to a force validated by nature.

THE NEEDLE'S EYE

The Needle's Eye, regarded by many readers as Drabble's finest novel, takes its title from Jesus' proverbial words to a rich young man: "It is easier for a camel to go through the eye of a needle, than for a rich man to enter into the kingdom of God" (Matthew 19:24). At the center of the novel are Simon Camish, a barrister from a poor background who would seem to have regretfully gained the world at the expense of his soul, and Rose Bryanston Vassiliou, a rich young woman who compulsively divests herself of the benefits of her inheritance but is not fully enjoying her flight into the lower classes.

Rose, a pale, timid girl, had created a tabloid sensation by marrying out of her class. Her choice was the disreputable, seedy, sexy Christopher Vassiliou, son of Greek immigrants whose pragmatic financial dealings are not solidly within the boundaries of the law. Rose sought to escape from the evils of wealth through Christopher, one of the downtrodden. Much to her consternation, however, Christopher is not a "happy peasant." He detests poverty, legitimately, and associates it not with virtue but with humiliation and deprivation, both of which he has endured.

Christopher's dream is to make something of himself. This dream is strengthened by the birth of their three children, for whom Christopher wants "only the best." He sees in Rose's war on wealth nothing but perverse self-destructiveness. His fury vents itself in physical abuse. Frail, pale Rose is equally adamant in the protection of her children's future. To her mind, "the best" means freedom from possessions. Again Rose and Christopher become figures of tabloid fantasy, this time in a dramatic divorce case.

Rose is working out her divorce settlement when she meets Simon. Simon is introduced to the reader on the same night that he is introduced to Rose; the reader first sees him in a store, buying liquor. Simon feels estranged from the lower-class types who frequent and staff the store. Soon thereafter, this isolation is established as a sharp discontinuity in Simon's life, for he has risen from these ranks. He has been pushed upward by a mother embarrassed by the meanness of her lower-class life and determined that her son will have what she never had. Ironically, the essential gap in his mother's life is also left unfilled in Simon's; that is, the need for warmth and affection. Simon tried to marry into an inheritance of warmth and wealth by his alliance with what he thought was a good-natured girl of the comfortable upper-middle class, Julie Phillips. Their marriage, however, only revealed her fear and insecurity, her essential coldness. What Simon had mistaken for warmth was merely superficial brightness, a by-product of the Phillipses' affluence.

Rose and Simon have attempted to gain what each personally lacked through marriage, as if one could graft onto oneself a human capacity with a wedding ring. Such marriages are doomed to failure. Also doomed has been Rose's attempt to meet human needs with "filthy lucre." She has given a huge portion of her inheritance to a schoolhouse in a lonely, little-known part of Africa. Within months, the school was demolished in the chaos of a civil war, along with approximately one hundred children. Rose does not attempt to deny the futility of what she has done.

Simon and Rose strike up a professional acquaintance, casually, it seems, because Christopher has begun some devious maneuvers to get his children away from Rose. As he becomes increasingly involved in helping Rose, Simon realizes that he is in love with her. Rose reveals but a few of her feelings on this issue, but she does indicate the joy she takes in his company. While Rose and Simon are chasing around after Christopher, who appears to be in the process of abducting the children and taking them out of England, Simon finally tells Rose that, were they at liberty, he would marry her. He blurts out this sentiment as they are walking in a woodland setting. The moment of his revelation finds them in sudden confrontation with a dead stoat hanging grotesquely in front of them, a dried-up little corpse. According to the narrator, this is "a warning" to Simon and Rose.

The satisfaction that Rose and Simon might find together is based on their shared concern for their obligations and duties. To turn to each other, a temptation for both of them, would be a betrayal of the very basis of their attraction to each other, as it would necessitate shirking their responsibilities. It is the grace in them that understands commitments beyond the self. Understanding this, Simon and Rose remain friends; Christopher and Rose are reunited. Rose has achieved a modus vivendi with Christopher, who goes to work for her father. There is no fully articulated happiness, but a kind of integrity exists at the heart of Rose's and Simon's arrangement.

In the novel's final tableau, Rose is looking at a vandalized plaster lion outside a second-rate British edifice called the Alexandra Palace. The lion's head is broken, revealing a hollow inside. It has been spray-painted red with the name of a local gang, but Rose decides that she likes it. Although it began life as an anonymous, mass-produced piece of kitsch, the lion has been worn into something unique: "It had weathered into identity. And this she hoped for every human soul." Rose's final wish accepts the uniqueness of life, the beauty of its mere being. She rejects the vision of a life that is continually being held up to an intellectual ideal, by which standards the lion, like her life, is an awful mess.

Drabble has said in an interview that, had she written *The Needle's Eye* after her husband left her, she might have altered Rose's destiny; perhaps she meant that Rose might have been sent off with Simon after all. Perhaps these words reveal something of the personal Drabble, but they are a betrayal of the novel. The delicacy of Simon and Rose's poise in front of the dead stoat and the final image of the lion resist second thoughts.

THE REALMS OF GOLD

Drabble has called *The Realms of Gold* her only comedy. It is the most elaborately plotted of her novels, and Drabble has observed that comedies are permitted such carefully structured plots. Perhaps Drabble defends her plot to excuse herself for pivoting the outcome of her story on the delay in the mail of a postcard, consciously parodying the tragic turn of William Shakespeare's *Romeo and Juliet* (pr. c. 1595-1596), when Romeo's letter from Friar Laurence is delayed. Unlike the passion of Romeo and Juliet, however, the passion of the lovers in *The Realms of Gold*, Frances Wingate and Karel Schmidt, is not "too swift, too unadvised." Frances and Karel are survivors, and it is for this reason that true love between them is possible.

The novel begins in a hotel room. Frances is on a lecture tour, giving talks about her discovery of an ancient city, Tizouk. One evening, in a fit of loneliness, she writes a postcard to Karel, whom she capriciously rejected six months previously. She now regrets her action. Impulsively, she writes on the card, "I miss you. I love you." She is bothered when she receives no response, ignorant of the fact that the card has not been delivered, having been mislaid by the European mail system. Frances is distraught, but she carries on as mother to her four children, as a professional, and as a member of her family.

Karel, too, carries on, thinking hopelessly about Frances, his lost love, puzzled by her rejection of him, suffering at the hands of his deranged wife and his students at the polytechnic, where he is a lecturer in history. Both wife and students continually take advantage of Karel's patience and good nature, and he, not quite understanding why, allows them to victimize him.

Karel and Frances's professional interests, history and archaeology, bring to the novel the long view of continuity. This view is partially what sustains Karel and Frances, whose families cannot or will not support them. Karel has been cut off from his family by the horrors of history. He is Jewish, the only member of his immediate family to survive World War II. Frances, on the other hand, has a large family, but it is wracked with odd and self-destructive behavior: alcoholism, suicide, depression. Frances's family is composed of two estranged branches, isolated from each other by an ancient quarrel—that no one can remember—between two brothers. During the course of the novel, the branches are reconciled. The healing begins when Frances discovers her cousin David, of whom she was previously unaware. She meets him professionally at a conference of the United Nations Educational, Scientific, and Cultural Organization (UNESCO) in Adra.

The conference has taken Frances away from England at a particularly crucial time in the life of her family. In Tockley, in the English Midlands, an old lady discovered dead of starvation turns out to be Frances's estranged great-aunt. As Frances's family is a prominent one, there is a scandal about this shocking neglect of a family member. Frances is called home from the conference and discovers another lost cousin, Janet Bird, the last person to see their great-aunt alive. Meanwhile, Frances's cousin David is surprised at the conference by the arrival of Karel, who, finally receiving the delayed postcard, flies heedlessly to join Frances at the conference and must be escorted by David back to Tockley. The results of these and more complications are the marriage of Karel and Frances and the reunification of Frances's family.

Frances and Karel synthesize stability and freedom; their marriage triumphantly asserts the victory of human freedom through history, continuity, and culture. The horrors of history—present in the Nazi persecution of the Jews, Frances's blighted family history, and the evidence of child sacrifice that Frances has found in her ancient city Tizouk—do not lead to a rejection of continuity but to the passion to grow through it and outlive the evil it contains.

The major image of *The Realms of Gold* incarnates the comic attitude necessary if one is to lay hands on that hard-won treasure known as life. Shortly before Frances had rejected Karel, causing the long separation that was to end in Tockley, Frances and Karel were enjoying a vacation together. Endeavoring to spend a pleasant day in the country, they had driven their car into the mud, resulting in the bespattering of their persons in a most unromantic way. In the midst of their predicament, they heard a strange, almost ominous sound. An investigation turned up hundreds of frogs simply honking away in a drainage pipe in a ditch. Frances and Karel were flooded with affection and amusement at this gratuitously joyous spectacle. The image of it never leaves them and becomes a sustaining force during their ordeal of separation. Perhaps this is Drabble's best image of a realistic optimism in a very flawed world: joy spontaneously uttered from a muddy ditch.

THE ICE AGE

In *The Ice Age*, Drabble considers the problem of survival within a dying tradition. England is enduring an ice age: Its social structure is collapsing. In a brilliantly dark vision, Drabble surveys the challenge this poses to personal resources.

As the novel begins, a reckless real estate speculator, Len Wincobank, is serving time in Scratby Open Prison for fraud. Len's technically innocent accomplice, Maureen Kirby, is wondering how to fit the pieces of her life back together again. A teenage girl, Jane Murray, daughter of an extremely beautiful former actor, Alison Murray, is on trial in the remote Communist country of Wallachia. Anthony Keating, a charming author of musical comedies turned real estate speculator, is recovering from a heart attack and the collapse of his financial empire.

All the characters are suffering through imprisonment in England. It is a time in which Max and Kitty Friedman are the victims of an Irish Republican Army (IRA) terrorist attack as they are having an anniversary dinner. England is plagued by degenerate youth, a situation frightening in what it portends for the future. Jane Murray is an angry, shallow child, seemingly incapable of love or of true civility. Anthony Keating finds two young squatters on the empty floor of his former home. The girl is a heroin addict, pregnant and in labor. The boy is drunk and stoned, unable to summon assistance for the girl. Anthony's chance visit to his old house means that the girl will get to the hospital, but she will die and her baby will be born suffering from prenatal heroin addiction.

Through the gloom of England's dark night, Drabble feels her way toward dawn, steadfastly refusing to deny the value of principle because history is suffering temporarily from chaos. She paints a damning picture of a contemporary of Anthony, Mike Morgan, a comedian who pointlessly and viciously ridicules his audience because he mistakes a bad patch for the end of coherence. She also, however, defends the human being as a flexible, creative source of energy not to be trapped within rigidities of principle.

Alison Murray emerges as the polar opposite to Mike Morgan. She too is a doomed soul, because as England flails about, she has chosen the sterility of a noble perfection over the struggles of possibility. Alison's choice has been to devote herself to her brain-damaged daughter, Molly, rather than to her normal daughter, Jane. Molly can never develop and grow, despite Alison's martyrdom, and Jane is wild and sullen as a result of her displacement. Drabble shows that Alison's choice is at least as bad as Mike's, leading directly to her own misery and indirectly to Jane's self-imposed troubles in Wallachia. Alison's choice also leads indirectly to Anthony Keating's downfall.

Anthony, Alison's lover, goes to Wallachia to escort Jane home when the authorities suddenly decide to return her to England. A civil war erupts, randomly freeing Jane and trapping Anthony. He is mistaken for a British spy and remanded to a Siberian-style forced-labor camp.

Between the extremes of Mike Morgan and Alison Murray lies the possibility of working one's way back to continuity by keeping the spirit free. The major examples of such survival in the novel are Maureen Kirby and Anthony Keating. Maureen is a lower-class girl, sexy rather than beautiful, who falls somewhat short of conventional morality. Hardly a person who eschews extremes, Maureen has been the partner of Len Wincobank in his whirlwind financial spree. She has also temporarily retreated into her own selfish, protected world when Len is imprisoned, but she is resilient. In a striking narrative device, Drabble looks into the future at the end of the novel, coolly summarizing the fates of her characters. Maureen is projected as a woman of the 1980's who ultimately marries well and becomes a role model to young women. Her coarse-grained vitality and common sense lack the charm of Alison's elegant self-immolation, but they radiate the warmth of survival.

Anthony Keating, in his frozen Wallachian prison, the ice age of England made palpable, turns also toward life in the only way that is available to him. He becomes enthralled with watching birds, symbols of his spirit, which, despite everything, remains untrammeled.

At the close of the novel, the state of the nation is given a good prognosis. It will recover, asserts the narrator. Anthony has come to terms. Len will surely go on to further development and a financial comeback. Maureen's trajectory is in ascent, but, asserts the narrator, Alison Murray will never recover. The doom of Alison Murray strongly suggests that her kind of retreat from possibility is the worst prison of all, subject to no reprieve or amelioration. Here Drabble seems to have found the limits of what critics have called her conservatism. Cutting off from one's roots to rise in the world brings peril, and denying one's context in order to acquire more brings suffering; these may reveal the flaws in the liberal dream. The ultimate horror, however, would seem to be turning away from growth, regardless of the reason.

THE RADIANT WAY

In her novels of the 1980's—*The Middle Ground*, *The Radiant Way*, and *A Natural Curiosity*—Drabble continued to work in the manner of *The Realms of Gold* and *The Ice Age*.

Her intrusive narrators continued to reflect on the nature of fiction and to make arch asides to the reader. All three of these novels center on well-educated characters of the upper middle class whose domestic concerns are intertwined with larger social issues.

The Radiant Way, *A Natural Curiosity*, and a long novel published in 1991, *The Gates of Ivory*, form a trilogy that follows a number of characters through the 1980's and beyond. *The Gates of Ivory* is not only a long book but also a demanding one. It moves from England to Thailand and back and seems to take as its subject not only the state of England but also the state of the world. In the book's opening sentence, Drabble understandably wonders whether it is a novel at all.

There is no doubt that the first two books in the trilogy are novels. As *The Ice Age* had shown Britain's suffering during a Labour government, so these novels show national life under Prime Minister Margaret Thatcher. At the center of the novels are three women friends: Liz Headleand, a psychotherapist; Alix Bowen, an idealistic social worker; and Esther Breuer, a mysterious art historian who focuses on minor figures of the Italian Renaissance. The title *The Radiant Way* refers both to a book that Liz's husband, Charles, read as a boy and to a television documentary he made in the 1960's. It also provides the novel's double-edged central symbol: the radiant personal sun of achievement that many of its youthful characters once envisioned and a radiant national future of justice and harmony. The novel's other pervasive symbol is a web—a vast and complicated web of interconnections in which the characters live.

The novel begins at Liz's New Year's Eve party in the last minutes of 1979. The 1980's get off to a bad start when Charles announces that he is leaving her. Things get worse nationally as relations between social classes deteriorate and as the gap between the North and South of England widens. Alix, the most political of the three friends, finds that her efforts to help the underprivileged not only bear no fruit but also lead to horrible violence. She loses faith in her husband's old-fashioned lower-class values and is content to sift through the papers of an old poet. Liz finds herself enmeshed in a personal web with her sister, Shirley Harper, unhappily married back in their home in the North of England, and with their mother, Rita. The Dickensian secret that Rita Ablewhite keeps is one of even more interrelationships.

A NATURAL CURIOSITY

By means of a loosely constructed narrative that shifts from plot thread to plot thread, *A Natural Curiosity* enables readers to follow the stories of the three women up to the point where *The Gates of Ivory* begins. In *A Natural Curiosity*, Liz and her former husband try to discover what has happened to a friend of theirs who is being held hostage. Liz also worries about the fate of another friend, a novelist named Stephen Cox. (The story of Stephen Cox forms the backbone of the plot of *The Gates of Ivory*.) Alix, now living in the North, visits the murderer who was introduced in the previous novel and brings him books. In order to try to understand him, she tracks down and confronts his unpleasant father and even more unpleasant mother. Shirley Harper is more prominent in this book; she finds herself free for the first time in her adult life and flees to Paris and a wild affair. Liz and Shirley find that the Ablewhite family mysteries deepen and go in new directions; these lead in turn to new revelations and new energy. Drabble's narrative voice is more intrusive in this novel than in her previous works.

THE GATES OF IVORY

The final novel of the trilogy that includes *The Radiant Way* and *A Natural Curiosity*, *The Gates of Ivory* follows Liz Headleand's investigation into the disappearance of Stephen Cox, who had traveled to Southeast Asia ostensibly to research Pol Pot in order to write a play. After a discursive section on "Good Time" and "Bad Time," the novel begins with the opening of a mysterious package delivered to Liz. The first items Liz finds are two finger bones. Also included are newspaper clippings, notebooks, postcards, a poem by Arthur Rimbaud, and photographs. One photograph is of a Khmer woman, Mme Savet Akrun, with the caption, "Where is my son?" In addition, Liz finds pages of an apparent novel in progress, which begins, "And he came to a land where the water flows uphill." Discovering the handwriting of Stephen Cox, Liz is propelled into the full mystery of Stephen's disappearance, the atrocities of a faraway land, and questions concerning the moral integrity of humanity itself.

In this novel, Drabble uses a nonchronological narrative from multiple points of view. A frequent ironic tone complicates the narration. Though largely told in third person through the perspectives of individual characters, primarily Liz Headleand, Alix Bowen, and Esther Breuer, in addition to a panorama of minor characters, *The Gates of Ivory* introduces a new character, Hattie Osborne, who speaks in first person. Hattie, whom Drabble describes as "dottie," is living in Stephen's apartment while he is away and serves as his unofficial literary executor. Interestingly, no one can remember how long ago Stephen left; was it one year, two years, or was it three? Though Liz is in charge, other characters take part as well; however, the entire investigation is frequently interrupted by the concerns of daily life in England. Within the narration, Drabble moves from England to Southeast Asia and back again, from present time to the past. One technique holding it all together is repetition—for example, the repeated image of Stephen's white suit, the caption "Where is my son," and phrases about water flowing uphill, as well as references to the sound of "spade on skull."

Finally Liz is on her way to Bangkok, following the same trail as Stephen Cox, staying in the same hotel, meeting the same characters. She travels to Site Ten, a refugee camp, where she meets Mme Savet Akrun, and back to Bangkok, learning nothing of Stephen's whereabouts. In a restaurant, she runs into old friends who tell her of Stephen's apparent death. They are thinking about making a documentary film of the Booker Prize-winning novelist's excursion to locate Pol Pot and his resulting death. Liz returns to England, where she organizes a memorial service for Stephen. Following the service, the novel closes anticlimactically, at a party at Liz's house, where she and Alix and Esther propose a vacation, bringing the trilogy full circle to where it began.

The Red Queen

The Red Queen, subtitled *A Transcultural Tragicomedy*, continues Drabble's exploration of the East. The novel is divided equally into two parts, the first titled "Ancient Times" and the second "Modern Times." In addition, a short section titled "Postmodern Times" concludes the novel. Part 1 is told in first person through the voice of the eighteenth century Korean crown princess Hong, who is apparently still in search of the meaning of her own story. Interestingly, she speaks with knowledge of late twentieth century intellectual theory and scholarship; death has not hindered her education, but neither has her continued education served to enlighten her. Part 2 is told in third person through the eyes of Barbara Halliwell, a twenty-first century scholar on sabbatical at Oxford, who reads Hong's memoirs on a flight to deliver a paper at an academic conference in South Korea. The immediate connection between Hong and Halliwell, and even between both and Drabble herself (as indicated by the novel's afterword), is a fondness for the color red. Each harbors a fondness for red clothing. In the novel, beginning with this one connection, Drabble attempts to collapse the dichotomies of East and West, past and present. Despite postmodern theory's demanding cultural relativism, Drabble attempts to locate a universal human personality.

The crown princess tells her story in the form of a chronological narrative. Hers is the story of a woman groomed from the age of nine to become a future queen of Korea. Korean life in the eighteenth century, based on Confucianism, was wrought with societal stresses; royal life was even more so. Hong begins her tale with a discussion of the pressure of examinations as experienced by her father. Quickly she is moved to the palace, where her daily behavior, even from childhood, is held to close scrutiny. She virtually grows up with her future husband and king, Prince Sado. Sado is constricted by his own pressures. He acquires a clothing fetish, which further creates economical stress. As pressure in the royal household mounts, his psychological problems escalate. He becomes a sadistic murderer, until he is, at last, forced to commit a ritual suicide by suffocation in a rice chest. All the while, Hong is cognizant of her own tenuous position in the royal household.

Barbara Halliwell's story is also told chronologically. On the plane, she is immediately captured by Hong's story. Arriving at her hotel in Korea, Barbara meets Dr. Oo, who is attending another local conference, through a mix-up in luggage. Dr. Oo serves as Barbara's escort as she visits locations significant in the memoir of the crown princess. At the conference, Barbara meets the scholar Professor Jan van Jost, with whom she has a brief affair. Van Jost delivers a paper filled with images of entombment; Barbara finds the work largely incomprehensible. Later, van Jost dies in her bed.

The novel ends happily with a meeting between Jan van Jost's wife, who has adopted an infant from China, and Barbara. Barbara returns to London, where she teaches and writes. Polly Usher, a character from earlier Drabble novels, makes an appearance. Margaret Drabble herself makes a cameo appearance at the novel's end, "looking older than she did on her book jackets."

Martha Nochimson; George Soule
Updated by Nettie Farris

Other major works

play: *Bird of Paradise*, pr. 1969.

screenplays: *Isadora*, 1969 (with Melvyn Bragg and Clive Exton); *A Touch of Love*, 1969 (also known as *Thank You All Very Much*; adaptation of her novel *The Millstone*).

teleplay: *Laura*, 1964.

nonfiction: *Wordsworth: Literature in Perspective*, 1966; *Arnold Bennett: A Biography*, 1974; *A Writer's Britain: Landscape in Literature*, 1979; *The Tradition of Women's Fiction: Lectures in Japan*, 1982; *Safe as Houses*, 1990; *Margaret Drabble in Tokyo*, 1991 (Fumi Takano, editor); *Angus Wilson: A Biography*, 1995.

children's literature: *For Queen and Country: Britain in the Victorian Age*, 1978.

edited texts: *Lady Susan; The Watsons; Sanditon*, 1974 (by Jane Austen); *The Genius of Thomas Hardy*, 1975; *The Oxford Companion to English Literature: New Edition*, 1985 (revised 6th edition, 2000).

Bibliography

Brownley, Martine Watson. "Mothers and Capitalists in International Politics: Margaret Drabble's *The Gates of Ivory*." In *Deferrals of Domain: Contemporary Women Novelists and the State*. New York: St. Martin's Press, 2000. Presents a sociopolitical analysis of *The Gates of Ivory* through the lens of feminist theory.

Leeming, Glenda. *Margaret Drabble*. Tavistock, England: Northcote House, 2006. Focuses on Drabble's use of narrative technique, often citing the author herself from published interviews. Includes a bibliography of interviews as well as critical works on Drabble.

Myer, Valerie Grosvenor. *Margaret Drabble: A Reader's Guide*. New York: St. Martin's Press, 1991. Informative volume identifies allusions in Drabble's works, places the works within historical and literary contexts, and summarizes critical opinions on them.

Rose, Ellen Cronan, ed. *Critical Essays on Margaret Drabble*. Boston: G. K. Hall, 1985. Collection includes important critical writings on Drabble's early works as well as an informative introduction that presents an overview of Drabble's career.

Rubenstein, Roberta. "Fragmented Bodies/Selves/Narratives: Margaret Drabble's Postmodern Turn." *Contemporary Literature* 35 (Spring, 1994): 136-155. Analyzes Drabble's novels of the 1980's and 1990's and shows how they are fragmented in postmodern ways.

Sadler, Lynn Veach. *Margaret Drabble*. Boston: Twayne, 1986. Offers a balanced and readable appraisal of Drabble's work. A brief biographical sketch is followed by a chronological survey of Drabble's novels through *The Middle Ground* and a coda titled "Drabble's Reputation." Includes an extensive bibliography.

Skoller, Eleanor Honig. "Margaret Drabble." In *The In-Between of Writing: Experience and Experiment in Drabble, Duras, and Arendt*. Ann Arbor: University of Michigan Press, 1993. Argues that many critics misread Drabble and asserts that, contrary to the popular opinion that she uses a traditional nineteenth century narrative approach to fiction, Drabble displays many postmodern techniques.

Soule, George. *Four British Women Novelists: Anita Brookner, Margaret Drabble, Iris Murdoch, Barbara Pym*. Lanham, Md.: Scarecrow Press, 1998. Annotated critical bibliography provides analysis and evaluation of most of the critical books and articles on Drabble's fiction through 1996.

Sullivan, Mary Rose. "Margaret Drabble: Chronicler, Moralist, Artist." In *British Women Writing Fiction*, edited by Abby H. P. Werlock. Tuscaloosa: University of Alabama Press, 2000. Provides a short chronological analysis of Drabble's novels through *The Gates of Ivory*. Includes both a bibliography of critical works on Drabble and an extensive bibliography of works by Drabble, including her scholarly publications and short stories.

Uniyal, Ranu. *The Fiction of Margaret Drabble and Anita Desai: Women and Landscape*. New Delhi: Creative Books, 2004. Analyzes Drabble's use of geography and images of landscape in her fiction. Also includes an interview between the author and Drabble.

HENRY FIELDING

Born: Sharpham Park, Somersetshire, England; April 22, 1707
Died: Lisbon, Portugal; October 8, 1754

PRINCIPAL LONG FICTION

An Apology for the Life of Mrs. Shamela Andrews, 1741 (commonly known as *Shamela*)
The History of the Adventures of Joseph Andrews, and of His Friend Mr. Abraham Adams, 1742 (commonly known as *Joseph Andrews*)
The History of the Life of the Late Mr. Jonathan Wild the Great, 1743 (revised 1754; commonly known as *Jonathan Wild*)
The History of Tom Jones, a Foundling, 1749 (commonly known as *Tom Jones*)
Amelia, 1751

OTHER LITERARY FORMS

Henry Fielding's literary output, aside from his novels, can be categorized into three groups: plays, pamphlets and miscellaneous items, and journals. In addition, the publication of his three-volume *Miscellanies* (1743) by subscription brought together a number of previously published items as well as new works, including the first version of *Jonathan Wild*, and an unfinished prose work, "A Journey from This World to the Next."

Fielding's dramatic works, many presented with great success at either London's Little Theatre in the Haymarket or the Drury Lane Theatre, include ballad opera, farce, full-length comedy, and adaptations of classical and French drama. Most are overtly political in theme. Because of their contemporary subject matter, few have survived as viable stage presentations, although *The Covent Garden Tragedy* (pr., pb. 1732) was presented by the Old Vic in London in 1968. Fielding also wrote a number of prologues, epilogues, and monologues that were performed in conjunction with other dramatic pieces.

The pamphlets and miscellaneous items that are currently attributed to Fielding, excluding those for which he merely wrote introductions or epilogues, are "The Masquerade" (1728), a poem; *The Military History of Charles XII King of Sweden* (1740), a translation; "Of True Greatness" (1741), a poem; "The Opposition: A Vision" (1741), a poem; "The Vernoniad" (1741), a poem; "The Female Husband" (1746); "Ovid's Art of Love Paraphrased" (1747); "A True State of the Case of Bosavern Penlez" (1749); "An Enquiry into the Causes of the Late Increase in Robbers" (1751); "Examples of the Interposition of Providence in the Detection and Punishment of Murder" (1752); "A Proposal for Making an Effectual Provision for the Poor" (1753); "A Clear State of the Case of Elizabeth Canning" (1753); and *The Journal of a Voyage to Lisbon*, which was published posthumously (1755).

Fielding edited and made major contributions to four journals: *The Champion* (November 15, 1739-June, 1741; the journal continued publication without Fielding until

1742); *The True Patriot* (November 5, 1745-June 17, 1746); *Jacobite's Journal* (December 5, 1747-November 5, 1748); and *The Covent-Garden Journal* (January 4-November 25, 1752).

ACHIEVEMENTS

Fielding's lasting achievements in prose fiction—in contrast to his passing fame as an essayist, dramatist, and judge—result from his development of critical theory and from his aesthetic success in the novels themselves. In the preface to *Joseph Andrews*, Fielding establishes a serious critical basis for the novel as a genre and describes in detail the elements of comic realism; in *Joseph Andrews* and *Tom Jones*, he provides full realizations of this theory. These novels define the ground rules of form that would be followed, to varying degrees, by Jane Austen, William Makepeace Thackeray, George Eliot, Thomas Hardy, James Joyce, and D. H. Lawrence, and they also speak to countless readers across many generations. Both novels, in fact, have been translated into successful films (*Tom Jones* was released in 1963; *Joseph Andrews*, in 1977).

The historical importance of the preface to *Joseph Andrews* results from both the seriousness with which it treats the formal qualities of the novel (at the time a fledgling and barely respectable genre) and the precision with which it defines the characteristics of the genre, the "comic epic-poem in prose." Fielding places *Joseph Andrews* in particular and the comic novel in general squarely in the tradition of classical literature and coherently argues its differences from the romance and the burlesque. He also provides analogies between the comic novel and the visual arts. Fielding thus leads the reader to share his conception that the comic novel is an aesthetically valid form with its roots in classical tradition and a form peculiarly suited to the attitudes and values of its own age.

With his background in theater and journalism, Fielding could move easily through a wide range of forms and rhetorical techniques in his fiction, from direct parody of Samuel Richardson in *An Apology for the Life of Mrs. Shamela Andrews* to ironic inversion of the great man's biography in *Jonathan Wild* to adaptation of classical structure (Vergil's *Aeneid*, c. 29-19 B.C.E.; English translation, 1553) in *Amelia*. The two major constants in these works are the attempt to define a good, moral life, built on benevolence and honor, and a concern for finding the best way to present that definition to the reader. Thus the moral and the technique can never be separated in Fielding's works.

Joseph Andrews and *Tom Jones* bring together these two impulses in Fielding's most organically structured, brilliantly characterized, and masterfully narrated works. These novels vividly capture the diversity of experience in the physical world and the underlying benevolence of the natural order, embodying them in a rich array of the ridiculous in human behavior. Fielding combines a positive assertion of the strength of goodness and benevolence (demonstrated by the structure and plot of the novels) with the sharp thrusts of the satirist's attack on the hypocrisy and vanity of individual characters. These elements are held together by the voice of the narrator—witty, urbane, charming—who serves as

Henry Fielding
(Library of Congress)

moral guide through the novels and the world. Thus beyond the comic merits of each of the individual novels lies a collective sense of universal moral good. The voice of the narrator conveys to the reader the truth of that goodness.

Although the novels were popular in his own day, Fielding's contemporaries thought of him more as playwright-turned-judge than as novelist. This may have been the result of the low esteem in which the novel as a form was held as well as of Fielding's brilliant successes in these other fields. These varied successes have in common a zest for the exploration of the breadth and variety of life—a joy in living—that finds its most articulate and permanent expression in the major novels.

Today Fielding is universally acknowledged as a major figure in the development of the novel, although there is still some debate about whether he or Richardson is the "father" of the British novel. Ian Watt, for example, has asserted that Richardson's development of "formal realism" is more significant than Fielding's comic realism. Other critics, notably Martin Battestin, have demonstrated that Fielding's broader, more humane moral vision, embodied in classical structure and expressed through a self-conscious narrator, is the germ from which the richness and variety of the British novel grows. This disagreement ultimately comes down to personal taste, and there will always be Richardson and

Fielding partisans to keep the controversy alive. There is no argument, however, that of their type—the novel of comic realism—no fiction has yet surpassed *Joseph Andrews* or *Tom Jones*.

BIOGRAPHY

Henry Fielding was born April 22, 1707, in Sharpham Park, Somersetshire, to Edmund and Sarah Fielding. His father, an adventurer, gambler, and swaggerer, was a sharp contrast to the quiet, conservative, traditional gentry of his mother's family, the Goulds. In 1710, the family moved to Dorset, where Fielding and his younger brother and three sisters (including the future novelist Sarah Fielding) would spend most of their childhood on a small estate and farm given to Mrs. Fielding by her father, Sir Henry Gould.

The death of Fielding's mother in April, 1718, ended this idyllic life. Litigation over the estate created a series of family battles that raged for several decades. In 1719, Fielding was sent to Eton College, partly because the Goulds wanted him influenced as little as possible by his father, who had resumed his "wild" life in London, and partly because Fielding disliked his father's new Catholic wife. Remaining at Eton until 1724 or 1725, Fielding made many friends, including George Lyttleton and William Pitt. At Eton he began his study of classical literature, which became a profound influence on his literary career.

Few details are known of Fielding's life during the several years after Eton. He spent a good deal of time with the Goulds in Salisbury, but he also led a hectic, boisterous life in London, spending much time at the theater, where the popular masquerades and burlesques influenced him greatly. His visits to the theater stimulated him to try his own hand at comedy, and in February, 1728, *Love in Several Masques*, based on his own romantic adventures of the previous year, was performed at Drury Lane. In March, 1728, Fielding enrolled in the Faculty of Letters at the University of Leyden (Netherlands), where he pursued his interest in the classics. In August, 1729, at the age of twenty-two, he returned to London without completing his degree.

It is clear from his literary output in the 1730's that Fielding was intensely involved in theatrical life. From 1730 through 1737 he authored at least nineteen different dramatic works (as well as presenting revivals and new productions of revised works), most with political themes, at both the Little Theatre in the Haymarket and the Drury Lane. In addition to writing ballad opera, full-length comedies, translations, and parodies, Fielding was also producing, revising the plays of other writers, and managing theater business. He also formed a new, important friendship with the artist William Hogarth.

His theatrical career came to an abrupt halt (although a few more plays appeared in the 1740's) with the passage of the Licensing Act of 1737 which resulted in the closing of many theaters. Fielding's political satire offended Prime Minister Sir Robert Walpole and had been part of the motivation for the government's desire to control and censor the theaters.

In addition to this theatrical activity with its political commentary, Fielding found time in the years 1733-1734 to court and marry Charlotte Cradock of Salisbury. Charlotte's mother died in 1735, leaving the entire estate to the Fieldings and alleviating many of the financial problems caused by the legal disputes over the estate in Dorset. The couple moved from London to East Stour the same year, although Fielding regularly visited London, because he was manager, artistic director, and controller in chief of the Little Theatre. The first of their three children, Charlotte, was born April 17, 1736.

Fielding's relentless energy (and desire to add to his income) compelled him to begin a new career in late 1737, whereupon he began to study law at the Middle Temple. He became a barrister on June 20, 1740, and spent the next several years in the Western Circuit. During this service he became friends with Ralph Allen of Bath. He remained active in the practice of justice, as attorney and magistrate, until he left England in 1754.

Fielding continued to involve himself in political controversy, even while studying law. He edited, under pseudonyms, *The Champion*, an opposition newspaper issued three times a week, directed against Prime Minister Walpole (a favorite subject of Fielding's satire). Later he would edit *The True Patriot* in support of the government during the threat of the Jacobite Rising, *Jacobite's Journal*, and *The Covent-Garden Journal*.

From theater to law to journalism—Fielding had already charged through three careers when the first installment of Richardson's *Pamela: Or, Virtue Rewarded* appeared on November 6, 1740. Deeply disturbed by the artificiality of the novel's epistolary technique, and appalled by its perversion of moral values, Fielding quickly responded with *An Apology for the Life of Mrs. Shamela Andrews*, often referred to as *Shamela*, an "antidote" to *Pamela*. Although published anonymously, Fielding's authorship was apparent and created ill feelings between the two authors that would last most of their lives.

The success of *Shamela* encouraged Fielding to try his hand at a more sustained satire, which eventually grew into *Joseph Andrews*. In 1743 he published, by subscription, the *Miscellanies*, a collection of previously published works, and two new ones: an unfinished story, "A Journey from This World to the Next," and the first version of *Jonathan Wild*.

Although the mid-1740's brought Fielding fame, success, and money, his personal life was beset with pain. He suffered continually from gout, and his wife died in November, 1744. In the following year he became involved in the propaganda battles over the Jacobite Rising. On November 27, 1747, he married his wife's former maid, Mary Daniel, and some sense of peace and order was restored to his private life. They would have five children.

While forming new personal ties and continuing strong involvement in political issues, Fielding was preparing his masterwork, *Tom Jones*. He also took oath as justice of the peace for Westminster and Middlesex, London, in 1748, and he opened an employment agency and estate brokerage with his brother in 1749. His last novel, *Amelia*, was not well received, disappointing those readers who were expecting another *Tom Jones*.

The early 1750's saw Fielding's health continue to decline, although he remained active in his judgeship, producing a number of pamphlets on various legal questions. In June of 1754, his friends convinced him to sail to Lisbon, Portugal, where the climate might improve his health. He died there on October 8, 1754, and is buried in the British Cemetery outside Lisbon. *The Journal of a Voyage to Lisbon*, his last work, was published one year after his death.

ANALYSIS

Analysis and criticism of Henry Fielding's fiction have traditionally centered on the moral values in the novels, the aesthetic structure in which they are placed, and the relationship between the two. In this view, Fielding as moralist takes precedence over Fielding as artist, since the aesthetic structure is determined by the moral. Each of the novels is judged by the extent to which it finds the appropriate form for its moral vision. The relative failure of *Amelia*, for example, may be Fielding's lack of faith in his own moral vision. The happy ending, promulgated by the deus ex machina of the good magistrate, is hardly consistent with the dire effects of urban moral decay that have been at work upon the Booths throughout the novel. Fielding's own moral development and changes in outlook also need to be considered in this view. The reader must examine the sources of Fielding's moral vision in the latitudinarian sermons of the day, as well as the changes in his attitudes as he examined eighteenth century urban life in greater detail, and as he moved in literature from *Joseph Andrews* to *Amelia*, and in life from the theater to the bench of justice.

As is clear from the preface to *Joseph Andrews*, however, Fielding was equally interested in the aesthetics of his fiction. Indeed, each of the novels, even from the first parody, *Shamela*, conveys not only a moral message but a literary experiment to find the strongest method for expressing that message to the largest reading public. This concern is evident in the basic plot structure, characterization, language, and role of the narrator. Each novel attempts to reach the widest audience possible with its moral thesis. Although each differs in the way in which Fielding attempts this, they all have in common the sense that the *how* of the story is as important as the *what*. The novels are experiments in the methods of moral education—for the reader as well as for the characters.

This concern for the best artistic way to teach a moral lesson was hardly new with Fielding. His classical education and interests, as well as the immediate human response gained from theater audiences during his playwriting days, surely led him to see that fiction must delight as well as instruct. Fielding's novels are both exemplars of this goal (in their emphasis on incidents of plot and broad range of characterization) and serious discussions of the method by which to achieve it (primarily through structure and through narrative commentary).

The direct stimulation for Fielding's career as novelist was the publication of Samuel Richardson's *Pamela*, a novel that disturbed Fielding both by its artistic ineptitude and by its moral vacuousness. Fielding was as concerned with the public reaction to *Pamela* as he was with its author's methods. That the reading public could be so easily misled by *Pamela*'s morals disturbed Fielding deeply, and the success of that novel led him to ponder what better ways were available for reaching the public with his own moral thesis. His response to *Pamela* was both moral (he revealed the true state of Pamela/Shamela's values) and aesthetic (he exposed the artificiality of "writing to the moment").

Sermons and homilies, while effective in church (and certainly sources of Fielding's moral philosophy), were not the stuff of prose fiction; neither was the epistolary presentation of "virtue rewarded" of *Pamela* (or the "objectively" amoral tone of Daniel Defoe's *The Fortunes and Misfortunes of the Famous Moll Flanders, Written from Her Own Memorandums*, 1722). Fielding sought a literary method for combining moral vision and literary pleasure that would be appropriate to the rapidly urbanizing and secular society of the mid-eighteenth century. To find that method he ranged through direct parody, irony, satire, author-narrator intrusion, and moral exemplum. Even those works, such as *Jonathan Wild* and *Amelia*, which are not entirely successful, live because of the vitality of Fielding's experimental methods. In *Joseph Andrews* and *Tom Jones*, he found the way to reach his audience most effectively.

Fielding's informing moral values, embodied in the central characters of the novels (Joseph Andrews, Parson Adams, Tom Jones, Squire Allworthy, Mr. Harrison) can be summarized, as Martin Battestin has ably done, as Charity, Prudence, and Providence. Fielding held an optimistic faith in the perfectability of humanity and the potential for the betterment of society, based on the essential goodness of human nature. These three values must work together. In the novels, the hero's worth is determined by the way in which he interacts with other people (charity), within the limits of social institutions designed to provide order (prudence). His reward is a life full of God's provision (Providence). God's Providence has created a world of abundance and plenitude; man's prudence and charity can guarantee its survival and growth. Both Joseph Andrews and Tom Jones learn the proper combination of prudence and charity. They learn to use their innate inclination toward goodness within a social system that ensures order. To succeed, however, they must overcome obstacles provided by the characters who, through vanity and hypocrisy, distort God's Providence. Thus Fielding's moral vision, while optimistic, is hardly blind to the realities of the world. *Jonathan Wild*, with its basic rhetorical distinction between "good" and "great," and *Amelia*, with its narrative structured around the ill effects of doing good, most strongly reflect Fielding's doubts about the practicality of his beliefs.

These ideas can be easily schematized, but the scheme belies the human complexity through which they are expressed in the novels. Tom Jones is no paragon of virtue, but he must learn, at great physical pain and spiritual risk, how to combine charity and prudence. Even Squire Allworthy is, as Sheldon Sacks has observed, a "fallible" paragon. These ideas do not come from a single source, but are derived from a combination of sources, rooted in Fielding's classical education; the political, religious, and literary movements of his own time; and his own experience as dramatist, journalist, and magistrate.

Fielding's familiarity with the classics, begun at Eton and continued at the University of Leyden, is revealed in many ways: through language (the use of epic simile and epic conventions in *Joseph Andrews*), through plot (the symmetry of design in *Tom Jones*), through theme (the importance of moderation in all the novels), and through structure (the relationship of *Amelia* to Vergil's *Aeneid*). The preface to *Joseph Andrews* makes explicit how much Fielding saw in common between his own work and classical literature. His belief in the benevolent order of the world, especially illustrated by country living, such as at Squire Allworthy's estate (Paradise Hall), is deeply rooted in the pastoral tradition of classical literature. These classical elements are combined with the beliefs of the latitudinarian homilists of the seventeenth and eighteenth centuries, who stressed the perfectibility of humankind in the world through good deeds (charity) and good heart (benevolence).

While Fielding's thematic concerns may be rooted in classical and Christian thought, his literary technique has sources that are more complex, deriving from his education, his own experience in the theater, and the influence of Richardson's *Pamela*. It is difficult to separate each of these sources, for the novels work them into unified and original statements. Indeed, *Joseph Andrews*, the novel most closely related to classical sources, is also deeply imbued with the sense of latitudinarian thought in its criticism of the clergy, and satire of Richardson in its plot and moral vision.

The London in which Fielding spent most of his life was a world of literary and political ferment, an age of factionalism in the arts, with the Tory wits (Jonathan Swift, Alexander Pope, John Gay, John Arbuthnot) allied against Colley Cibber, the poet laureate and self-proclaimed literary spokesman for the British Isles. Swift's *Gulliver's Travels* (1726) and Gay's *The Beggar's Opera* (1728) had recently appeared; both were influential in forming Fielding's literary methods—the first with its emphasis on sharp political satire, the second with the creation of a new literary form, the ballad opera. The ballad opera set new lyrics, expressing contemporary political and social satire, to well-known music. Fielding was to find his greatest theatrical success in this genre and was to carry it over to his fiction, especially *Jonathan Wild*, with its emphasis on London low life and its excesses of language.

It was a time, also, of great political controversy, with the ongoing conflicts between the Tories and Jacobites about the questions of religion and succession. Prime Minister Walpole's politics of expediency were a ripe subject for satire. Fielding's career as journalist began as a direct response to political issues, and significant portions of *Joseph Andrews* and *Tom Jones*, as well as *Jonathan Wild*, deal with political issues.

These various sources, influences, and beliefs are molded into coherent works of art through Fielding's narrative technique. It is through the role of the narrator that he most clearly and successfully experiments in the methods of teaching a moral lesson. Starting with the voice of direct literary parody in *Shamela* and moving through the varied structures and voices of the other novels, Fielding's art leads in many directions, but it always leads to his ultimate concern for finding the best way to teach the clearest moral lesson. In

Tom Jones he finds the most appropriate method to demonstrate that the world is a beautiful place if people practice charity and prudence.

Shamela

The key to understanding how *Shamela* expresses Fielding's concern with both the moral thesis and the aesthetic form of fiction is contained in the introductory letters between Parsons Tickletext and Oliver. Oliver is dismayed at Tickletext's exuberant praise of *Pamela* and at the novel's public reception and popularity. The clergy, in particular, have been citing it as a work worthy to be read with the Scriptures. He contends that the text of *Shamela*, which he encloses, reveals the "true" story of Pamela's adventures and puts them in their proper moral perspective. By reading Oliver's version, Tickletext will correct his own misconceptions; by reading *Shamela* (under the guidance of the prefatory letters), the public will laugh at *Pamela* and perceive the perversity of its moral thesis.

Shamela began, of course, simply as a parody of Richardson's novel, and, in abbreviated form, carries through the narrative of the attempted seduction of the young serving girl by the squire, and her attempts to assert her virtue through chastity or marriage. Fielding makes direct hits at Richardson's weakest points: His two main targets are the epistolary technique of "writing to the moment" and the moral thesis of "virtue rewarded" by pounds and pence (and marriage).

Fielding parodies the epistolary technique by carrying it to its most illogical extreme: Richardson's technical failure is not the choice of epistolary form, but his insistence on its adherence to external reality. Shamela writes her letters at the very same moment she is being attacked in bed by Squire Booby. While feigning sleep she writes: "You see I write in the present tense." The inconsistency of Pamela's shift from letters to journal form when she is abducted is shown through Fielding's retention of the letter form throughout the story, no matter what the obstacles for sending and receiving them. He also compounds the criticism of Richardson by including a number of correspondents in addition to Shamela (her mother, Henrietta Maria Honora Andrews, Mrs. Jewkes, Parson Williams) and including various complications, such as letters within letters within letters.

Fielding retains the essential characters and key scenes from *Pamela*, such as Mr. B's hiding in the closet before the attempted seduction, Pamela's attempted suicide at the pond, and Parson Williams's interference. For each character and scene Fielding adopts Richardson's penchant for minute descriptive detail and intense character response to the event; he also parodies the method and seriousness of the original by revealing the motives of the characters.

The revealing of motives is also Fielding's primary way of attacking the prurience of Richardson's presentation as well as the moral thesis behind it. He debunks the punctilio (decorum) of the central character. Shamela's false modesty ("I thought once of making a little fortune by my person. I now intend to make a great one by my virtue") mocks Pamela's pride in her chastity; the main difference between them is Shamela's recognition and acceptance of the mercenary motives behind her behavior and Pamela's blindness to her own motivation. Richardson never examines the reliability of Pamela's motivations, although he describes her thoughts in detail. Fielding allows Shamela to glory in both her ability to dupe the eager Squire Booby and her mercenary motives for doing so. The reader may, as Parson Oliver wants Tickletext to do, easily condemn Shamela for a villain but never for a hypocrite.

Fielding also attacks Richardson's refusal to describe the sexual attributes of his characters or to admit the intensity of their sexual desires, particularly in the case of Pamela herself. Pamela always hints and suggests—and, Fielding claims, wallows in her suggestiveness. Fielding not only describes the sexual aspects directly, but exaggerates and reduces them to a comic level, hardly to be taken sensually or seriously. *Shamela* quickly, fully, and ruthlessly annihilates the moral thesis of "virtue rewarded" through this direct exaggeration. Fielding does not, however, in his role as parodist, suggest an alternative to *Pamela*'s moral thesis; he is content, for the time, with exposing its flaws.

This first foray into fiction served for Fielding as a testing ground for some of the rhetorical techniques he used in later works, especially the emphasis on satiric inversion. These inversions appear in his reversal of sexual roles in *Joseph Andrews*, the reversal of rhetoric in the "good" and "great" in *Jonathan Wild*, and the reversal of goodness of motive and evil of effect in *Amelia*. Fielding's concern to find a rhetorical method for presenting a moral thesis was confined in *Shamela* to the limited aims and goals of parody. He had such success with the method (after all, he had his apprenticeship in the satiric comedy of the theater), that he began his next novel on the same model.

JOSEPH ANDREWS

Like *Shamela*, *Joseph Andrews* began as a parody of *Pamela*. In his second novel, Fielding reverses the gender of the central character and traces Joseph's attempts to retain his chastity and virtue while being pursued by Lady Booby. This method of inversion creates new possibilities, not only for satirizing Richardson's work but for commenting on the sexual morality of the time in a more positive way than in *Shamela*. The most cursory reading reveals how quickly Fielding grew tired of parody and how *Joseph Andrews* moved beyond its inspiration and its forerunner. Even the choice of direct narration rather than epistolary form indicates Fielding's unwillingness to tie himself to his model.

Most readers agree that the entrance of Parson Adams, Joseph's guide, companion, and partner in misery, turns the novel from simple parody into complex fiction. Adams takes center stage as both comic butt, preserving Joseph's role as hero, and moral guide, preserving Joseph's role as innocent.

Adams's contribution is also part of Fielding's conscious search for the best way to convey his moral thesis. The narrative refers continually to sermons, given in the pulpit or being carried by Adams to be published in London. These sermons are generally ineffectual or contradicted by the behavior of the clergy who pronounce them. Just as experience and the moral example of Adams's life are better teachers for Joseph than sermons—what could be a more effective lesson than the way he is treated by the coach passengers after he is robbed, beaten, and stripped?—so literary example has more power for Fielding and the reader. Adams's constant companion, his copy of Aeschylus, is further testament to Fielding's growing faith in his exemplary power of literature as moral guide. In *Joseph Andrews*, narrative art takes precedence over both parody and sermon.

Fielding's concern for method as well as meaning is given its most formal discussion in the preface. The historical importance of this document results from both the seriousness with which it treats the formal qualities of the novel and the precision with which it defines the characteristics of the genre, the "comic epic-poem in prose." The seriousness is established through the careful logic and organization of the argument and through the parallels drawn between the new genre and classical literature (the lost comic epic supposedly written by Homer) and modern painting (Michelangelo da Caravaggio and William Hogarth).

Fielding differentiates the "comic epic-poem in prose" from contemporary romances such as *Pamela*. The new form is more extended and comprehensive in action, contains a much larger variety of incidents, and treats a greater variety of characters. Unlike the serious romance, the new form is less solemn in subject matter, treats characters of lower rank, and presents the ludicrous rather than the sublime. The comic, opposed to the burlesque, arises solely from the observation of nature, and has its source in the discovery of the "ridiculous" in human nature. The ridiculous always springs from the affectations of vanity and hypocrisy.

Within the novel itself, the narrator will continue the discussion of literary issues in the introductory chapters to each of the first three of four books: "of writing lives in general," "of divisions in authors," and "in praise of biography." These discussions, although sometimes more facetious than serious, do carry through the direction of the opening sentence of the novel: "Examples work more forcibly on the mind than precepts." Additionally, this narrative commentary allows Fielding to assume the role of reader's companion and guide that he develops more fully in *Tom Jones*.

While the preface takes its cue from classical tradition, it is misleading to assume that *Joseph Andrews* is merely an updating of classical technique and ideas. Even more than *Shamela*, this novel brings together Fielding's dissatisfaction with Richardson's moral thesis and his support of latitudinarian attitudes toward benevolence and charity. Here, too, Fielding begins his definition of the "good" man in modern Christian terms. Joseph redefines the place of chastity and honor in male sexuality; Parson Adams exemplifies the benevolence all people should display; Mrs. Tow-wowse, Trulliber, and Peter Pounce, among others, illustrate the vanity and hypocrisy of the world.

The structure of the novel is episodic, combining the earthly journey and escapades of the hero with suggestions of the Christian pilgrimage in John Bunyan's *The Pilgrim's Progress* (1678, 1684). Fielding was still experimenting with form and felt at liberty to digress from his structure with interpolated tales or to depend on coincidence to bring the novel to its conclusion. The immediate moral effect sometimes seems more important than the consistency of rhetorical structure. These are, however, minor lapses in Fielding's progression toward unifying moral thesis and aesthetic structure.

JONATHAN WILD

In *Jonathan Wild*, Fielding seems to have abandoned temporarily the progression from the moral statement of parody and sermon to the aesthetic statement of literary example. *Jonathan Wild* was first published in the year immediately following *Joseph Andrews* (revised in 1754), and there is evidence to indicate that the work was actually written before *Joseph Andrews*. This is a reasonable assumption, since *Jonathan Wild* is more didactic in its method and more negative in its moral vision. It looks back toward *Shamela* rather than ahead to *Tom Jones*.

Jonathan Wild is less a novel, even as Fielding discusses the form in the preface to *Joseph Andrews*, than a polemic. Critic Northrop Frye's term "anatomy" may be the most appropriate label for the work. Like other anatomies—Sir Thomas More's *De Optimo Reipublicae Statu, deque Nova Insula Utopia* (*Utopia*, 1551), Swift's *Gulliver's Travels*, and Samuel Johnson's *Rasselas, Prince of Abyssinia* (1759)—it emphasizes ideas over narrative. It is more moral fable than novel, and more fiction than historical biography, altering history to fit the moral vision.

More important, it was Fielding's experiment in moving the moral lesson of the tale away from the narrative (with its emphasis on incident and character) and into the rhetoric of the narrator (with its emphasis on language). Fielding attempted to use language as the primary carrier of his moral thesis. Although this experiment failed—manipulation of language, alone, would not do—it gave him the confidence to develop the role of the narrative voice in its proper perspective in *Tom Jones*.

Fielding freely adapted the facts of Wild's life, which were well known to the general public. He chose those incidents from Wild's criminal career and punishment that would serve his moral purpose, and he added his own fictional characters, the victims of Wild's "greatness," especially the Heartfrees. Within the structure of the inverted biography of the "great" man, Fielding satirizes the basic concepts of middle-class society. He differentiates between "greatness" and "goodness," terms often used synonymously in the eighteenth century. The success of the novel depends on the reader's acceptance and understanding of this rhetorical inversion.

"Goodness," characterized by the Heartfrees, reiterates the ideals of behavior emphasized in *Joseph Andrews:* benevolence, honor, honesty, and charity, felt through the heart. "Greatness," personified in Wild, results in cunning and courage, characteristics of the will. The action of the novel revolves around the ironic reversal of these terms. Although Wild's actions speak for themselves, the ironic voice of the narrator constantly directs the reader's response.

Parts of *Jonathan Wild* are brilliantly satiric, but the work as a whole does not speak to modern readers. Fielding abandoned the anatomy form after this experiment, recognizing that the voice of the narrator alone cannot carry the moral thesis of a novel in a convincing way. In *Jonathan Wild*, he carried to an extreme the role of the narrator as moral guide that he experimented with in *Joseph Andrews*. In *Tom Jones*, he found the precise balance: the moral voice of the narrator controlling the reader's reaction through language and the literary examples of plot and character.

TOM JONES

In *Tom Jones*, Fielding moved beyond the limited aims of each of his previous works into a more comprehensive moral and aesthetic vision. No longer bound by the need to attack Richardson or by the attempt to define a specific fictional form, such as the moral fable or the "comic epic-poem in prose," Fielding dramatized the positive values of the good man in a carefully structured narrative held together by the guiding voice of the narrator. This narrator unifies, in a consistent pattern, Fielding's concern for both the truthfulness of his moral vision and the best way to reach the widest audience.

The structure of *Tom Jones*, like that of *Joseph Andrews*, is based on the secularization of the spiritual pilgrimage. Tom must journey from his equivocal position as foundling on the country estate of Squire Allworthy (Paradise Hall) to moral independence in the hellish city of London. He must learn to understand and control his life. When he learns this lesson, he will return to the country to enjoy the plenitude of paradise regained that Providence allows him. He must temper his natural, impetuous charity with the prudence that comes from recognition of his own role in the larger social structure. In precise terms, he must learn to control his animal appetites in order to win the love of Sophia Western and the approval of Allworthy. This lesson is rewarded not only by his gaining these two goals, but by his gaining the knowledge of his parentage and his rightful place in society. He is no longer a "foundling."

Unlike the episodic journey of *Joseph Andrews*, *Tom Jones* adapts the classical symmetry of the epic in a more conscious and precise way. The novel is divided into eighteen books. Some of the books, such as 1 and 4, cover long periods of time and are presented in summary form, with the narrator clearly present; others cover only a few days or hours, with the narrator conspicuously absent and the presentation primarily scenic. The length of each book is determined by the importance of the subject, not the length of time covered.

The books are arranged in a symmetrical pattern. The first half of the novel takes Tom from his mysterious birth to his adventures in the Inn at Upton; the second half takes him from Upton to London and the discovery of his parentage. Books 1 through 6 are set in Somerset at Squire Allworthy's estate and culminate with Tom's affair with Molly. Books 7 through 12 are set on the road to Upton, at the Inn, and on the road from Upton to London; the two central books detail the adventures at the Inn and Tom's affair with Mrs. Waters. Books 13 through 18 take Tom to London and begin with his affair with Lady Bellaston.

Within this pattern, Fielding demonstrates his moral thesis, the education of a "good man," in a number of ways: through the narrative (Tom's behavior continually lowers his moral worth in society); through characters (the contrasting pairs of Tom and Blifil, Allworthy and Western, Square and Thwackum, Molly and Lady Bellaston); and through the voice of the narrator.

Fielding extends the role of the narrator in *Tom Jones*, as teller of the tale, as moral guide, and as literary commentator and critic. Each of these voices was heard in *Joseph Andrews*, but here they come together in a unique narrative persona. Adopting the role of the stagecoach traveler, the narrator speaks directly to his fellow passengers, the readers. He is free to digress and comment whenever he feels appropriate, and there is, therefore, no need for the long interpolated tales such as appeared in *Joseph Andrews*.

To remind his readers that the purpose of fiction is aesthetic as well as moral, the narrator often comments on literary topics: "Of the Serious in Writing, and for What Purpose it is introduced"; "A wonderful long chapter concerning the Marvelous"; "Containing Instructions very necessary to be perused by modern Critics." Taken together, these passages provide a guide to Fielding's literary theory as complete as the preface to *Joseph Andrews*.

Although in *Tom Jones* Fielding still schematically associates characters with particular moral values, the range of characters is wider than in his previous novels. Even a minor character, such as Black George, has a life beyond his moral purpose as representative of hypocrisy and self-servingness.

Most important, *Tom Jones* demonstrates Fielding's skill in combining his moral vision with aesthetic form in a way that is most pleasurable to the reader. The reader learns how to live the good Christian life because Tom learns that lesson. Far more effective than parody, sermon, or moral exemplum, the combination of narrative voice and literary example of plot and character is Fielding's greatest legacy to the novel.

Lawrence F. Laban

OTHER MAJOR WORKS

PLAYS: *Love in Several Masques*, pr., pb. 1728; *The Author's Farce, and the Pleasures of the Town*, pr., pb. 1730; *Rape upon Rape: Or, Justice Caught in His Own Trap*, pr., pb. 1730 (also known as *The Coffee-House Politician*); *The Temple Beau*, pr., pb. 1730; *Tom Thumb: A Tragedy*, pr., pb. 1730 (revised as *The Tragedy of Tragedies: Or, The Life and Death of Tom Thumb the Great*, pr., pb. 1731); *The Letter-Writers: Or, A New Way to Keep a Wife at Home*, pr., pb. 1731; *The Welsh Opera: Or, The Grey Mare the Better Horse*, pr., pb. 1731 (revised as *The Grub-Street Opera*, pb. 1731); *The Covent Garden Tragedy*, pr., pb. 1732; *The Lottery*, pr., pb. 1732; *The Mock Doctor: Or, The Dumb Lady Cur'd*, pr., pb. 1732 (adaptation of Molière's *Le Medecin malgré lui*); *The Modern Husband*, pr., pb.

1732 (five acts); *The Old Debauchees*, pr., pb. 1732; *The Miser*, pr., pb. 1733 (adaptation of Molière's *L'Avare*); *Don Quixote in England*, pr., pb. 1734; *The Intriguing Chambermaid*, pr., pb. 1734 (adaptation of Jean-François Regnard's *Le Retour imprévu*); *An Old Man Taught Wisdom: Or, The Virgin Unmask'd*, pr., pb. 1735; *The Universal Gallant: Or, The Different Husbands*, pr., pb. 1735 (five acts); *Pasquin: Or, A Dramatic Satire on the Times*, pr., pb. 1736; *Tumble-Down Dick: Or, Phaeton in the Suds*, pr., pb. 1736; *Eurydice Hiss'd: Or, A Word to the Wise*, pr., pb. 1737; *Eurydice: Or, The Devil's Henpeck'd*, pr. 1737 (one act); *The Historical Register for the Year 1736*, pr., pb. 1737 (three acts); *Miss Lucy in Town*, pr., pb. 1742 (one act); *The Wedding-Day*, pr., pb. 1743 (five acts; also known as *The Virgin Unmask'd*); *The Fathers: Or, The Good-Natured Man*, pr., pb. 1778 (revised for posthumous production by David Garrick).

NONFICTION: *The Journal of a Voyage to Lisbon*, 1755.

TRANSLATION: *The Military History of Charles XII King of Sweden*, 1740.

MISCELLANEOUS: *Miscellanies*, 1743 (3 volumes).

BIBLIOGRAPHY

Battestin, Martin C. *A Henry Fielding Companion*. Westport, Conn.: Greenwood Press, 2000. Comprehensive reference work covers the life and writings of Fielding in a thorough fashion. Includes sections on where Fielding lived, his family, and significant historical figures and literary influences, in addition to material on Fielding's works, themes, and characters. Includes bibliography and index.

Battestin, Martin C., with Ruthe R. Battestin. *Henry Fielding: A Life*. New York: Routledge, 1989. The *Sunday Times* of London voted this work one of the four best biographies of the year. Based on fourteen years' research, this detailed biography provides a definitive story of Fielding. Includes a useful bibliography of Fielding's writings.

Bertelsen, Lance. *Henry Fielding at Work: Magistrate, Businessman, Writer*. New York: Palgrave, 2000. Presents analysis of Fielding in his roles as writer, magistrate, and businessman, discussing how his various work experiences affected the form and content of his writing. Includes bibliography and index.

Dircks, Richard J. *Henry Fielding*. Boston: Twayne, 1983. Provides a useful introduction to Fielding, integrating his central ideas and vision of life as they are experienced in his works as a novelist, dramatist, journalist, and pamphleteer. Focuses on Fielding's major works. Includes an excellent bibliography and a chronology.

Mace, Nancy A. *Henry Fielding's Novels and the Classical Tradition*. Newark: University of Delaware Press, 1996. Examines the classical influence on Fielding's novels and other writings, discussing his knowledge of classical literature and his use of classical allusions and quotations.

Pagliaro, Harold E. *Henry Fielding: A Literary Life*. New York: St. Martin's Press, 1998. Excellent work presents an interesting account of Fielding's life and writings, with one chapter devoted to his novels and other prose fiction. Includes bibliographical references and index.

Paulson, Ronald. *The Life of Henry Fielding: A Critical Biography.* Malden, Mass.: Blackwell, 2000. Examines how Fielding's literary works—novels, plays, and essays—all contained autobiographical elements. Each chapter begins with an annotated chronology of the events of Fielding's life in the period covered within the chapter. Includes bibliography and index.

Rawson, Claude, ed. *The Cambridge Companion to Henry Fielding.* New York: Cambridge University Press, 2007. Collection of essays, commissioned for this volume, includes an examination of Fielding's life and discussion of his major novels, his style, his theatrical career, and his journalism work.

Rivero, Albert J., ed. *Critical Essays on Henry Fielding.* New York: G. K. Hall, 1998. Interesting collection of essays about Fielding that were published originally in the 1980's and 1990's, including discussions of the novels *Joseph Andrews*, *Tom Jones*, *Amelia*, and *Jonathan Wild.* Includes bibliographical references and index.

Watt, Ian. *The Rise of the Novel: Studies in Defoe, Richardson, and Fielding.* 2d American ed. Berkeley: University of California Press, 2001. Focuses on three novelists—Fielding, Daniel Defoe, and Samuel Richardson—in tracing the social conditions, public attitudes, and literary practices in eighteenth century England that contributed to the emergence of the novel as an important literary genre. Includes a chapter titled "Fielding and the Epic Theory of the Novel" as well as a chapter analyzing *Tom Jones.*

JOSEPH HELLER

Born: Brooklyn, New York; May 1, 1923
Died: East Hampton, New York; December 12, 1999

PRINCIPAL LONG FICTION

Catch-22, 1961
Something Happened, 1974
Good as Gold, 1979
God Knows, 1984
Picture This, 1988
Closing Time, 1994
Portrait of an Artist, as an Old Man, 2000

OTHER LITERARY FORMS

Joseph Heller's first published piece was a short story in *Story Magazine* (1945), and in the late 1940's, he placed several other stories with *Esquire* and *The Atlantic Monthly*. Heller's enthusiasm for the theater accounts for the topic of his master's thesis at Columbia University, "The Pulitzer Prize Plays: 1917-1935," and he wrote three plays that deal directly or indirectly with the material he used in *Catch-22*. *We Bombed in New Haven*, a two-act play, was first produced by the Yale School of Drama Repertory Theater in 1967. It later reached Broadway and was published in 1968. *Catch-22: A Dramatization* (1971) was first produced at the John Drew Theater in East Hampton, Long Island, where Heller spent his summers. *Clevinger's Trial*, a dramatization of chapter 8 of *Catch-22*, was produced in London in 1974. Only *We Bombed in New Haven* enjoyed a modicum of critical and commercial success. Heller also contributed to a number of motion-picture and television scripts, the best known of which is *Sex and the Single Girl* (1964), for which he received his only screen credit.

ACHIEVEMENTS

Joseph Heller's reputation rests largely on his first novel, *Catch-22*, the publication of which vaulted him into the front ranks of postwar American novelists. Critics hailed it as "the great representative document of our era" and "probably the finest novel published since World War II." The expression "Catch-22" quickly entered the American lexicon. More than eight million copies of the novel have been printed, and it has been translated into more than a dozen languages. In 1970, Mike Nichols's film adaptation of Heller's tale sparked renewed interest in the novel itself and launched it onto the best-seller lists.

Catch-22 was one of the most widely read and discussed novels of the 1960's and early 1970's; its blend of humor and horror struck a responsive chord, particularly with the young, during the upheavals of the Vietnam era. The critic Josh Greenfield, writing in

1968, claimed that it had "all but become the chapbook of the sixties." Within the context of Vietnam, the novel seemed to be less about World War II than about that Asian war over which Americans were so furiously divided. *Catch-22*, then, remains the classic fictional statement of the antiwar sentiments of its time.

Although some have compared *Catch-22* to Norman Mailer's *The Naked and the Dead* (1948), James Jones's *The Thin Red Line* (1962), and other essentially naturalistic war tales written by Heller's contemporaries, its conception of war in basically absurdist terms and its crazy-quilt structure suggest affinities rather with such works as Kurt Vonnegut's *Slaughterhouse-Five* (1969). Heller's fiction is frequently described as "black comedy." In the tradition of Nathanael West, Günter Grass, Ralph Ellison, and Thomas Pynchon, Heller stretches reality to the point of distortion.

In his novels, as well as in his plays, Heller displays a worldview that shares much with twentieth century existentialist thought: The world is meaningless, it simply exists; humankind by its very nature seeks meaning; the relationship between humanity and its world is thus absurd; when a person recognizes these facts, he or she experiences what Jean-Paul Sartre termed the "nausea" of modern existence. In all of his work, Heller argues for "massive resistance" to routine, regimentation, and authority in whatever form. He affirms, no matter how much that affirmation may be qualified by pain and defeat, the sanctity of the individual. He writes not so much about the life of a soldier (as in *Catch-22*), the life of a businessman (as in *Something Happened*), or the life of a would-be politician (as in *Good as Gold*) as about the threats posed to individual identity by the institutions of modern life.

BIOGRAPHY

Joseph Heller was born in Brooklyn, New York, on May 1, 1923, the son of Russian-Jewish immigrants only recently arrived in the United States. His mother then barely spoke English; his father drove a delivery truck for a bakery until, when Heller was only five years old, he died unexpectedly during a routine ulcer operation. The denial of this death in particular and the bare fact of mortality in general were to color Heller's later life and work. The youngest of three children, Heller spent his boyhood in the Coney Island section of Brooklyn, an enclave of lower-and middle-class Jewish families, in the shadow of the famed amusement park. Both his family and his teachers recognized Heller as a bright but bored student; he tinkered with writing short stories while still in high school.

In 1942, at the age of nineteen, Heller joined the U.S. Army Air Corps. He spent one of the war years flying sixty missions as a wing bombardier in a squadron of B-25's stationed on Corsica in the Mediterranean. This proved to be the crucial year of his life; it provided him with the materials, and the bitterly sardonic attitude, out of which he forged his major work—*Catch-22*—as well as his three plays. Moreover, his sixty missions, many of them brutal and bloody (including the series of raids on Bologna that form the core of *Catch-22*), profoundly affected the attitude toward death that informs all of his work.

Demobilized in 1945, having achieved the rank of first lieutenant, Heller married fellow Brooklynite Shirley Held, with whom he had two children. Heller spent the next seven years within academe. Under the G.I. Bill, he attended college, first at the University of Southern California and then at New York University, where he received his bachelor of arts degree in 1948. Heller then traveled uptown to earn a master's degree at Columbia University before receiving one of the first Fulbright scholarships to study at Oxford. He returned to the United States to teach English at Pennsylvania State University between 1950 and 1952.

During the remainder of the 1950's, Heller was employed in the advertising departments of *Time*, *Look*, and *McCall's* magazines successively. In 1954, he began writing, at night and during odd hours, the manuscript that would be published eight years later as *Catch-22*. Almost forty years old when *Catch-22* finally appeared, Heller ironically referred to himself as an "aging prodigy."

Heller abandoned his successful advertising career during the 1960's and returned to teaching. His position as distinguished professor of English at the City University of New York (CUNY) afforded him both the salary to support his family and the free time to devote to his writing. In these years, he began work on a second novel, wrote several motion-picture and television scripts (usually adaptations of the work of others and often using a pseudonym), and completed his first play, *We Bombed in New Haven*.

Something Happened, Heller's second novel, took thirteen years to complete before appearing in 1974. Never fully at ease with academic life, Heller resigned his chair at CUNY in 1975, and in 1979 he published his third novel, *Good as Gold*. Although he occasionally lectured on the college circuit and served as writer-in-residence at both Yale University and the University of Pennsylvania, Heller was basically a reclusive writer, uncomfortable at literary gatherings and suspicious of the trappings of literary success. His life and work seemed guided by Ralph Waldo Emerson's dictum that "a foolish consistency is the hobgoblin of little minds."

In December, 1981, Heller was diagnosed as having Guillain Barré syndrome, a sometimes fatal condition involving progressive paralysis. He was hospitalized for several months but eventually recovered. The experience resulted in a book, *No Laughing Matter* (1986), written with his friend Speed Vogel, describing Heller's condition and its resolution; the illness also led to his second marriage, to one of his nurses, Valerie Humphries, in 1987.

God Knows returns to the irreverence and defiance of logic that characterized *Catch-22*. Its narrator, the biblical King David, speaks in modern jargon and in his extended version of his life and career displays knowledge of events long after his own time. *Picture This* is a protracted meditation on the ironies of history and of human life, focusing on the Netherlands of Rembrandt's time and the Athens of Aristotle.

In 1994, more than thirty years after the release of *Catch-22*, Heller published *Closing Time*, a sequel to *Catch-22*. Set in the late 1980's, this novel revisits both the characters from Heller's first novel and the experiences of Heller's generation of New York Jews, for whom World War II was a formative experience. In *Closing Time*, both groups come face-to-face with their own mortality and the fate of a world governed by flawed human institutions.

Now and Then: From Coney Island to Here (1998) is an autobiographical account of Heller's life from his boyhood days in Coney Island through the period following the publication of *Catch-22*. Devotees of *Catch-22* may be disappointed to find that Heller spends only part of a chapter on his wartime experience, while much of the early sections of the memoir chart the geography of Coney Island in elaborate detail. Heller would make his home in East Hampton, Long Island, New York. He died there on December 12, 1999.

ANALYSIS

At first glance, Joseph Heller's novels seem quite dissimilar. Heller's manipulation of time and point of view in *Catch-22* is dizzying; it is a hilariously macabre, almost surreal novel. *Something Happened*, on the other hand, is a far more muted book composed of the slow-moving, pessimistic broodings of an American business executive. *Good as Gold* is part remembrance of family life in the impoverished sections of Coney Island and part savage satire of contemporary American political life. Throughout Heller's work, however, all his characters are obsessed with death and passionately searching for some means to deny, or at least stay, their mortality. Heller's characters, like those of Saul Bellow, cry out to assert their individuality, their sense of self, which seems threatened from all sides. For example, Captain John Yossarian in *Catch-22* finds the world in conspiracy to blow him out of the sky. The worlds of *Catch-22*, *Something Happened*, and *Good as Gold* are not so much chaotic as absurdly and illogically routinized. In such an absurd world of callous cruelty, unalloyed ambition, and blithe disregard for human life, Heller maintains, the individual has the right to seek his own survival by any means possible.

CATCH-22

While *Catch-22*'s most obvious features are its antiwar theme and its wild, often madhouse humor, the novel itself is exceedingly complex in both meaning and form. In brief, the plot concerns a squadron of American airmen stationed on the fictional Mediterranean island of Pianosa during World War II. More specifically, it concerns the futile attempts of Captain Yossarian, a Syrian American bombardier, to be removed from flying status. Every time he approaches the number of missions necessary to complete a tour of duty, his ambitious commanding officers increase it. Yossarian tries a number of ploys to avoid combat. He malingers, feigns illness, and even poisons the squadron's food with laundry soap to abort one mission. Later, after the gunner Snowden dies in his arms during one particularly lethal mission, Yossarian refuses to fly again, goes naked, and takes to walking backward on the base, all in an attempt to have himself declared insane.

Yossarian is motivated by only one thing—the determination to stay alive. He sees his life threatened not only by the Germans who try to shoot him out of the sky but also by his superior officers, who seem just as intent to kill him off. "The enemy," he concludes at one point, "is anybody who's going to get you killed, no matter which side he's on." When Yossarian attempts to convince the camp's medical officer that his fear of death has driven him over the brink and thus made him unfit to fly, he first learns of the "catch" that will force him to keep flying: "There was only one catch and that was Catch-22, which specified that a concern for one's own safety in the face of dangers that were real and immediate was the process of a rational mind." As Doc Daneeka tells Yossarian, "Anyone who wants to get out of combat duty isn't really crazy."

Most of the large cast of characters surrounding Yossarian are, by any "reasonable" standard, quite mad. They include Colonel Cathcart, who keeps raising the number of missions his troops are required to fly not for the sake of the war effort but for his own personal glory; Major Major Major, who forges Washington Irving's name to official documents and who is pathologically terrified of command; and Milo Minderbinder, the mess officer, a black marketeer who bombs his own base under contract with the Germans. These supporting characters most often fall into one of four categories. The ranking officers—Cathcart, Dreedle, Korn, Black, Cargill, and Scheisskopf—appear more concerned with promotion, neat bombing patterns, and their own petty jealousies than with the war itself or the welfare of their men. A second group, including Doc Daneeka, Minderbinder, and Wintergreen, are also concerned with pursuing the main chance. They are predatory but also extremely comic and very much self-aware. Another group, including Nately, Chief Halfoat, McWatt, Hungry Joe, and Chaplain Tappman, are (like Yossarian himself) outsiders, good men caught within a malevolent system. The dead—Mudd, Snowden, Kraft, and "the soldier in white"—constitute a final group, one that is always present, at least in the background.

It is the military system—which promulgates such absurdly tautological rules as "Catch-22"—that is Yossarian's real enemy. He and the other "good" men of the squadron live in a world that is irrational and inexplicable. As the company's warrant officer explains, "There just doesn't seem to be any logic to their system of rewards and punishments. . . . They have the right to do anything we can't stop them from doing."

As the novel progresses, the victims, increasingly aware of the menace posed by this system, carry their gestures of rebellion to the point of open defiance. Yossarian is the most blatant in this regard: He moans loudly during the briefing for the Avignon mission; he insists that there is a dead man in his tent; he goes naked during the Avignon mission itself and then again during the medal ceremony afterward; he halts the Bologna raid by putting soap in the squadron's food and by moving the bomb-line on the squadron's map; and he requests that he be grounded and eventually refuses to fly. Finally, he deserts, hoping to reach sanctuary in neutral Sweden.

In the world of *Catch-22*, then, the reader is forced to question the very nature of sanity. Sanity is commonly defined as the ability to live within society and to act appropriately according to its rules. If those rules—such as Catch-22—are patently false, however, then adhering to them is in truth an act of insanity, for the end result may be death or the loss of freedom. The world of *Catch-22* is, to Yossarian, a spurious culture, as anthropologists would call it, one that does not meet the basic needs of its members—above all, the need to survive. Authority, duty, and patriotism are all called into question, and Heller demonstrates that when those in authority lack intelligence or respect for life, as is the case with Yossarian's commanding officers, obeying authority can only be self-defeating. Heller thus argues that in an absurd universe, the individual has the right to seek his own survival; he argues that life itself is infinitely more precious than any cause, however just. When Yossarian decides that he has done his part to defeat the Nazis (and after all, he has flown many more missions than most other airmen), his principal duty is to save himself. Yossarian's desertion, then, is a life-affirming act.

As one critic noted, *Catch-22*

> speaks solidly to those who are disaffected, discontented, and disaffiliated, and yet who want to react to life positively. With its occasional affirmations couched in terms of pain and cynical laughter, it makes nihilism seem natural, ordinary, even appealing.

Thus the surface farce of *Catch-22*, when peeled away, reveals a purpose that is literally deadly serious.

If the basic plot of *Catch-22* is fairly simple, its narrative technique and structure most certainly are not. The novel appears to be a chronological jumble, flashing forward and backward from the central event—the death of Snowden—that marks Yossarian's final realization of the mortal threat posed by Catch-22. Time in the novel exists not as clock time but rather as psychological time, and within Yossarian's stream-of-consciousness narrative, events in the present intermingle with cumulative repetitions and gradual clarifications of past actions. For example, in chapter 4, the bare facts of Snowden's death are revealed, that he was killed over Avignon when Dobbs, his copilot, went berserk and grabbed the plane's controls at a crucial moment. Yossarian returns to this incident throughout the novel, but it is not until the penultimate chapter that he reconstructs the story in full. In this fashion, Heller seeks to capture the real ways in which people apprehend the world, incompletely and in fragments.

Catch-22 is intricately structured despite its seeming shapelessness. Until chapter 19, almost everything is told in retrospect while Yossarian is in the hospital; chapter 19 itself begins the movement forward in time leading to Yossarian's desertion. The gradual unfolding of the details of Snowden's death provides another organizing device. Such structural devices as parallelism, doubling, and—most important—repetition, force the reader to share Yossarian's perpetual sense of déjà vu, the illusion of having previously experienced something actually being encountered for the first time. The ultimate effect of such devices is to reinforce the novel's main themes: Yossarian is trapped in a static world, a world in which nothing seems to change and in which events seem to keep repeating themselves. He does not move through his experiences but rather seems condemned to a treadmill existence. The only way to resist this world is to escape it, to desert.

SOMETHING HAPPENED

Heller himself once revealed that he considered Bob Slocum, the protagonist-narrator of his second novel, *Something Happened*, to be "the antithesis of Yossarian—twenty years later." Indeed, the scene shifts dramatically from the dusty, littered airfields of Pianosa to the green, well-kept lawns of suburban Connecticut. In *Something Happened*, Heller details—some say monotonously details—the inner life of an outwardly successful man and, in doing so, seeks to expose the bankruptcy of contemporary middle-class American culture.

Slocum works as a middle-level marketing research manager in a large company. He is middle-aged, married, and the father of three children. Although he is by all appearances successful, Slocum's extended monologue of memories, self-analysis, and carpings at the world reveal that he is anything but happy: "I keep my own counsel and drift speechlessly with my crowd. I float. I float like algae in a colony of green scum, while my wife and I grow old." He sees his life as a series of humiliating failures of nerve, of unfulfilled expectations and missed opportunities. Slocum harks back repeatedly and with regret to his adolescent yearnings for an office girl—later a suicide—with whom he had worked shortly after finishing high school. He now wishes in vain that he could desire someone or something as desperately as he once desired her.

Slocum despises his present job and mistrusts his associates yet politics shamelessly for promotion; he feels bound to his family yet commits numerous adulteries. He is hopelessly at odds with himself and his life. For example, he loves his family in a temporizing kind of way, but he also fears that he has made them all unhappy. His wife, bored and restless, feels isolated in the suburbs and turns to alcohol. His sixteen-year-old daughter is sullen and promiscuous. One son is hopelessly brain-damaged and an insufferable burden to Slocum; the other, Slocum seems truly to want to love, but he cannot help browbeating him. The novel reaches its bleak climax when this latter son is hit by a car and lies bleeding in the street. Slocum cradles the boy in his arms and, at the moment when he feels he can express his love, inadvertently smothers him.

There is no real resolution in *Something Happened*. At novel's end, Slocum has not changed or learned anything of importance. Unlike Yossarian, who is threatened from without, Slocum is his own worst enemy. His sense of alienation, of loss, of failure, is unrelieved.

Critical opinion of *Something Happened* has been mixed. Those who admire the novel most often praise its exact and mercilessly honest replication of the banality and vacuousness of everyday life among the American middle classes, and they argue that Heller, as in *Catch-22*, nicely fuses form and meaning. Others find the novel irritatingly tedious and pessimistic and consider the character of Slocum seriously flawed, unlikable, and unheroic by any standard. Many reviewers could not resist quipping that a more appropriate title for Heller's novel would be *Nothing Happens*.

Good as Gold

Heller's third novel, *Good as Gold*, savagely satirizes the aspirations of the Jewish intellectual community in America. The comic dimension of *Catch-22*, so absent from *Something Happened*, returns. Bruce Gold is a forty-eight-year-old Brooklyn-born English professor who desperately wants to make—or at least have—money. Like Bob Slocum, Gold has problems with his family, which, he knows, considers him a failure because he is not rich. Much of the novel takes place within the Gold family itself, which Gold finds oppressive, if at times amusingly so.

Gold is in most ways a fool—albeit a cynical one—a hypocrite, and a congenital social climber. He is a 1970's version of Budd Schulberg's Sammy Glick. Evidence of this is his engagement to a wealthy WASP socialite with political connections. Gold himself harbors political ambitions. He hungers to replace his alter ego and archnemesis Henry Kissinger as secretary of state and hopes that his fiancé's tycoon father will help him in his quest for political power. Heller savages both Gold and Kissinger, and for precisely the same reason: They represent to him those in the Jewish community who want to escape their heritage while at the same time exploiting it. (To further his financial, academic, and political fortunes, Gold wants to write a "big" book about the Jewish experience in America, about which he knows next to nothing.)

Gold understands his own hypocrisy but promptly dismisses it. Yet, when Gold is eventually offered Kissinger's former cabinet position, he experiences a change of heart. Prompted by the death of his older brother, Gold refuses the post and returns to New York and his family. Like Yossarian, Gold is able to restore his own integrity by deserting.

Heller's work has been compared to that of artists as varied as Eugène Ionesco and the Marx Brothers; *Good as Gold* lies closer to the latter than to the former. Until his decision to renounce his political ambitions, Gold is very much the comic intellectual, pathetically incapable of coping with the difficulties in which he finds himself. The humor of *Good as Gold* is painted with the broadest brush of Heller's career, but its target is his familiar one: the means by which institutions in the modern world coerce the individual and the way in which individuals—such as Slocum and, until his turnabout, Gold—become coconspirators in their own demise.

God Knows

God Knows is Heller's rewriting of a major element of the Old Testament, the story of David. As in all of his fiction, Heller focuses here on the human insistence on repeating earlier mistakes and on the ironies of life. His David is a prototypical wise guy, looking back over his life from his death bed; his language veers from that of the King James version of the Bible to twentieth century slang as he presents his side of various stories, from his encounter with Goliath to his problems with King Saul to his troubles with his children and his various wives.

His first wife—Saul's daughter, Michal—was a shrew to whom he refers as the first

Jewish American Princess. He misses Abigail, his second wife, the only one who loved him completely; she has been dead for many years. Bathsheba, the great passion of his life, has turned into an overweight nag, bored with sex and interested only in trying to convince David to name their son, Solomon, as his successor. Solomon, in David's eyes, is an idiot, a humorless man with no original thoughts who writes down everything his father says and later pretends that they are his ideas. The old king's only solace is the young virgin, Abishag the Shunnamite, who waits on him and worships him.

David complains about his present state, remembers his days of glory, and rationalizes his deeds, avoiding responsibility for any evil that has befallen others but claiming credit for benefits. His knowledge is modern. He maintains, for example, that Michelangelo's famous statue of him is a nice piece of work but it is not "him." His language is laden with quotations from William Shakespeare, Robert Browning, T. S. Eliot, and many others, and he seems to have direct knowledge of most of ancient and modern history.

God Knows is Heller's most engaging fiction since *Catch-22*. Suspense is maintained by David's reluctance to name Solomon as his successor, as he must do, and by the question of whether he will ever hear the voice of God, which he desperately wants. Heller's David is not an admirable man, but he is a fascinating one and an interesting commentator not only on his own life but on human frailty and ambition as well. He is cynical, his faith in God and humanity having left him years before, but even as he complains about the pains of old age, his memory keeps reminding him of the enjoyments of the life he has led.

Picture This

Picture This is neither conventional fiction nor history but a kind of extended meditation on human weakness. Its inspiration is the famous painting *Aristotle Contemplating the Bust of Homer*, by Dutch painter Rembrandt van Rijn. Heller presents many historical facts, chiefly about the Greece of the time of Aristotle, Plato, and Socrates, as well as the Netherlands of the time of Rembrandt, and he draws frequent parallels between events of those periods and those of the modern age. In discussing the Athenian wars, for example, he makes clear his conviction that the motivations, the mistakes, and the stupidities are parallel to those made by the United States in the years since World War II.

Picture This contains much authentic information, most of which is intended to demonstrate human greed and weakness. Heller seems to be fascinated by the financial aspects of Rembrandt's life, in which great success was frittered away and in which a life of luxury ended with enormous debts; he also writes at length about Rembrandt's marriage and his mistresses. In writing about Greece in the Golden Age, he focuses on the failings of government. The great leader Pericles, in his view, led Athens into self-destructive wars. Pericles was personally noble, but he did his city no good. The tyrant Creon was even worse. Much of what Plato wrote about he could not have observed.

Unlike either *Catch-22* or *God Knows*, *Picture This* fails to provide a leavening of irreverent humor to lighten Heller's dark view of human existence. The only fictional elements in the book are imaginary dialogues between some of the historic figures and the fantasy that Aristotle exists in the painting of him and can observe Rembrandt and his labors; these imaginary flights are only occasionally humorous. Otherwise, the irony in *Picture This* is unrelenting and bitter.

CLOSING TIME

Though *Closing Time* is more humorous, Heller's irony remains bitter, as a World War II generation contemplating the later years of their lives takes the whole world down with them, courtesy of an incompetent U.S. president who, at the novel's conclusion, launches a nuclear strike under the mistaken impression that he is playing a video game. Prior to that apocalyptic finale, readers are reintroduced to Yossarian, who, in the thirty years since the events of *Catch-22*, has been working as an ethics adviser for Milo Minderbinder's multinational corporation. He has been married, had four children, and divorced. As he faces retirement and realizes he is not long for the world, he worries about the future of his children, begins an affair with a younger nurse, and resolves "to live forever, or to die trying."

In terms of genre, *Closing Time* is a difficult book to characterize. As a sequel to *Catch-22*, it takes familiar characters such as Yossarian, Chaplain Tappman, and Milo Minderbinder through an absurdist parody of business, medicine, government, and the military. The addition of two World War II veteran characters (Sammy Singer and Lew Rabinowitz) with only ancillary connections to the main plot brings a nostalgic realism to the novel, more in keeping with Heller's subsequent memoir, *Now and Then*, than with the Yossarian sections of the novel. *Closing Time* also is Heller's most self-consciously postmodern novel, as real-life figures, such as author Kurt Vonnegut, are intertwined with fictional ones; references are made to not only the events of *Catch-22* but also the novel itself and the entry of the term "Catch-22" into the popular lexicon. At its best, this generic combination allows Heller to range widely in his criticism of contemporary society (as in a priceless explanation Yossarian is given of the Freedom of Information Act). Too often, however, these various formats seem at odds with each other, leading to a novel that moves both slowly and in too many directions.

Richard A. Fine
Updated by Jim O'Loughlin

OTHER MAJOR WORKS

PLAYS: *We Bombed in New Haven*, pr. 1967; *Catch-22: A Dramatization*, pr. 1971; *Clevinger's Trial*, pb. 1973.

SCREENPLAYS: *Sex and the Single Girl*, 1964 (with David R. Schwartz); *Casino Royale*, 1967 (with others); *Dirty Dingus Magee*, 1970 (with others).

NONFICTION: *No Laughing Matter*, 1986 (with Speed Vogel); *Now and Then: From Coney Island to Here*, 1998.

Bibliography

Aldridge, John W. *The American Novel and the Way We Live Now.* New York: Oxford University Press, 1983. Aldridge's overview of American fiction after World War II gives Heller's work high marks, praising his skeptical view of modern society and the imaginative qualities of his novels.

Bloom, Harold, ed. *Joseph Heller's "Catch-22."* New ed. New York: Bloom's Literary Criticism, 2008. A collection of critical assessments of the novel, including pieces by respected writers and literary critics, such as Nelson Algren, Christopher Buckley, and Norman Podhoretz, and an introduction by Bloom.

Cacicedo, Alberto. "'You Must Remember This': Trauma and Memory in *Catch-22* and *Slaughterhouse-Five*." *Critique* 46, no. 4 (Summer, 2005): 357-368. A comparison of the novels by Heller and Kurt Vonnegut, focusing on the writers' ability to depict the horrors of World War II while creating a sense of indignation in readers that could result in ethical social action. Critics generally agree that Heller's novel was able to do this, while there is disagreement about the ethical engagement of Vonnegut's novel.

Craig, David M. *Tilting at Mortality: Narrative Strategies in Joseph Heller's Fiction.* Detroit, Mich.: State University Press, 1997. An examination of the ethical dimensions of Heller's work, linking his distinctive stylistic features to his preoccupation with questions of death, meaning, and identity. Includes separate chapters on each of Heller's first six novels.

Klinkowitz, Jerome. *The American 1960's: Imaginative Acts in a Decade of Change.* Ames: Iowa State University Press, 1990. This analysis of American fiction in political terms suggests that Heller's *Catch-22* introduces a distinctively new kind of politics, that of withdrawal from impossible situations, and that in this sense the novel is one of the truly original works of its time.

LeClair, Thomas. "Joseph Heller, *Something Happened*, and the Art of Excess." *Studies in American Fiction* 9 (Autumn, 1981): 245-260. This essay focuses on Heller's second novel, defending its repetitive quality as a stylistic device that is necessary to the portrayal of the dullness and mediocrity of the life of its protagonist and the other characters.

Potts, Stephen W. *From Here to Absurdity: The Moral Battlefields of Joseph Heller.* 2d ed. San Bernardino, Calif.: Borgo Press, 1995. This insightful and accessible overview of Heller's novels and plays emphasizes the continuities throughout Heller's writings, despite the various genres within which he has worked. As a moralist and political cynic, Heller creates characters whose personal crises drive them either to confront or to conform to governing orthodoxy.

Saurian, Adam J. *Conversations with Joseph Heller.* Jackson: University Press of Mississippi, 1993. A collection of interviews conducted during the 1960's, 1970's, and 1980's, in which Heller discusses the themes, structure, and satire in his fiction, the writers who influenced his work, and his political opinions, among other topics. Includes two humorous "anti-interviews" with his friends Mel Brooks and George Mandel.

Seed, David. *The Fiction of Joseph Heller: Against the Grain*. New York: St. Martin's Press, 1989. Analyzes Heller's work published through the late 1980's, demonstrating how the writer's absurdist vision is present in his novels, plays, and essays.

Woodson, Jon. *A Study of Joseph Heller's "Catch-22": Going Around Twice*. New York: Peter Lang, 2001. Uses the New Criticism and mythological criticism that Heller was familiar with to argue that *Catch-22* is in essence a retelling of the epic of Gilgamesh in much the same way that James Joyce's *Ulysses* is a retelling of Homer's *Odyssey*.

GISH JEN

Born: New York, New York; August 12, 1955
Also known as: Lillian Jen

PRINCIPAL LONG FICTION

Typical American, 1991
Mona in the Promised Land, 1996
The Love Wife, 2004

OTHER LITERARY FORMS

In *Who's Irish? Stories* (1999), Gish Jen (jehn) has collected short stories that are both a part of the origins of the central themes in her fiction and a continuance of their implications. Her first novel, *Typical American*, developed from the short story "In the American Society" (1987), whereas her novel *Mona in the Promised Land* was first begun while she was working on *Typical American*. She was uncertain about how to finish the second novel and decided instead to explore her teenage years with the short story "The Water-Faucet Vision" (1988) after meeting a friend from her high school days.

ACHIEVEMENTS

Gish Jen's work has been instrumental in introducing Asian American cultures to a reading public that, for the most part, has been casually familiar with an ethnic community that remains stereotyped in the United States. Asian Americans and Asian immigrants are often derided as not just different but as representative of a kind of evil in direct conflict with European values. Jen's presentations of Chinese families in the United States are so fully human, humorous, and admirable that they counteract these bigoted preconceptions.

Jen's goal as a writer has been to demonstrate that the essence of the American experience is one of forced accommodation to a narrow, constricting model of behavior. She also has sought ways to demolish the model itself by showing how much more there can be to life for all if the full range of a diverse, transnational population is permitted to flourish. With insight, humor, and clarity, her books have transformed conceptions of Chinese Americans and expanded the entire concept of what it means to be "typically American." In recognition of her achievements, Jen received the Lannan Literary Award in 1995 and a prestigious Strauss Living Award from the American Academy of Arts and Letters for 2003-2008.

BIOGRAPHY

Gish Jen, born Lillian Jen in 1955, is the daughter of Chinese immigrants who came to the United States separately in the 1940's. Jen grew up in the suburb of Scarsdale, north of New York City. Her father was a hydraulics engineer who had been invited to the United

States to assist in the war effort and her mother was a young socialite who had been sent to the United States for graduate education. Neither was able to return to China following the communist takeover there. Now permanently in the United States, her father felt he was living "in no world"; he did not become a U.S. citizen for many years.

Jen has said that she and her brother were beaten and insulted regularly as children because they were part of the only Chinese family in the neighborhood. She soon began to introduce herself as Gish Jen, named for film star Lillian Gish, in "a spirit of adventure." Jen's parents wanted her to earn an M.B.A. after majoring in English at Harvard, but she "had to be a writer or die." She took a job at Doubleday, which did not pay well or advance her aspirations to write. She then applied to Stanford University's business school only because Stanford had a graduate writing program. She managed to pass her business courses while "taking great courses across the street." Her mother did not speak to her for one year after she graduated from Stanford. Jen then taught English at a coal-mining school in China before applying to the Iowa Writers' Workshop at the University of Iowa; she graduated in 1983. She and her husband David O'Connor lived in California until 1985 then moved to Cambridge, Massachusetts, where Jen was awarded a fellowship to Radcliffe's Bunting Institute. She wrote her first novel, *Typical American*, while at Radcliffe. The novel was a finalist for the National Book Critics Circle Award in 1991.

Jen's two children with O'Connor inspired the title of her short-story collection *Who's Irish?* and her increasing interest in the traditional culture of mainland China formed the basis for *The Love Wife*, which explores how a visitor from China affected an acculturated Chinese American family.

ANALYSIS

Gish Jen's novels, while introducing many readers to the details of a Chinese family adjusting to life in the United States in the last decades of the twentieth century, present not only portraits of an ancient culture both in collision and in coordination with mainstream American culture; her novels present as well portraits of individual characters of considerable depth whose lives are part of an expansion and revision of what it means to be a U.S. citizen. As Jen has said, "I think that something about the complexities of our times makes me want to hear every voice I can hear" as a part of a new American family.

Jen's long fiction traces the developing arc of involvement in American life for Chinese Americans. Her novels are wide-ranging and explore the earliest arrivals of a family trying to understand a new environment, a second generation with concerns and interests that could not be anticipated, and the problems faced by a multigenerational family whose members have moved from a relatively single-minded focus on specific issues to a full range of difficulties common to an American family near the start of the twenty-first century. When she began to work on *Typical American*, Jen recalls, "matters of ethnicity as a great theme of literature were not on anybody's list." She has said that the act of naming oneself Asian American was "not something that comes down to us straight from our heritage." She set her first novel at a "time when ethnicity as we know it was suddenly being invented." The transition from the popular designation "Oriental" to the preferred term "Asian American" takes place in the novel during the years that Chang family members seek success in the United States without completely compromising their sense of themselves as Chinese.

TYPICAL AMERICAN

In the years following the end of World War II, the rise to power in China by the Communist government of Mao Zedong prevented many Chinese citizens involved with the United States in the war effort from returning to their homeland. *Typical American* follows Yfeng Chang from his boyhood in China to his arrival in the United States with his sister Theresa. They struggle to adjust to life in America while Ralph studies for a Ph.D. in mechanical engineering and Theresa enters medical school. They are joined by Theresa's friend Helen (named Hailan, "sea blue," at birth), whom Yfeng (now Ralph) eventually marries.

Initially skeptical about almost everything Americans take seriously—a skepticism that turned "typically American" into a slur—and contemptuous of various enthusiasms of postwar popular culture, the Changs become less alienated and steadily more comfortable with their life as U.S. citizens. Jen handles the transition with insight and comic verve, sympathetically evoking the real pain that the Changs feel while gently casting their predicaments in a humorous fashion. That Yfeng accepts the name Ralph from a girlfriend is one example of Jen's wit: Jen took the assumption that Chinese speakers have problems pronouncing "r" and "l," named a character Ralph (which contains both letters), and thus faced the assumption with mild mockery and defiant pride.

The Changs' expectation that they can succeed in America with substantial credentials enabling Ralph to find suitable work, a comfortable if modest home, and a sense of independence for Theresa as a modern woman in the 1960's is a typically American expectation. Also typically American is the expansion of the family's ambitions to include status, wealth, and privilege beyond respect. Jen does not avoid the embarrassment and rejection that is a part of their lives, but her depiction of the ways in which the Changs respond to the challenges of their new world is tempered by a kind of antic outlook that is one of her signature stylistic devices. At the conclusion of the novel, the Changs are part of the newly recognized Asian American community, the identifying term itself as much an evolving construct as their lives.

MONA IN THE PROMISED LAND

If *Typical American* covers a familiar narrative in new ways, *Mona in the Promised Land* moves far beyond the traditional adjustments-to-America model of second-generation children of immigrants. Set in the affluent Scarshill suburb north of New York City, the Chang children are enthusiastically involved in the re-creation and establishment of individual identities that their parents, now comfortable as Americans, cannot have imagined. Mona and Callie, in their teens, have not so much rejected their heritage as explored ways to expand it.

Mona is beguiled by the lives of her friends in the Jewish community, while Callie is attempting to recover a Chinese identity by studying Mandarin at Harvard and cooking rice while her parents have developed a taste for organic foods. Ralph's instinctive distrust of the African American and Latino employees at the restaurant he owns is altered as he discovers how much they contribute to the business.

The novel is somewhat episodic as chapters alternate among narrative threads that follow the main character's situations. As Mona becomes involved with Seth Mandel, a Jewish student entranced by multicultural complexities, her mother's displeasure is gradually dispelled and the couple's marriage leads to a very optimistic and joyous conclusion to the novel. In keeping with Jen's unabashed comic technique, Mona takes Changowitz as a surname. Callie has become more traditionally Chinese than her parents, although she has also chosen to become a Roman Catholic. Ralph and Helen have weathered all sorts of crises and have completed a kind of cycle, now beginning to reclaim the elements of their Asian heritage that were set aside when they entered the United States.

As Jen told an interviewer asking about the comedy inherent in the Chang's lives, she did not "manage to make them funny—they simply turn funny at the most inappropriate times," a good description of the tone of the novel and an indication of the outlook of a writer who says "My natural facility is to find the laugh. I'm very aware of incongruity."

THE LOVE WIFE

The Love Wife tells the story of an Asian American family firmly established in American society. Individual versions of the family's fortunes are presented, as Jen put it, "as if told by various Wongs at a very long family therapy session, only without the therapist." Jen's intention was to create individual realities expressed by many voices—two children adopted by Carnegie Wong (Chinese American) and Janie "Blondie" Wong (Anglo-American) prior to the unexpected arrival of their biological son, and the Wongs themselves. The family arrangement, rife with possibilities for confusion about parentage, is complicated further by the arrival of their cousin Lan from China to help with childcare. Lan is insecure in the United States, and her philosophy of child rearing is often distinctly different from that of the Wongs.

Jen has said that "There is really no such thing as one who is purely Chinese American or anything else." *The Love Wife* is an exploration of the implications of this position, particularly with respect to the fear among the Wongs about who really belongs to the family, or to the United States.

The multivocal structure of the novel reads like a script for a dramatic performance, with each character speaking in a distinctive manner. Their responses to each other illuminate their psychological foundations and express their moods with empathy. One of the most distinctive features of the narrative is Lan's voice, which is rendered in italics to represent the Mandarin language and the cultural mind-set from which it evolved. Lan's stories about the Cultural Revolution in China are taken from accounts Jen heard when visiting China herself. Lan's arrival compels the formation of alliances within the family, fracturing what has been a somewhat tenuous unity and forcing a kind of introspection that has been largely absent due to the family's successes "in the American society" (the title of one of Jen's short stories).

Carnegie Wong's mother is in the early stages of Alzheimer's disease, representing the fading of a traditional Asian outlook. She has given her children a financial and psychological foundation based on her own determination to thrive in the United States, and her loss of memory causes her son to search for as much of his Asian heritage as he can recover, an ironic reversal of his lifelong rebellion against her "Chineseness." Jen has observed that the United States as an "invented nation based on shared ideals" continues to bring together families "by choice rather than by circumstance and biology." *The Love Wife* reveals the ways in which three generations of a kind of mixed or hybrid family attempts to deal with the fluidity of identity.

Leon Lewis

Other major works

SHORT FICTION: "In the American Society," 1987 (in *The New Generation: Fiction for Our Time from America's Writing Programs*; Alan Kaufman, editor); "The Water-Faucet Vision," 1988 (in *Best American Short Stories, 1988*); "The White Umbrella," 1990 (in *Home to Stay: Asian American Women's Fiction*; Sylvia Watanabe and Carol Bruchac, editors); *Who's Irish? Stories*, 1999.

Bibliography

"About Gish Jen." *Ploughshares* 26, nos. 2/3 (2000): 217-222. Brief but comprehensive profile of Jen in a well-known and respected literary journal.

Brada-Williams, Noelle, and Karen Chow. *Crossing Oceans: Reconfiguring American Literary Studies in the Pacific Rim*. Hong Kong: Hong Kong University Press, 2004. Examines the "identity switch" in *Mona in the Promised Land* from a multicultural perspective that takes individual identification as a fluid concept.

Chen, Shu-ching. "Disjuncture at Home: Mapping the Domestic Cartographies of Transnationalism in Gish Jen's *The Love Wife*." *Tamkang Review* 37, no. 2 (Winter, 2006): 1-32. Grounded in theoretical concepts that the author handles competently. Discussion of the characters, themes, and concepts of the novel is incisive and illuminating. A serious, scholarly study of the essence of Jen's work.

Feng, Pin-Chia. "Reinventing a Chinese American Women's Tradition in Gish Jen's *Mona in the Promised Land*." *EurAmerica: The Journal of European and American Studies* 32, no. 4 (December, 2002): 675-704. Instructive analysis of the ways in which identity is constructed in Jen's novel, considering the conflict between the vertical (generational) model and the horizontal model (overlooking race, class, and gender) of identity and Jen's handling of these issues.

Lee, Rachel C. *The Americas of Asian American Literature: Gendered Fictions of Nation and Transnation*. Princeton, N.J.: Princeton University Press, 1999. Includes the chapter "Gish Jen and the Gendered Codes of Americanness," which discusses *Typical American* from the perspective of postcolonial theory.

Zhou Xiaojing, "Becoming Americans: Gish Jen's Typical American." In *The Immigrant Experience in North American Literature: Carving Out a Niche*, edited by Katherine Payant and Toby Rose. Westport, Conn.: Greenwood Press, 1999. Considers the ways in which cultural conditions influence the creation of a literature about the immigrant experience in Jen's early work.

DIANE JOHNSON

Born: Moline, Illinois; April 28, 1934
Also known as: Diane Lain; Diane Lain Johnson Murray

PRINCIPAL LONG FICTION

Fair Game, 1965
Loving Hands at Home, 1968
Burning, 1971
The Shadow Knows, 1974
Lying Low, 1978
Persian Nights, 1987
Health and Happiness, 1990
Le Divorce, 1997
Le Mariage, 2000
L'Affaire, 2003
Lulu in Marrakech, 2008

OTHER LITERARY FORMS

Diane Johnson's nonfiction works often complement her fictional subjects by exploring similar settings and themes. Her book *The True History of the First Mrs. Meredith and Other Lesser Lives* (1972) is a biography of Mary Ellen Nicolls Meredith, the daughter of novelist and poet Thomas Love Peacock and the first wife of novelist and poet George Meredith. Johnson also wrote the first published full-length biography of Dashiell Hammett, *Dashiell Hammett: A Life* (1983).

Terrorists and Novelists, a collection of Johnson's book reviews and essays that appeared originally in *The New York Times Book Review* and *The New York Review of Books*, was published in 1982. Her autobiographical works include *Natural Opium: Some Travelers' Tales* (1993) and *Into a Paris Quartier: Reine Margot's Chapel and Other Haunts of St. Germain* (2005). Johnson has also published articles in such periodicals as the *San Francisco Chronicle*, *The Times* of London, and *Bon Appétit*; has contributed forewords to works such as *Americans in Paris: Great Short Stories of the City of Light* (2002), edited by Steven Gilbar, and photographer Philip Trager's *Changing Paris: A Tour Along the Seine* (2000); and has written introductions for reprint editions of literary classics, including Charlotte Brontë's *Jane Eyre* (1847) and Mary Shelley's *Frankenstein* (1818). In addition, Johnson has written scripts for both film and television. She collaborated with film director Stanley Kubrick on the 1980 screenplay adaptation of Stephen King's 1977 novel *The Shining*, and in 1979 she adapted her 1971 short story "An Apple, an Orange" for television.

ACHIEVEMENTS

Diane Johnson's novels have achieved both popularity and critical acclaim for their portrayals of insecure women grasping for a sense of identity amid chaotic surroundings. Her biography *The True History of the First Mrs. Meredith and Other Lesser Lives* was nominated for a National Book Award in 1973. Johnson received a Guggenheim Fellowship in 1977-1978, and in 1979 her novel *Lying Low* was a National Book Award nominee for fiction; also in that year, the American Academy of Arts and Letters presented Johnson with the Rosenthal Foundation Award. Johnson's essay anthology *Terrorists and Novelists* was a finalist for the 1983 Pulitzer Prize, and her biography of Dashiell Hammett was nominated for the Los Angeles Times Book Prize in 1984. *Persian Nights* was a Pulitzer Prize finalist in 1988. From 1988 through 1992, the American Academy of Arts and Letters gave Johnson the Mildred and Harold Strauss Living Stipend. In 1992, Johnson received the Los Angeles Times Robert Kirsch Award for her overall literary accomplishments. Her book *Le Divorce* was a National Book Award finalist in the fiction category in 1997; the novel also received a California Book Awards Gold Medal. *Le Divorce* has been distributed internationally, and its film adaptation, directed by James Ivory, was released in 2003. Many of Johnson's works have been best sellers and have been published in numerous European and Asian languages.

BIOGRAPHY

Diane Johnson was born Diane Lain on April 28, 1934, in Moline, Illinois, to Dolph Lain, an educator, and Frances Eloise Lain (née Elder). She had one younger brother and attended local schools in that community adjacent to the Mississippi River. Johnson's orderly and stable midwestern background influenced her writing. Her fascination with French culture began when a librarian at the Moline public library suggested that she read books written by Alexandre Dumas, *père*. His novels *The Three Musketeers* (1844) and *The Count of Monte-Cristo* (1844-1845) especially impressed Johnson, as did such literary classics as Jane Austen's *Pride and Prejudice* (1813). She began writing stories as a child.

Johnson attended Stephens College in Columbia, Missouri, from 1951 to 1953. In July, 1953, she married Byron Lamar Johnson, Jr., and took a job with the University of California, Los Angeles, library system to earn income while her husband attended medical school. She graduated from the University of Utah in 1957 with a B.A. in English. Before Johnson and her husband divorced in August, 1966, she gave birth to two daughters and two sons.

Johnson received an M.A. degree in 1966 from the University of California, Los Angeles, and pursued doctoral studies at that school, funded with a Woodrow Wilson grant in 1967 and an American Association of University Women fellowship in 1968. There she befriended author Alison Lurie, who urged Johnson to write fiction. While she was a student, Johnson wrote two manuscripts, including her debut novel, *Fair Game*.

Johnson first visited Paris, France, in 1967, when she was living in London, England, while conducting research about George Meredith and his wife Mary Ellen Peacock, whose life she later documented in a biography. Two years later, she completed her Ph.D. at the University of California, Los Angeles. She joined the English faculty at the University of California, Davis, in 1968 as an assistant professor, focusing on Victorian literature.

Johnson married Dr. John Frederic Murray, a physician, on November 9, 1969. The couple lived in Berkeley, California, and Johnson also rented an apartment where she wrote. During the late 1970's, Johnson collaborated with film director Stanley Kubrick—who had admired her 1974 novel *The Shadow Knows*—on the screenplay for the motion-picture version of Stephen King's novel *The Shining*. Promoted to the rank of full professor, Johnson taught through 1987, resigning the next year, when the Mildred and Harold Strauss Living Stipend provided her sufficient funds annually that she could focus on writing.

Johnson often accompanies her husband on international travels related to his research in the field of infectious diseases, and she has incorporated her experiences of other cultures and nations into her fiction and nonfiction. The couple has homes in both Northern California and Paris, and Johnson's observations of Americans in Paris inspired a series of novels, starting with *Le Divorce*, featuring expatriates in that city.

ANALYSIS

In Diane Johnson's novels, the central characters are often women caught in circumstances in which they feel trapped and insecure; inevitably, the pressures of contemporary life and social problems contribute to their frustrations and cause them to fight to extricate themselves. Usually suffering more than men from loss of identity and dehumanization, they reach out to experiences beyond their confined lives in the hope of finding a new paradigm for surviving. Men in Johnson's novels frequently become impediments and adversaries, for these women's difficulties arise partly from unsatisfactory relationships with men. Johnson's characters share a desire to be free from the wife-mother syndrome, to make choices, and to break through the complexities of relationships that keep them mired in unhappiness. They are intensely aware of the limited circumference of their lives as they are held in an emotional abyss.

The novels' settings intensify the difficulties and predicaments of the characters: for example, the unrest and impending revolution in the last days of the shah of Iran; the decadent, atrophying Los Angeles subculture; the confusion of French society; the chaos of violent African communities; and the social unrest of the 1960's. Although Johnson's early novels are light and satiric in tone, the subsequent works become increasingly serious as the characters are forced to reevaluate their lives and make compromises about their futures.

Fair Game

In *Fair Game*, Johnson's first novel, Dabney Wilhelm is a creative young woman who has her own business making children's clothes and who has also written a children's book. She must grapple with the nature of a woman's ultimate responsibility: marriage, children, husband, or a creative commitment. Several letters by Dabney to Mr. Trager, a famous young poet, are interspersed throughout the novel and reveal her search for an identity and her concerns. Dabney is acquainted with men who seek to guide her, and the narrative is told from their alternating points of view. The guru-philosopher Emerson Kado seeks to control Dabney intellectually and to protect her creativity. A symbolic key scene is an orgy at Kado's home where, in a ritual of fertilization, real blood is thrown and he gives a speech on evil. Frightened by the event, Dabney retreats into her more ordered existence. Marcus Stein, a psychiatrist, wants to make love to Dabney in order to free her emotions; he accuses her of not wanting to take chances and says that she is too concerned with ensuring her success. The young man to whom Dabney is engaged, Charles Earse, wonders whether she will be a good wife and is distressed by her literary aspirations. The various emotional harnesses these men try to fit on Dabney come to nothing when she runs off at the end with the poet.

The novel is satiric in tone; it does not have the underlying intensity that develops in Johnson's later novels, or the later works' sense of despair. Although Dabney is searching for and exploring options in her life, she is able to assess the difficulties, make a decision, and seek her identity with confidence.

Loving Hands at Home

Unlike Dabney, Karen Fry in *Loving Hands at Home* is already trapped in a stultifying situation. She has no particular talent and is a middle-class housewife with two children who has married into a Mormon family only to find herself stifled by their expectations of a perfect wife-mother role for her. She finds continual frustration in trying to meet the high demands of her home-economist mother-in-law, Mrs. Fry, and to break the indifference of her husband, Garth. For Mrs. Fry, a lopsided cake that Karen bakes for the ritual family Sunday dinner symbolizes Karen's unworthiness.

Karen seeks escape in a "secret life." She applies for jobs that she has no intention of accepting—interesting, strange jobs such as fortune-telling. When she is offered a job, the approval this suggests diminishes her feelings of inadequacy. Whenever Karen breaks out of her structured life, however, she meets with an incident that frightens her, forcing her back into the role she hates. Remembering her childhood in a small midwestern town, she thinks of Alma, the girl nobody was permitted to play with, a member of the "shiftless poor." Alma's rebelliousness and recklessness look increasingly appealing to Karen, caught as she is in a rigid structure where domestic accomplishments represent the ideal of femininity. When she learns that Alma has died from a reaction to a drug, however, she sees such freedom as less appealing.

Karen becomes aware that all the Fry family togetherness is beginning to break down. She catches Mrs. Fry, the mother of seven children, making love with a deliveryman. Sebastian Fry, who is the curator for Paris Pratt, a wealthy, mysterious benefactor of artists, is in love with Karen's poetic image, while his wife, Patty, a convert to Mormonism, valiantly tries to keep their home together. Feeling a closeness to the sensitive, creative Sebastian, Karen, in a moment of recklessness, makes love to him on the floor of Mrs. Pratt's bedroom. To Karen, this act is another attempt to free herself. When Mrs. Fry hears of the incident, she chides Karen for not living up to the Mormon role of womanhood and for ignoring the sanctity of marriage. Karen again takes flight, only to return, unable to face the uncertainties of the future on her own.

The novel's climactic scene occurs at one of the Frys' regular Sunday-night dinners. Mrs. Fry insists on eating some suspicious-looking mushrooms, while the others refuse to eat them, signifying a waning of her influence. Suddenly distraught, Mrs. Fry confesses her infidelities in a wild scene. She becomes violently ill and ultimately blames all the dissension on Karen, the outsider, and locks her in the bedroom, telling her that she is not "allowed to walk out on this life." When Garth and the other family members fail to come to her rescue, Karen escapes by climbing out the window, realizing now that she must reassess her life.

Earlier, Mrs. Pratt, another of Johnson's guru-type characters, has told Karen that she looks as if she has "not made the important decision yet"—is it possible to be happy? She tells Karen that she must discover an "organizing motif." In the novel's final scene, Karen and her children are on the beach, totally absorbed in building a sand castle. They know that they are "doing an important thing," and it is "an extraordinary, inspired sand castle." Karen is not running or waiting; she is "reorganizing."

Burning

Johnson focuses on social institutions in *Burning*, a satiric attack on the Los Angeles subculture and particularly on social welfare agencies. A historic event, the 1961 Bel Air fire, is the backdrop for the climax and parallels the social disintegration of this world.

The novel covers one day in the life of Barney and Bingo, a middle-class couple with two children who live in the hills of the wealthy Los Angeles neighborhood of Bel Air. When the hedge separating them from their neighbors—psychiatrist Hal Harris, Harris's wife, and his patient Max—is cut down by the fire department as a fire hazard, there is a symbolic breaking down of the barrier between Barney and Bingo's "calm and orderly" world and that of the guru psychiatrist, drug dependents, an unfit mother, and group therapy. Barney and Bingo go through a rite of passage, gradually losing their illusions in a "jungle" that they cannot comprehend. The novel's point of view alternates between Barney and Bingo; indeed, Barney is one of Johnson's more fully realized male characters.

The world of this novel is askew. The psychiatrist provides drugs, followed by sex, to his patients, but he really prefers his plants. Having given up on his patients, he gives them drugs to sedate them, insulating them from the life he himself avoids; he has retreated from society because he no longer believes in human improvement. Despite Harris's attitude, Max, an unfit mother and drug addict, looks up to him as a father, and his other patients depend on his therapy to keep them going. When Bingo is persuaded to substitute for Max in an appearance at a child-welfare agency hearing, Bingo assumes that because she is stable she will pass the test. Her interview with the child-welfare worker is the incisive satiric scene of the novel. Although Bingo gives honest answers, she fails the test and is declared an unfit mother. She is indignant but shaken, and she is further disturbed by the fact that she believes the social worker's judgment. She begins to look at herself with less certainty, feeling isolated and inadequate in this environment.

Barney expresses the novel's central metaphor when he comments that one must experience the "pains and exaltations of life" and likens these to a "hard, gemlike flame." Thus he admonishes Bingo, when, at the end, as the fire is raging and water is needed desperately, she wants to take a shower. He accuses her of not caring, of not being committed.

There is a symbolic moment in the book's final scene, when Barney and Bingo are faced with the changes in their lives and the loss of their illusions. She laments, "Terrible, terrible. What shall we do?" He replies, "We have each other." The ironic distance in their responses indicates that they are more apart than they realize; Bingo's ability to deal with the changes in her life is dubious.

THE SHADOW KNOWS

In *The Shadow Knows*, Johnson skillfully depicts the psychology of a woman fearing for her life and beset with other anxieties, who panics. Similar to a detective story, the novel begins with the remembrance of a violent crime and ends with a rape. *The Shadow Knows* covers one week in the life of "N," who is a victim of terror and acts of violence. A young, divorced mother of four, a graduate student, involved in a love affair with a married man, she gradually reveals her uncertainties about herself in her search for the criminal identity of her pursuer. Abandoned by her husband, feeling the pain of loneliness, and resentful of her new situation, she declines into misery and paranoia, nursing a foreboding that something violent is going to happen. Adopting a wryly ironic tone to blunt her fear, she thinks that "murder would spoil everything" and that anticipating one's murder "gives you something to live for." She also imagines the "Famous Inspector," a figure who will investigate the murder, and she fantasizes how it will be reported in the newspaper.

Two black women, Osella and Ev, play significant roles in the story, and the protagonist's attitudes toward them reflect truths about herself. She is suspicious of "mad" Osella, who served as N's housekeeper when she was married. She recognizes similarities between herself and Osella: They are both left-handed, and they have the same birthday. There is the implication that Osella represents an alter ego of N—but N hates her for her dominance over the household, for her power. She also realizes that she does not like "fat and black" people and regards Osella as an "insignificant animal." Still, when Osella calls

N a "whore," a "taker," and "hard-hearted" and "cold," N is affected, because she sees truth in these accusations. She knows that Osella's presence enabled her to have the freedom she wanted. Ev, N's current housekeeper, also shares qualities with N: Her husband has deserted her, she lives in permanent fear, and she feels victimized. N admires Ev's courage, for somehow Ev can face her life calmly in spite of these difficulties.

In N's ruminations, she wonders whether a person who is an intended murder victim perhaps deserves to be killed. She accepts that there is some evil in herself. She knows that she has exploited Osella and admits that she wanted her as a "slave." She also realizes that she can act without principles; she has considered inducing an abortion of the child she is carrying. In her self-absorption she thinks of suicide, a "wild card." When she is betrayed by her lover, who returns to the wife he does not love, she knows that she must deal with her misery. In the final climactic moment, when N is raped, the metaphorical implications are suggested by her reactions. She feels a "strange elation" and wonders who the rapist was, but she realizes that she has changed, that she has the "lightness of a shadow, like a ghost" leaving the body.

Lying Low

A sense of foreboding also permeates the lives of three women in *Lying Low.* Theo and her two boarders, Marybeth and Ouida, are women struggling without men in uncertain times; their lives have reached intense levels of frustration and dissatisfaction. Victims of circumstances they cannot control, they look back on the past, struggle in the present, and fear the future. They are engulfed by their problems: Marybeth, a fugitive radical of the 1960's, is wanted for blowing up a napalm plant; Ouida, an alien Brazilian student, fears deportation and has difficulty understanding English; and Theo, a nonconformist, laments the lack of moral values in society and fights against social injustice. Dreams and memories link these women to the past, which becomes more real than the present. Covering four days, the novel conveys a sense of futility and violence, beginning with the death of a chicken, which foreshadows the death of Theo at the end.

Disillusioned women who have lost their identities, Theo and Marybeth have been committed to principles in their past lives but are now both "lying low." Remembering herself as "vital and alive" and "committed to a cause six years ago," Marybeth sees herself now as a "drowning person reviewing [her] life." Although Theo was a talented dancer, she never used that gift to accomplish anything, and she speaks of her past as "withered." The present for Ouida, too, is uncomfortable; she seeks solace in her messianic religion, keeping a candle lit in her room, and in her memories of Brazil. The women's concerns about their lost identities leave them suspended in apprehension. Marybeth has assumed a new name to protect her from arrest and is always ready to move on when she fears discovery. Ouida's lack of a passport makes her fearful in a strange country; her passport becomes her security. Theo's concern about her identity is revealed in the end, when she calls out her name to prove that she exists and asks, "Who knows her?"

The final irony for Theo comes when she goes to teach dancing to prison inmates, to give them the "power of dance" and participate in the cleansing of their souls—"black men, graceful, in cages": She becomes a victim of the random violence she laments when she is taken hostage in a van with escaped prisoners. The police shoot at the van, despite their awareness that it contains explosives; this parallels Marybeth's crime of blowing up a factory even though she knew that a man was inside. Marybeth also recognizes the irony in the fact that Theo is the victim: "I always thought it would be me." In the end, Marybeth considers turning herself in, while Ouida realizes that she does not have the ability to protect herself, that she has "great ignorance."

Persian Nights

Chloe Fowler, in *Persian Nights*, is another Johnson character who is faced with uncertainties in her life. Chloe is an attractive wife of an American doctor with two children, living a stable, ordered existence. Arriving alone in Iran—her husband, Jeffrey, has been detained to attend a patient—she is frightened and lonely, although she expects to continue her affair with Hugh Monroe, a colleague of her husband. Even though Chloe admits to a few affairs, she also realizes that she is dependent on her husband and feels more secure because she is married. She is aware that safety is important to her and has always been one of her problems: She stays married because that way she feels safer.

Chloe is linked with other Americans who are satirized in this novel. When she arrives at her quarters in the Azami compound, she is distressed at the shabbiness of the apartment: Americans expect a standard of living that assures their comfort. Americans can also do things in Iran that they would not do at home; they have no respect for Iranian law. Thus they buy antiques that are illegal to sell to foreigners. Chloe feels guilty because she has taken plants from a neighbor, something she would not do at home, and she wonders why. Like the other residents living in the compound, she is isolated from the real Iran.

As the wild dogs bark at night and the Savak (secret police) make arrests, however, Chloe gradually becomes aware of the intensity of Iran's conflict and begins to feel fear. The suspicion and paranoia around her ironically heighten her sensibilities. She believes that she has no reason to be there, but she begins to be stimulated by her situation.

As the pressures intensify, Chloe admits that she cannot "grasp the tragic," so she goes on "with egotism and vanity." Her actions indicate how well she defines herself in this respect. When Chloe's husband, who had no intention of joining her in Iran, writes her that he is divorcing her, that there is someone else, she feels betrayed. Chloe thinks of herself as abandoned, without a home, but she also observes that she would like to have been the one who decided to leave the marriage. In a climactic scene at the ruins of Persepolis, Abbas Mowlavi, an Oxford-educated doctor, dies trying to save the treasures from plunderers; Chloe cannot react to the tragedy of his death and wonders whether she is the one who is dead. Earlier in the story, she and Abbas had been attracted to each other and had made love.

Chloe begins to be aware that she is not without purpose, that she is searching for a conclusion. She asks herself questions that show her concerns about moral issues. As she departs on an airplane at the end of the novel, unhappy to be leaving Iran, she believes that in her experience there she found something, but she does not know what it was. Meanwhile, eating tins of caviar, she is comforted by the thought that she will not save one for Jeffrey.

LATER NOVELS

Since the publication of *Persian Nights*, Johnson has continued to address the reactions of expatriate American women to cultural differences, particularly in *Le Divorce*, *Le Mariage*, *L'Affaire*, and *Lulu in Marrakech*. Anticipation, naïveté, and vulnerability are common themes in these four books. Some critics have referred to *Le Divorce*, *Le Mariage*, and *L'Affaire* as a trilogy, but the novels do not present a continuous story line. These books and *Lulu in Marrakech* share some literary elements, including epigraphs introducing chapters, the use of foreign phrases, and recurring minor characters.

Motivated by adventure and desire for change, and possibly love, Johnson's displaced American protagonists immerse themselves in foreign cultures, which can be bewildering and unpredictable. Despite their efforts to assimilate, they often are rebuffed by the people from whom they seek approval and find themselves outsiders, sometimes rejected merely because they are Americans and so are considered unworthy. These characters live double lives, divided not only by their nationality and expatriate status but also by how they perceive themselves and how others view them. Their identities blurring, they occasionally feel as if they do not belong to either their native or their adopted countries.

Johnson's satirical characterizations of both people and countries are these novels' strength. American and foreign attitudes concerning socioeconomic class, money, and family reinforce the authenticity of the characters. Johnson enhances her frequently comical presentations by emphasizing characters' flaws, arrogance, clumsiness, innocence, and awkward attempts to adjust. Her incorporation of stereotypes and clichés as literary elements contributes to the effectiveness of the humorous and frequently absurd situations portrayed. Misunderstandings and faulty translations by people who are confident that they comprehend foreign terms complicate already tenuous relationships and further isolate expatriates; film references illuminate different cultural perceptions. Many of Johnson's expatriates share similar crises during their self-imposed exiles, including the loss of passports and involvement in legal conflicts; their situations occasionally involve danger and violence, which may escalate into international news stories broadcast on television. Differences between U.S. laws and foreign laws aggravate perplexed characters who agonize when they are stymied by foreign laws that seem to them unjust or when French judges define truth in ways that differ from the definitions of their American counterparts.

Isabel Walker in *Le Divorce* personifies Johnson's expatriate heroine. She reveals her experiences through first-person narrative, which intensifies readers' awareness of

Isabel's excitement, frustration, and disappointment as she tries to separate from her American identity. In her twenties, Isabel perseveres despite obstacles posed by her sister Roxeanne, brother-in-law Charles-Henri de Persand, and their associates when she travels to Paris to assist Roxeanne in surviving a pregnancy and a divorce complicated by division of property, particularly an expensive painting that both spouses seek to control. Although Isabel babysits her niece and interacts with the entitled Persand family, she pursues her own interests in Paris, engaging in a love affair with Charles-Henri's uncle Edgar and securing employment. The resilient Isabel nurses her suicidal sister and survives the enraged husband of Charles-Henri's mistress. Affected by her foreign experiences, Isabel discusses people's responsibility to improve oppressive situations in the world and considers performing aid work in Bosnia.

In *Le Mariage*, American actor Clara Holly seems passive in comparison with the intrepid Isabel. This novel, which explores themes of fidelity and commitment, is told in the third person, exposing various characters' points of view. Living in Paris, unhappily married to film director Serge Cray, Clara frets about her elderly mother in Oregon and shelters Delia, also an Oregonian, who is waiting for a replacement passport so she can leave France after inadvertently becoming involved in a murder investigation. When Serge travels to the United States, Clara begins a satisfying affair with a neighbor, lawyer Antoine de Persand (brother of Charles-Henri of *Le Divorce*). Other plot developments involve a stolen medieval manuscript and the engagement of American journalist Tim Nolinger to Parisian Anne-Sophie d'Argel. Aware of his wife's affair, Cray threatens to kill Clara at Tim and Anne-Sophie's wedding rehearsal dinner, revealing both Antoine's cowardice and Clara's loyalty. Johnson depicts the contrasting cultures of the Americans and the French through characters' reactions to such issues as the historical integrity of architecture.

In *L'Affaire*, which is also presented in the third person, Johnson alternates scenes among a large cast of characters. Wealthy dot-com entrepreneur Amy Hawkins blends aspects of Isabel in *Le Divorce* and Clara in *Le Mariage*. Vacationing at the Hôtel Croix St. Bernard at Valméri in the French Alps, Amy interferes in an inheritance dispute after an avalanche injures English publisher Adrian Venn. While he is comatose, Adrian's four children, adults Posy, Rupert, and Victoire and toddler Harry, the offspring of three mothers from three countries, stay at the resort as the adults among them vie for Adrian's riches. Where Adrian dies will determine his heirs' inheritance rights. Amy, not comprehending the legal complexities, arranges for Adrian to be airlifted to a British hospital, where he dies. Unsettled by the chaos she has provoked, Amy indulges in an affair with a married man, Emile Abboud. She defends Americans when people blame U.S. bomber vibrations for triggering the avalanche. Realizing that she will never belong in France, Amy decides to return home.

Lulu Sawyer, the spy protagonist using a false name in *Lulu in Marrakech*, could be a previous Johnson expatriate. Narrating her story in the first person, Lulu reveals background details similar to Isabel's description. Lulu travels from Kosovo, where she conducted aid work and was Ian Drumm's lover, to her Moroccan assignment. She settles into Ian's Marrakech estate, hoping to continue their romance, while publicly posing as a literacy worker and covertly trying to identify donors to Islamic terrorists. Lulu interacts with Ian's guests, including Posy from *L'Affaire*, and questions whether any of the expatriates and servants might be terrorism supporters or spies. The theme of duty exemplifies Lulu's dedication even after the library she established is bombed. Although Ian proposes marriage, Lulu leaves Morocco to escape punishment for her role in a deadly kidnapping. Like many of Johnson's protagonists, Lulu represents women who flee familiar settings to test possibilities in exotic places.

Millicent Sharma
Updated by Elizabeth D. Schafer

OTHER MAJOR WORKS

SCREENPLAY: *The Shining*, 1980 (adaptation of Stephen King's novel; with Stanley Kubrick).

TELEPLAY: *An Apple, an Orange*, 1979 (adaptation of her short story).

NONFICTION: *The True History of the First Mrs. Meredith and Other Lesser Lives*, 1972; *Terrorists and Novelists*, 1982; *Dashiell Hammett: A Life*, 1983; *Natural Opium: Some Travelers' Tales*, 1993; *Into a Paris Quartier: Reine Margot's Chapel and Other Haunts of St. Germain*, 2005.

BIBLIOGRAPHY

Durham, Carolyn A. "Cataclysmic Relations: Franco-American Discord in Diane Johnson's *L'Affaire*." *Contemporary French and Francophone Studies* 8, no. 4 (Fall, 2004): 379-389. A professor of French and comparative literature presents a scholarly examination of the novel's plot developments and characterizations and provides examples of the stereotypes, assumptions, and biases that Johnson incorporates in her text to provoke cultural complications and patriotic responses.

_______. "The Franco-American Novel of Literary Globalism: The Case of Diane Johnson." *French Politics, Culture, and Society* 21, no. 2 (Summer, 2003): 64-80. Assesses how Johnson's novels *Le Divorce* and *Le Mariage* achieve cultural credibility. Discusses the literary elements, including use of idioms, that enhance the two novels' depictions of French and American characters and settings.

Greiner, Donald J. "Joan Didion, Diane Johnson, and the Novel of Female Bonding in the 1970's." In *Women Without Men: Female Bonding and the American Novel of the 1980's*. Columbia: University of South Carolina Press, 1993. Focuses on Johnson's book *The Shadow Knows* and Didion's novel *A Book of Common Prayer* (1977) in discussing the two authors' portrayals of women's interactions with other women and with men.

James, Caryn. "An American in Valmeri." Review of *L'Affaire*, by Diane Johnson. *The*

New York Times Book Review, October 12, 2003. Asserts that Johnson excels at characterization because of her insights regarding cultural misunderstandings, motivations, and relationships.

Johnson, Diane. "Diane Johnson." Interview by Diane Osen. In *The Book That Changed My Life: Interviews with National Book Award Winners and Finalists*, edited by Diane Osen. New York: Modern Library, 2002. Johnson identifies the literature that influenced her development as a writer, revealing how specific authors and books shaped her awareness of literary techniques.

_______. "Diane Johnson." Interview by Susan Groag Bell. In *Women Writers of the West Coast: Speaking of Their Lives and Careers*, edited by Marilyn Yalom. Santa Barbara, Calif.: Capra Press, 1983. In a wide-ranging interview with Bell, a friend, Johnson discusses her life, the literary and social influences on her work, the creative process, and memorable experiences connected with her writing projects.

_______. "An Interview with Diane Johnson." Interview by Carolyn A. Durham. *Contemporary Literature* 45, no. 2 (Summer, 2004): 189-217. Johnson discusses a variety of topics, including her life as an expatriate, her literary activities in France, and the film adaptation of *Le Divorce.*

Kakutani, Michiko. "A Goody-Two-Shoes Trips the Spy Fantastic." Review of *Lulu in Marrakech*, by Diane Johnson. *The New York Times*, October 24, 2008. Asserts that character and plot flaws weaken the novel's plausibility and argues that Johnson portrays Islamic culture more accurately in her 1987 novel *Persian Nights*.

ALISON LURIE

Born: Chicago, Illinois; September 3, 1926

PRINCIPAL LONG FICTION

Love and Friendship, 1962
The Nowhere City, 1965
Imaginary Friends, 1967
Real People, 1969
The War Between the Tates, 1974
Only Children, 1979
Foreign Affairs, 1984
The Truth About Lorin Jones, 1988
The Last Resort, 1998
Truth and Consequences, 2005

OTHER LITERARY FORMS

In addition to writing fiction, Alison Lurie has distinguished herself in two other areas, children's literature and the semiotics of dress, and her novels reflect both concerns as well. Her interest in children's literature is reflected in *Only Children*, in which two little girls pose their fantasies against the reality exposed to them by their parents, and in *Foreign Affairs*, in which one of the two central characters spends her sabbatical in England collecting playground rhymes. Real children's rhymes, Lurie observes, are surprisingly subversive, not like the "safe" literature written for children by adults. She develops this insight in the nonfiction work *Don't Tell the Grown-Ups: Subversive Children's Literature* (1990). Lurie's fascination with the semiotics of clothing, which she addresses in *The Language of Clothes* (1981), is reflected frequently in the novels, where she pursues the relationship between clothing and personal identity. An especially provocative example can be found in *Imaginary Friends*, where Roger Zimmern, forced by a strange religious group to abandon his academic dress in favor of cheap suits, loses his sense of identity.

Two literary memoirs by Lurie, published thirty-five years apart, deserve mention. The writing of the first in 1966, the memoir of a friend, an ill-fated young poet-playwright, proved life-changing. In 2001, Lurie published *Familiar Spirits: A Memoir of James Merrill and David Jackson*. She had befriended the two poets while at Amherst College during a lonely time in her life as a faculty wife. Merrill and Jackson were companions whose mercurial life together Lurie traces with compassion throughout.

ACHIEVEMENTS

Alison Lurie's fiction has received much praise from critics, and her work has been very popular with the broader reading public. Her first novel, *Love and Friendship*, appeared in 1962 and was followed by several prestigious grants and fellowships: Yaddo Foundation Fellowships in 1963, 1964, and 1966; a Guggenheim grant in 1965-1966; a Rockefeller Foundation grant in 1967-1968; and a New York State Cultural Council Foundation grant in 1972-1973. *The War Between the Tates* in 1974 brought Lurie a popular audience and more critical acclaim. An American Academy of Arts and Letters award followed in 1978, and for *Foreign Affairs* she received a Pulitzer Prize in 1985. All of Lurie's fiction displays a remarkable control of language, a style that surprises and amuses. Both for her wit and for her sharp-edged, satiric depiction of human follies, Lurie has often been compared to Jane Austen, and her following in England is among the largest of any living American novelist.

Biography

Alison Lurie was born September 3, 1926, in Chicago, Illinois, but grew up in White Plains, New York. Her Latvian-born father was a scholar, a teacher, and a socialist who later became the founder and executive director of the Council of Jewish Federations. Lurie's mother, also a socialist, was a former journalist for a Chicago newspaper. Lurie suffered a minor birth injury that affected the hearing in her left ear and also caused some damage to her facial muscles. An avid reader as a child, she began at about the age of thirteen to read such authors as Charles Dickens, George Bernard Shaw, and Jane Austen. In 1947, she graduated from Radcliffe College, where she had met many people who later became important literary figures, including Jonathan Peale Bishop, a teacher, critic, and essayist. She married Bishop in 1948, and they had three children. In 1975, Lurie separated from Bishop, divorcing him ten years later.

Lurie struggled with many discouraging rejections of her writing when she was in her twenties, and she regards 1966 as the turning point in her life, when she wrote and published privately a memoir of an eccentric friend, V. R. "Bunny" Lang. Thereafter came a succession of novels that garnered high praise, including a Pulitzer Prize for *Foreign Affairs*. A professor of children's literature at Cornell University in Ithaca, New York, where she began teaching in 1969, Lurie divides her time among Ithaca, Key West, and London.

Analysis

Alison Lurie's novels are known for their comedy and satire, and her acute observation is most often trained on the complications of love, marriage, and friendship as they affect the lives of the upper classes, the educated, and the academic. Many of her novels take place at the fictional Convers College in New England or at Corinth University in upstate New York (based on Cornell University) or concern characters who teach at or have been associated with Corinth. These novels are not, however, all academic satire; the academics often travel to other places or become involved in issues beyond the campus.

Lurie's style is most often detached and ironic, a treatment that has won for her both blame and praise. Her novels, except for *Only Children*, explore the time in which they are written and reflect the events and culture of Lurie's own adult years. The novels typically cover a short space of time, a crisis point in the lives of the characters, but several of the characters are seen at different points in their lives because of Lurie's use of the same characters in different novels—sometimes as major characters, sometimes as minor ones. Lurie works successfully with a variety of narrative points of view: omniscient narration in *The War Between the Tates*, first-person narration in *Real People*, third-person focus narration in *Imaginary Friends* (expanded to include two focus characters in *Foreign Affairs*). She shows no penchant for either the happy or the unhappy ending, realistically leaving her characters to continue to work out their lives as best they can.

Love and Friendship

At the heart of Lurie's first two novels are couples trying to work out their relationships. Her first novel, *Love and Friendship* (a title taken from Jane Austen), draws out the main lines of the issue. What is love and what is friendship? Are they different in what is best and most enduring? In this novel, the main character, Emmy Turner, "loves" her lover more than she does her husband. In the end, however, she chooses her husband over her lover because he needs her and to him she can be a friend. Indeed, what first led her to enter into a love affair was a frustration with her husband's failure to make a friend of her, to discuss with her his work and his concerns. Ultimately, Lurie suggests, friendship is more satisfying and lasting than love; indeed, love at its best is friendship at its best.

The Nowhere City

In her second novel, *The Nowhere City*, the ending is the opposite, but the implication seems the same. Paul Cattleman rediscovers his wife at the end after much neglect and many adulteries. It is too late, however: Friendship is lost, and with it love; she tells him that she is not angry with him, but she just does not know him anymore.

Real People

While the love and friendship theme becomes a secondary issue in *Imaginary Friends*, the novel Lurie published after *The Nowhere City*, she makes it once again the central focus of *Real People*. In this novel, Janet Belle Spencer, a writer, has taken up residence at Illyria, a haven for writers and artists. Although she published a book of stories six months before, she is enduring writer's block, which she is unable to break out of at Illyria. She is also drawn there by her love for an artist, Ken, with whom she believes she has much more in common than with her insurance-executive husband. The artists' colony of Illyria is an unreal world, however, and Janet discovers that she and Ken are not really friends; she learns much about her writing that she resolves to change. It is at home with her husband, Clark, not at Illyria, she finally realizes, that she will be able to put to work her new understandings.

The War Between the Tates

Love and friendship in marriage are explored most intensively in Lurie's next and most celebrated novel, *The War Between the Tates*. Erica and Brian Tate, a young academic couple, are in their own eyes and in the eyes of their friends the perfect couple, but as middle age looms, Brian becomes increasingly frustrated at not being famous, and the couple's children become rebellious teenagers. True love and friendship appear to be lacking. Finally, Brian has an affair with a student whom he makes pregnant, Erica befriends the student, and both Brian and Erica, but especially Erica, wander through a bewildering maze of events that leaves their earlier sense of themselves and their marriage damaged. As the novel ends, they drift back together, confused, "out of love," but basically seeking a peace they can find only with each other.

Only Children

Love and friendship in marriage is the topic once again of *Only Children*, but this time the actions of the adults are seen through the eyes of two little girls, Lolly and Mary Ann, who respond to what they see in the behavior of their elders, especially their parents. In each set of parents there is one serious, deeply dedicated person (Lolly's mother, Mary Ann's father) and one shallow, egotistical, flamboyant hunter of the other sex. The two sets of parents ultimately stay together, but, lacking love based on friendship, they are merely maintaining a facade, and their example will cripple their children's ability to love. Novelist Mary Gordon has called *Only Children* "the most interior of Lurie's novels." Lurie is especially skilled at evoking the traumas that adult crimes and misdemeanors work on youngsters.

Foreign Affairs

The love and friendship theme appears again in *Foreign Affairs*, which juxtaposes two main characters, one married and one not. Vinnie Miner, a middle-aged professor, finds love surprisingly where she had least expected it, in a friendship with a man totally unlike her, a retired sanitary engineer. The other main character, a handsome young man in Vinnie's academic department, begins the novel estranged from his wife, is temporarily dazzled and infatuated by a far more glamorous Englishwoman, but returns to his wife at the end, finding her superior in trust, honesty, and common decency.

The Truth About Lorin Jones

Love and friendship are very complicated and contradictory in *The Truth About Lorin Jones*, a novel that is a departure from Lurie's earlier novels for a number of reasons. Instead of an academic setting, the setting is the contemporary art world, and the primary relationship in the novel is one that essentially exists within the mind of Polly Alter, a failed painter who is researching the life of the late Lorin Jones, an artist whose life and loves seem to speak to Polly's own situation. Lorin, who was once Lauren "Lolly" Zimmern, one of the little girls in *Only Children*, has lived a life of professional and personal frustration and is possibly still haunted by the demons of her childhood. The contemporary issues of feminism and lesbian sexuality complicate the lives of both Polly and Lorin, but Lurie adds a new twist to the feminist argument by suggesting that it was Lorin who exploited the men in her life, using them as a means to serve her own ambitions. Polly's discovery of the truth about Lorin permits her a new lease on life, as does her romance with Hugh Cameron, a onetime hippie poet who had been Lorin's first husband.

THE LAST RESORT

In Lurie's ninth novel, *The Last Resort*, Jenny Walker, formerly a subservient wife to her distinguished academic husband, faces a crisis in her marriage when she increasingly comes under the sway of the charismatic lesbian Lee Weiss. Jenny's attraction to Lee is heightened by the respect and attention Lee accords her, whereas her husband, Wilkie, is content to see her merely as a passive supporter of his plans. Wilkie himself, under the impression that he is terminally ill, begins to detach himself emotionally from his wife but has a brief flirtation with a young female admirer even as he prepares to commit suicide. Although the couple are reunited at the end of the novel, their relationship has changed. Jenny acquires greater self-confidence and feels she is now in charge of her own life. Wilkie's "greatness" is no longer allowed to dominate their relationship as it once did.

TRUTH AND CONSEQUENCES

Truth and Consequences, Lurie's tenth novel, appeared in 2005, the same year as Philip Caputo's *Acts of Faith*, a massive novel about the civil war in Sudan whose various plots turn on the disasters of unintended consequences on the well-meaning. In *Truth and Consequences*, two couples, each pairing a caregiver and a "caregetter," enact outcomes that are predictable—in other words, intended consequences. The first couple, Jane and Alan Mackenzie, until recently have been congratulating themselves on how well everything is going, how much they love each other, how respected they are in the Corinth University community—he a professor, she an administrator. However, when Alan painfully injures his back playing volleyball, Jane is forced into a caretaking role. As the book opens, Jane no longer recognizes the invalid who once was her sturdy partner. The second couple consists of Delia Delaney, a famous and narcissistic poet, and her mate, Henry Hull, a freelance editor whose only role is the care and feeding of his wife's ego. The expected happens—the caregetters are attracted to each other, as are the caregivers. What saves the story is how convincingly Lurie deconstructs what happens to love, marriages, and people when important role changes take over their lives. Her foursome, often shrill, are never cardboard cutouts of philandering husbands and wives. Just as she deepens rather than chastens the Tates in their war, Lurie adds the depth of empathy to her foursome under siege. She asks readers to see themselves in the characters.

THE ACADEMIC MICROCOSM

Lurie's novels concern themselves with relationships between people, and these relationships are at the center of all of her work, but the lives of Lurie's characters are affected by more than personal forces alone. Context, temporal and physical alike, is also central to these novels, and the directions of the lives of Lurie's characters are profoundly affected by the times and the places in which they live. The most persistent context, moreover, is academic, since many of these characters, like Lurie herself, are university professors or members of their families. In this case again, *Love and Friendship* sets a pattern that later novels follow.

The academic world is also a factor in *The Nowhere City*, although the story takes place in a Los Angeles setting that dominates the novel. Paul, in the end, will retreat to the eastern academic world that he knows (remaking his relationships with his old Harvard friends and taking a teaching post at Convers College), while Katherine, who had initially seemed the more eastern academic of the two, refuses to return there with him and seems to find a new self in Los Angeles.

The War Between the Tates again makes the academy not only a strong backdrop but also an actor in the events. Brian Tate is a highly successful sociology professor at Corinth University in upstate New York; Erica Tate is a faculty wife. Their two closest friends, who divorce in the novel, are Leonard Zimmern, an English professor, and Danielle Zimmern, Erica's closest female friend, a part-time faculty member in the French department. The convulsions of American academe in the late 1960's interfere directly in Brian's and Erica's lives. Brian, though very successful academically, has always dreamed of fame as an adviser to governments and presidents, and his middle-aged frustration makes him susceptible to trying to recover his lost youth by mixing socially with his graduate students, increasingly adapting his clothing and other styles to theirs, finally indulging himself in an affair with Wendy. Erica, like Katherine Cattleman in *The Nowhere City*, attempts to preserve her traditional moral values in the face of all this upheaval and tries not only to adapt herself to these values but also to give direction to Brian and Wendy, even to the point of insisting that Brian divorce her and marry Wendy. She becomes peripherally involved, through her friend Danielle, in the Hens, a local feminist group, and finding the local Hare Krishna guru of the students to be an old school friend, under his guidance has her own adventure with LSD. Brian and Erica, then, experience their marital troubles amid the student rebellions of the 1960's. Though the novel does not probe as deeply as *Imaginary Friends* into the political and intellectual doubts and troubles of academe, these influences are present, shaping their reaction.

In *Foreign Affairs*, the two main characters are again college professors, both from the English department at Corinth University: the middle-aged, internationally famous expert in children's literature, Vinnie Miner, and the young specialist in the eighteenth century, Fred Turner, both on leave to do scholarly work in London. The novel for the most part tells their stories separately, their paths crossing significantly only twice. While their common background does make their lives cross in significant ways, and while both their lives are shaped by their academic backgrounds, the primary focus of the novel is on other aspects of their lives.

The American macrocosm

The university campus, then, demonstrates the importance of time and place in Lurie's novels. This is also true in a larger sense, since American culture itself, with its regional and sociological tensions, plays just as important a role as do the characters. If *Love and Friendship*, the first novel, works off a Jane Austen theme, it also echoes a peculiarly American, Fitzgeraldian theme in which the different regions and classes of the United States become important players in the conflicts of the novel. Emmy is New Jersey rich; her lover, Will Thomas, is southern shabby genteel; and her husband, Holman, is Chicago shabby-but-respectable poor. As the marital couple work out their conflicts with traditions of Convers College playing an important role, these different regional and class conflicts do much to shape their actions and reactions.

In *The Nowhere City*, 1960's America, with its new and strange customs and dress, almost overpowers its characters' ability to work out their human problems. Here, Los Angeles is the city in which "nowhere" comes to mean "present but lacking history and future." Mixed new forms of architecture in both house and public building design, styles of hair and dress, sexual lifestyles, artistic forms, even subjects being studied in the universities are all strange, macabre, and new, dividing Katherine and Paul Cattleman as they respond to them so differently. Setting plays just as important a role in *Imaginary Friends*, which brings two very traditional strongholds, the enclosed small town and the principles of academic inquiry, together with the strains of the world without.

Real People, again, though it removes its main characters to an isolated, protected, ideal world of the artists' colony, nevertheless shows that the best work cannot be done in an artificial atmosphere but only when the artists are living and writing truthfully about the world in which they are "real people." Again, too, despite all the 1960's campus shenanigans of *The War Between the Tates* (drugs; strange new lifestyles, clothes, and hairstyles), the novel presents a strong sense that the campus is only reflecting all the major movements, confusions, and displacements of the society at large.

In *Only Children*, which is set during the Great Depression, the characters reflect the concerns of that time, including its powerful economic and political conflicts. Bill Hubbard, for example, is an example of the President Franklin D. Roosevelt-type liberal Democrat, dedicated to social reforms that will lift the poor, while Dan Zimmern represents the nascent Madison Avenue type, flamboyant and driven to succeed. *Foreign Affairs*, in the experiences of both Vinnie Miner and Fred Turner, discloses the tensions of many cultural mores, especially different class and sexual expectations, complicated further by differences between Great Britain and the United States.

In her eighth and ninth novels, Lurie abandons both the international theme and academic settings, returning to the world of art and the artist that was her subject in *Real People. The Truth About Lorin Jones* and *The Last Resort* introduce another setting into Lurie's work—that of Key West, the southernmost point in the continental United States and the site of Lurie's second home. Lurie uses the remoteness and luxury of Key West to place her characters in a distinct setting where they can work out their problems before returning, altered and refreshed, to the "real" world. In this way, Key West operates much like the island in William Shakespeare's *The Tempest* (pr. 1611). Lurie also sketches cultural and political differences on the island, delineating the way Key West's sizable homosexual community comes under attack from wealthy, right-wing Republicans who also reside in the area. Issues such as aging and acquired immunodeficiency syndrome (AIDS) also are given extended, if sometimes lighthearted, examination.

LITERARY INFLUENCES

Lurie additionally sets the lives of her individual characters against the backdrop of the world of literature itself. In *Real People*, Janet Belle Spencer imagines Ken as the ideal reader of her fiction, largely because he recognizes every literary reference—which in turn is reminiscent of Lurie's own rich texture of literary allusion. In this regard, as already observed, she uses the "love and friendship" theme from Jane Austen. Another novelist to whom Lurie is greatly indebted is Henry James, especially in *Imaginary Friends* and *Foreign Affairs*. Indeed, *Imaginary Friends* in many ways duplicates the plot of James's *The Bostonians* (1886), in which a young woman named Verena leads a band of truth seekers through an extraordinary gift for public speaking, which seems to proceed from a trancelike ability to contact higher powers.

Foreign Affairs enlarges on the Jamesian theme not only by explicitly introducing James's work by name but also by exploring one of his most insistent themes: what happens when basically good, decent Americans encounter a far more culturally sophisticated European society. In James's novels of this type, the balance is struck in favor finally of the basic, honest decency of Americans against the more sophisticated but possibly corrupt world of the Europeans, and Lurie's novel arrives at the same resolution. This exploration is complicated by the fact that, of the two Americans, Vinnie Miner is very sophisticated in the ways of the English, knowing their ways and customs so well that she really feels more culturally at home in England than in the United States. Fred Turner, on the other hand, despite his great physical charms and handsomeness and his knowledge of eighteenth century literature, is basically a raw recruit to European culture. Both, however, have "foreign affairs": Vinnie with an almost illiterate Oklahoman whom she meets on the plane on the way over, so embarrassingly crude that she dreads presenting him to her friends; and Fred with an English aristocrat and actor so elegant and sophisticated that his American life appears crude by comparison. Despite this structural converse—in which Vinnie loves an American who is far less presentable than her European friends, and Fred loves an Englishwoman who is far more sophisticated than his American wife and friends—both find, despite all of their differences, their American loves superior after all, and their European friends, for all of their sophistication, less satisfying morally as friends and lovers than their American friends. Thus the pattern of James's international novels, in which superior American decency confronts and ultimately wins out over superior European elegance and sophistication, is repeated here in Lurie's fiction.

The influence of James can also be discerned in *The Truth About Lorin Jones*, which, like *Imaginary Friends*, recalls James's *The Bostonians*. In this case, the competition between male and female for the loyalty of a talented woman is enlarged into an exploration of the politics of lesbian feminist separatism, something only hinted at in the James novel.

Characters

If Lurie's readers often spot resonances from other fiction, they also have the pleasure of recognizing characters they have met in other Lurie novels, for Lurie frequently works with recurring characters. Emmy Turner's four-year-old boy Freddy from *Love and Friendship* is one of the grown-up main characters in *Foreign Affairs*, while Fred's wife Roo in that same novel appears as a child in the earlier *The War Between the Tates*. Sometimes Lurie will, in a later novel, go back to an earlier period in a character's life: Miranda, the grown-up, married mother of three children in *Love and Friendship*, is seen as a child in the later novel *Only Children*.

Of all the characters that recur, the most persistent one is Leonard Zimmern, first seen in *Real People* as a middle-aged, distinguished critic of American literature living in New York; later, he appears in *The War Between the Tates* as a friend of Brian and Erica. He is also the father of Roo, a child here but an adult in *Foreign Affairs*. In *Only Children*, the Depression-era story, Zimmern is a teenager, and in *Foreign Affairs* he is the father of a grown-up Roo, the famous critic whose harsh article on Vinnie Miner's work in children's literature haunts Vinnie as she goes to England.

Roger Zimmern of *Imaginary Friends* is mentioned briefly in *The War Between the Tates* as Leonard Zimmern's cousin. L. D. Zimmern also surfaces in *The Truth About Lorin Jones* as the legal owner of his half sister Lorin's unsold paintings. In addition, *The Truth About Lorin Jones* features the return of Lorin's father, Dan Zimmern of *Only Children*, and Danielle Zimmern, divorced wife of Leonard and Erica's best friend in *The War Between the Tates*. In *The Last Resort*, L. D. Zimmern returns as the cousin of Lee Weiss, the lesbian who befriends Jenny Walker. Another continuity in *The Last Resort* is the return of the character of Barbara Mumpson, who first appears in *Foreign Affairs*. This remarkable amount of recurrence suggests Lurie's strong interest in understanding how her characters have come to be who they are, despite her novels' time frames. Given that the events of each novel cover only a short period of time—one, *Only Children*, takes place in a single weekend—Lurie often spreads out characters' lives over several novels in order to continue developing the characters and to tie their lives together.

IMAGINARY FRIENDS

All the themes discussed so far are treated as well in *Imaginary Friends*. Their treatment in this novel, however, represents perhaps Lurie's broadest and deepest effort, for the academic backdrop she uses so often elsewhere is broadened here to embrace the most fundamental of human questions, questions of knowledge, of identity, of sanity, and finally of madness. The main character in this novel, sociologist Roger Zimmern—a young, brand-new Ph.D. at a large upstate New York university—goes to Sophis, a nearby small town, as the research assistant of Thomas McMann, a famous senior professor in his department whom Roger admires, despite rumors he has heard about McMann from other young faculty members and despite the realization that McMann's form of empirical sociology (the case-study method) is passé.

To investigate McMann's hypothesis that small groups can build a belief system so powerful that it can withstand, rationalize, and incorporate doubting attacks from within and without, Roger infiltrates, under the cover of a public opinion seeker, a group of religious fundamentalists called the Truth-seekers, whose young leader, Verena, leads and directs the group through automatic writing from superior beings on another planet, named Varna. Roger introduces McMann to the group as a businessman friend who is also interested in their theories. Roger's secure identity is overset by his mentor's unscientific attempt to control the experiment in the direction of his hypothesis rather than merely to observe and record. Also tormented by his sexual attraction for Verena, Roger reaches a point where he no longer knows what he believes in, no longer knows who he is, no longer knows whether there is in his discipline any objective basis for scientific inquiry. He believes that he is going mad but decides that it is, rather, his mentor who is insane, and he unwillingly becomes the primary witness whose testimony results in McMann's being committed to an asylum. The novel ends with Roger maintaining a tenuous but commonsensical hold on his own sanity. Here, Lurie touches on questions central not only to academic life but to the lives of everyone else as well: How can one truly observe and know? How real is our own sense of self?

Taken as a whole, Lurie's novels reveal a remarkable uniformity. Her own background in academe provides the most common setting for her novels, and frequently this setting is broadened to reflect the central questions with which Lurie is concerned. Her interest in clothing and identity, in the lives of children, indeed in the lives of all of her characters, is unusual. Her work is best considered not as a series of separate novels but as a continuity in which her characters' lives go on, not ceasing with the end of a particular novel but continuing as do all our lives—growing and changing through time.

June M. Frazer; Margaret Boe Birns
Updated by Richard Hauer Costa

OTHER MAJOR WORKS

SHORT FICTION: *Women and Ghosts*, 1994.

NONFICTION: *The Language of Clothes*, 1981; *Don't Tell the Grown-Ups: Subversive*

Children's Literature, 1990; *Familiar Spirits: A Memoir of James Merrill and David Jackson*, 2001; *Boys and Girls Forever: Children's Classics from Cinderella to Harry Potter*, 2003.

children's literature: *The Heavenly Zoo: Legends and Tales of the Stars*, 1979; *Clever Gretchen, and Other Foreign Folktales*, 1980; *Fabulous Beasts*, 1981; *The Black Geese: A Baba Yaga Story from Russia*, 1999 (with Jessica Souhami).

edited text: *The Oxford Book of Modern Fairy Tales*, 1993.

Bibliography

Costa, Richard Hauer. *Alison Lurie*. New York: Twayne/Macmillan, 1992. First book-length study of Lurie's work, written with her cooperation, is an essential resource. Provides a biographical sketch as well as discussion of all her writing, including a thorough examination of her major novels through *The Truth About Lorin Jones*. Features an extensive bibliography.

Newman, Judie. *Alison Lurie: A Critical Study*. Atlanta: Rodopi, 2000. Presents a chapter of biography and then discusses in turn each of Lurie's novels through *The Last Resort*.

_______. "Paleface into Redskin: Cultural Transformations in Alison Lurie's *Foreign Affairs*." In *Forked Tongues: Comparing Twentieth Century British and American Literature*, edited by Ann Massa and Alistair Stead. London: Longman, 1994. Particularly valuable for its discussion of Lurie's theme of transatlantic cultural differences. Offers insights into why Lurie's fiction is so popular in England.

Rogers, Katherine M. "Alison Lurie: The Uses of Adultery." In *American Women Writing Fiction: Memory, Identity, Family, Space*, edited by Mickey Pearlman. Lexington: University Press of Kentucky, 1989. Important study of Lurie's novels through *Foreign Affairs* explores the works from a feminist perspective, focusing especially on the theme of self-examination on the part of Lurie's heroines.

Stark, John. "Alison Lurie's Career." In *Twayne Companion to Contemporary Literature in English*, edited by R. H. W. Dillard and Amanda Cockrell. New York: Twayne, 2003. Reprint of a 1989 contribution to *The Hollins Critic* discusses Lurie's career as an instance of maturation within the same fictional territory.

Stern, Carol Simpson. "Alison Lurie." In *Contemporary Novelists*. 4th ed. New York: St. Martin's Press, 1986. Argues that the usual "influence" tie-ins from Lurie to Jane Austen and Henry James are "misleading" and asserts that Lurie's long fiction is more aptly compared with the works of feminist novelists Marilyn French, Erica Jong, Doris Lessing, and Joyce Carol Oates.

Waxman, Barbara Frey. "A New Language of Aging: 'Deep Play' in Carol Shield's *The Stone Diaries* and Alison Lurie's *The Last Resort*." *South Atlantic Quarterly* 67, no. 2 (Spring, 2002): 25-51. Analyzes two novels by prizewinning authors in which beliefs and practices regarding later life have the power to change readers' attitudes toward aging and death.

MARY MCCARTHY

Born: Seattle, Washington; June 21, 1912
Died: New York, New York; October 25, 1989
Also known as: Mary Therese McCarthy

PRINCIPAL LONG FICTION

The Oasis, 1949
The Groves of Academe, 1952
A Charmed Life, 1955
The Group, 1963
Birds of America, 1971
Cannibals and Missionaries, 1979

OTHER LITERARY FORMS

First known as a book reviewer, drama critic, and essayist, Mary McCarthy also wrote short stories, collected in *The Company She Keeps* (1942), *Cast a Cold Eye* (1950), and *The Hounds of Summer, and Other Stories* (1981). Her drama criticism is collected in *Sights and Spectacles, 1937-1956* (1956) and in *Mary McCarthy's Theatre Chronicles, 1937-1962* (1963). *Venice Observed* (1956) and *The Stones of Florence* (1959) are books of travel and art history. *The Writing on the Wall, and Other Literary Essays* (1970) and *Ideas and the Novel* (1980) are literary essays and lectures. *On the Contrary: Articles of Belief* (1961) contains autobiographical essays and literary criticism. *Memories of a Catholic Girlhood* (1957) and *How I Grew* (1987) are memoirs of her childhood and youth. Her books *Vietnam* (1967) and *Hanoi* (1968) oppose U.S. involvement in the Vietnam War, an interest that she continued in *Medina* (1972) and in *The Seventeenth Degree* (1974). *The Mask of State* (1974) presents impressions of the Watergate affair hearings.

ACHIEVEMENTS

From the appearance of her first book reviews, when she was just out of college, to the time of her death, Mary McCarthy was one of the leading figures of the American literary scene. In her novels as much as in her essays and reviews, she was above all a critic, a sharp observer of contemporary society. For students of twentieth century American culture, her work is indispensable.

BIOGRAPHY

Mary Therese McCarthy was born into an affluent family of mixed Irish and Jewish heritage on June 21, 1912, in Seattle, Washington, and had a segmented childhood. After six years of what she called a "fairy-tale" existence of happiness, both parents died of influenza in 1918 during a move to Minneapolis. McCarthy and her three younger brothers, placed with their grandaunt and uncle, then entered a bleak phase of intense, strict Catholicism, which McCarthy described in *Memories of a Catholic Girlhood.*

In 1923, McCarthy's grandparents moved her to a convent school in Seattle for the seventh and eighth grades; she spent her ninth grade year in a public school and then her remaining high school years at the Annie Wright Seminary in Tacoma, Washington, from which she graduated in 1929 at the top of her class. In the same year of her graduation as a Phi Beta Kappa from Vassar College in 1933, she married Harold Johnsrud, a marriage that lasted three years. She reviewed novels and biographies for *The New Republic* and *The Nation*, worked for the left-wing publishing company Covici Friede, and, in 1937, participated in Trotskyite politics. In 1937, she also became drama editor for *Partisan Review.*

The next year, McCarthy married Edmund Wilson and gave birth to a son, Reuel Wilson; also, at Wilson's urging, McCarthy wrote her first work of fiction, a short story. Thereafter, the stories she wrote for *Southern Review, Partisan Review*, and *Harper's Bazaar* were collected in 1942 in *The Company She Keeps*. She separated from Wilson in 1945, the same year that she was teaching literature at Bard College. In 1946, she married Bowden Broadwater, and in 1948, she taught one semester at Sarah Lawrence College. In 1949, she was a Guggenheim Fellow (a fellowship she received again in 1959) and also received the *Horizon* literary prize from the publishers of her novel *The Oasis*. In 1961, she was divorced from Broadwater, married James Raymond West—a U.S. State Department official assigned to Paris—and lived with him in France.

Two events dominated the 1960's for McCarthy. The first was the enormous popular success of her novel *The Group*, which became a best seller. The second was the Vietnam War; she was an outspoken critic of U.S. policy in Vietnam. In the 1970's, she published two novels with social and political themes: *Birds of America* in 1971 and *Cannibals and Missionaries* in 1979; the latter, she said, would be her last novel.

In 1980, an offhand remark on *The Dick Cavett Show* embroiled McCarthy in a prolonged legal battle that became a cause célèbre in the literary community. McCarthy said of dramatist Lillian Hellman that "every word she writes is a lie, including [the words] 'and' and 'the.'" Hellman responded by suing McCarthy. The resulting legal maneuvering was costly for McCarthy (in contrast, the wealthy Hellman did not count the cost), ending only in 1984, when, after Hellman's death, the suit was dropped before going to trial. Meanwhile, legal issues aside, the controversy brought several of Hellman's autobiographical works under close scrutiny, and the consensus was that McCarthy's judgment, clearly stated in hyperbolic terms, was vindicated.

In 1987, McCarthy published *How I Grew*, the first installment in what was projected to be a multivolume intellectual autobiography. In general, critics found it inferior to *Memoirs of a Catholic Girlhood*, which had covered some of the same territory from a different perspective. McCarthy died in New York City on October 25, 1989.

ANALYSIS

Mary McCarthy's novels often feature herself, with an assumed name, as protagonist; she also exploited her husbands and other people close to her for fictional purposes. Her characters generally have a superior education or intellect, or both, so that citations and quotations from learned sources—mainly classical or artistic—spring into their conversations. This heightened discourse promotes compact paragraphs of dialogue, in which several persons speak to the same topic, in contrast with the usual fictional technique of a separate paragraph for each speaker. Yet, in the close conceptual unity of McCarthy's novels, lengthy paragraphs of extensive character analyses frequently fill several pages without interruption. As a result, the technique of several speakers in one paragraph seems to support the general schema. It supports, also, the paradigm of the group.

Structurally, the three novels preceding *The Group* develop around separate chapters, each presenting the viewpoints and the consciousness of the different characters; their point of unity is the common awareness of the social group. A protagonist, often a reflection of the author, generally emerges from among these peripheral persons, but the effect of each chapter remains that of the portrait or sketch.

Several factors of McCarthy's work can be inferred from this structure. As an orphan and a Catholic among Protestants, she no doubt had an early sensitivity to the significance of the group and the outsider. Furthermore, the intensely autobiographical nature of her work blurs the lines of genre, so that her essays read like short stories and her short stories like essays. Genre distinction, then, becomes a problem in any analysis of her work. An example is *The Company She Keeps*, short stories that are pulled into book form and revolve around a central theme—the quest—and parallel the structure of her novels. Also, McCarthy did not term *The Oasis* a "novel" but called it a *conte philosophique*, and several chapters of her novels were published individually as short stories before being incorporated in the novels. The effect of this technique raises the question of whether she pushed the boundaries of the traditional novel outward or merely retreated to its earliest phases of development. She lamented the loss of a "sense of character" in modern novels, saying it began to fade with D. H. Lawrence. She admired Leo Tolstoy, Gustave Flaubert, George Eliot, Charles Dickens, and "all the Elizabethans."

The dominant quality of McCarthy's work is satire, and much of it is achieved by exaggeration and generalization. The dominant organization is the pairing of a separate character with each chapter, infused with an occasional chorus of viewpoints. McCarthy compared the technique to ventriloquism: The author throws her voice into various characters who speak for her. The long paragraphs of explication or character analysis tend to minimize plot; the concentration is on the psychological effects of what are frequently trivial incidents—as in *The Oasis*, when a couple illegally picking berries on the group's farm destroys the group.

The themes of McCarthy's novels generally concern the social failures of a group—of utopian communities in *The Oasis*, of progressive education in *The Groves of Academe*, or of cultural progress in *The Group*. The interest in group attitudes can be best observed in the political content of McCarthy's novels, many of which feature a person who had some affiliation with the Communist Party and defected or failed to become a member. Her work also shows a persistent aversion to the efforts of Senator Joseph McCarthy to eradicate communists in the United States.

The Oasis

McCarthy's first novel, *The Oasis*, was published serially in *Horizon* magazine as *A Source of Embarrassment*. The work puts into practice the theories of Arthur Koestler about "oases," small libertarian groups that would try, as McCarthy said, "to change the world on a small scale." Set at Pawlet, Vermont, at an abandoned hotel on an isolated mountain in 1946 or 1947, the novel brings together a group of about fifty people of varying backgrounds and motives. The characters seek to revive the concept of utopian communities and welcome defectors from Europe. Their efforts, however, remain confined to the daily problems of food gathering and management and fall short of the larger goals.

First, the group fails to agree on its purpose. The purists aspire to a millennium but the realists seek only a vacation or a retreat from atomic warfare. They disagree, also, about who should be permitted to join the group, and some oppose the admission of businessman Joe Lockman. Next, they find that intellect, good intentions, and the simple life without electricity do not bring about moral reform: Personal relationships and property ownership intrude. Lockman leaves oil in the kitchen stove that singes the eyebrows of Katy Norell, and then, as a prank, he frightens Will Taub by pointing a gun at him. Later, when intruders pick their wild strawberries (the stolen fruit in their Eden), Katy is highly offended at the theft of her property, and Joe is indignant about the other colonists' attempts to drive away the berry pickers until he realizes that it was his property, the gun, they used in the assault.

The first to defect from the community is Taub, in whom many readers recognized Philip Rahv, and Katy, who resembles McCarthy, dreams of the dissolution of the community at the book's end. With Lockman cast in the role of the outsider, with little plot and with incident minimized, and with much explication of philosophical theory and discussion of ideals and goals, the book sets the style for McCarthy's other novels.

The Groves of Academe

Suspense is greatly improved in McCarthy's next novel, *The Groves of Academe*, set in a small Pennsylvania college called Jocelyn and resembling Bard College. Directing its satire at progressive education, this novel pits the progressive against the classical, satirizes the small college in general, and exposes the evils of McCarthyism, focusing on Joseph McCarthy's House Committee on Un-American Activities. The group here is the English Department faculty, from which Professor Henry Mulcahy finds himself dismissed. He rallies the faculty to his support, although he is a poor academician and deserves dismissal, and gains it through an appeal for sympathy for his wife and children. McCarthyism brought him to the position—the president hired him because he had been unjustly accused of being a Communist sympathizer—and, finally, it accounts for his retention. Mulcahy loses his chief faculty supporter when she discovers that he lied about his wife's illness, but he gains another weapon through a visiting poet who recognizes him from Communist Party meetings.

At the climax of the novel, the Joseph McCarthy scare is shown at its most evil: Protecting the college, the well-meaning president conducts an interview into Mulcahy's past, which results in his being charged with libel. The unstable Mulcahy triumphs and secures his position at Jocelyn—certain to continue bullying students and colleagues alike—and the president resigns.

A Charmed Life

In *A Charmed Life*, Martha Sinnott returns to a group of artistic people at New Leeds, a small New England village based on Wellfleet, Cape Cod, where she had lived with her former husband (much like McCarthy had lived at Wellfleet and returned with a second husband). Martha returns determined to be different from and independent of the New Leedsians who live a charmed life of many accidents, none of which kills them. Here, time, which signifies the mortal, is askew and awry, as indicated by the many problems with clocks and calendars. Part of Martha's anxiety about her return to New Leeds is the possibility of meeting her former husband (based on McCarthy's former husband, Edmund Wilson) with his new wife and child and the fear that he will reestablish domination over her. When he seduces her and she later finds herself pregnant, she cannot remember the date well enough to determine whether her former or present husband is the father. Her moral decision to have an abortion because she cannot live a lie results in her death; returning from borrowing money for the abortion, she drives on the right side of the road, contrary to New Leeds custom, and meets another car head-on. The charmed life of New Leeds goes on, but Martha lives and dies an outsider.

McCarthy called this novel a fairy tale. Loosely analogous to "Sleeping Beauty," Sinnott pricks her hand at the beginning of the novel, lives in self-doubt on the fringes of the immortality of New Leeds (the timelessness of a century of sleep), and is awakened to the new existence of pregnancy and decision. The prince who wakens her with a kiss (the seduction), however, is an evil prince.

The Group

With a theme of the failure of modern progress, *The Group* was published in November, 1963. At that time, Betty Friedan's *The Feminine Mystique* (1963) and other feminist writings had focused on the problems of women, and the public was responsive to works focused on the problems of the emancipated woman. Although *The Group* is set in the seven years from 1933 to 1940, the progressiveness of the eight-cum-nine young Vassar women seemed to be the progress that was engulfing women of the 1960's. Like gleanings from an alumnae bulletin, the random appearances, different voices, and loose ends are not expected to be resolved. The undistinguished occupations of the group, also, confirm the alumnae magazine reports of most women graduates, but somehow more is expected of Vassar women. Not only the money but also increased competition for admission meant that, by 1963, most women could not get into Vassar. For the general public, there is some comfort in the failure of the culturally advantaged.

The novel begins with the wedding of Kay Strong in 1933 and ends with her death seven years later at the age of twenty-nine. Of the eight members of the group who had lived in the same dormitory, plus one outsider, Kay seemed to be most forward-looking and progressive. Like McCarthy, she comes from the West and, immediately upon graduation, she marries her lover of some time, a mostly unemployed playwright named Harald Petersen who resembles Harold Johnsrud. Part of McCarthy's personality is dispersed among the other characters, especially Libby MacAusland, a woman of formidable intellect who writes book reviews and becomes a literary agent.

The elegant, beautiful, and wealthy Elinor Eastlake disappears into Europe and reemerges as a lesbian prior to Kay's death. Polly Andrews becomes attached to a married man who is obviously well adjusted except that he pays twenty-five dollars a week for psychiatric counseling. Working in a hospital, Polly becomes engaged to another man, a psychiatrist who has defected from the profession and thus augments the satiric attack on psychiatry. Helena Davison, in Cleveland, remains the stable rich girl, highly intelligent and analytic. Priss Hartshorn marries a pediatrician, and, attempting to breast-feed her son and train him by modern theories, provides the satire on this aspect of progressivism. Pokey Prothero, from a household organized and represented by an invaluable butler, plans to become a veterinarian.

Kay, during a fight with Harald, gets a black eye and finds herself committed to a mental hospital. Despite Harald's admission that she does not belong there, she decides to stay for a rest and then disappears from the story until she reemerges after a divorce and a year in the West. Back East, ready to start a career again, she falls to her death while spotting planes from her window and becomes the first casualty of the war. Representing a culmination of the group philosophy and the disjointed voices of the earlier novels, *The Group*, with its timely feminist content, earned for McCarthy a great deal of money and many appearances on talk shows and in magazines. Some Vassar alumnae were recognizable in the book, and the film version did not name the college. This novel established McCarthy as a popular writer, but she did not attempt to capitalize on it with a follow-up novel. Instead, eight years later, she brought out a novel of a different sort altogether.

BIRDS OF AMERICA

Departing from the group structure, McCarthy's next novel, *Birds of America*, begins in 1964 with Peter Levi's return at age nineteen to Rocky Port, Maine, after an absence of five years. During his absence, his favorite horned owl died. With his divorced and remarried mother Rosamund, he searches for a waterfall that they cannot find—the victim of a highway project. In their respective ways, the village and the mother cling to fashions of the past but rapidly succumb to modern times.

Peter goes to the Sorbonne for his junior year in college but finds his ideals of French culture in conflict with the realities. His friends are American; he has a painful Thanksgiving dinner at an American general's home discussing vegetarianism and the war in Vietnam; he runs afoul of the French police while watching a demonstration; and he spends Christmas vacation in Rome where the masses of tourists interfere with his appreciation of the Sistine Chapel. Returned to Paris, he attempts in his Kantian way—"Behave as if thy maxim could be a universal law"—to help the street drunkards. Everywhere he goes, he tangles with human refuse, which is best revealed in a long letter home about the filth of Parisian toilets. Clinging to his preferences for nature, however, he grows vegetables and other plants in his apartment and joins a bird study group. At a zoo at the close of the novel, he is attacked by a swan while attempting to feed it from his hand. He wakens, later, in a hospital recovering from a reaction to a penicillin shot. At this point, Kant speaks to him, saying that "nature is dead, my child."

Peter (obviously modeled on Reuel Wilson) calls his father babbo, is familiar with Italy, speaks both French and Italian, and is an intellectual like his mother. This novel, much different from the other seven, is the only one with a clear and unmistakable protagonist. The group Peter satirizes are tourists as a group; but the group does not make up the novel's characters.

CANNIBALS AND MISSIONARIES

The group of *Cannibals and Missionaries*, originally formed as a committee of six to fly by Air France to Iran to investigate reports of the shah's torturing of prisoners, expands, by the time the plane is hijacked to Holland, to twenty-four hostages and eight terrorists. Set during the administration of U.S. president Gerald R. Ford, the novel takes its title from the puzzle in which three cannibals and three missionaries must cross a river in a boat that will hold only two people, and if the cannibals outnumber the missionaries, they might eat the missionaries. In the novel, however, there is no clear indication as to which group represents the cannibals and which the missionaries.

In one passage of explication, McCarthy points out that the terrorists' demands accomplish nothing but the reabsorption into the dominant society of whatever they demanded; prisoners released, for example, are eventually returned to prison. Confined in a Dutch farmhouse, hostages learn of their terrorists' demands from television: $1.25 million, Holland's withdrawal from the North Atlantic Treaty Organization (NATO), the breaking of relations with Israel, and the release of "class war" prisoners from Dutch jails. Like the other groups in McCarthy's fiction, the members of this group are pulled together in a common cause; even though divided between hostages and terrorists, the hostages willingly aid the terrorists in some efforts and feel triumphant in the successful completion of a task, such as hiding the helicopter that brought them to the farmhouse. At the novel's conclusion, however, all but four are killed, one of whom claims that she has not been changed by the experience.

The European settings of the last two novels reflect McCarthy's travel experiences and utilize her interest in art. In *Cannibals and Missionaries*, McCarthy returned to her early interest in communism and to the group structure with separate narrative voices.

While *The Groves of Academe* is still highly esteemed as an example of the academic novel, and *The Group* is read by students of popular fiction and women's studies, McCarthy's novels considered by themselves do not make up a lasting body of work. Rather, they derive their lasting significance from their place in the life and work of an exemplary woman of letters.

Grace Eckley

OTHER MAJOR WORKS

SHORT FICTION: *The Company She Keeps*, 1942; *Cast a Cold Eye*, 1950; *The Hounds of Summer, and Other Stories*, 1981.

NONFICTION: *Sights and Spectacles, 1937-1956*, 1956; *Venice Observed*, 1956; *Memories of a Catholic Girlhood*, 1957; *The Stones of Florence*, 1959; *On the Contrary: Articles of Belief*, 1961; *Mary McCarthy's Theatre Chronicles, 1937-1962*, 1963; *Vietnam*, 1967; *Hanoi*, 1968; *The Writing on the Wall, and Other Literary Essays*, 1970; *Medina*, 1972; *The Mask of State*, 1974; *The Seventeenth Degree*, 1974; *Ideas and the Novel*, 1980; *Occasional Prose*, 1985; *How I Grew*, 1987; *Intellectual Memoirs: New York, 1936-1938*, 1992; *Between Friends: The Correspondence of Hannah Arendt and Mary McCarthy, 1949-1975*, 1995 (Carol Brightman, editor); *A Bolt from the Blue, and Other Essays*, 2002 (A. O. Scott, editor).

BIBLIOGRAPHY

Abrams, Sabrina Fuchs. *Mary McCarthy: Gender, Politics, and the Postwar Intellectual.* New York: Peter Lang, 2004. Abrams examines McCarthy the fiction writer and McCarthy the cultural critic, discussing how her marginalized identity as a Catholic woman among the Jewish, male-dominated New York intelligentsia influenced her view of post-World War II American culture.

Brightman, Carol. *Writing Dangerously: Mary McCarthy and Her World.* New York: Clarkson Potter, 1992. Supplements but does not supersede Carol W. Gelderman's earlier biography. Like Gelderman, Brightman was able to interview her subject, and her book reflects not only inside knowledge but also, as its subtitle suggests, a strong grasp of the period in which McCarthy published. Includes a biographical glossary and notes.

Ebest, Sally Barr. "Mary McCarthy: Too Smart to Be Sentimental." In *Too Smart to Be*

Sentimental: Contemporary Irish American Women Writers, edited by Ebest and Kathleen McInerney. Notre Dame, Ind.: University of Notre Dame Press, 2008. This collection of essays on twelve writers begins with Ebest's discussion of McCarthy. Ebest says it is "fitting" that her essay comes first in the collection because McCarthy "single-handedly reformulated the Irish American literary tradition characterizing her female predecessors," and she describes how McCarthy updated the traditional depiction of women characters.

Epstein, Joseph. "Mary McCarthy in Retrospect." *Commentary* 95 (May, 1993): 41-47. Provides a summary of McCarthy's work. Comments on her role in intellectual life in America, and discusses the relationship of her life to her fiction.

Freeman, Kimberly A. "Mary McCarthy's *A Charmed Life*: Divorcing Fiction from Fact." In *Love American Style: Divorce and the American Novel, 1881-1976*. New York: Routledge, 2003. Freeman analyzes McCarthy's book as well as novels by William Dean Howells, Edith Wharton, and John Updike to examine these authors' treatment of divorce and how that depiction reflects conflicting ideas about American identity. Includes notes, a bibliography, and an index.

Gelderman, Carol W. *Mary McCarthy: A Life*. New York: St. Martin's Press, 1988. Gelderman offers an objective biography of McCarthy. Although much of the narrative is familiar, the book is well written and amply documented. The photographs provide important perspective on McCarthy's childhood and a satisfying glimpse into her adult life. This biography is appropriate for general readers as well as students studying McCarthy.

Kiernan, Frances. *Seeing Mary Plain: A Life of Mary McCarthy*. New York: W. W. Norton, 2000. A comprehensive biography full of vivid details and anecdotes but marred by a lack of focus on certain essential aspects of McCarthy's life and work.

Kufrin, Joan. *Uncommon Women*. Piscataway, N.J.: New Century, 1981. In a book that examines women who have succeeded within several different fields, McCarthy is "The Novelist" in the chapter so named. The portrayal of the writer is friendly and informal, largely the transcription of an interview in McCarthy's home in Maine. McCarthy comments on her writing process of extensive revision. The two photographs capture a sense of fun and humor in McCarthy.

McKenzie, Barbara. *Mary McCarthy*. New York: Twayne, 1966. McKenzie offers a one-page chronology of McCarthy's life as well as an opening chapter titled "The Fact in Biography." She analyzes McCarthy's novels and short stories and assesses McCarthy's overall contribution to literature. McKenzie's book, with notes, a bibliography, and an index, would benefit serious students of McCarthy's work.

Pierpont, Claudia Roth. *Passionate Minds: Women Rewriting the World*. New York: Alfred A. Knopf, 2000. Evocative, interpretive essays on the life paths and works of twelve women, including McCarthy, connecting the circumstances of their lives with the shapes, styles, subjects, and situations of their art.

Stwertka, Eve, and Margo Viscusi, eds. *Twenty-Four Ways of Looking at Mary McCarthy: The Writer and Her Work.* Westport, Conn.: Greenwood Press, 1996. Based on papers originally presented at a conference in 1993, this book includes discussions of McCarthy's position as a public intellectual, Edmund Wilson's role in McCarthy's career, political dilemma in *The Groves of Academe*, and other aspects of her work and career.

VLADIMIR NABOKOV

Born: St. Petersburg, Russia; April 23, 1899
Died: Montreux, Switzerland; July 2, 1977
Also known as: Vladimir Vladimirovich Nabokov; V. Sirin

PRINCIPAL LONG FICTION

Mashenka, 1926 (*Mary*, 1970)
Korol', dama, valet, 1928 (*King, Queen, Knave*, 1968)
Zashchita Luzhina, 1929 (serial), 1930 (book; *The Defense*, 1964)
Kamera obskura, 1932 (*Camera Obscura*, 1936; revised as *Laughter in the Dark*, 1938)
Podvig, 1932 (*Glory*, 1971)
Otchayanie, 1934 (serial), 1936 (book; *Despair*, 1937; revised 1966)
Priglashenie na kazn', 1935-1936 (serial), 1938 (book; *Invitation to a Beheading*, 1959)
Dar, 1937-1938 (serial), 1952 (book; *The Gift*, 1963)
The Real Life of Sebastian Knight, 1941
Bend Sinister, 1947
Lolita, 1955
Pnin, 1957
Pale Fire, 1962
Ada or Ardor: A Family Chronicle, 1969
Transparent Things, 1972
Look at the Harlequins!, 1974

OTHER LITERARY FORMS

Vladimir Nabokov (nah-BO-kof) began, as many novelists do, as a poet. As a youth, he published privately what now would be called a chapbook and a full book of poetry before emigrating from Russia. Throughout his life, he continued to publish poetry in periodicals and several book-length collections, including *Stikhotvorenia, 1929-1951* (1952), *Poems* (1959), and *Poems and Problems* (1970). Some critics even consider the long poem "Pale Fire" (an integral part of the novel *Pale Fire*) a worthy neo-Romantic poem in itself. Nabokov also published a good deal of short fiction, first in a variety of short-lived émigré publications such as *Rul'*, *Sovremennye Zapiski*, and *Russkoe ekho*, and later in such prominent magazines as *The New Yorker*, *The Atlantic Monthly*, *Playboy*, *Harper's Bazaar*, and *Tri-Quarterly*. His stories were collected in *Vozrashchenie Chorba* (1930; the return of Chorb), which also included twenty-four poems, *Soglyadatay* (1938; the eye), *Nine Stories* (1947), and *Nabokov's Dozen* (1958), among others. His plays include *Smert'* (pb. 1923; death), *Tragediya gospodina Morna* (pb. 1924; the tragedy of Mister

Vladimir Nabokov
(Library of Congress0

Morn), *Chelovek iz SSSR* (pb. 1927; the man from the USSR), *Sobytiye* (pr., pb. 1938; the event), and *Izobretenie Val'sa* (pb. 1938; *The Waltz Invention*, 1966). He also worked on a screenplay for the film version of *Lolita* (1962). In addition to translating his own works from Russian to English (and vice versa, as well as occasionally from French to Russian to English), he often translated the works of other writers, including Lewis Carroll's *Alice's Adventures in Wonderland* (1865) and poetry of Rupert Brooke, Alexander Pushkin, Arthur Rimbaud, William Shakespeare, and Alfred de Musset. In nonfiction prose, Nabokov's fascinating life is recalled in three volumes of memoirs, *Conclusive Evidence* (1951), *Drugie Berega* (1954; other shores), and *Speak, Memory: An Autobiography Revisited* (1966, a revision and expansion of the earlier works). Throughout his life, his often idiosyncratic criticism was widely published, and the publication after his death of several volumes of his lectures on world literature provoked much discussion among literary scholars. As a lepidopterist, Nabokov published a number of scholarly articles in such journals as *The Entomologist*, *Journal of the New York Entomological Society*, *Psyche*, and *The Lepidopterists' News*.

ACHIEVEMENTS

Vladimir Nabokov's strength as a writer lay in his control and mastery of style. Writers are sometimes successful in a language other than their native language, but only a select few are capable of writing equally well in two languages, and Nabokov may be alone in his ability to master the insinuations of two such extraordinarily different and subtle languages as Russian and English. Under the pen name "V. Sirin," Nabokov was recognized as a noteworthy émigré novelist and poet in Berlin and Paris. After fleeing the rise of Nazism and settling in the United States, he became recognized as a major English-language author with the publication of *Lolita* in 1955. As was the case with Gustave Flaubert, James Joyce, and D. H. Lawrence, all of whose international sales were aided by the controversies surrounding their works, Nabokov received worldwide attention as critics debated the morality of *Lolita*, prompting the republication and translation of many of his earlier works. Few writers with such an uncompromising style achieve such popularity. Nabokov was often in financial difficulty before *Lolita*, yet he always remained the consummate craftsman. He has come to be regarded as one of the literary giants of his generation.

BIOGRAPHY

Vladimir Vladimirovich Nabokov was born to Vladimir Dmitrievich and Elena Rukavishnikov Nabokov in St. Petersburg, Russia, the eldest of five children. He grew up in comfortable circumstances, tracing his ancestry back to a Tartar prince of the 1380's and through a number of military men, statesmen, Siberian merchants, and the first president of the Russian Imperial Academy of Medicine. His father was a noted liberal who had helped found the Constitutional Democratic Party, was elected to the first Duma, and coedited the sole liberal newspaper in St. Petersburg. In his childhood, the young Nabokov was taken on trips to France, Italy, and Spain, and he summered on the country estate of Vyra, accumulating memories that would become woven into his later writings. His father, an Anglophile, provided governesses who taught the boy English at a very early age. He once remarked that he had learned to read English even before he had learned Russian. He was also taught French.

Entering puberty, Nabokov attended the liberal Prince Tenishev School, where he first developed a hatred of coercion but played soccer and chess, started collecting butterflies, and showed some artistic talent. He began writing poetry, and a now lost brochure of a single poem "in a violet paper cover" was privately published in 1914. In 1916, he privately published a recollection that provoked his cousin to beg him to "never, never be a writer," and in 1918, he collaborated on a collection with Andrei Balashov. Nabokov inherited an estate and the equivalent of two million dollars when his Uncle Ruka died and seemed to be on his way to the comfortable life of a Russian bourgeois when history intervened. His father became part of the Provisional Government in the March Revolution of 1917, but in October, when the Bolsheviks displaced the Alexander Kerensky government, the

Nabokov family fled, first to the Crimea and then, in 1919, into permanent exile in the West on an old Greek ship ironically named *Nadezhda* ("Hope").

Nabokov studied at Trinity College, Cambridge University, paying little attention to anything but soccer, tennis, and girls. He did, however, do many translations (of Rupert Brooke, Seumas O'Sullivan, William Butler Yeats, Lord Byron, and others) and came under the influence of English poetry. He also read and was influenced by James Joyce. Despite his claim that he never once visited the library, he graduated with honors in French and Russian literature in 1923. This was shortly following his father's assassination in Berlin in March, 1922, as two reactionaries shot the elder Nabokov in error as he was introducing their intended victim. After Cambridge, the twenty-five-year-old Nabokov moved to Berlin, where, in 1925, he married Vera Evseevna Slonim, and a year later he published his first novel, *Mary*, under a pseudonym. He felt that his father had prior claim to the name "Vladimir Nabokov," and he wrote all of his early Russian works as "V. Sirin."

With very little money, Nabokov published poems, stories, and essays in Berlin's émigré newspapers, and later, as the Nazis grew in power (his wife was Jewish), in similar Parisian publications. He survived by teaching tennis, devising crossword puzzles in Russian, making up chess problems, teaching Russian, and translating. He sold the Russian translation of *Alice's Adventures in Wonderland* (*Anya v strane chudes*, 1923), for example, for the equivalent of five dollars. In 1934, his only son, Dmitri, was born, and four years later, Nabokov fled to Paris. As early as 1935, he decided to immigrate to the United States, probably recognizing that Europe was no longer safe. He was invited by the Soviet government during the 1930's to return to Russia several times, but he refused.

Nabokov's novels published in Berlin and Paris had been relatively successful, and several had been translated into English with and without his assistance. He made the remarkable and difficult decision to abandon the language in which he had written so well. "My private tragedy," he later wrote, "which cannot, indeed should not, be anybody's concern, is that I had to abandon my natural idiom, my untrammeled, rich, and infinitely docile Russian tongue for a second-rate brand of English." Stanford University invited him to teach in the summer of 1940, and he set sail for the United States on the liner *Champlain* in May, just ahead of the German invasion. He had already begun writing his first English novel, *The Real Life of Sebastian Knight*, while in Paris, and, in 1941, it was published in the United States after several friends helped him edit it. He taught Russian grammar and literature at Wellesley College from 1941 to 1948, also serving as a research fellow at the Museum of Comparative Zoology at Harvard University. He became a prominent lepidopterist, publishing many monographs, articles, and reviews. He spent summers roaming the United States searching for butterflies and discovered several species and subspecies, including one that came to be called Nabokov's wood nymph. After seeing praise for his work on the *Lycaeides* genus in a field guide, Nabokov is said to have remarked, "That's real fame. That means more than anything a literary critic could say."

In 1944, Nabokov published a critical book on Nikolai Gogol, and in 1947, his first novel written in the United States, *Bend Sinister*, appeared. From 1948 to 1959, he taught at Cornell University, carefully writing out his lectures, combining his attacks on such intellectual touchstones as Karl Marx, Charles Darwin, and especially Sigmund Freud with dramatic classroom readings. Well before the publication of *Lolita*, he was recognized as a remarkable talent in certain quarters, as is indicated by his receipt of grants from the Guggenheim Foundation in 1943 and 1953 and by an award from the American Academy of Arts and Letters in 1953; students in his classes at Cornell, however, were often unaware that their teacher was also a writer, although he published stories and articles in *The New Yorker*, *The Atlantic Monthly*, *Hudson Review*, and other periodicals. *Lolita* changed all that. Rejected by several American publishers, it was brought out by publisher Maurice Girodias's Olympia Press in Paris in 1955. As one of the most controversial books ever published—banned for a while in France, debated in Parliament in England, and forbidden in many American libraries—it swept the best-seller lists and freed Nabokov from teaching. In addition to the royalties, he received $150,000 and a percentage from the sale of the film rights. He also wrote a screenplay (which was later substantially changed) for the film version to be directed by Stanley Kubrick, which was released in 1962. (A second film version of *Lolita*, directed by Adrian Lyne, was released in 1997.)

In 1960, Nabokov moved to Montreux, Switzerland, where he and his wife lived in a sixth-floor apartment in the Palace Hotel overlooking Lake Geneva, in order to be near their son Dmitri, who was having some success as an opera singer. In the wake of *Lolita*, Nabokov and his son translated many of his earlier novels into English and introduced several collections of his short stories to American readers. His novels *Pale Fire*, *Ada or Ardor*, *Transparent Things*, and *Look at the Harlequins!* were all published during this period. He was regularly discussed as a possible recipient of the Nobel Prize until his death of a viral infection in 1977.

Analysis

In 1937, Vladeslav Khodasevich, an émigré poet and champion of "V. Sirin's" work, wrote, "Sirin [Nabokov] proves for the most part to be an artist of form, of the writer's device, and not only in that . . . sense of which . . . his writing is distinguished by exceptional diversity, complexity, brilliance, and novelty." Khodasevich went on to say that the key to all Sirin's work was his ability to put all his literary devices on display, with little or no attempt to conceal them, thus entertaining his readers more with the revelation of how the magician performs his tricks, than with the trick itself. "The life of the artist and the life of a device in the consciousness of an artist—this is Sirin's theme." Khodasevich, although he had not yet read *The Gift*—purported to be Vladimir Nabokov's greatest Russian novel—had discovered the most important element of Nabokov's fiction.

Throughout his entire life, although Nabokov underwent great changes in his circumstances, he was consistent, whether writing in Russian or English, in his unflagging delight in literary devices of all sorts, art for its own sake, and a contempt for mimetic conventions, simplistic psychological motivation, ordinary plot structure, and anything that inhibits the literary imagination. He can, in many respects, be called an aesthete, but his rejection of most schools of thought makes him difficult to classify. He strove for and achieved a uniqueness that runs as a thread throughout his oeuvre. Clarence Brown once commented in a critical essay that "for well over a quarter of a century now . . . [Nabokov] has been writing in book after book about the same thing," and Nabokov is said to have admitted that Brown was probably correct.

MARY *and* KING, QUEEN, KNAVE

Nabokov's first novel, *Mary*, is rather sentimental and probably based on Nabokov's regret for a lost love, but it already contains two elements he would use repeatedly—the love triangle and uncertain identity. *King, Queen, Knave*, however, is an even more obvious reflection of the Nabokov canon. In it, a character named Franz Bubendorf, a country bumpkin on his way to the city, apparently to be corrupted by the bourgeois life, is, in fact, already corrupted by his distaste for his own class, which distorts his perception. As if to emphasize this distortion of perception, Franz steps on his glasses and Berlin becomes a blur. Again, there is a love triangle, and each of the participants is, in his or her own way, unable to perceive reality. The melodrama of a love triangle and a planned murder is handled with the authorial detachment that is one of Nabokov's hallmarks. The novel becomes a parody of traditional forms, and the characters become obvious contrivances of the author. Derived from a Hans Christian Andersen work of the same title, the novel consists of thirteen chapters, as there are thirteen cards in each suit in a deck of cards. The card metaphor is carried throughout the work, even in the description of clothes.

LAUGHTER IN THE DARK

Laughter in the Dark opens with a parody of the fairy tale revealing the entire plot, here a relatively conventional bourgeois love story that Nabokov typically manipulates. The main character, blinded by love, becomes literally blinded and trapped in a love triangle, which results in his murder (accomplished in a scene that is a parody of motion-picture melodrama). This type of parody, which partially represents Nabokov's delight in mocking inferior art, can also be seen as a parody of the reader's expectations. Nabokov constantly thwarts the reader who wants a nice, comfortable, conventional novel. The writer is always in control, always tugging the reader this way and that, never allowing a moment of certainty. Perceptions are distorted on all levels. The characters have distorted perceptions of one another. The reader's perception of events is teasingly distorted by the author. Nabokov operates a house of mirrors. If a reader expects realism, there will be no pleasure in the warped mirrors Nabokov presents. One must delight instead in the odd shapes and obvious deformities in the mirrors he has shaped.

NABOKOV'S CHARACTERS

Character types in the Russian novels also recur throughout Nabokov's career, so much so that some critics have attempted to pair earlier Russian novels with later English ones. Usually, the central figure is an outsider, an unusual person in his milieu. Bubendorf of *King, Queen, Knave* is a country boy in the city. In *The Defense*, the chess master Luzhin does not fit in with his family or his school, and is sent into exile after the Revolution. Martin Edelweiss of *Glory* is in exile in London.

What is more important, however, is that these and many more of Nabokov's characters are isolated as much by their mental states as by their physical surroundings. Their fantasies, dreams, ambitions, and obsessions set them utterly apart from the ordinary world. Luzhin, for example, is so obsessed with chess that he cannot deal with the disorder of life. Cincinnatus in *Invitation to a Beheading* is thought peculiar by his fellow workers in the doll factory. In later English novels, immigrant Timofey Pnin is thought mad by his academic colleagues, Humbert Humbert and Adam Krug are seen as dangers to society, and Charles Kinbote intrudes and imposes on people. Generally, the main characters of Nabokov's novels are perceived as talented men, in some sense more valuable than the soulless people and society that persecute them. They are outsiders because they are extraordinary. They are free, imaginative, and capable of a kind of heroism that ordinary people lack: the ability to remake the world according to their own obsessions.

THE GIFT

The Gift is generally thought of as Nabokov's best Russian novel. It was originally published serially in *Sovremennye Zapiski*, an émigré periodical, and the fourth section was not included (for political reasons) in a complete edition until 1952. In *The Gift*, the central figure is Fyodor Godunov-Cherdyntsev, a brilliant émigré poet. As the book opens, he has just published a collection of poems, and much of the early part concerns his literary career. Later, his obsession with the memory of his father begins to dominate his everyday life, and he becomes caught in the typical confusions of the biographer: What is the truth and how can one see it? He feels an obligation to write a biography of his father but becomes trapped in assessing the various versions of his father's life. Later, he does succeed in writing a biography of Nikolai Gavrilovich Chernyshevski, a so-called poetic history based on the idea that reconstructing the past is essentially a creative act—history exists only in the historian's imagination—and that the best biographies are literary creations.

The Gift has been seen as the summing up of Nabokov's experiences as an émigré writer, and similarities have been seen between the author's biography and the events and people in the novel. The book is heavy with allusions to Russian literature and has been called the Russian counterpart to *Ada or Ardor*, an extremely allusive and complex book that also focuses on the nature of the writer. In *The Gift*, many of Nabokov's favorite devices are employed: the love triangle, the ironic suicide, and the heightened perception of the hero, in which he imagines conversations with the dead.

The Real Life of Sebastian Knight

After his decision to begin writing in English, Nabokov produced two novels before the *succès de scandale* of *Lolita*. *The Real Life of Sebastian Knight* was begun in Paris and is ostensibly the biography of a fiction writer, Sebastian, narrated by his brother, "V." V. is shocked to discover upon his brother's death in 1936 that there was more to learn of Sebastian from his novels than he had learned in person. Once again, Nabokov introduces the theme that art surpasses reality. V. fights the various distortions of Sebastian's life yet, at the end of his biography, confesses that "Sebastian's mask clings to my face." V. created Sebastian, so Sebastian is V. (as both characters were created by Nabokov). Again, the novel is characterized by the use of parodistic techniques and distorted characters. One can easily recognize this novel as a Nabokov work, yet because of Nabokov's uncertainty at writing in the English language at this stage, the work is not completely satisfying. Nabokov admitted, for example, to having had native speakers help him with the editing, something he would never permit later.

Bend Sinister

Many resemblances have been noted between Nabokov and his brother Sergei, and V. and his brother Sebastian. Sergei, unlike Vladimir, stayed in Europe during the Nazi period and died of starvation in a concentration camp near Hamburg on January 10, 1945. These events perhaps explain the harsh allegorical tone of *Bend Sinister*, a novel that is, in some ways, better than its predecessor and perhaps one of the most accessible of Nabokov's novels. The hero, Adam Krug, is an intellectual whose ideas are largely responsible for the new regime in an Eastern European country. Krug, however, refuses to swear allegiance to the ruler of the regime, a fellow student from childhood named Paduk. "I am not interested in politics," he says. Inexorably, the ring of tyranny tightens around Krug, resulting in the arrest of friends, the death of his son, and Krug's death as he attempts to attack Paduk in a mad vision of schoolyard life.

The artist, the literary craftsman in Nabokov, was incapable, however, of writing a straightforward novel of outrage against Fascists or Communists. The country is not specified; numerous vague descriptions of setting give the work a Kafkaesque flavor. The regime is tyrannical—it wants the souls of its people as well as their cooperation (not unlike Big Brother in George Orwell's *Nineteen Eighty-Four*, 1949)—yet it is not a specific ideology that is being attacked. Any form of coercion that limits the imagination of the artist or the intellectual is the target. Although some critics have argued that Krug's flaw is that he refuses to become involved in politics, it is difficult to imagine *Bend Sinister*, in the light of other works, as being a call to commitment. Krug has made a commitment to his own intellectual life. He, like many Nabokov heroes, does not "fit in" and, like many Nabokov heroes, comes to a tragic end. The supremacy of the individual imagination is Nabokov's "message"; art is his morality. There is an abundant helping of satire and parody directed against the intellectual community and the "great" political leaders of the world. Paduk is shown as a sniveling, ugly weakling who craves Krug's approval, but the alternatives to his tyranny are shown to be equally preposterous. Even in reacting to the horrors of dictatorship, Nabokov remains the detached artist.

LOLITA

Lolita, the novel that would provide a comfortable living for the author for the rest of his life, has been called everything from pornography to one of the greatest novels of the twentieth century. Today, when virtually every sexual predilection has been the subject of motion pictures and television, it is hard to appreciate the whirlwind of controversy that was stirred up by *Lolita*'s publication. Humbert Humbert, the central character and narrator, has an obsession with young girls that he has hidden by unhappy affairs with older women. He comes to the United States after inheriting a business and separating from his childish wife Valeria. Eventually, he becomes the boarder of Charlotte Haze and becomes sexually obsessed with her twelve-year-old daughter, Lolita. He marries Mrs. Haze to be near Lolita, and when the mother is killed, he takes the girl on a trip across the United States. She is eventually stolen by Clare Quilty, who is, in many ways, Humbert's double, and Humbert goes on a two-year quest to rescue the girl. He finds the sad, pregnant Lolita married to a man named Richard Schiller and, in revenge, shoots Quilty. The novel is allegedly Humbert's manuscript, written as he awaits trial. According to the foreword, Humbert died in jail of a coronary thrombosis, and the manuscript was transmitted to one John Ray, Jr., Ph.D., who prepared it for publication.

As in all of Nabokov's works, however, a plot summary is absurdly inadequate in characterizing the book. *Lolita* is protean in its directions and effects. It has been seen as a satire on the United States (though Nabokov denied it), as a psychological study (although Nabokov called Freud a "medieval mind"), and as a parody of the Romantic novel. Lionel Trilling argued that, since adultery was such a commonplace in the modern world, only a perverse love could cause the adequate passion mixed with suffering characteristic of great Romantic loves: Tristan and Isolde, Abélard and Héloise, Dante and Beatrice, Petrarch and Laura. Humbert often justifies his pedophilia by references to the courtly love tradition. There is also much reference to the story of Edgar Allan Poe's love for Virginia Clemm (Humbert's first teenage love was a girl named Annabel Leigh).

Although many critics attempted to justify *Lolita* as having an important moral message, Nabokov rebuked the notion by saying, "I am no messenger boy." His aesthetic philosophy would never have permitted him to subordinate his art to a moral. He once said that Lolita was about his love for the English language, but even that is an oversimplification of an immensely complex book. Among the various elements critics have noted are the doppelgänger relation of Quilty to Humbert, chess metaphors, puns on names, the question of the masks of the narrator (the probably unreliable Humbert through the clinical Ray through the mischievous Nabokov), and the supposed immortality of Humbert's love, a love that becomes timeless through a work of art. It has even been argued that

Nabokov's description of Lolita very much resembles his description of a certain species of butterfly in his scientific studies. While *Lolita*'s place in the canon of world literature is still debated, there is little doubt that it may be the finest example of the author's "game-playing" method of artistic creation.

PALE FIRE

With the publication of *Pale Fire*, readers were once again amused, perplexed, or horrified by Nabokov's ironic wit. This experimental novel inspired extremes of praise—such as Mary McCarthy's judgment that "it is one of the great works of art of this century"—and mockery. The novel is presented in the form of a scholarly edition of a poem titled "Pale Fire" by John Shade, with commentary by Charles Kinbote. Both worked at Wordsmith University, where Kinbote seems to have believed that Shade was writing a poem about Kinbote's obsession with Charles Xavier Vseslav, "The Beloved," the king of Zembla who was forced to flee the revolution that replaced him.

Pale Fire can be described as a series of Russian dolls, one enclosed within another. John Shade's poem (as edited by Kinbote) is explained by Kinbote, who intends to give life to the extraordinary personality of Shade. He writes in the foreword, "Without my notes Shade's text simply has no human reality at all," but the reader soon recognizes that Kinbote is a madman who either is or imagines himself to be the displaced king of Zembla, and whatever human reality Shade may have exists only through his colleague's warped interpretation of events. On another level, the reader finds some of Shade's "reality" in the text of his poem and reads much into and between Kinbote's lines as the madman gradually exposes his own madness.

Nabokov never wants his reader to forget, however, that all this invention is entirely of his making. The author intends much more in *Pale Fire* than a mere parody of scholarly editions, scholars, and neo-Romantic poetry. Once more, Nabokov wittily develops his lifelong theme that reality exists only in the eyes of its interpreter.

J. Madison Davis

OTHER MAJOR WORKS

SHORT FICTION: *Vozrashchenie Chorba*, 1930; *Soglyadatay*, 1938 (title novella and short stories); *Nine Stories*, 1947; *Vesna v Fialte i drugie rasskazy*, 1956; *Nabokov's Dozen: A Collection of Thirteen Stories*, 1958; *Nabokov's Quartet*, 1966; *A Russian Beauty, and Other Stories*, 1973; *Tyrants Destroyed, and Other Stories*, 1975; *Details of a Sunset, and Other Stories*, 1976; *The Stories of Vladimir Nabokov*, 1995.

PLAYS: *Dedushka*, pb. 1923; *Smert'*, pb. 1923; *Polius*, pb. 1924; *Tragediya gospodina Morna*, pb. 1924; *Chelovek iz SSSR*, pb. 1927; *Izobretenie Val'sa*, pb. 1938 (*The Waltz Invention*, 1966); *Sobytiye*, pr., pb. 1938.

POETRY: *Stikhi*, 1916; *Dva puti*, 1918; *Gorny put*, 1923; *Grozd'*, 1923; *Stikhotvorenia, 1929-1951*, 1952; *Poems*, 1959; *Poems and Problems*, 1970.

SCREENPLAY: *Lolita*, 1962 (adaptation of his novel).

NONFICTION: *Nikolai Gogol*, 1944; *Conclusive Evidence: A Memoir*, 1951; *Drugie berega*, 1954; *Speak, Memory: An Autobiography Revisited*, 1966 (revision of *Conclusive Evidence* and *Drugie berega*); *Strong Opinions*, 1973; *The Nabokov-Wilson Letters: Correspondence Between Vladimir Nabokov and Edmund Wilson, 1940-1971*, 1979 (Simon Karlinsky, editor); *Lectures on Literature*, 1980; *Lectures on Russian Literature*, 1981; *Lectures on Don Quixote*, 1983; *Vladimir Nabokov: Selected Letters, 1940-1977*, 1989.

TRANSLATIONS: *Anya v strane chudes*, 1923 (of Lewis Carroll's novel *Alice's Adventures in Wonderland*); *Three Russian Poets: Translations of Pushkin, Lermontov, and Tiutchev*, 1944 (with Dmitri Nabokov); *A Hero of Our Time*, 1958 (with Dmitri Nabokov; of Mikhail Lermontov's novel); *The Song of Igor's Campaign*, 1960 (of the twelfth century epic); *Eugene Onegin*, 1964 (of Alexander Pushkin's novel).

BIBLIOGRAPHY

Alexandrov, Vladimir E. *Nabokov's Otherworld*. Princeton, N.J.: Princeton University Press, 1991. Argues that "the central fact of both Nabokov's life and his art was something that could be described as an intuition about a transcendent realm of being." Shows how an awareness of this "otherworld" informs Nabokov's works, focusing on the autobiography *Speak, Memory* and on six of Nabokov's novels. Seeks to correct the widely accepted view of Nabokov as an aloof gamesman preoccupied with verbal artifice for its own sake. Includes notes, a secondary bibliography, and an index.

Bloom, Harold, ed. *Vladimir Nabokov*. New York: Chelsea House, 1987. Collection of essays addresses such topics as Nabokov's handling of time, illusion and reality, and art. Includes an informative editor's introduction, essays on Nabokov's major novels, chronology, and bibliography.

Boyd, Brian. *Vladimir Nabokov: The Russian Years*. Princeton, N.J.: Princeton University Press, 1990.

_______. *Vladimir Nabokov: The American Years*. Princeton, N.J.: Princeton University Press, 1991. Prodigiously researched two-volume biography is based in part on material found in Nabokov's archives, to which Boyd gained unprecedented access. Recounts the events of Nabokov's life and charts his development as a writer. Each volume includes illustrations, extensive notes, and an exceptionally thorough index.

Connolly, Julian W., ed. *The Cambridge Companion to Nabokov*. New York: Cambridge University Press, 2005. Collection of essays offers a good introduction to Nabokov's life and writings. Topics addressed include Nabokov as a storyteller, a Russian writer, a modernist, and a poet; also covered are his transition to writing in English and the reception of *Lolita*.

De la Durantaye, Leland. *Style Is Matter: The Moral Art of Vladimir Nabokov*. Ithaca, N.Y.: Cornell University Press, 2007. Focuses on *Lolita* but also looks at some of Nabokov's other works to discuss the ethics of art in Nabokov's fiction. Asserts that although some readers find Nabokov to be cruel, his works contain a moral message—albeit one that is skillfully hidden.

Field, Andrew. *VN: The Life and Art of Vladimir Nabokov.* New York: Crown, 1986. Critical biography recounts the events of Nabokov's life and places his works within personal and historical context. Includes discussion of *Lolita, Pale Fire, The Gift,* and other works.

Foster, John Burt. *Nabokov's Art of Memory and European Modernism.* Princeton, N.J.: Princeton University Press, 1993. Scholarly work divides discussion of Nabokov's work into three parts: Nabokov's early years in Russia, his period in Europe, and his prolonged period in the United States. Intended for advanced students.

Glynn, Michael. *Vladimir Nabokov: Bergsonian and Russian Formalist Influences in His Novels.* New York: Palgrave Macmillan, 2007. Glynn disagrees with other critics who have called Nabokov a Symbolist writer, arguing that he was an anti-Symbolist who was influenced by the philosopher Henri Bergson and by Russian Formalism. Useful for advanced students of Russian literature and philosophy.

Grayson, Jane, Arnold B. McMillin, and Priscilla Meyer, eds. *Nabokov's World: Reading Nabokov.* New York: Palgrave Macmillan, 2002.

_______. *Nabokov's World: The Shape of Nabokov's World.* New York: Palgrave Macmillan, 2002. Two-volume collection of essays written by an international group of Nabokov scholars provides comprehensive discussion of his work. Presents analyses of individual novels as well as coverage of topics such as intertextuality in Nabokov's works and the literary reception of his writings.

Parker, Stephen Jan. *Understanding Vladimir Nabokov.* Columbia: University of South Carolina Press, 1987. Introductory guide to Nabokov for students and nonacademic readers focuses on individual analyses of five of his Russian novels and four of his American novels. Begins with a chapter on the self-reflexive aspects of Nabokov's narrative technique.

Pifer, Ellen, ed. *Vladimir Nabokov's "Lolita": A Casebook.* New York: Oxford University Press, 2002. An interview with Nabokov and a collection of essays provide a range of approaches to the reading of *Lolita*, including discussions of the novel and the art of persuasion, the Americanization of Humbert Humbert, and *Lolita* and the poetry of advertising.

Wood, Michael. *The Magician's Doubts: Nabokov and the Risks of Fiction.* Princeton, N.J.: Princeton University Press, 1995. Close readings of Nabokov's works show the power and beauty of his language and subtlety of his art. This examination also reveals the ethical and moral foundations of his work, which Nabokov denied existed.

GEORGE ORWELL
Eric Arthur Blair

Born: Motihari, Bengal, India; June 25, 1903
Died: London, England; January 21, 1950
Also known as: Eric Arthur Blair

Principal long fiction
Burmese Days, 1934
A Clergyman's Daughter, 1935
Keep the Aspidistra Flying, 1936
Coming Up for Air, 1939
Animal Farm, 1945
Nineteen Eighty-Four, 1949

Other literary forms

Since the mid-1940's, George Orwell has been considered one of the world's premier essayists. Combining reportage, the polemical essay, fictional techniques, and refracted autobiographical detail, his works defy precise generic definition. Orwell's numerous nonfiction works have been compiled in *The Collected Essays, Journalism, and Letters of George Orwell* (1968), edited by Sonia Orwell and Ian Angus.

Achievements

Although George Orwell is widely recognized as one of the best essayists of the twentieth century, his reputation as a novelist rests almost entirely on two works: the political allegory *Animal Farm* and the dystopian *Nineteen Eighty-Four.* Both have been translated into so many other languages and have been read so widely that the adjective "Orwellian" has international currency—synonymous, as Bernard Crick has put it, with the "ghastly political future." Indeed, Jeffrey Meyers has asserted that Orwell, the writer of essays, political tracts, and fiction, "is more widely read than perhaps any other serious writer of the twentieth-century."

Biography

George Orwell was born Eric Arthur Blair, the son of Richard Walmesley Blair and Ida (Limouzin) Blair. Orwell was born in India and lived there for four years, until his father moved the family back to England, to a small house named Nutshell, located in Henley-on-Thames. After a short leave, Orwell's father returned alone to India; his wife and children remained in England, where he rejoined them later, upon his retirement. With his father's return, Orwell, like most male members of the upper middle class, was sent away to boarding school, St. Cyprian's, located at Eastbourne on the Sussex coast. After several

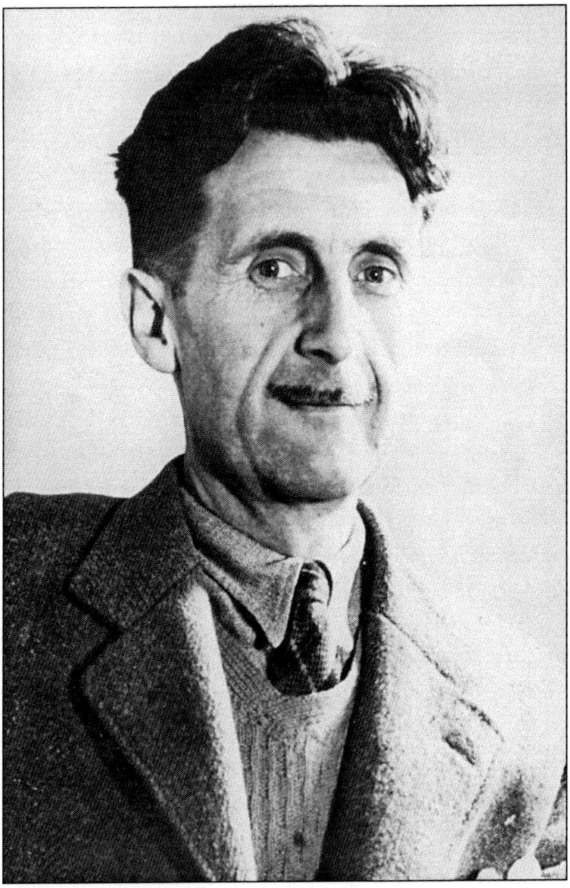

George Orwell
(Library of Congress)

miserable years, as Orwell describes them in his autobiographical *Such, Such Were the Joys* (1953), he won a scholarship to Eton, the public school that would forever set him apart from the working classes about which he was so concerned during most of his adult life.

Considered rather unacademic at Eton, Orwell graduated in December, 1921, and, after a decision not to attend university, he applied to the India Office for the position of imperial police officer. Five years in Burma, from 1922 to 1927, shaped the impressionable young man so as to make him forever sympathetic to individuals victimized by governmental bureaucracy and imperialistic power. Orwell left Burma in the summer of 1927, ostensibly on sick leave (he suffered from a lung condition most of his life). At some point early in his leave, Orwell wrote a letter of resignation to the India Office and explained to his skeptical parents that all he really wanted to do was to write.

In 1928, Orwell commenced a long, five-year apprenticeship as a writer, time spent as a tramp in both Paris and London and in the writing and rewriting of countless manuscripts. By 1933 he had assumed the name by which he is known and had produced, in addition to at least two destroyed novels, the nonfictional *Down and Out in Paris and London* (1933) and his first novel, *Burmese Days*, published one year later.

From 1933 to 1937, Orwell continued to develop his literary talents, producing two more novels, a nonfiction book about his experiences with poverty-stricken coal miners in Wigan (*The Road to Wigan Pier*, 1937), and several essays, occasional pieces, and book reviews. By the end of this period, he had also married for the first time and, within a year or so of that, gone to Spain. In perhaps the most singular experience of his life to date, the Spanish Civil War found Orwell on the front lines, a member of a Partido Obrero de Unificación Marxista (a Marxist worker's party) brigade; from that time on, Orwell passionately declared himself a fighter for "democratic Socialism." In that context, he wrote his most famous nonfictional work, *Homage to Catalonia* (1938). After being wounded (and nearly imprisoned), Orwell escaped Spain with the help of his wife, returned to England, and continued his literary career. Within another year, his lungs still causing him problems, Orwell moved to the dry climate of Morocco, where he wrote much of *Coming Up for Air*.

His fourth novel was buried under mounting war concerns and preparations. Orwell, unable to join the military because of his health, became a spokesman for the British Broadcasting Corporation (BBC). During the last years of the war, Orwell finished writing *Animal Farm*, only to see it rejected by almost every major publisher in England and the United States. Finally brought out in August, 1945, during the last days of the Pacific War, *Animal Farm* was a work of near perfection, making Orwell's name internationally known, so that when *Nineteen Eighty-Four* was published four years later, the world came to realize that both works would henceforth be considered literary classics, satires ranking with Sir Thomas More's *De Optimo Reipublicae Statu, deque Nova Insula Utopia* (1516; *Utopia, 1551*) and Jonathan Swift's *A Tale of a Tub* (1704). Orwell's death in 1950 at the age of forty-six was a tragic loss to the world of letters and to the larger world with which he always kept in touch.

ANALYSIS

Excepting *Animal Farm*, most critics view George Orwell's fictions as aesthetically flawed creations, the work of a political thinker whose artistry was subordinate to his intensely didactic, partisan passions. This reaction to Orwell's novels was generally promoted posthumously, since his fiction in the 1930's was often ignored by the larger reading public and panned by those reviewers who did pick up one of his books. The early academic critics—up to the late 1960's—were often Orwell's personal friends or acquaintances, who tended to see his early novels as conventionally realistic and strongly autobiographical. Even his masterpieces, *Animal Farm* and *Nineteen Eighty-Four*, were viewed as formally undistinguished, however powerful their message. It was not until the second generation of critics began looking at Orwell's fiction that a more balanced assessment was possible.

BURMESE DAYS

Orwell's first published novel, *Burmese Days*, concerns the life of John Flory, an English policeman in Burma during the early 1920's. The plot is fairly straightforward. After a lengthy introduction to Flory's personality and daily life, Orwell dramatizes him as a man blemished with a physical stigma, a birthmark, and puzzled by moral dilemma—how to deal with the increasingly rebellious natives, to whom he is secretly sympathetic but against whom he must wield the club of imperialistic authority. In the middle of this dilemma, Elizabeth arrives, a young English woman who is fresh faced but decidedly a traditional "burra memsahib." Flory attempts to win both her heart and mind—much to the dismay of his Burmese mistress, Ma Hla May—and succeeds in doing neither, even though he manages to half succeed in proposing marriage during an earthquake. With a mind too closed to anything not properly British, and a heart only to be won by someone very English, Elizabeth forgets Flory's attentions with the arrival of Verrall, an English military policeman, who will in turn reject her after his billet is completed. A humble Flory waits for Elizabeth, and after Verrall has left takes her to church services, confident that he has outlasted his rival. Unfortunately, Flory is humiliated by Ma Hla May, is repulsed yet again by Elizabeth, and, in a mood of despair, commits suicide, killing both his dog and himself.

In such a world, Flory is emphatically not meant to be a sympathetic character, but rather a victim of the very political order he has sworn to uphold. In effect, Orwell has laid a trap for the unwary reader. Too close an identification with Flory, too intense a desire to have him succeed in marrying Elizabeth—an unholy alliance of imperialistic Englishwoman and revolutionary, thinking pariah—will prevent the reader from recognizing the irreconcilable contradictions inherent in the British presence in Burma.

COMING UP FOR AIR

Orwell's fourth published novel, *Coming Up for Air*, was written in Marrakesh, Morocco, shortly after the author had recovered from yet another bout with tubercular lesions of the lungs. Although the novel sold moderately well for the time (a first printing of two thousand copies and a second printing of one thousand), many critics were vaguely condescending toward the hero, George Bowling, a middle-class insurance salesman who longs for the golden country of the past while simultaneously dreading the horrors of a second world war, then only months away. Many of the themes more fully developed in *Nineteen Eighty-Four* find their initial expression in Orwell's last conventional novel, set before the outbreak of the devastation that the next six years would bring.

Coming Up for Air is set in London during the late 1930's; Orwell employs a first-person narrative to describe the life of George Bowling, a middle-aged, middle-class salesman, whose first set of false teeth marks a major milestone in his life. Musing in front of a mirror while he prepares for work one morning, George's mind wanders back to the past, the golden England of thirty years earlier when he was growing up. As he goes about his day, disgusted with all the evidence of modern life in front of him—the casual brutalities, the tasteless food, the bombers overhead—George forms a plan to return to Lower Binfield, his childhood home, and, by extension, the simple life he had once led. Unfortunately, his return only confirms the all-pervasive slovenliness of the modern world: Lower Binfield has been swallowed by a sprawling suburb, his adolescent sweetheart has become a frowsy old married woman (she is all of two years older than he), and the fishing hole (once filled with huge finny dreams) has been emptied of water and filled with trash. Shocked and completely disenchanted, Bowling makes plans to get at least a relaxing few days from the trip when a bomber accidentally drops a bomb close by, killing and wounding several people. In thorough disgust, Bowling packs, leaves, and returns home to face his wife, who has somehow found out where he has gone, although his motives for going will be forever incomprehensible to her.

A plot summary of the novel fails to do justice to the subtle tonal shifts and complicated psychological changes Orwell employs in presenting his portrait of the average man waiting for the Apocalypse. Orwell uses the ancient theme of the double (or doppelgänger) to illustrate the self-fragmentation of European man prior to the outbreak of the war. George Bowling is divided into two "selves." Tubby is the outwardly fat, insensitive insurance tout who is able to function successfully in a fast-paced, competitive world that would eat up less hardened personalities, but his character can survive only at the cost of any sort of satisfying inner life. Georgie, on the other hand, would be lost in the modern rat race and so is protected by Tubby; nevertheless, Georgie can give expression to the memories, the sensitivities, the love for natural pleasures that Tubby (and George Bowling) would have to forgo to remain functional. Thus, George Bowling devised a strategy for living both materially successfully and psychologically well in the modern world, doing so by splitting his identity into Tubby and Georgie. *Coming Up for Air* details the ongoing dialogue between these two "selves"—a conversation that reflects the strains of modern living as well as any other novelist has done in the twentieth century.

Furthermore, Orwell has modified the literary conventions of the doppelgänger to suit his own needs. Whereas the death of one-half of the double usually means the destruction, ultimately, of both, Orwell has Tubby live on after Georgie is symbolically destroyed by the bombing plane. The tonal change at this point, rather like the tonal change in Joseph Heller's *Catch-22* (1961) with the death of Kid Sampson, shows the reader the world that Orwell envisioned between 1938 and 1939, one horrible enough to prevent total escape even by death. It is, however, typically Orwellian that however horrible human bondage can make the cultural world, nature, of which humankind is a part, has enough ebullient energy to wait out any social mess—a wait without immediate hope, without idols, but also without hopeless despair. George Bowling leaves Lower Binfield, returning to his scold of a wife, Hilda; to the everlasting round of bills, worries, war clouds on the horizon, and a death-in-life without Georgie—but, as the novel's epigraph states, "He's dead, but he won't lie down."

ANIMAL FARM

Animal Farm is one of those rare books before which critics lay down their pens. As a self-contained "fairy story," the book can be read and understood by children not old enough to pronounce most of the words in an average junior high school history text. As a political satire, *Animal Farm* can be highly appreciated by those who actually lived through the terrible days of World War II. As an allegory concerned with the limitations and abuses of political power, the novel has been pored over eagerly by several generations of readers.

The novel is built around historical events in the Soviet Union from before the October Revolution to the end of World War II; it does this by using the frame of reference of animals in a farmyard, the Manor Farm, owned by a Mr. Jones. Drunk most of the time and, like Czar Nicholas II of Russia in the second decade of the twentieth century, out of touch with the governed, Jones neglects his farm (allegorically representing the Soviet Union, or by extension, almost any oppressed country), causing much discontent and resentment among his animals. One day, after Jones does his nightly rounds, Major, an imposing pig (Vladimir Ilich Lenin), tells the other animals of a dream he has had concerning theories about the way they have been living. Animals have been exploited by Mr. Jones and humankind generally, but Major has dreamed of a time when they will throw over their yokes and live free, sharing equally both the profits and the hazards of their work. Major teaches the animals the words to a song, "Beasts of England" (The Internationale), and tells them to look to the future and the betterment of all animals; three days later he dies.

The smartest of the animals, the pigs, are aroused by his speech and by the song; they secretly learn to read and write, developing a philosophical system called animalism (Communism, Bolshevism) whose principles are taught to all the animals. When Jones forgets one day to feed them (as Russians starved near the end of their involvement in World War I), the animals revolt spontaneously, driving out Jones, his wife (Russian nobility), and Moses, the raven (the Russian Orthodox Church). The animals rejoice, feeling a sense of camaraderie and esprit de corps, and set about to build a new life.

The pigs, however, by taking on the responsibility of organization, also take over certain decision-making processes—as well as all the milk and apples; in fact, Orwell has himself stated that the first sign of corruption, the taking of the cow's milk, led to the inevitable destruction of everything else. Two pigs in particular, Snowball (Leon Trotsky) and Napoleon (Joseph Stalin), argue constantly, while a third, Squealer (*Pravda*, Tass) appears more than happy to endorse any course of action with his adroit use of language and his physical habit of skipping from side to side as he speaks. After changing the name from Manor Farm to Animal Farm, the pigs paint on the side of the barn the seven commandments of animalism, the most important being: "All animals are equal." Meanwhile, Napoleon has been privately raising puppies born on the farm after the overthrow of Jones, puppies that develop into savage attack dogs (secret police, People's Commissariat of Internal Affairs, or NKVD); with these, he will one day drive off the farm all of his personal enemies, especially the brilliant theoretician Snowball. Also soon to be lost to Animal Farm is Mollie (the bourgeoisie), who shows up at Pilkingtons (the West, England).

At this point, the work becomes more difficult, the pigs assume practical control, and the arguments become more intense. Even though Benjamin, the donkey (Tolstoyan intellectuals), remains cynical about the supposed heaven on earth, Boxer, the horse (the peasantry), vows to work harder; nevertheless, the animals continue to lose their spirit and cohesiveness until attacked by Farmer Jones, who tries to regain the Farm. Because of Snowball's brilliant strategy, Jones is driven off in what is thereafter called the Battle of the Cowshed (the Civil War).

Following the victory celebration, Snowball and Napoleon move toward a decisive parting: The former wants to move full speed ahead with the building of the windmill (permanent revolution), while the latter thinks the most important task immediately ahead is the increase in food production (develop socialism in Russia first). After much debate and just before what could be an affirmative vote for Snowball's policies, Napoleon unleashes his secretly kept dogs on his rival, chasing him out of Animal Farm forever. Henceforth, the unchallenged leader abolishes Sunday meetings, increasingly changes rules at will, and even announces that the building of the windmill was his idea.

The animals continue to work hard, still believing that they are working for themselves. The changes Napoleon institutes, however, are so at variance with the initial rules of Animal Farm, and life gets to be so much drudgery, that no one has the memory to recall the ideals of the past, nor the energy to change the present—even if memories were sound.

Very soon, life at Animal Farm seems indistinguishable from the life the animals led at Manor Farm. Orwell is not so much ultimately pessimistic as he is realistically moral: Institutionalized hierarchy begets privilege, which begets corruption of power. The first mistake of the animals was to give over their right to decide who got the milk and apples. Lord Action's famous statement could not be more appropriate: "Power tends to corrupt; absolute power corrupts absolutely."

NINETEEN EIGHTY-FOUR

Nineteen Eighty-Four is Orwell's most famous work. As a fantasy set in the future, the novel has terrified readers for more than thirty years—frightened them into facing the prospect of the ultimate tyranny: mind control. As a parody of conditions in postwar England, it is, as Anthony Burgess argues in his novel *1985* (1978), a droll, rather Swiftean exaggeration of then current trends straining the social and political fabric of British culture. As a critique of the way in which human beings construct their social reality, the novel has so affected the modern world that much of its language (like that of its predecessor, *Animal Farm*) has entered into the everyday language of English-speaking peoples everywhere: "doublethink," "newspeak," "thoughtcrime," and "Big Brother." Bernard Crick has argued that *Nineteen Eighty-Four* is intimately related to *Animal Farm* and that both works convey Orwell's most important message: Liberty means telling people what they do not want to hear. If the vehicle for the telling gets corrupted, then the message itself will always be corrupted, garbled; finally, the very thoughts that led to the utterances in the first place will be shackled, constrained not only from the outside but also from the inside. To think clearly, to speak openly and precisely, was a heritage Englishmen received from their glorious past; it was a legacy so easily lost that it needed to be guarded fiercely, lest those who promulgated ideologies of right or left took away what had been won with such difficulty. That was where the danger lay, with those who practiced the "smelly little orthodoxies" that are still "contending for our souls."

The story begins with a man named Winston Smith, who is hurrying home on a cold, windy April day as the clocks are striking thirteen. With this ominous beginning, the reader is quickly plunged into a gritty, decaying world where the political order so dominates everyday life that independent thought is a crime, love is forbidden, and language seems to say the opposite of what one has normally come to expect. As Winston's daily life unfolds, the reader quickly learns that the whole world has been divided into three geographical areas: Oceania, Eurasia, and Eastasia. All are engaged in perpetual warfare with one or both of the others, not for territorial or religious reasons but primarily for social control. At some point, atomic warfare had made total war unthinkable, yet it suits the political leaders of Oceania (the same is also true of the other two political areas) to keep the population in a general state of anxiety about foreign attack. Under the guise of national concern, Oceania's leaders keep the population under their collective thumb through the use of propaganda (from the Ministry of Truth), through outright, brutally applied force (from the Ministry of Love), through eternally short rations (Ministry of Plenty), and through the waging of perpetual war (Ministry of Peace). The ruling elite, called the Inner Party, make up only 2 percent of the population; the Outer Party, the next 13 percent. The remainder, some 85 percent of the population, make up the oppressed masses; those in this group are called Proles.

Winston, a member of the Outer Party, has been disturbed by strange thoughts of late, and one day he purchases a small, bound volume of blank paper, a diary in which he can record his most private thoughts without being observed by the omnipresent telescreen manned by members of the Thought Police. In his diary, he records his first thought: "Down with Big Brother!" To compound such a heinous thoughtcrime, he begins a liaison with a pretty young woman, a member of the Anti-Sex League, named Julia. After their affair has progressed for some time, they are contacted by a man named O'Brien, who enlists their aid in combating Big Brother by joining a group called the Brotherhood. O'Brien gives Winston a book, written by a man named Emannuel Goldstein, called *The Theory and Practice of Oligarchical Collectivism*. Having made love to Julia in a room rented from an old Prole (secretly a member of the Thought Police), Winston begins reading to her from Goldstein's book, actually an exposition of the theory that Orwell has used to construct *Nineteen Eighty-Four*.

Although Winston is fascinated, Julia, a rebel from the waist down only, falls asleep, and, after a while, so does Winston. They awake many hours later, are captured by the Thought Police, who apparently knew of their hideaway from the first, and are taken to rooms in the Ministry of Love. There, they find that O'Brien is in reality a member of the Thought Police; he alternately tortures and debates with Winston, trying to convince him that he must love Big Brother.

When torture fails, Winston is taken to Room 101, where he will be subjected to that which he fears most—in his case, rats. He gives in, begs them to "do it to Julia," and is ultimately convinced that he loves Big Brother. The novel ends as Winston, having exchanged mutual conversations of betrayal with Julia, sits at the Chestnut Café drinking Victory Gin, completely brainwashed and committed to Big Brother.

Much has been said about the ultimate pessimism of *Nineteen Eighty-Four* being related to Orwell's fatal illness, which he fought unsuccessfully during the composition of the novel. If, however, one thinks of Orwell's fiction less in biographical terms and more in relation to artistic intention, then such a conclusion could be subject to argument. Although the novel ends with Winston in what Northrop Frye called the sixth level of irony, unrelieved bondage, one should draw a distinction, as Orwell does in his other writings (most notably in the essay "A Good Word for the Vicar of Bray"), between humans' actions as cultural beings and their activities as creatures of planet Earth, natural beings.

As political creatures, humans and their purely cultural institutions could, Orwell believes, develop a world such as the one portrayed in *Nineteen Eighty-Four.* This would be impossible, however, for humans as biological residents of the planet Earth. Humankind never displays hubris more graphically than does O'Brien in his speech about the party's supposed control of nature. In Orwell's view, human beings will never fully control nature, because they are only a part of what they wish to control. The great chestnut tree blossoming over Winston and his degeneration as a free being is Orwell's symbol indicating that the natural world can outlast humankind's cultural and political aberrations. "The planting of a tree," says Orwell, "if [it] takes root . . . will far outlive the visible effect of any of your other actions, good or evil." If there is hope for Oceania in the Proles, perhaps it is because they are instinctively closer to the natural world symbolized by the chestnut tree. Nevertheless, whether one thinks there is any hope for the people of that world or not, their existence has served as a warning to the larger world: The price of the right to tell people what they do not want to hear is never too high to pay.

John V. Knapp

OTHER MAJOR WORKS

NONFICTION: *Down and Out in Paris and London*, 1933; *The Road to Wigan Pier,* 1937; *Homage to Catalonia*, 1938; *Inside the Whale, and Other Essays*, 1940; *The Lion and the Unicorn*, 1941; *Critical Essays*, 1946 (also known as *Dickens, Dali, and Others*); *Shooting an Elephant, and Other Essays*, 1950; *Such, Such Were the Joys*, 1953;

The Collected Essays, Journalism, and Letters of George Orwell, 1968 (4 volumes; Sonia Orwell and Ian Angus, editors); *Orwell: The War Broadcasts*, 1985 (also known as *Orwell: The War Commentaries*, 1986); *The Lost Orwell*, 2006 (Peter Davison, editor).

MISCELLANEOUS: *Orwell: The Lost Writings*, 1985; *The Complete Works of George Orwell*, 1986-1998 (20 volumes; Peter Davison, editor).

BIBLIOGRAPHY

Bloom, Harold, ed. *George Orwell*. Updated ed. New York: Chelsea House, 2007. Collection of essays provides analyses of Orwell's works, including the novels *Animal Farm*, *Nineteen Eighty-Four*, and *Coming Up for Air*. Includes bibliography, chronology, and index.

Bowker, Gordon. *Inside George Orwell*. New York: Palgrave Macmillan, 2003. Biography presents the "human face" of Orwell, describing his inner emotional life and its relationship to his political activities and ideas. One of the better books about Orwell to be published in the centenary year of his birth.

Crick, Bernard. *George Orwell: A Life*. Boston: Little, Brown, 1980. Important full-scale biography considers all phases of Orwell's career, drawing on extensive use of the writer's archives and other manuscript sources as well as numerous publications. Crick was the first biographer of Orwell to benefit from unlimited rights of quotation from Orwell's works held under copyright.

Davison, Peter. *George Orwell: A Literary Life*. New York: St. Martin's Press, 1996. Follows the course of Orwell's career as a writer. Includes background chapters explaining Orwell's origins, but focuses chiefly on his literary influences and relationships, such as those with his publishers and editors.

Hitchens, Christopher. *Why Orwell Matters*. New York: Basic Books, 2002. Emphasizes Orwell's criticism of Nazism and Stalinism—philosophies toward which he never softened his view in order to sell books. Argues that Orwell's analyses of those two governmental systems continue to apply in the early twenty-first century.

Holderness, Graham, Bryan Loughrey, and Nahem Yousaf, eds. *George Orwell*. New York: St. Martin's Press, 1998. Collection of essays on Orwell's novels covers topics such as his use of allegory, his politics, his view of England, and his handling of form, character, and theme. Includes bibliography.

Meyers, Jeffrey. *Orwell: Wintry Conscience of a Generation*. New York: W. W. Norton, 2000. Well-researched biography provides a balanced look at Orwell's life and work. Vividly describes the contrast between Orwell the writer and Orwell the man.

Reilly, Patrick. *"Nineteen Eighty-Four": Past, Present, and Future*. Boston: Twayne, 1989. Spirited defense of Orwell's last novel upholds the author's conceptions against the claims of modern detractors. Contains a detailed chronology and an annotated bibliography.

Rodden, John, ed. *The Cambridge Companion to George Orwell.* New York: Cambridge University Press, 2007. Collection of essays provides information on a wide range of Orwell's works and literary influences. Some of the essays analyze *Animal Farm* and *Nineteen Eighty-Four*; others discuss Orwell's response to the political events of his time.

Sandison, Alan. *George Orwell After "Nineteen Eighty-Four."* New York: Macmillan, 1986. Interpretive work views Orwell's writings as a reflection of a long intellectual tradition of religious and philosophical individualism. A lengthy postscript presents Sandison's views on other works about Orwell.

Saunders, Loraine. *The Unsung Artistry of George Orwell: The Novels from "Burmese Days" to "Nineteen Eighty-Four."* Burlington, Vt.: Ashgate, 2008. Offers reappraisal of all of Orwell's novels, arguing that the novels published in the 1930's deserve as much credit as the subsequent works. Examines the influences of writer George Gissing and of 1930's politics on Orwell's work, and also discusses Orwell's depictions of women.

Shelden, Michael. *Orwell: The Authorized Biography.* New York: HarperCollins, 1991. Extensive, detailed work helps to place Orwell's works within the context of the events of his life. Includes notes and a bibliography.

DAWN POWELL

Born: Mount Gilead, Ohio; November 28, 1897
Died: New York, New York; November 14, 1965

PRINCIPAL LONG FICTION

Whither, 1925
She Walks in Beauty, 1928
The Bride's House, 1929
Dance Night, 1930
The Tenth Moon, 1932
The Story of a Country Boy, 1934
Turn, Magic Wheel, 1936
The Happy Island, 1938
Angels on Toast, 1940, 1989 (revised as *A Man's Affair*, 1956)
A Time to Be Born, 1942, 1991
My Home Is Far Away, 1944, 1995
The Locusts Have No King, 1948, 1990
The Wicked Pavilion, 1954, 1990
A Cage for Lovers, 1957
The Golden Spur, 1962
Novels, 1930-1942, 2001 (Tim Page, editor)
Novels, 1944-1962, 2001 (Page, editor)

OTHER LITERARY FORMS

Though Dawn Powell is known primarily as a novelist, she had originally intended to write for the theater. Her play *Big Night* was produced by the Group Theatre in 1933, and *Jig Saw: A Comedy* had a short run in 1934. Powell also wrote a musical comedy and scripts for radio, television, and film and published essays, reviews, and short stories in distinguished national magazines. A number of her short stories were collected in *Sunday, Monday, and Always* (1952).

ACHIEVEMENTS

While such contemporaries as Ernest Hemingway and John Dos Passos considered Dawn Powell one of the finest writers of their time, she never attained their popularity. Shortly before her death in 1965, Powell was honored with an honorary doctorate and an award from the National Institute of Arts and Letters, but despite occasional attempts by her admirers, such as Edmund Wilson, to call attention to her achievements, she remained relatively obscure, and her sixteen novels, all out of print, were difficult to find. Fortunately, in the next two decades, there was a revolution in the American sensibility. One of

Dawn Powell
(Library of Congress)

the results of the feminist movement was that critics and publishers had to admit sins of omission; they had minimized the talent of many fine women writers simply because they were women. Powell, who has been called an American equivalent to English satiric novelists such as Evelyn Waugh and Anthony Powell, is an obvious example.

In 1987, author and critic Gore Vidal launched the campaign to obtain proper recognition for Powell. In a lengthy essay published in *The New York Review of Books*, he traced her life and her literary career and concluded by bemoaning the fact that the novels of the person he considered America's best comic novelist were all out of print. As a result of his article, several of her later books were reprinted, all with Vidal's essay as an introduction, and the reviews that followed suggest that Powell may at last receive the recognition denied her during her lifetime.

Biography

Dawn Powell was born in Mount Gilead, Ohio, on November 28, 1897, the daughter of Roy K. Powell, a traveling salesman, and Hattie B. Sherman Powell. For six years, after the death of her mother when Powell was six, she and her two sisters lived with various relatives on farms and in small towns. After her father's remarriage, the girls went to live with him and their stepmother on a farm. Powell already was a dedicated writer; indeed, after her stepmother punished her by burning her stories, Powell fled to the home of an aunt. After graduating from high school, Powell went to Lake Erie College, where she received her bachelor of arts degree in 1918. That year she moved to New York to serve in the U.S. Navy auxiliary, remaining there working in public relations and in advertising.

In 1920, Powell married Joseph Roebuck Gousha, an executive with an advertising agency, with whom she had one son, Joseph Roebuck Gousha, Jr. Failing in her attempts to break into the theatrical world as a playwright, Powell began writing novels, publishing the first, *Whither*, in 1925. Over the next four decades, she published fifteen more novels, the early ones set in her native Ohio, most of the later ones in New York City's Greenwich Village, in what became her world, the small circle of writers, publishers, actors, producers, artists, and critics who were at the intellectual center of the United States. Still without wide recognition, Powell died of cancer at St. Luke's Hospital in New York City on November 14, 1965.

Analysis

The primary purpose of a Dawn Powell novel is to describe a society. To do so, Powell brings a number of characters together, perhaps in an Ohio boardinghouse, perhaps at a New York party or a bar. Then the characters seem to take over, as if they are determined to dramatize their own world. They act and interact, they talk, they boast, they scheme, they lie, and they confess to one another. To this extent, Powell's novels could be called realistic. They also, however, include an element of satire. It is primarily noticeable in the characters' inner deliberations, which Powell reveals to her readers in illuminating detail. The characters' confusion about facts, their muddled reasoning, and above all their clearly selfish motivations, reported with such painstaking care, leave the reader no doubt as to Powell's satiric intentions, which are further stressed in her occasional wry and witty comments.

Although Powell's first book, *Whither*, was set in New York City, all but one of the six novels published during the next six years were placed in the rural Midwest. These works introduce the themes that would dominate Powell's later work: the alienation of an individual from society, the frustration of the failing artist, the random nature of love, the limits of friendship, and above all the rule of money. Beginning with *Turn, Magic Wheel*, Powell wrote a series of seven novels to which Vidal refers as her "New York cycle." Most critics consider these novels to represent Powell's highest artistic achievement and, indeed, a unique contribution to American literature.

Angels on Toast

The third of these novels, *Angels on Toast*, illustrates Powell's approach. The world that she both summarizes and satirizes is defined in the first chapter of the book. The story begins with two businessmen, Jay Oliver and Lou Donovan, on a train from Chicago to New York. The self-absorption that marks most of Powell's characters is evident from the first.

Their world is neither abstract nor cosmopolitan. At its simplest it is made up of their own bodies and their own clothes. Jay admires his own shoes, which he thinks reflect his polished personality, and his socks, which are so dazzling that he must mention how expensive they were. Lou contemplates and assesses his weight, his shoulders, then is delighted to tell Jay how much his shirt cost and to invite him to feel the material. For men so fascinated with the most trivial details about themselves, it is not surprising that both friendship and love are limited in depth. From the facile comment that Jay is his best friend, Lou soon has moved to the notion that Jay may know too much about him; indeed, it is Jay's company that is his best friend, not Jay himself, Lou muses. If Jay were replaced, the new man would become Lou's best friend. Lou's capacity for love is similarly limited by circumstances. For example, when he married above himself, he found it convenient to forget having been married before, and he is now worried because that former wife has turned up in Chicago. In a typical Powell passage, however, Lou congratulates himself because he has been faithful to his wife, except for casual encounters in places where she would never go. Jay, on the other hand, is shockingly unfaithful, picking up his regular mistress on the train and taking her to New York with him. It is not adultery, but taking such chances, that Lou considers immoral.

Thus, by re-creating conversations and by reporting her characters' thoughts, Powell reveals their attitudes and values. Her satiric intention is clear, when she lets Lou congratulate himself for what are in fact very low moral standards; it is obvious that for him and his society, love and friendship will never stand in the way of making money.

In Powell's later novels, New York itself might as well be listed as one of the characters. It is symbolic that the first chapter takes place on the way to New York, instead of on the way back to Chicago. In New York, the businessmen think they can get away with anything. It is, of course, ironic that the city proves to be much smaller than the out-of-town visitors think it is; unfortunately, paths do cross, and wives do find out what is occurring.

In *Angels on Toast*, the compelling attraction of New York is also dramatized in the attitude of an eccentric old lady who lives in a seedy hotel. When her daughter suggests that they both move to Connecticut, the idea is greeted with horror. Obviously, even a dingy hotel in New York is better than a mansion anywhere else. Actually, the old lady's real home is the hotel bar; its inhabitants are the only people she needs or wishes to know.

Except for the fact that Ebie Vane is a commercial artist, the conflict between the creator and his crass, indifferent world is not as important in *Angels on Toast* as it is in Powell's last three novels, in which the alienation of the artist from society is a major theme. The cohesiveness of New York's literary and theatrical world is suggested by the title of the first of these books, *The Locusts Have No King*. The quotation, which comes from the biblical Proverbs, emphasizes the idea that although there is no single leader among locusts, they seem to have a mysterious single direction. They move in hordes and, it should be added, destructive hordes. It is such mindless human groups that can destroy the will and the hopes of an artist or, perhaps worse, turn an artist into a commercial success at the cost of creative integrity and personal relationships.

The Locusts Have No King

At the beginning of *The Locusts Have No King*, there seems to be no possibility that the protagonist, Frederick Olliver, a writer of scholarly books, will ever become successful enough to find his soul endangered. In contrast, his mistress, Lyle Gaynor, a successful playwright, is a celebrity who knows every other celebrity in the literary world. Lyle is completely devoted to Frederick. Indeed, she would marry him except that she feels a duty to remain with her ill-tempered husband because he is disabled. To help Frederick, Lyle includes him in every party she gives and arranges for him to be invited to every party she attends. Nevertheless, Frederick always feels that he is an alien in Lyle's world. In response, he voices his scorn of the successful, including his generous mistress. The fact that one lover is inside the magic circle and the other is outside clearly imperils their relationship.

Powell's theme of alienation appears in three different typical situations. The first involves characters such as Frederick, who, though they are not new to New York, have simply not had enough success to be accepted. The second involves a young person who, like Jonathan Jaimison in *The Golden Spur* and like the young Powell herself in 1918, has recently arrived in New York, usually from the Midwest, and must be initiated into its ways. Although the misunderstandings and mistakes of the innocent can be highly comic, they do not provide the occasions of satire that Powell sees in the third kind of alienation. Like all the great satirists, she delights in exposing the pretensions of characters who attempt to be accepted in a complex, cultivated society but who are too foolish to master its mannerisms or even its idiom.

An example of this kind of alienated character, who unlike the other types has no hope of being accepted as a result of eventual success or deliberate adaptation, is Dodo Brennan in *The Locusts Have No King*. Dodo has chosen to think of herself as a southern belle, and she has come from Baltimore to conquer New York with cuteness. Unfortunately, her poses and her baby talk make her ludicrous. Although Frederick becomes involved with Dodo and introduces her into Lyle's circle, Dodo's vulgarity, her stupidity, and her inability to realize that her idiotic speeches have no resemblance to wit ensure her status as a permanent alien in the literary world.

In *The Locusts Have No King*, however, the theme of alienation is most important as it relates to the central love story. When by chance Frederick and Lyle reverse their places in society, when Lyle's fortunes decline and Frederick becomes a commercial success, ironically the psychological barriers to their union disappear. Unlike most of Powell's lovers, whose short-term entanglements are motivated by chance, lust, and ambition, Frederick and Lyle prove to be capable of profound attachment, which only grows stronger in the face of change.

The Wicked Pavilion

Even though sexual liaisons are important in Powell's novels, the real action takes place not in bedrooms but in the living rooms and bars where her characters gather. Although the title of her next novel, *The Wicked Pavilion*, is taken from a reference to the Brighton Pavilion in England, Powell's pavilion is simply a New York café, where many of the characters from her preceding books reappear, now older but hardly wiser. The book is carefully crafted, with two plots that are intertwined, both of which depend on frequent appearances in the Café Julien. One of them involves an incomplete love story. Haunted by the memory of his passion for a young woman whom he met at the café during the war, Rick Prescott has returned to search for her and for the happiness he believes that he somehow lost. In developing this plot, Powell again emphasizes the transitory nature of most human relationships, especially love, which, despite lovers' illusions, depends heavily on chance and on the imagination.

The second plot exposes the phoniness of the artistic world. When a painter dies, two of his unsuccessful fellow artists discover that they can make a large amount of money by forging works supposedly painted by him; their scheme is complicated, however, when they find that he is not dead but has pretended to die and is now profiting by the greatly increased value of his old paintings, as well as of the new ones he is producing, which he can market as lost masterpieces. It is evident that Powell is in sympathy with the artists, who on at least one occasion have thus triumphed over the commerciality of art dealers and the arrogant stupidity of art critics.

The Golden Spur

In Powell's final novel, *The Golden Spur*, it is not the artist but the innocent who triumphs over the glittering and corrupt world that Powell knew, loved, and satirized. Again, the title refers to a bar, but in this case the reference is not oblique. The Golden Spur is indeed the name of a bar that has a special significance to a young man from the Midwest. In her youth, his mother, then Constance (Connie) Birch, had come to New York as a real innocent, had fallen in love with the city and with one of its residents, and then, pregnant, had returned to Ohio to marry an unsuspecting flour salesman named John Jaimison. Now another innocent, Connie's son, has come to New York.

In his response to the city, the son is like his mother. Within eighteen hours he is hopelessly in love with it. Unlike her, however, he is not destined to become a victim. As he seeks out the various men mentioned in his mother's diaries, any of whom might possibly be his father, he finds that instead of being horrified at the prospect of scandal, they are all pleased. Even those who cannot remember Connie would like to talk themselves into the memory of an affair with her, which could have produced this appealing son. Yet the prospective son is less than enthusiastic about the various candidates, who, though they may be rich and famous, do not live up to the dream father who has appeared in his imagination.

Certainly, Powell is pointing out that reality rarely equals illusion. In this final book, however, there is a special significance in Jonathan's disenchantment. Like Powell herself, in her sixties at the time *The Golden Spur* appeared, the people of the magic circle have aged, and the old New York is dead. At the end of *The Wicked Pavilion*, the Café Julien was torn down; at the end of *The Golden Spur*, an artist insists that the real money of the twenty-first century will be not in creation but in demolition. His ambition does not stop with seedy hotels and run-down cafés; he yearns to take the big ball to the Metropolitan Museum of Art. Thus, Powell's final book does not mark merely the end of a young man's dream; it commemorates the end of the world Powell knew.

In Robert van Gelder's book of interviews, *Writers and Writing* (1946), Powell answered the repeated criticism of her work—that she did not deal with significant people—by pointing out that most people have no real goals in life. The answer was that of a realist. Still, she might better have appealed to the standards of her genre. The satirist causes readers to laugh at people, not to revere them. In her last and best novels, Powell points out the follies and the vices of New Yorkers like those she knew: the vulnerable or vulgar innocence of newcomers, the desperate need of the alien to become accepted, the misuse of reason to justify lust and ambition, the betrayal of love and friendship, and above all, the enslavement to greed.

It is appropriate that Powell has had a revival. Certainly she immortalized a society forever gone, but more important, she created characters whose weaknesses are all too universally human.

Rosemary M. Canfield Reisman

Other major works

Short fiction: *Sunday, Monday, and Always*, 1952; *Dawn Powell at Her Best*, 1994 (Tim Page, editor).

Plays: *Big Night*, pr. 1933; *Jig Saw: A Comedy*, pr., pb. 1934; *The Lady Comes Across*, pr. 1941; *Four Plays*, 1999 (Michael Sexton and Tim Page, editors).

Nonfiction: *The Diaries of Dawn Powell, 1931-1965*, 1995 (Page, editor); *Selected Letters of Dawn Powell, 1913-1965*, 1999 (Tim Page, editor).

Bibliography

Levy, Barbara. "Forerunners: Dorothy Parker, Dawn Powell, Betty MacDonald." In *Ladies Laughing: Wit as Control in Contemporary American Women Writers*. Amsterdam: Gordon and Breach, 1997. Levy analyzes the use of wit in the works of seven contemporary American writers. The study includes a biographical chapter about Powell.

Page, Tim. *Dawn Powell: A Biography.* New York: Holt, 1998. Page, one of Powell's finest critics and the major force behind her literary resurrection, provides the first comprehensive account of her life and work. Includes detailed notes and an extensive bibliography.

Rice, Marcelle Smith. *Dawn Powell.* New York: Twayne, 2000. More of an overview than a traditional biography, this book concentrates on Powell's novels, their creation, and their relation to the author's life experiences. Includes an index and bibliographical references.

Rovit, Earl. "A Memorable Reality." *Sewanee Review* 110, no. 2 (Spring, 2002). An overview of Powell's life and literary career, discussing the work that Powell herself described as her "Ohio novels" and her "New York stories." Rovit speculates on why Powell never attained significant success as a novelist.

Vidal, Gore. "Dawn Powell, the American Writer." *The New York Review of Books*, November 5, 1987. This essay, which also serves as the introduction to the Vintage Press editions of *Angels on Toast*, *The Golden Spur*, and *The Wicked Pavilion*, is an important work of Powell criticism. In it, Vidal summarizes Powell's life, suggests reasons for her obscurity, presents a chronological summary of her novels, and discusses her importance to American literature.

_______. "Dawn Powell: Queen of the Golden Age." In *The Last Empire: Essays, 1992-2000.* New York: Doubleday, 2001. Vidal admired Powell and called her America's "best mid-century novelist." This analysis of her work is included in his collection of essays about literature, politics, and American society and culture.

Wetzsteon, Ross. *Republic of Dreams: Greenwich Village, the American Bohemia, 1910-1960.* New York: Simon & Schuster, 2002. Wetzsteon recounts the history of the New York City neighborhood in the chapter "Dawn Powell: The Village as an Idea of Itself." Recounts stories about some of Greenwich Village's most creative residents, including Powell, Eugene O'Neill, and Edna St. Vincent Millay.

Wilson, Edmund. "Greenwich Village in the 50's." *The New Yorker*, November 17, 1962. A review of *The Golden Spur* by one of the literary giants who shared Powell's world. Wilson compares her genius to that of Anthony Powell, Evelyn Waugh, and Muriel Spark.

Wilson, Edmund, and Leon Edel, eds. *The Thirties: From Notebooks and Diaries of the Period.* New York: Farrar, Straus and Giroux, 1980. An excellent source, not only because of the references to Powell but also because it provides a full picture of the period in which she lived. Edel's introduction is also illuminating. Includes illustrations.

FRANCINE PROSE

Born: Brooklyn, New York; April 1, 1947

PRINCIPAL LONG FICTION

Judah the Pious, 1973
The Glorious Ones, 1974
Marie Laveau, 1977
Animal Magnetism, 1978
Household Saints, 1981
Hungry Hearts, 1983
Bigfoot Dreams, 1986
Primitive People, 1992
Hunters and Gatherers, 1995
Guided Tours of Hell: Novellas, 1997 (includes *Guided Tours of Hell* and *Three Pigs in Five Days*)
Blue Angel, 2000
A Changed Man, 2005
Goldengrove, 2008

OTHER LITERARY FORMS

Francine Prose is a prolific writer who, in addition to her novels, has published critically acclaimed short stories, translations, children's books, collections of Jewish folktales, and essays that explore topics that range widely from art history and the power of writing to gluttony. Over the course of her career as a writer, Prose has published articles, stories, and book reviews in numerous magazines and journals as diverse as *Hudson Review*, *The Atlantic Monthly*, *The New Yorker*, *People*, *Redbook*, *The New York Times Book Review*, *The New Republic*, *Yale Review*, and *Art News*, among others. She has written several novels for young adults, including *After* (2003) and *Bullyville* (2007), which deal with the pervasiveness of violence in American society and explore themes of power, authority, and security.

Prose has contributed to Oxford University Press's series of books on the seven deadly sins with the satiric volume *Gluttony* (2003), and her books *Caravaggio: Painter of Miracles* (2005) and *The Lives of the Muses: Nine Women and the Artists They Inspired* (2002) not only offer powerful insights into artists and their worlds but also provide moving meditations on the nature of art and on the little-explored role of women in the history of art. In *Reading Like a Writer: A Guide for People Who Love Books and for Those Who Want to Write Them* (2006), Prose invites readers to explore with her the writings of Jane Austen, Marcel Proust, Charles Dickens, Gustave Flaubert, and others as a way of demonstrating that becoming a good writer requires being a close and observant reader. Prose's nonfiction is marked by the same close observation of the world that characterizes her novels.

Achievements

From the beginning of her career, Francine Prose has been critically acclaimed as a splendid writer and often regarded by critics as a prophet for her wise and deep social observation. She has won four Pushcart Prizes for her short stories, and many of her books, novels and nonfiction, have been national best sellers. Her first novel, *Judah the Pious*, was awarded the Jewish Book Council Award for 1973. Two years later, in 1975, she was *Mademoiselle* magazine's Mademoiselle Award winner and was recognized as one of "Twelve Women Working to Make Things Better" in an article accompanying the announcement of the award.

Prose often gets her inspiration from her travels, and in 1989 she was awarded a Fulbright grant for travel to Yugoslavia. She won grants from the National Endowment for the Arts in 1979 and 1985, and she received a Guggenheim Fellowship in 1991. Her contribution to children's literature was recognized when she received the Sydney Taylor Award for books for younger children. Prose's novel *Blue Angel* was a finalist for the National Book Award in 2000, and her young adult novel *After* was nominated for the Los Angeles Times Book Prize in 2003. Prose was awarded the first Dayton Literary Peace Prize in fiction for her novel *A Changed Man* in 2006. The film adaptation of her novel *Household Saints*, starring Tracey Ullman and directed by Nancy Savoca, was released in 1993.

Biography

Francine Prose began reading when she was four years old and never stopped. She has told numerous interviewers that the only reason she wanted to become a writer was that she was such an avid reader and that she could not imagine any other career. Born on April 1, 1947, in Brooklyn, New York, to two physicians, Philip Prose and Jessie Rubin Prose, the young Francine grew up listening to her father discuss medical cases with his colleagues. She learned the knack of narrative storytelling from these sessions, and she also learned how to be closely observant of details from her parents. In addition, she developed her keen ear and eye by paying close attention to the lives of her family's neighbors and to the larger social world in which she grew up.

Prose graduated summa cum laude with a bachelor's degree in English in 1968 from Radcliffe College. In 1969, she entered an M.A. program at Harvard, but she soon grew tired of the claustrophobic atmosphere there. In 1971, she left the program to travel for almost a year in Bombay (now Mumbai), India, where she read the classic novels of authors from Fyodor Dostoevski to Marcel Proust. During that year, she scrapped the autobiographical novel on which she had been working and started writing what would become her first published novel, *Judah the Pious*. After that novel appeared, her career as a writer was launched, and she never looked back, producing a new book almost every three years and also writing articles and stories.

In 1976, Prose married Howard "Howie" Michaels, an artist and sculptor. The couple's first son, Bruno, was born in 1978, and their second, Leon, was born in 1982. After Leon's birth, Prose embarked on a teaching career, and, between 1982 and 1989, she taught at the University of Arizona, the Iowa Writers' Workshop, Sarah Lawrence College, the Bread Loaf Writers' Conference, and the Sewanee Writers' Conference. During these years she continued to write and publish novels, including *Household Saints*, *Hungry Hearts*, and *Bigfoot Dreams*. In 1999, Prose was a director's fellow at the New York Public Library's Center for Scholars and Writers, and she has been a fellow of the New York Institute of the Humanities. She continues to teach and has held the position of visiting professor of literature at Bard College. In 2007, she became president of the PEN/American Center in New York.

Analysis

In her book *Reading Like a Writer*, Francine Prose provides some insights into her own life as a writer as she analyzes the writings of other writers she admires. Reading and rereading writers whom she loves—Dostoevski, Flaubert, Austen, Dickens, Philip Roth, Franz Kafka—Prose admits that writing, like reading, puts every word on trial for its life. Much as she reads her favorite writers closely for the ways they use words and language, in writing her own novels Prose weighs every word, every phrase, for the way it tells the story, the way it expresses emotions, the way it shocks or surprises a reader, the way it elicits a snicker or a belly laugh, the way it haunts the spirit, or the way it evokes the beauty of the world and the human soul.

In her early fiction, such as *Judah the Pious*, Prose turned a folklorist's eye to the stories of rabbis and their families that she retold in her fiction. She preserved the traditions of these folktales by weaving colorful narratives of the modern world around them. While she has never abandoned the use of these tales in her fiction (she has published several books of them for children), her later novels have focused on the modern world. *Bigfoot Dreams*, for example, features Vera (whose name means "truth"), a writer for a supermarket tabloid who composes stories about UFO sightings, Elvis Presley's being alive and well on Mars, and a ninety-one-year-old woman bearing a child; the novel explores the challenges that writing such fictions presents to Vera's real life. In almost all of Prose's novels, the characters struggle to distinguish between the real world and imaginary worlds, worlds they have very often created for themselves as places of retreat from the real world. In both *Blue Angel* and *Goldengrove*, the main characters often delude themselves about their real lives and create for themselves, if only momentarily, alternate universes in which they feel safe and secure. Much like Kafka, Prose creates a universe in which life is often turned upside down with no reason and in which men and women must right themselves in order to move through life.

Prose's novels also often deal with the spiritual. *Judah the Pious* follows the adventures of the Polish Rabbi Eliezer and his attempts to help his people. *Marie Laveau* chronicles the life of the great New Orleans voodoo queen and her magic. In *Hunters and Gatherers*, Prose narrates the exploits of New Age priestess Isis Moonwagon and her followers, and *Household Saints* recounts the story of a Catholic family striving to understand the ways in which the spiritual impinges on the ordinary. Through the use of satire and comedy, Prose explores the spiritual longings of human beings and their attempts to reconcile those longings with everyday life. Prose's sharp and cunning long fiction provides incisive glimpses into various situations, reflecting the humor, the sorrow, and the pathos in human lives.

HOUSEHOLD SAINTS

Like many of Prose's early writings, *Household Saints* weaves elements of folklore and legend into a tale of revelation and hope. In this stunning novel, Prose captures the intensity of family life lived in close quarters as well as the details that shape the everyday lives of the members of a close-knit social community. Her prose evokes the smells, sights, and sounds of Little Italy in New York in the 1950's so that the setting becomes as much of a character in the novel as the men and women who live on the neighborhood's streets. This splendid little morality tale, as many critics have observed, is reminiscent of the powerful stories of Isak Dinesen and Isaac Bashevis Singer. The novel offers readers a study in character and confronts readers with troublesome questions about the nature of evil, the character of the good, and the promise of hope. Above all, it asks readers to consider the ways in which human beings' mundane lives can be transformed by ancient ways and by something beyond themselves.

The novel opens with the startling and comic assertion that Joseph Santangelo has won his wife, by the grace of God, in a game of pinochle. As in most of the rest of his life, Joseph, a butcher in Little Italy, has had to depend on some power outside himself to help him navigate life's waters. Since he often discovers that little help is forthcoming from those quarters, he cheats his customers at his butcher shop and he cheats at cards. Joseph's mother sees evil in every aspect of the world around her and prays to her saints for good health and wealth from the sausages that her son sells in his store. Joseph's wife, Catherine, is caught between the old world and the new as she tries to teach her daughter, Theresa, the lessons of the saints of old and the lessons the girl will need to survive in the modern world. Theresa, much like her namesake, Theresa of Avila, does discover the ways in which the mundane is infused with the sacred. Although the novel ends in surprising ways, the events depicted confirm that the veneration of everyday objects can keep alive the memory of those household saints who have graced our lives.

Household Saints depicts one family's struggles to reconcile the ordinary and the extraordinary, in this case, the spiritual. Prose offers readers a beautiful little morality tale of despair and hope, loss and redemption, and family and society.

A CHANGED MAN

What happens when a former skinhead walks into a human rights organization and declares that he is a changed man? What happens when this young man declares that he wants to help prevent other young men from making the choices he made in the past? Should the organization be extremely wary and suspicious that the newly changed individual is lying, or should the organization and its founders embrace this person and allow him to work to bring about good in the world? In her typically satiric fashion, Prose raises these and other questions in her often hilarious, and always bitingly incisive, novel *A Changed Man*.

One spring afternoon, young Vincent walks into the offices of World Brotherhood Watch, a human rights organization run by Meyer Maslow, a Holocaust survivor. Vincent, a former neo-Nazi whose arms are covered with Nazi tattoos, claims to have been transformed and wants to change his life. Vincent tells Maslow that he would like to convince other young men not to choose the life of a neo-Nazi but instead to choose a life of moderation and charity. Can Maslow afford to believe him? Vincent appears at a time in Maslow's life when Maslow himself is beginning to question his own effectiveness at stopping intolerance and injustice. As the plot progresses, Vincent begins to transform everyone around him. Much like Albert Camus's Dr. Rieux in *La Peste* (1947; *The Plague*, 1948), Vincent transforms the world around him through his actions and his active commitment to social justice. He is no mere cheerleader for the right ways; rather, he leads others to perform those right actions. Maslow himself is eventually transformed and regains and renews his dedication to bringing an end to anti-Semitism and intolerance. Bonnie Kalen, the fund-raiser for the organization, who has been devoted to Maslow over the years, warily eyes Vincent from the beginning but is won over by his commitment and honesty. Bonnie's son, Danny, also changes his life after an encounter with Vincent.

With her characteristic humor, Prose raises challenging questions about human nature and the nature of the world. Is it possible to overcome evil? Is it possible to change for the good and for that change to last and to influence the lives of others? What is the nature of morality? What does it mean to be human? How can one determine what it means to live a moral life? Prose couches these questions in a fast-paced, satiric narrative that asks readers to consider how they live their own lives.

BLUE ANGEL

From Kingsley Amis's *Lucky Jim* (1954) and Lionel Trilling's *The Middle of the Journey* (1947) to Randall Jarrell's *Pictures from an Institution* (1954) and Richard Russo's *Straight Man* (1997), the academic novel has often comically portrayed the ways in which power relations between professors and students go awry. Most of the main characters in these novels are older males who take advantage of younger female students who have become enamored of them. These professors find themselves losing not only their sexual fire but also their desire for the subjects about which they were once passionate. Prose's *Blue Angel* joins the rank of these campus novels, but her novel is more than simply a story about the lust of an older professor for a younger student; it revolves around themes of loneliness and insecurity. In this work Prose also explores the banality of an educational system that at once encourages such relationships by the passions inherent in its very structure and condemns these dynamic relationships through static sets of rules that do not account for human passions.

Ted Swenson, a professor of creative writing at a small, rural New England college, is going through the motions of teaching and writing. It has been years since he has written a novel, and his fame has steadily declined as his name has disappeared from the bookstore shelves. His new class is more frustrating than exciting, and most of his students are writing stories about having sex with dead animals. Living with his wife in an isolated wooded area near the campus and estranged from his only child, Swenson exists in a bubble, striving vainly now and then to work on a new novel and to impart some wisdom to his students. His life is revived by one of those students, Angela Argo, a purple-haired waif whose own novel seduces Swenson with its mature prose and its depiction of a relationship between an older man and a younger woman. As Angela seeks his help with her novel, Swenson becomes more and more entangled in a web of lust and infatuation. Filled with stereotypical characters from a college campus—the haughty dean, the feminist English professor, the English professor who tried to live as if his real life were determined by the elements of literary theory—*Blue Angel* is a compelling satire of academic novels as well as an examination of loss and loneliness.

Prose ingeniously takes Josef von Sternberg's 1930 movie *The Blue Angel*, starring Marlene Dietrich, as the model for her campus novel. In the film, an older professor becomes so enamored of a burlesque dancer that he loses everything. In Prose's novel, Swenson watches this film over and over for some clue to his own demise and ponders how one man can so easily lose everything in the quest for the unreachable. Unlike other campus novels, Prose's novel astutely explores the challenges of life in an artificial environment such as a college campus and the foibles of the men and women who live there.

GOLDENGROVE

Coming of age in a small town where everyone knows your every move is hard enough to do, but coming of age in such an environment grows even harder when you must face that experience without your best friend, who has died unexpectedly. Such is the life that thirteen-year-old Nico must face in Prose's novel *Goldengrove*. One Sunday in early May, Nico and her older sister, Margaret, are spending the afternoon lazily drifting on Mirror Lake, as they have on many Sunday afternoons before. The novel's opening sentence almost warns of the ominous events to follow, for Nico reflects that for many years her and her sister's lives were as calm and transparent as the waters. On this Sunday afternoon, the waters open to swallow Margaret forever—she drowns while making the short swim back to the dock near their house. Suddenly, Nico must navigate life's rough waters alone, and she struggles to understand the mysteries of life and death that have left her alone and that have snatched her sister from her.

Nico's mother escapes into drugs and drink as she tries to blunt her feelings of loss, and

Nico's father, who runs a bookstore called Goldengrove in their town, retreats into his attempts to write a novel about an apocalyptic religious sect. Both parents are so engrossed in their own grief that neither can help Nico with her own struggles. Seeking refuge from the tragedy that has changed her life, Nico starts to hang around with Margaret's boyfriend, Aaron, as both of them try to grow closer to her dead sister. In a summer full of halting attempts to recover from her monumental loss, Nico learns about the inadequacy of love, the disappointments of hope, the shortcomings of family and friends, and the insufficiency of both emotional and rational responses to loss.

Prose wrote *Goldengrove* as her own mother was dying (the novel is dedicated to her) and as she was struggling with her own losses. The novel takes its name from Gerard Manley Hopkins's poem "Spring and Fall: To a Young Child," which features a young woman whose mourning over the falling of leaves in Goldengrove is actually a mourning over the loss of her youth. Prose effectively uses this poem as a springboard into an extended meditation on a young girl's realization that she is alone in this world and must face its joys and sorrows without the consolation of her parents or her friends.

Henry L. Carrigan, Jr.

OTHER MAJOR WORKS

SHORT FICTION: *Women and Children First, and Other Stories*, 1988; *The Peaceable Kingdom*, 1993.

NONFICTION: *The Lives of the Muses: Nine Women and the Artists They Inspired*, 2002; *Gluttony: The Seven Deadly Sins*, 2003; *Sicilian Odyssey*, 2003; *Caravaggio: Painter of Miracles*, 2005; *Reading Like a Writer: A Guide for People Who Love Books and for Those Who Want to Write Them*, 2006.

TRANSLATIONS: *A Scrap of Time, and Other Stories*, 1987 (with Madeline Levine; of Ida Fink's novel); *The Journey*, 1992 (with Johanna Weschler; of Fink's novel).

CHILDREN'S/YOUNG ADULT LITERATURE: *Stories from Our Living Past*, 1974; *Dybbuk: A Story Made in Heaven*, 1996; *The Angel's Mistake: Stories of Chelm*, 1997; *You Never Know: A Legend of the Lamedvavniks*, 1998; *The Demon's Mistake: A Story from Chelm*, 2000; *After*, 2003; *Leopold, the Liar of Leipzig*, 2005; *Bullyville*, 2007; *Touch*, 2009.

EDITED TEXTS: *The "Mrs. Dalloway" Reader*, 2003; *Best New American Voices, 2005*, 2004.

BIBLIOGRAPHY

Aarons, Victoria. "Responding to an Old Story: Susan Fromberg, Leslea Newman, and Francine Prose." In *Daughters of Valor: Contemporary Jewish American Writers*, edited by Jay L. Halia and Ben Siegel. Newark: University of Delaware Press, 1997. Helpful essay explores the works of Prose and two other writers and discusses these authors' canny abilities to retell Jewish folktales for a new generation of children.

Hogan, Randolph. "The Butcher Won a Wife." Review of *Household Saints*, by Francine Prose. *The New York Times Book Review*, July 12, 1981. Positive review provides an overview of the novel and praises Prose as a splendid writer.

Hooper, Brad. Review of *Blue Angel*, by Francine Prose. *Booklist* 96, no. 16 (April 15, 2000). Positive review observes that Prose breathes new life into the standard story of academe.

Maslin, Janet. "An Aura of Grief Surrounds a Stunned Family." Review of *Goldengrove*, by Francine Prose. *The New York Times*, September 11, 2008. Thoughtful review describes *Goldengrove* as one of Prose's gentler books and praises Prose's "mostly effortless narrative verve."

Nebroso, Donna L. Review of *Household Saints*, by Francine Prose. *Library Journal* 106, no. 11 (June 1, 1981). Describes the novel as a simple but powerful tale that elevates the commonplace into the mythic.

Potok, Rena. "Francine Prose." In *Jewish-American Women Writers: A Bio-Bibliographical and Critical Sourcebook*, edited by Sara R. Horowitz. Westport, Conn.: Greenwood Press, 1994. Informative article provides a biographical sketch and offers an overview of Prose's early work.

Prose, Francine. "Francine Prose." Interview by Mickey Pearlman. In *Inter/View: Talks with America's Writing Women*, edited by Mickey Pearlman and Katherine Usher Henderson. Lexington: University of Kentucky Press, 1990. Prose discusses her early novels and stories and provides insights into her writing methods.

Publishers Weekly. Review of *Household Saints*, by Francine Prose. May 8, 1981. Positive review summarizes the novel and praises Prose for her insight into families and their shortcomings.

Tierney, William G. "Interpreting Academic Identities: Reality and Fiction on Campus." *Journal of Higher Education* 73, no. 1 (January, 2002): 161-173. Compares Prose's *Blue Angel* with two other campus novels, Philip Roth's *The Human Stain* (2000) and Saul Bellow's *Ravelstein* (2000), and describes Prose's novel as a masterpiece of comic despair.

FRANÇOIS RABELAIS

Born: La Devinière, near Chinon, France; c. 1494
Died: Paris, France; April, 1553

PRINCIPAL LONG FICTION

Pantagruel, 1532 (English translation, 1653)
Gargantua, 1534 (English translation, 1653)
Tiers Livre, 1546 (*Third Book*, 1693)
Le Quart Livre, incomplete 1548, complete 1552 (*Fourth Book*, 1694)
Le Cinquième Livre, 1564 (*Fifth Book*, 1694)
Gargantua et Pantagruel, 1567 (includes all previous titles; *Gargantua and Pantagruel*, 1653-1694, 1929)

OTHER LITERARY FORMS

In preparation for his doctoral degree, François Rabelais (RAHB-uh-lay) composed commentaries on the *Aphorisms* of Hippocrates and the *Ars medicinalis* of Galen in editions of these works that Rabelais published in 1532. After his first trip to Rome, he edited a *Topographia antiquae Romae*, based on a work by Bartolome Marliani, which was published by Sébastien Gryphe in 1534. *La Sciomachie et festins* (simulated combats and feasts), published in Lyons by Gryphe in 1549, also refers to Rabelais's journeys. It is also known that Rabelais composed poetry. Many of his letters, especially letters that he wrote while in Rome, are available in various editions.

ACHIEVEMENTS

With François Rabelais, French literature entered into a new phase. After the great medieval epics and romances of the twelfth and thirteenth centuries, there had been a steady decline until the sixteenth century. In France, the new learning brought about by the rediscovery of ancient Greek manuscripts, the invention of printing, and the great voyages of discovery found its first expression in Rabelais. *Gargantua and Pantagruel* breathes the spirit of enthusiasm, liberation, and discovery that inspired the rebirth of culture and learning.

Nevertheless, there is in Rabelais much of the medieval. In fact, he chose as his inspiration a book popular at the time, *Grandes et inestimables cronicques du grant et énorme géant Gargantua* (1532; great and inestimable chronicles of the great and enormous giant Gargantua), based on the story of a giant associated with King Arthur, Merlin, Morgan, and Mélusine. Rabelais proposed a sequel in which he continued the popular comic of the *cronicques*. He enriched his legend with notes on history, geography, local custom, and theater; his is a Renaissance interpretation of a medieval carnival.

As the critic Jean Plattard noted, Rabelais maintained the medieval spirit of the farces

François Rabelais
(Library of Congress)

and fabliaux in his violent imagery, his vulgarity, and his preoccupation with sexual matters. At the same time, Rabelais introduced the spirit of the Renaissance with his rejection of Scholasticism, his confidence in antiquity, his faith in science, and his belief in human progress.

Rabelais did not write a novel in the modern sense of the word, nor did he intend to compose one. As Jacques Boulenger observed, Rabelais wanted to embroider a vast canvas both with fantasies and with scenes from real life; in his encyclopedic ambition, he was typical of the Renaissance. Rabelais's achievement lies above all in his style, in a remarkable exploitation of all the possibilities of language. His giants are polyglots, and so is their creator. He uses French and Latin with ease; he creates words in torrents. He is equally adept in dialect, patois, argot, and scientific terminology. Boulenger described Rabelais's styles as "verbal intoxication in the dionysiac sense," yet when the occasion demands, as in the description of Badebec's death, Rabelais is a master of economy. The first French prose writer with genuine artistic talent and one of the greatest examples of the *esprit gaulois* found in the *Roman de Renart* (c. 1175-1205), the fabliaux, Molière, and Voltaire, Rabelais was truly a turning point in French literature.

Biography

Much of François Rabelais's biography is lost in obscurity, but modern scholars have established the principal events of his life. The year of Rabelais's birth, believed to be 1494, is still uncertain, but it is known that his father, Antoine, was a lawyer at the royal court of Chinon and was associated with the most enlightened men of his day. Rabelais spent his childhood at Chinon, especially at the family's country home, La Devinière, often mentioned in his works, and at Angers, his mother's birthplace. He was probably educated at the Benedictine abbey of Seuillé, evoked in Friar John's monastery in *Gargantua and Pantagruel.*

By 1521, Rabelais was a Franciscan monk at Fontenay-le-Comte in Bas Poitou; it was there that he met Pierre Amy, one of the outstanding Hellenists of the time, and entered into correspondence with the eminent French Hellenist Guillaume Budé. Rabelais translated some of Herodotus from Greek into Latin, and also contributed to André Tiraqueau's treatise on the laws of marriage, "De legibus connubialibus," echoes of which appear in book 3.

In 1523, the Greek books of the monastery were confiscated under orders from the Sorbonne, and shortly afterward Rabelais transferred to the Benedictines of Saint-Pierre-de-Maillezain, where he came into contact with the scholarly bishop Geoffroy d'Estissac. In 1527, Rabelais left the monastery and toured the same universities his Pantagruel visits in book 2. In 1532, he received his bachelor's degree in medicine from the University of Montpellier and assumed a post in Lyons, at that time the capital of the Renaissance. He also continued his classical commentaries and the same year published *Pantagruel*, censured by the Sorbonne for obscenity. Jean du Bellay, bishop of Paris, became Rabelais's protector in 1534, taking him to Rome as his personal physician. It was upon Rabelais's return that he published *Gargantua*, likewise censured because of its unfortunate coincidence with the Affair of the Placards.

Rabelais attempted briefly the life of a secular priest; by 1537, he was a doctor of medicine in Lyons. In 1541, he published a new edition of *Gargantua and Pantagruel*, with the attacks against the Sorbonne expurgated. The publication of book 3 in 1546 still provoked censure, as did that of the complete book 4 in 1552. His later days included more travel in Italy, especially with du Bellay. It is fairly certain that Rabelais died in Paris, at the beginning of April, 1553.

Analysis

François Rabelais is universally regarded as one of the major figures in the Western literary tradition, in the company of Dante, Geoffrey Chaucer, William Shakespeare, and Miguel de Cervantes, yet he is more often praised than read. Indeed, in the judgment of scholar Mikhail Bakhtin, "Of all the great writers of world literature, Rabelais is the least popular, the least understood and appreciated."

The difficulty of Rabelais, the quality that discourages many modern readers from making headway in his work, is not the strategic obscurity of a James Joyce or an Ezra Pound; rather, it resembles the difficulty that one experiences in "getting" a joke, the humor of which is not immediately apparent. To read Rabelais is essentially to laugh, but humor is notoriously elusive, dependent on a wide range of local cultural assumptions and linguistic practices and thus quick to be lost in time and in translation. Here, there is a comparison with Shakespeare: One vein of Shakespearean humor, closely related to the humor of Rabelais, is accessible to the modern reader only via scholarly explication of wordplay, allusions, implicit cultural assumptions, and so on, but Shakespeare remains highly readable even when many of his bawdy puns, for example, are entirely missed.

The difficulty in grasping the spirit of Rabelais's jokes, their underlying intent, is confirmed by ongoing critical debate. Even such a fundamental issue as Rabelais's attitude toward Christianity and the Church has been the subject of bitter controversy. Throughout *Gargantua and Pantagruel* there are frequent satiric jabs at the rites and institutions of the Church. While Rabelais ridicules monasticism and the Papacy, however, and while his parodies of Christian ritual could be deemed sacrilegious if not blasphemous, he stops short of the open atheism of the Enlightenment.

Critics such as Abel Lefranc have argued that Rabelais was in fact a thoroughgoing rationalist who, unable to express his convictions openly, presented them in a humorous guise. According to such critics, Rabelais thus anticipated the skepticism of the Enlightenment. On the other hand, critics such as Lucien Febvre, who devoted a massive volume to a refutation of Lefranc, have argued that Rabelais's satire was directed against institutional abuses of the Church, not against the heart of Christian belief.

Although such questions may never be definitively resolved, one helpful approach to Rabelais's humor is that taken by Bakhtin, who places Rabelais in what he calls the carnival tradition, a tradition of folk humor with roots in the ancient past, encompassing such festivities as the Roman Saturnalia and still vital in the Middle Ages: "Celebrations of a carnival type represented a considerable part of the life of medieval men, even in the time given over to them. Large medieval cities devoted an average of three months a year to these festivities."

Bakhtin suggests that it is Rabelais's indebtedness to this folk tradition, an expression of popular culture still largely unexplored by literary scholars, that accounts for the relative failure of modern readers to appreciate his work. In the carnival atmosphere, all of the sacred values of medieval society were parodied in a ritualistic manner—often with the full participation of the clergy. Rabelais's humor is thus characterized by the systematic inversion typical of carnival: parody, blasphemy, gross physical images, and so on.

By placing *Gargantua and Pantagruel* in this context, Bakhtin shifts the emphasis from an interpretation of Rabelais's values—that is, the personal beliefs informing his work—to the folk tradition of which his work was the supreme expression even as it marked the decisive break between the Renaissance and the Middle Ages.

GARGANTUA AND PANTAGRUEL

Rabelais's Renaissance spirit is nowhere more apparent than in his style, an overflowing fountain of verbal exuberance, a rich compound of slang, odd words, jargon of the various professions, interminable lists, and other heterogeneous elements. *Gargantua and Pantagruel* is full of puns that are difficult to translate: *service du vin/service divin* (the wine service/the divine service); Grandgousier's name, from *Que grand tu as (gosier)* (What a big gullet you have); or Epistemon, who has *la coupe têtée* (his chop headed off).

This exuberance is also evident in Rabelais's characterizations. Although he created types rather than flesh-and-blood people, his characters are unforgettable. Grandgousier, the progenitor of the illustrious family of giants, is the most shadowy. He appears as the noble lord, just and forgiving after the Picrocholine Wars and a good father to Gargantua. His son is curious, witty, garrulous, and loving. After the beginning of book 2, Grandgousier appears rarely, but always with concern for his son. Pantagruel, Gargantua's son, is the real hero of the story. After a well-delineated education, he becomes a kind lord, and his earlier wit changes to wisdom. Perhaps the best-portrayed characters are Friar John and Panurge. Friar John is the garrulous monk who always has something of the cloister about him; kind, generous, and witty, he enlivens all the adventures from the Picrocholine Wars to the voyage for the Divine Bottle. Panurge, the perpetual trickster and inventor of farces, changes his character in book 3 to that of a man caught in a dilemma: to marry or not to marry? To choose action or inaction? There are few female characters in *Gargantua and Pantagruel*; they are limited to Gargamelle, Grandgousier's wife, and Badebec, Gargantua's wife, who dies as she is giving birth to Pantagruel. Basically, the story is a very masculine one; as in the medieval farces, women are little more than bearers of children and objects of sexual desire.

GARGANTUA

Although published two years after *Pantagruel*, in 1534, *Gargantua* is known as book 1 because of its chronology. Gargantua is the father of Pantagruel, and the book tells of his miraculous birth, adolescence, education, and maturity. The prologue describes a *silenus*, a little box for rare drugs, which Rabelais compares to Socrates, and indeed to his own work: ugly from the outside but precious on the inside.

After Rabelais has made a Genesis-like presentation of Gargantua's genealogy, birth, and naming, the reader learns his first words: *à boire* (drink), symbolic of the thirst of the Renaissance man for the new learning. Much of book 1 is concerned with education; the critic Thomas M. Greene considers its essential theme to be the process of development in the young giant as he progresses from the "random equality of childhood experience . . . to poise and sophistication without losing his capacity for naïve joy." First educated in a haphazard manner by the Sophists, he is purged by Ponocrates and learns more by ear than by eye to integrate all activities—physical, mental, and spiritual—and grow from chaos to discipline and from ignorance to truth and justice.

A lengthy episode treats the wars between Picrochole, King of Lerné, and Grandgousier, Gargantua's father, a noble and peace-loving lord. Lefranc sees historical and biographical material in this unjust war, as it takes place around La Roche-Clamard, near Seuillé, in Rabelais's native Chinon. As the war progresses, Friar John of the Funnels, the vibrant and impetuous monk, becomes Grandgousier's staunch ally. In the words and actions of Friar John, one finds some of Rabelais's finest satire of the monastic life he knew so well.

In recompense for his help in the war won by Grandgousier, Friar John receives the Abbey of Thélème, Rabelais's ideal for an elite community. This semiutopian monastery, modeled on the château of Bonnivet, admits both men and women of outstanding physical and moral traits, inviting them to spend their time in pursuit of culture and eventually to leave and marry. It is governed by only one rule: "Fay ce que voudras" (do what you wish). An enigmatic inscription in poetry concludes the book and invites the reader to continue the search for truth in the Renaissance spirit.

PANTAGRUEL

Book 2, *Pantagruel*, is the least coherent of the first four volumes. It reveals the author's unmistakable style and wit and gives promise of more adventures in the future. As in *Gargantua*, Rabelais traces the genealogy of Pantagruel in a burlesque parody of the Bible and Pliny the Elder's *Natural History* (77 C.E.), as he emphasizes his hero's gigantic appetite and prodigious strength. Because Pantagruel will later liberate himself and others from the bonds of ignorance, he frees himself as a child from the constraint of his cradle.

Education plays an important role here also, especially in chapter 8, in which Gargantua tells his son Pantagruel to become "an abyss of knowledge." Pantagruel also tours the famous universities of his day: Toulouse, a center of dance and fencing; Montepellier, noted for its wine; Avignon, for its women; Bourges, for its poor laws; and Angers, which he avoids because it is infested with the plague. He visits libraries, which Rabelais uses to satirize many spiritual texts and the immoral lives of those who read them.

In book 2, Pantagruel meets Panurge, who is to become his friend for life. Panurge is one of a long line of picaros; he introduces himself in many languages, a performance typical of his pranks, which, as Greene observes, "mingle in various measures humor, cunning, perversity, creative inspiration and malice." Rabelais describes Panurge as proper-looking, a bit of a lecher, always short of money (which he always finds by cunningly perpetrated larceny), and a perpetual trickster. His clever and often crude tricks form much of the wit of books 2 and 4.

In the courtly tradition, Panurge and Pantagruel go off to battle in Utopia, where Gargantua has been transferred by the fairy Morgue. Rabelais seems to return to the spirit of the *cronicques* as he ends his disjointed but highly original portrayal of the giants.

In contrast to the looseness of book 2, book 3 is the most unified of the entire series. In the prologue, Rabelais compares himself to Diogenes, who, though physically unfit for war, rolled his tub so as not to appear lazy. In the first six chapters, Panurge appears as the traditional spendthrift; having inherited an estate, he rapidly squanders his inheritance on feasting. In the remainder of the book, he engages in lengthy discussions on whether to marry. Many critics trace Rabelais's treatment of marriage and cuckoldry in book 3 to the medieval farces; others, such as Greene, see the search for truth and the importance of action as forming the real subject of the book.

Panurge consults various sources to resolve his dilemma: the *sortes vergilianae* (a book of Vergil opened at random), a fortune-teller, the poet Raminagrobis, the magician Herr Trippa. All give him the same response: If he marries, he will be cuckolded, beaten, and robbed. The theologian Hippothadée encourages him to choose someone like Solomon's "valiant woman"; the doctor Rondibilis tells him of woman's foibles; the philosopher Trouillogan has no definite answer. After a final consultation with the fool Triboulet, no more satisfactory than all the others, Pantagruel convinces Panurge to consult the Oracle of the Divine Bottle in Cathay. Thus, the stage is set for the adventures that occupy books 4 and 5.

In book 4, inspired by the accounts of navigation so prominent at the time, especially those of Jacques Cartier, Rabelais composed the travelogue or odyssey of his heroes—a fantastic account of imaginary places and allegorical people, filled with the marvelous and touching on science fiction, such as the frozen words that melt and begin to speak. There are many realistic allusions to Rabelais's own day, such as the Decretals, the base of canonical jurisprudence; the officers of law and justice, portrayed in the Chicanous; and the wars between Protestants and Catholics, symbolized by the battle with the Andouilles.

Rabelais also satirizes perennial vices such as gluttony and its opposite, a sterile asceticism based on pride rather than on genuine piety. Panurge reassumes the character of the trickster and in a famous episode drowns the sheep of the avaricious merchant Dindenault. The travelers have not reached the Divine Bottle by the end of book 4, but Rabelais's imagination and invention are here at their height.

Originally published posthumously as *L'Isle sonante* in 1562, book 5 differs so radically from the preceding ones that critics today still question its authenticity; it is bitter, rambling, and far less creative than its predecessors. In it, the story of the navigation continues through many more fantastic islands.

The Isle Sonante (ringing island), with its perpetually clanging bells, is inhabited by birds that resemble men and women and whose names refer to the clergy and members of religious orders. The Chats-fourrés (furry cats) are the officers of the Parlement of Paris, who refused Michel de l'Hospital's proposal for an edict of toleration for the Protestants. The Apedeftes, or ignoramuses, are the tax collectors and clerks in the counting houses.

After many other such adventures, the travelers finally reach the Divine Bottle and admire the magnificent temple in which it is located. The priestess Bacbuc invites Panurge to hear the long-awaited pronouncement, which consists of one word: "Drink." The priestess has another word of wisdom: *in vino veritas* (in wine is truth). The engimatic conclusion has as many interpretations as there are critics, for essentially it tells readers to interpret their own destinies for themselves.

Irma M. Kashuba

OTHER MAJOR WORKS

NONFICTION: *La Sciomachie et festins*, 1549.

EDITED TEXTS: *Aphorisms*, 1532; *Ars medicinalis*, 1532; *Topographia antiquae Romae*, 1534.

MISCELLANEOUS: *Pantagruéline Prognostication*, 1532 (occasional verses and letters).

BIBLIOGRAPHY

Berry, Alice Fiola. *The Charm of Catastrophe: A Study of Rabelais's "Quart Livre."* Chapel Hill: University of North Carolina, Department of Romance Languages, 2000. Analyzes *Le Quart Livre*, the last novel by Rabelais published in the author's lifetime, demonstrating how the work expresses the elderly writer's despair over failing to achieve his youthful dreams.

Bowen, Barbara C. *Enter Rabelais, Laughing*. Nashville: Vanderbilt University Press, 1998. Focuses on the humor in Rabelais's work, describing why it was funny to his sixteenth century contemporaries and placing him within the tradition of Renaissance comic writings. Includes notes and bibliography.

Carron, Jean-Claude, ed. *François Rabelais: Critical Assessments*. Baltimore: Johns Hopkins University Press, 1995. Selection and revision of papers concerning Rabelais that were delivered at a 1991 symposium at the University of California, Los Angeles. Among the topics addressed are realism, feminism, and cultural connections in Rabelais's works.

Chesney, Elizabeth A., and Marcel Tetel. *Rabelais Revisited*. New York: Twayne, 1993. Provides a good introduction to the novels, with an annotated bibliography of important studies on Rabelais. Examines the relationships between men and women in Rabelais's works.

Coleman, Dorothy Gabe. *Rabelais: A Critical Study in Prose Fiction*. New York: Cambridge University Press, 1971. Presents a meticulous analysis of Rabelais as a prose stylist and of the genres in which he wrote. Includes bibliography.

Frame, Donald M. *François Rabelais: A Study*. New York: Harcourt Brace Jovanovich, 1977. Detailed study of Rabelais's life and work includes several chapters on his major fiction and on topics such as obscenity, comedy, satire, fantasy, storytelling, giantism, humanism, evangelism, characters, and fortunes in Rabelais's writings. Supplemented with detailed notes and an annotated bibliography.

Gauna, Max. *The Rabelaisian Mythologies*. Madison, N.J.: Fairleigh Dickinson University Press, 1996. Rabelais described his novels as "mythologies," and this study analyzes the mythological elements in *Pantagruel*, *Gargantua*, *Tiers Livre*, and *Le Quart Livre*. Includes bibliography.

Greene, Thomas M. *Rabelais: A Study in Comic Courage*. Englewood Cliffs, N.J.: Prentice-Hall, 1970. Excellent analysis of Rabelais's works is often cited as the best introductory study of the writer. Includes bibliography.

O'Brien, John, and Malcolm Quainton, eds. *Distant Voices Still Heard: Contemporary Readings of French Renaissance Literature*. Liverpool, England: Liverpool University Press, 2000. Collection of paired essays on five major authors applies modern critical theories to French Renaissance literature. The two essays on Rabelais provide a structuralist reading of *Pantagruel* and examine the methodology of *Tiers Livre*.

Zegura, Elizabeth Chesney, ed. *The Rabelais Encyclopedia*. Westport, Conn.: Greenwood Press, 2004. Alphabetically arranged collection of articles covers a wide range of topics, including Rabelais's characters, references to Renaissance and historical figures in Rabelais's works, themes and allusions in his works, and key influences on his writing. Also features a chronology of major events in his life and literary career.

LAURENCE STERNE

Born: Clonmel, Ireland; November 24, 1713
Died: London, England; March 18, 1768

PRINCIPAL LONG FICTION

The Life and Opinions of Tristram Shandy, Gent., 1759-1767 (commonly known as *Tristram Shandy*)
A Sentimental Journey Through France and Italy, 1768

OTHER LITERARY FORMS

Laurence Sterne began his literary career with political pieces in the *York-Courant* in 1741. Two years later, he published a poem, "The Unknown World," in *The Gentleman's Magazine* (July, 1743). His song "How Imperfect the Joys of the Soul," written for Kitty Fourmantel, appeared in Joseph Baildon's *Collection of New Songs Sung at Ranelagh* (1765), and a four-line epigram, "On a Lady's Sporting a Somerset," was attributed to Sterne in *Muse's Mirror* (1778). His sermons were published in three installments: two volumes in 1760, another two in 1766, and a final three volumes in 1769. A satire titled *A Political Romance* was published in 1759 but quickly suppressed. After Sterne's death, *Letters from Yorick to Eliza* appeared in 1773, and his daughter arranged for the publication of the three-volume *Letters of the Late Rev. Mr. L. Sterne to His Most Intimate Friends* (1775). These volumes include an autobiographical *Memoir* and the *Fragment in the Manner of Rabelais*. In 1935, Oxford University Press published the definitive edition of Sterne's letters, edited by Lewis Perry Curtis. The *Journal to Eliza*, composed in 1767, was not published until 1904.

ACHIEVEMENTS

When Laurence Sterne went to London in March, 1760, he was an obscure provincial parson. He rode as a guest in Stephen Croft's cart, and he brought with him little more than his "best breeches." Two months later, he returned to York in his own carriage. Robert Dodsley, who the year before had refused the copyright of *The Life and Opinions of Tristram Shandy, Gent.* (commonly known as *Tristram Shandy*) for 50 pounds, now gladly offered Sterne 250 pounds for the first two volumes, 380 pounds for the next two, as yet unwritten, and another 200 pounds for two volumes of sermons. The famous artist William Hogarth agreed to provide a frontispiece to the second edition of volume 1 and another for volume 3; Joshua Reynolds painted Sterne's portrait. Like Lord Byron, Sterne could have said that he awoke to find himself famous. As Sterne did say, in a letter to Catherine Fourmantel, "I assure you my Kitty, that Tristram is the Fashion." Despite the carpings of a few—Horace Walpole thought *Tristram Shandy* "a very insipid and tedious performance," and Samuel Richardson thought it immoral—the novel was the rage of

Laurence Sterne
(Library of Congress)

London, inspiring so many continuations and imitations that Sterne had to sign the later volumes to guarantee their authenticity.

After the novel's initial popularity, sales did drop off. In book 8, Tristram complains that he has "ten cart-loads" of volumes 5 and 6 "still unsold." Dodsley abandoned publication of the work after volume 4, and Sterne's new publisher, Thomas Becket, complained in April, 1763, that he had 991 copies of volumes 5 and 6 unsold (from a printing of 4,000). Samuel Johnson's famous comment, though ultimately incorrect, probably reflected the opinion of the day: "Nothing odd will do long. *Tristram Shandy* did not last." Even Sterne may have tired of the work; the volumes grew slimmer, and volume 9 appeared without its mate, volume 10 having, in Sterne's apt words for an obstetrical novel, "miscarried."

Tristram Shandy has lasted, however. It retains a readership, even if it has continued to justify Sterne's complaint of being "more read than understood." Some modern-day readers have made great, perhaps exaggerated, claims for the novel, seeing it as the harbinger of the works of Marcel Proust, James Joyce, and Albert Camus, who, it is said, derived from Sterne the concept of relative time, the stream of consciousness, and a sense of the absurd. Even if one discounts such assertions, there can be no question of the work's importance in the development of the novel or of *Tristram Shandy*'s place in the first rank of eighteenth century fiction.

Less has been claimed for *A Sentimental Journey Through France and Italy* (commonly known as *A Sentimental Journey*), yet this work, apparently so different from and so much simpler than *Tristram Shandy*, greatly influenced Continental, especially German, literature of the Romantic period. Though critics debate the sincerity of the emotions in the work, eighteenth century readers generally did not question Yorick's sentimentality, which contributed to the rise of the cult of sensibility exemplified by such works as Henry Mackenzie's *The Man of Feeling* (1771). Because of its brevity, its benevolence, and its accessibility, *A Sentimental Journey* has enjoyed continued popularity since its first appearance. Although lacking the stature of *Tristram Shandy*, it remains a classic.

BIOGRAPHY

Laurence Sterne was born in Clonmel, Tipperary, Ireland, on November 24, 1713. On his father's side, he could claim some distinction: His great-grandfather, Richard Sterne, had been Archbishop of York, and his grandfather, Simon Sterne, was a rich Yorkshire country squire. Roger Sterne, Laurence's father, was less distinguished. Sterne described his father as "a little smart man—active to the last degree, in all exercises—most patient of fatigue and disappointments, of which it pleased God to give him full measure." Sterne added that his father was "of a kindly, sweet disposition, void of all design." Many have seen Roger Sterne as the model for Uncle Toby Shandy. At the age of sixteen, Roger joined the Cumberland Regiment of Foot, and on September 25, 1711, he married Agnes Nuttall. Agnes, according to her son, was the daughter of "a noted sutler in Flanders, in Queen Ann's wars," whom Roger married because he was in debt to her father. Actually, she may have been the daughter of a poor but respectable family in Lancashire.

From his birth to the age of ten, Sterne led a nomadic life, wandering from barracks to barracks across Great Britain. During these years, he may have acquired some of the military knowledge that appears throughout *Tristram Shandy*, or at least that fondness for the military that marks the work. When Sterne was ten, his uncle Richard sent him to school near Halifax, in Yorkshire, and in 1733, Sterne's cousin sent him to Jesus College, Cambridge, where his great-grandfather had been a master and where both his uncle Jaques and his cousin had gone. At Cambridge, Sterne met John Hall, who later renamed himself John Hall-Stevenson. Hall-Stevenson was to be one of Sterne's closest friends throughout his life; his library at "Crazy Castle" would furnish much of the abstruse learning in *Tristram Shandy*, and he would himself appear in both that novel and *A Sentimental Journey* as Eugenius, the sober adviser. While at Cambridge, Sterne suffered his first tubercular hemorrhage.

After receiving his bachelor's degree in January, 1737, Sterne had to choose a profession. Because his great-grandfather and uncle had both gone into the clergy, Sterne followed their path. After Sterne served briefly in St. Ives and Catton, his uncle Jaques, by then archdeacon of Cleveland and canon and precentor of the York Cathedral, secured for him the living of Sutton on the Forest, a few miles north of York. A second post soon followed; Sterne received the prebend of Givendale, making him part of the York Cathedral chapter and so allowing him to preach his turn there.

At York, Sterne met Elizabeth Lumley, a woman with a comfortable fortune. Their courtship had a strong sentimental tinge to it. Indeed, if Sterne actually wrote to Elizabeth the letters that his daughter published after his death, his is the first recorded use of the word "sentimental," and the emotions expressed in these letters foreshadow both *A Sentimental Journey* and the *Journal to Eliza*. Even if these letters are spurious, Sterne's description of his courtship in the *Memoirs* is sufficiently lachrymose to rival the death of Le Fever in *Tristram Shandy*. Unfortunately for Sterne, he, unlike Tristram, did go on; on March 30, 1741, he married Elizabeth. The unfavorable portrait of Mrs. Shandy owes much to Sterne's less than sentimental feelings toward his wife, whom he called in March, 1760, the "one Obstacle to my Happiness."

The year 1741 was also important for Sterne because it marked his first appearance in print. His uncle Jaques was a strong Whig, and he recruited his nephew to write in support of the Whig candidate for York in that year's election. Sterne wrote, the Whig won, and Sterne received the prebend of North Newbold as a reward. The Whig success was, however, short-lived. When the Walpole government fell in 1742, Sterne wrote a recantation and apology for his part in "the late contested Election," and thereby earned the enmity of his uncle, an enmity that ended only with Jaques's death in 1759.

For eighteen years, Sterne lived as a typical provincial clergyman, attending to the needs of his parishioners and publishing two sermons. One of these, "For We Trust We Have a Good Conscience," Sterne reprints in its entirety in the second volume of *Tristram Shandy*. In 1751, he received the commissaryship of Pickering and Pocklington, despite his uncle's efforts to secure this position for Dr. Francis Topham. Sterne and Topham collided again in 1758, when Topham attended to include his son in a patent and thus secure for him a post after his own death. When the dean of York Cathedral blocked the inclusion, a pamphlet war ensued. Sterne fired the final shot; his pamphlet *A Political Romance* so squashed Topham that he agreed to abandon the fray if Sterne would withdraw the work. Sterne did withdraw *A Political Romance*, but he was not finished with Topham, who was to appear in *Tristram Shandy* as Phutatorius and Didius.

A Political Romance is little more than a satiric squib, but it shows that Sterne was familiar with the works of Jonathan Swift. In its use of clothes symbolism as well as in its severity it recalls *A Tale of a Tub* (1704), and it shows that Swift's work was running in Sterne's head between 1758 and 1759. He was making other use of Swift, too. On May 23, 1759, Sterne wrote to Robert Dodsley, "With this You will receive the Life & Opinions of

Tristram Shandy, which I choose to offer to You first." By this time, the first volume of the novel was finished. Although Dodsley refused the copyright for the sum of 50 pounds that Sterne requested, Sterne continued to write, completing a second volume and revising the first to remove "all locality" and make "the whole . . . more saleable," as he wrote to Dodsley several months later.

Salable it was. The York edition sold two hundred copies in two days when it appeared in December, 1759, and when Sterne went up to London, he was told that the book was not "to be had in London either for Love or money." Dodsley, who had been unwilling to risk 50 pounds on the copyright, now purchased it for 250 pounds, gave another 380 pounds to publish the still-unwritten volumes 3 and 4, and yet another 200 pounds for two volumes of Sterne's sermons. Sterne was honored by the great. Thomas Gray wrote to Thomas Wharton, "Tristram Shandy is still a greater object of admiration, the Man as well as the Book. One is invited to dinner, where he dines, a fortnight beforehand."

In March, 1760, Sterne also succeeded to the curacy of Coxwold, a better position than his earlier one at Sutton. In May, 1760, he therefore settled at Coxwold, renting Shandy Hall from Earl Fauconberg. Here he worked on the next two volumes of *Tristram Shandy*, which he brought to London at the end of the year. In 1761, he repeated this pattern, but he did not return to Yorkshire after delivering the manuscript of volumes 5 and 6. Having suffered a tubercular hemorrhage, he set off for the warmer, milder air of France.

There he repeated his earlier triumph in London, and he incidentally acquired materials for book 7 of *Tristram Shandy* and *A Sentimental Journey*. Sterne remained in France for almost two years; when he returned to England, he hastily wrote the next two volumes of *Tristram Shandy*, which appeared in January, 1765. In October of that year, he brought twelve sermons to London rather than more of his novel. After leaving the manuscript with his publisher, he again set off for the Continent; he would combine the adventures of this trip with those of his earlier one in writing *A Sentimental Journey*.

In June, 1766, Sterne was back in Coxwold, where he wrote what proved to be the last installment of *Tristram Shandy*. This he brought with him to London in late December; shortly after his arrival, he met Eliza Draper, the wife of an East India Company clerk twenty years her senior. Though initially unimpressed with her, Sterne was soon madly in love. When Sterne met her, she had already been in England some two years, and she was to return to India less than three months later, yet she was to color Sterne's last year of life. Before she sailed on the *Earl of Chatham* on April 3, 1767, Sterne visited her daily, wrote letters to her, drove with her, and exchanged pictures with her. After their separation, Sterne continued his letters; those he wrote between April 13 and the beginning of August, 1767, constitute the *Journal to Eliza*. When he broke off this journal with the words "I am thine—& thine only, & for ever" to begin *A Sentimental Journey*, her spirit haunted that work, too, as the Eliza upon whom Yorick calls.

By December, Sterne had finished the first half of *A Sentimental Journey* and again set off for London and his publisher. On February 27, 1768, *A Sentimental Journey*, volumes 1 and 2, appeared. Less than a month later, on March 18, Sterne died. He was buried in London on March 22; on June 8, 1769, he was reinterred in the Coxwold churchyard in Yorkshire.

Analysis

Readers may be tempted to see Laurence Sterne's works either as sui generis or as eighteenth century sports that had no mate until Marcel Proust and James Joyce. In fact, Sterne was very much a product of his age. His humor owes much to such earlier writers as François Rabelais, Miguel de Cervantes, Michel Eyquem de Montaigne, Sir Thomas Browne, and Jonathan Swift, all of whom influenced his experimentation with the form of the newly emerged novel. Even this experimentation is typical of the age. Thomas Amory's *The Life and Opinions of John Buncle Esquire* (1756-1766) may have suggested to Sterne his complete title *The Life and Opinions of Tristram Shandy, Gent.* Like *Tristram Shandy*, Amory's book is full of digressions, and its narrator is conceited.

Sterne's experimentation did go beyond the traditional; one need look no farther than the typography, the varying length of the chapters in *Tristram Shandy*—from four lines to sixty pages—or the unusual location of certain conventional elements—for example, the placing of *Tristram Shandy*'s preface after the twentieth chapter of book 3 or Yorick's writing the preface to *A Sentimental Journey* after chapter 6. At the same time, Sterne relied on the conventions of the novel. He is meticulous in his descriptions of clothing, furniture, and gesture. His characters are fully developed: They walk, sometimes with a limp, they cough, they bleed, they dance. From Swift, Daniel Defoe, and Samuel Richardson, Sterne took the first-person narrator. From Richardson, he adopted the technique of writing to the moment; from Henry Fielding, he got the idea of the novel as a comic epic in prose. From numerous sources—Rabelais, Cervantes, and Swift, to name but three—he learned of the satiric potential of the genre.

A Political Romance reveals Sterne's powerful satiric abilities, but this work has little in common with the novels. True, the personal satire of the pamphlet does persist in the novels. Sterne lampoons Dr. Burton (Dr. Slop), Dr. Richard Meade (Dr. Kunastrokius), and Francis Topham (Phutatorius, Didius) in *Tristram Shandy*; Tobias Smollett (Smeldungus) and Samuel Sharp (Mundungus) in *A Sentimental Journey*. For the most part, however, Sterne is after bigger game. As he wrote to Robert Dodsley, the satire is general; and, as he wrote to Robert Foley some years later, it is "a laughing good tempered Satyr," another distinction between the novels and the pamphlet.

The objects of this general satire are several: system-makers of all types, pedants, lawyers, doctors, conceited authors, prudes, and self-deceivers. A common thread uniting all these satiric butts is folly, the folly of believing that life should conform to some preconceived notion, of trying to force facts to fit theories rather than the other way around.

Sterne's insistence on common sense and reason is consistent with the Augustan tradition, which itself is rooted in Anglican beliefs that Sterne emphasized in his sermons as well as in his fiction. Although Sterne's satire is good-tempered, it attacks people's tendency to evil, a tendency noted in Article IX of the Thirty-nine Articles of the Anglican Church. Like his fellow Augustans, Sterne saw this tendency to evil in many spheres. Like them, therefore, he attacked these deviations from the norm as established by religion and reason (which for Sterne are the same), by nature, by tradition, and by authority. The characters in *Tristram Shandy* and Yorick in *A Sentimental Journey* (who is the only sustained character in that work) are laughable because they deviate from the norm and because they refuse to accept their limitations.

Sterne repeatedly reminds the reader of people's finiteness. Thus, death haunts the novels: In *Tristram Shandy*, Toby, Walter, Mrs. Shandy, Yorick, Trim, and Bobby are all dead, and Tristram is dying. In *A Sentimental Journey*, a resurrected Yorick sees death all around him—a dead monk, dead children, a dead ass, dead lovers. Another, less dramatic symbol of the characters' limitation is their inability to complete what they begin. *Tristram Shandy* and *A Sentimental Journey* remain fragments. Trim never finishes his tale of the King of Bohemia and his seven castles. Walter never finishes the *Tristrapaedia*. Obadiah never goes for yeast. Yorick never finishes the story of the notary. Nor can characters communicate effectively with one another: Walter's wife never appreciates his theories, Toby's hobbyhorse causes him to understand all words in a military sense, Dr. Slop falls asleep in the middle of Trim's reading, and Yorick in *A Sentimental Journey* never pauses long enough to develop a lasting friendship.

Death, the prison of the self, the petty and great disappointments of life—these are the stuff of tragedy, yet in Sterne's novels they form the basis of comedy, for the emphasis in these novels is not on the tragic event itself but rather on the cause or the reaction. Bobby's death, for example, is nothing to the reader, not only because one never meets Bobby alive but also because one quickly becomes involved in Walter's oration and Trim's hat. In *A Sentimental Journey*, Sterne focuses on Yorick's reaction to Maria rather than on her poignant tale: Consequently, one laughs at Yorick instead of crying with Maria. The prison of words that traps the characters is not the result of people's inherent isolation but rather of a comic perversity in refusing to accept the plain meaning of a statement. The tragic is further mitigated by its remoteness. Though Tristram writes to the moment, that moment is long past; Tristram's account is being composed some fifty years after the events he describes, and Yorick, too, is recollecting emotions in tranquillity. The curious order of *Tristram Shandy* and the rapid pace of *A Sentimental Journey* further dilute the tragic. Yorick dies in book 1 but cracks the last joke in book 9. Yorick has barely begun a sentimental attachment with a *fille de chambre*, or lady's maid, in Paris when he must set off for Versailles to seek a passport. Though the disappointments, interruptions, failures, and deaths recur, individually they quickly vanish from view. What remains are the characters, who are comic because they refuse to learn from their failures.

Sterne's world is therefore not tragic; neither is it absurd. In the world of the absurd, helpless characters confront a meaningless and chaotic world. For Sterne, the world is reasonable; he shares the Augustan worldview expressed so well by Alexander Pope: "All Nature is but Art, unknown to thee,/ All Chance Direction which thou canst not see." The reasonableness of the world is not, however, to be found in the systematizing of Walter Shandy or the sentimentalism of Yorick. People can live in harmony with the world, Sterne says, only if they use common sense. The comedy of these novels derives in large part from people's failure or laziness to be sensible.

TRISTRAM SHANDY

In *Aspects of the Novel* (1927), E. M. Forster writes: "Obviously a god is hidden in *Tristram Shandy* and his name is Muddle." There is no question that the muddle is present in the novel. Chapters 18 and 19 of book 9 appear as part of chapter 25. The preface does not appear until the third volume. There are black, marbled, and white pages. In book 4, a chapter is torn out and ten pages dropped. Uncle Toby begins knocking the ashes out of his pipe in book 1, chapter 21, and finishes this simple action in book 2, chapter 6. The novel begins in 1718 and ends, if it may be said to end, in 1713. Although called *The Life and Opinions of Tristram Shandy, Gent.*, the novel recounts the life of Uncle Toby and the opinions of Walter Shandy.

One must distinguish, however, between the muddle that the narrator, Tristram, creates and the ordered universe that Sterne offers. Theodore Baird has demonstrated that one can construct an orderly sequence of events from the information in *Tristram Shandy*, beginning with the reign of Henry VIII (III, xxxiii) through the wounding of Trim in 1693 (VIII, xix; II, v), the siege of Namur at which Toby is wounded in 1695 (I, xxv), the conception and birth of Tristram Shandy in 1718 (I-III), the death of Bobby (1719; IV, xxxii, and v, ii), the episode of Toby and the fly (1728; II, xii), the death of Yorick (1748; I, xii), and the composition of the novel (1759-1766). Tristram does attempt to impose some order on these events; the first five and a half books trace his life from his conception to his accident with the window sash and his being put into breeches. He then breaks off to recount the amours of Uncle Toby, which again appear essentially in sequence, with the major exception of book 7, Tristram's flight into France.

Although Tristram attempts to order these events, he fails. He fails not because life is inherently random or absurd, but because he is a bad artist. He pointedly rejects the advice of Horace, whose *The Art of Poetry* (c. 17 B.C.E.) was highly respected among eighteenth century writers. He will not pause to check facts and even refuses to look back in his own book to see whether he has already mentioned something; this is writing to the moment with a vengeance. He refuses to impose any order at all on his material, allowing his pen to govern him instead of acting the part of the good writer who governs his pen.

In governing his pen, the good writer carefully selects his material. Many a person has told a plain, unvarnished tale in less space than Tristram, but Tristram cannot decide what is important. Must one know what Mrs. Shandy said to Walter on the night of Tristram's begetting, which, incidentally, may not be the night of Tristram's begetting at all, since the night described is only eight months before Tristram's birth rather than nine—does Tristram realize this fact? Does one need so vivid an account of how Walter falls across the bed upon learning of Tristram's crushed nose? Is it true that one cannot understand Toby's statement, "I think it would not be amiss brother, if we rung the bell," without being dragged halfway across Europe and twenty-three years back in time? Such details serve the purpose of Tristram's creator by highlighting the follies of a bad writer, but they hardly help Tristram proceed with his story.

Tristram's failure to select his material derives in part from laziness. "I have a strong propensity in me to begin this chapter very nonsensically, and I will not balk my fancy," he writes (I, xxiii), for it requires intellectual effort to balk a fancy. In part, too, this failure to select reflects Tristram's belief that everything concerning himself is important. His is a solipsistic rendering of the humanist's credo, "*Homo sum, humani nihil a me alienum puto*"—I am a man, and nothing that relates to man can be foreign to me. He is confident that the more the reader associates with him, the fonder he (the reader) will become. Hence, the reader will want to know about his failure with Jenny, about his aunt Dinah's affair with the coachman, about his attire as he writes, about his casting a fair instead of a foul copy of his manuscript into the fire. Tristram sets out to write a traditional biography, beginning with a genealogy and proceeding to birth, education, youthful deeds that foreshadow later achievements, marriage, children, accomplishments, death, and burial. He becomes so bogged down in details, however, that he cannot get beyond his fifth year. The episode of Toby and the fly must substitute for a volume on education, and the setting up of his top replaces an account of his youthful deeds.

Although Tristram refuses to impose any system on his writing, he is a true son of Walter Shandy in his willingness to impose systems on other aspects of his world. He devises a scale for measuring pleasure and pain, so that if the death of Bobby rates a five and Walter's pleasure at delivering an oration on the occasion rates a ten, Walter proves the gainer by this catastrophe. Tristram has another scale for measuring his own writing; he awards himself a nineteen out of twenty for the design of the novel. Tristram attaches much significance to the way he is conceived, believing that one's conception determines his entire life. His declared method of describing character is similarly reductive, focusing strictly on the individual's hobbyhorse. He has a theory on knots, on window sashes, and on the effect of diet on writing. Tristram thus serves as a satire on systematizers as well as on bad writers.

The more obvious butt of Sterne's satire on system-makers is Walter Shandy. The Augustan Age has also been called the Age of Reason, and Sterne recognizes the importance of reason. At the same time, the Augustans recognized that a person's reason alone is often an insufficient guide because it can be corrupted by a ruling passion, as Yorick's sermon in *Tristram Shandy* reveals. Tristram fails as an author because he trusts exclusively to his own logic instead of following conventional guidelines. Walter Shandy is another example of one who becomes foolish because of his reliance on his own reason. Like Pope's dunces, Walter is well read, and like Pope's dunces, he fails to benefit from his learning because he does not use common sense. He will look in the Institutes of Justinian instead of the more obvious, and more reliable, catechism—part of Sterne's joke here is that the source Walter cites does not contain what he wants. Walter will consult Rubenius rather than a tailor to determine of what cloth Tristram's breeches should be made. From his reading and reasoning he develops a host of theories: that cesarean birth is the best way of bringing a child into the world, that Christian names determine one's life, that auxiliary verbs provide a key to knowledge. Each of these theories rests on a certain logic. Walter is correct that no one would name his child Judas. From this true observation, however, he erects a most absurd theory, proving Tristram's statement that "when a man gives himself up to the government of a ruling passion,—or, in other words, when his Hobby-Horse grows headstrong,—farewell cool reason and fair discretion" (II, v). Neither Walter nor his son will rein in his hobbyhorse, and, as a result, they become ridiculous.

They may also become dangerous. While Walter is busily engaged in composing his *Tristrapaedia* that will codify his theories of child rearing, Tristram grows up without any guidance at all. Walter is willing, indeed eager, to have his wife undergo a cesarean operation because he believes that such an operation will be less harmful to the infant than natural childbirth. That such an operation will cause the death of Mrs. Shandy is a fact that apparently escapes him.

Even the benign and lovable Uncle Toby makes himself ridiculous by yielding to his hobbyhorse. Not only does this hobbyhorse lead him into excessive expense and so deprive him of money he might put to better use, but also it keeps his mind from more worthwhile occupations. Repeatedly, Sterne, through Tristram, likens Toby's garden battlefield to a mistress with whom Toby dallies; the Elizabethan sense of hobbyhorse is precisely this—a woman of easy virtue. As Tristram notes early in the novel, when "one . . . whose principles and conduct are as generous and noble as his blood" is carried off by his hobbyhorse, it is better that "the Hobby-Horse, with all his fraternity, (were) at the Devil" (I, viii). Deluding himself that he is somehow contributing to the defense of England, Toby blinds himself to the real horrors of war. Wrapped up in his military jargon, he isolates himself verbally from those around him; a bridge or a train has only one meaning for him. No less than Tristram, he is betrayed by words, but in his case as in Tristram's the fault lies not with the words but with the individual betrayed.

Nor is Toby's hobbyhorse dangerous to himself alone. It keeps him away from the Widow Wadman and so prevents his fulfilling his legitimate social responsibilities of marrying and begetting children; his hobbyhorse renders him sterile even if his wound has not. This hobbyhorse also comes close to rendering Tristram sterile, for Trim removes the weights from the window sash to make cannon for Toby's campaigns.

Each of the major characters is trapped in a cell of his own making. Tristram can never finish his book because his theory of composition raises insurmountable obstacles. The more he writes, the more he has to write. Walter's and Toby's hobbyhorses blind them to reality and prevent their communicating with each other or anyone else. The Shandy family is well named; "shandy" in Yorkshire means crackbrained. Significantly, the novel begins with an interrupted act of procreation and ends with sterility. As in Pope's *The Dunciad* (1728-1743), the uncreating word triumphs because of human folly.

Sterne's vision is not quite as dark as Pope's, however; the novel ends not with universal darkness but with a joke. Yorick, the voice of reason and moderation, remains to pull the reader back to reality. Yorick is a jester, and the role of the jester is to remind his audience of the just proportion of things as well as to make them laugh. Yorick does not put a fancy saddle on a horse that does not deserve one. He will destroy a sermon because it is too bad (unlike Tristram, who destroys a chapter because it is too good). He makes only modest claims for his sermons and is embarrassed even by these (unlike Tristram, who repeatedly proclaims himself a genius). Yorick thus offers in word and deed an example of living reasonably and happily.

Sterne offers a second consolation as well. Even though characters isolate themselves with their hobbyhorses, even though they cannot or will not understand one another's words, they can and do appreciate one another's feelings. These emotional unions are short-lived, but they are intense and sincere. Walter will continue to make fun of Toby even after promising not to, but at the moment the promise is made, the two are united spiritually and physically. Tristram and Jenny quarrel, but they also have their tender moments. Trim looks for a carriage in a book by shaking the leaves, and he mistakes fiction for reality in a sermon, but he allows his parents three halfpence a day out of his pay when they grow old. The benevolence that Sterne urged in his sermons is capable of bridging self-imposed isolation. Although one laughs at the characters in *Tristram Shandy*, one therefore sympathizes with them as well, seeing their weaknesses but also their underlying virtue. Though they have corrupted that virtue by yielding to a natural tendency to evil, they redeem themselves through their equally natural tendency to kindness.

Tristram Shandy offended many contemporary readers because of its bawdy tales; reviewers much preferred such seemingly sentimental episodes as the death of Le Fever and urged Sterne to refine his humor. *A Sentimental Journey* superficially appears to have been written to satisfy these demands. It is full of touching scenes, of tears, of charity, of little acts of kindness. Moreover, in a letter to Mrs. William James in November, 1767, Sterne describes the novel as dealing with "the gentle passions and affections" and says his intention is "to teach us to love the world and our fellow creatures better than we do." Sterne's letters, and especially his *Journal to Eliza*, reveal him as a man of feeling, and *Tristram Shandy* satirizes all aspects of human life except for benevolence. Sterne's sermons reinforce his image as a believer in the importance of charity. As a Latitudinarian, he believed that the Golden Rule constitutes the essence of religion, that ritual and church doctrine, while important, are less significant than kindness. Because Yorick in *Tristram Shandy* is Sterne's spokesman, it is tempting to see Yorick in *A Sentimental Journey* as having the same normative function. Though the narrator of *Tristram Shandy* is a dunce and a satiric butt, can one not still trust the narrator of *A Sentimental Journey*?

No. In a famous letter to Dr. John Eustace, Sterne thanks Eustace for the gift of a curious walking stick: "Your walking stick is in no sense more shandaic than in that of its having *more handles than one*." Readers could regard *Tristram Shandy* as total nonsense, as a collection of bawdy stories, as a realistic novel, as a satire on the realistic novel, or as a satire on the follies of humankind. Sterne's second novel, too, is "shandaic." The reader can see it as a tribute to the popular spirit of sentimentality or can view it as a satire of that spirit, yet a careful reading of the book will demonstrate why Sterne wrote to the mysterious "Hannah" that this novel "shall make you cry as much as ever it made me laugh." In other words, Sterne is sporting with rather than adopting the sentimental mode.

A SENTIMENTAL JOURNEY

The object of Sterne's laughter is Yorick. The Yorick who recounts his travels is not the same normative parson as appears in *Tristram Shandy*. He is by now twice dead—dead in William Shakespeare's *Hamlet* (pr. c. 1600-1601) and dead again in *Tristram Shandy* some fifteen years prior to the events of *A Sentimental Journey*. This second resurrection may itself be a joke on the reader, who should recall Yorick's death in book 1 of the earlier novel.

This revived Yorick bears a great similarity to Tristram. He is, for one thing, a systematizer. He establishes three degrees of curses; he discovers "three epochas in the empire of a French woman" ("Paris"), he is able to create dialogues out of silence, and he derives national character not from "important matters of state" but rather from "nonsensical minutiae" ("The Wig—Paris"). Like Tristram, too, Yorick is vain. He gives a sou to a beggar who calls him "My Lord *Anglois*" and another sou for "*Mon cher et très charitable Monsieur*." He does not worry about being unkind to a monk but is concerned that as a result a pretty woman will think ill of him.

Even his style, though less difficult to follow than Tristram's, bears some similarities to that of Sterne's earlier narrator. In the midst of the account of his adventures in Versailles, Yorick introduces the irrelevant anecdote of Bevoriskius and the mating sparrows, thus combining Tristram's habit of digressing with Walter's love of abstruse learning. Yorick later interpolates an account of the Marquis d'E****, and while telling about Paris he presents a "Fragment" that does nothing to advance the story. Like Tristram, too, Yorick cannot finish his account, breaking off in midsentence. Apparently, he is more governed by his pen than governing.

Yorick also reminds the reader of the narrator in Swift's *A Tale of a Tub*, who believes that happiness is the state of being well deceived. Yorick is disappointed to learn that his small present to Le Fleur has been sufficient only to allow his servant to buy used clothes: "I would rather have imposed upon my fancy with thinking I had bought them new for the fellow, than that they had come out of the *Rue de friperie*" ("Le Dimanche—Paris"). Instead of inquiring about the history of the lady at Calais, he invents a pleasant account of her until he gets "ground enough for the situation which pleased me" ("In the Street—

Calais"). He deceives himself into believing that he is accompanying a pretty *fille de chambre* as far as possible to protect her when actually he wants her company. Even his benevolence is self-deception. He conjures up images to weep over—a swain with a dying lamb, a man in the Bastille, an imaginary recipient of charity. When in this last instance he confronts the reality, his behavior is hardly benevolent, though.

Sterne is not satirizing benevolence as such. In his sermons "The Vindication of Human Nature" and "Philanthropy Recommended" he rejects the notion that people are inherently selfish and stresses his belief in humankind's natural benevolence, yet he had to look no farther than his own nose to discover that benevolence can become a hobbyhorse that can carry a person away from the path of reason. Yorick's hobbyhorse of benevolence is no less dangerous than Uncle Toby's or Walter Shandy's. Yorick will weep over a carriage, over a dead ass, or over a caged starling. He admits that he does not even need an object for his sympathy: "Was I in a desert, I would find out wherewith in it to call forth my affection" ("In the Street—Calais"). Real human misery, however, he cannot understand. He can weep over his imagined prisoner in the Bastille, but he cannot imagine the real suffering there. He can be callous to the poor, but never to a pretty young woman.

Yorick's benevolence is thus a compound of self-deception and lust. He will give no money to the poor monk until he wants to impress a pretty woman. He gives a sou to a beggar with a dislocated hip, but he gives an unsolicited crown to a pretty *fille de chambre*, and he gives three *louis d'or* to a pretty grisette. He imagines that in offering to share his chaise with another pretty young lady, he is fighting off "every dirty passion" such as avarice, pride, meanness, and hypocrisy. Actually, he is yielding to desire.

True benevolence is guided by reason, and it is not a thing of the moment only, as Sterne points out in his sermon on the Good Samaritan. Yorick's benevolence is impulsive and short-lived. The cry of a caged starling moves him greatly: "I never had my affections more tenderly awakened," he says ("The Passport—The Hotel at Paris"). The hyperbole of the language is itself a warning of Yorick's inability to temper emotion with reason. After such a reaction, his attitude changes abruptly; Yorick buys the starling but never frees it. After tiring of it, he gives it away to another as callous as himself. At Namport, he mourns for a dead ass and praises its owner for his kindness, adding, "Shame on the world! . . . Did we love each other, as this poor soul but loved his ass—'twould be something" ("Namport—The Dead Ass"). By the next page, Yorick is sending his postilion to the devil. Yorick goes out of his way to find the mad Maria, whom Sterne had introduced in book 7 of *Tristram Shandy*. He weeps with Maria at Moulines; she makes such an impression on him that her image follows him almost to Lyon—an entire chapter.

Yorick is humorous because, like Tristram, Walter, and Toby, he is the victim of his hobbyhorse. He gallops away from reason, failing to examine his motivation or to temper his sudden fanciful flights. In "Temporal Advantages of Religion," Sterne provides a picture of the ideal Christian traveler. "We may surely be allowed to amuse ourselves with the natural or artificial beauties of the country we are passing through," Sterne notes, but he warns against being drawn aside, as Yorick is, "by the variety of prospects, edifices, and ruins which solicit us." More important, Yorick forgets the chief end of people's earthly sojourn: "Various as our excursions are—that we have still set our faces towards Jerusalem . . . and that the way to get there is not so much to please our hearts, as to improve them in virtue." Yorick has come to France for knowledge, but he learns nothing. His benevolence is much closer to wantonness than to virtue; it is fitting that he ends his account in the dark.

In *A Sentimental Journey*, as in *Tristram Shandy*, Sterne mocks excess. He shows the folly that results from the abdication of reason. Though he introduces norms such as Yorick in *Tristram Shandy* or the old soldier in *A Sentimental Journey*, the ideal emerges most clearly from a depiction of its opposite—perverted learning, bad writing, and unexamined motives. When Sterne arrived in London in 1760, Lord Bathurst embraced him as the heir to the Augustan satirists.

Joseph Rosenblum

OTHER MAJOR WORKS

NONFICTION: *A Political Romance*, 1759; *The Sermons of Mr. Yorick*, 1760 (volumes 1-2), 1766 (volumes 3-4); *Sermons by the Late Rev. Mr. Sterne*, 1769 (volumes 5-7); *Letters from Yorick to Eliza*, 1773; *Letters of the Late Rev. Mr. L. Sterne to His Most Intimate Friends*, 1775 (3 volumes); *Sterne's Letters to His Friends on Various Occasions, to Which Is Added His History of a Watch Coat*, 1775; *In Elegant Epistles*, 1790; *Journal to Eliza*, 1904.

BIBLIOGRAPHY

Bowden, Martha F. *Yorick's Congregation: The Church of England in the Time of Laurence Sterne*. Newark: University of Delaware Press, 2007. Examines the religious environment in which Sterne wrote his novels and sermons, explicating passages from his work to demonstrate how his experience of life in rural parishes informed his novels.

Cash, Arthur Hill. *Laurence Sterne*. 2 vols. London: Methuen, 1975-1986. Considered the definitive biography of the author. The first volume follows Sterne's life to early 1760 and offers many details about his role in the religious and political affairs of York. The second volume treats Sterne the author. Presents a realistic picture, freed from Victorian strictures and romantic glosses. Interesting appendixes provide a series of portraits and letters that were previously unpublished.

Cash, Arthur Hill, and John M. Stedmond, eds. *The Winged Skull: Papers from the Laurence Sterne Bicentenary Conference*. Kent, Ohio: Kent State University Press, 1971. Collection of essays covers a wide range of subjects, including Sterne's style, his reputation outside England, and his fictional devices. Includes some helpful illustrations.

Gerard, W. B. *Laurence Sterne and the Visual Imagination*. Burlington, Vt.: Ashgate, 2006. Study focuses on the illustrations by William Hogarth and other artists that complemented Sterne's work in the original editions. Examines the pictorial quality of Sterne's writing, describing how it inspires the visual imagination, and analyzes some of the illustrations for *Tristram Shandy* and *A Sentimental Journey*.

Keymer, Thomas, ed. *The Cambridge Companion to Laurence Sterne*. New York: Cambridge University Press, 2009. Collection of specially commissioned essays provides analyses of all of Sterne's works and their key issues of sentimentalism, national identity, and gender. Some of the essays consider Sterne's life and milieu, his literary career, and his subsequent influence on modernism; others analyze *Tristram Shandy* and *A Sentimental Journey*.

Kraft, Elizabeth. *Laurence Sterne Revisited*. New York: Twayne, 1996. Provides a short biography and then devotes individual chapters to specific works. Closes with a discussion of Sterne's changing critical reputation. Includes a selected bibliography.

New, Melvin. *"Tristram Shandy": A Book for Free Spirits*. New York: Twayne, 1994. Begins with background on the literary and historical milieu of Stern's most famous work and then explores five different methods of approaching *Tristram Shandy* in sections headed "Satire," "Heads" (viewing the work intellectually), "Hearts" (viewing it emotionally), "Joy," and "Tartuffery" (examining it as a humorous attack on hypocrisy).

Ross, Ian Campbell. *Laurence Sterne: A Life*. New York: Oxford University Press, 2001. Thorough and well-researched biography concentrates on the events of Sterne's life rather than on the analysis of his literary works. Includes bibliography and index.

Stedmond, John M. *The Comic Art of Laurence Sterne: Convention and Innovation in "Tristram Shandy" and "A Sentimental Journey."* Toronto, Ont.: University of Toronto Press, 1967. Provides helpful readings of Sterne's novels and describes how the works highlight the comic distance between aspiration and attainment that is endemic in human existence. Includes an appendix recording Sterne's direct borrowings.

Walsh, Marcus, ed. *Laurence Sterne*. New York: Longman, 2002. Sterne's works are particularly amenable to poststructuralist interpretation; this collection pulls together a stimulating group of essays that take modern theoretical approaches to the work.

JONATHAN SWIFT

Born: Dublin, Ireland; November 30, 1667
Died: Dublin, Ireland; October 19, 1745

PRINCIPAL LONG FICTION

A Tale of a Tub, 1704

Gulliver's Travels, 1726 (originally titled *Travels into Several Remote Nations of the World, in Four Parts, by Lemuel Gulliver, First a Surgeon, and Then a Captain of Several Ships*)

OTHER LITERARY FORMS

Jonathan Swift's oeuvre includes a large and important body of verse, best assembled in *The Poems of Jonathan Swift* (1937, 1958), edited by Harold Williams. His letters may be found in *The Correspondence of Jonathan Swift* (1963-1965), also edited by Williams. Outstanding among a variety of political writings are Swift's contributions to *The Examiner* (1710-1711), the treatise called *The Conduct of the Allies and of the Late Ministry, in Beginning and Carrying on the Present War* (1711), and the important *The Drapier's Letters to the People of Ireland* (1735).

His prose writings have been published together in *The Prose Works of Jonathan Swift* (1939-1968), a fourteen-volume collection edited by Herbert Davis.

ACHIEVEMENTS

It is generally conceded that Jonathan Swift is the greatest satirist among English-language writers, possibly the most brilliant ironist and acerb wit in any language. The force of his satiric barbs has rendered him controversial, however, and many critics have retaliated against his potent quill by claiming that Swift is reckless, uncontrolled, spiteful, insensate, heathenish, and insane. Such rash responses merely demonstrate the powerful effects of his writing.

Swift is not an overt lampooner, diatribe-monger, or name-caller. Curiously, he never utilizes the direct approach; he almost always speaks through a defective mouthpiece, a flawed, self-incriminating persona who forges a case against himself. Indeed, Swift is to be remembered as a grand satiric mimic, finely shaping and generating the voices of knaves and fools alike (the "modern" hack writer in *A Tale of a Tub*, the ignorant servingwoman Frances Harris, the idiot astrologer Isaac Bickerstaff, the callous and mathematical Modest Proposer, the proud but demented simpleton Lemuel Gulliver).

Swift's ear for clichés and inflections of dullness is almost perfect, and authors such as Herbert Read (in *English Prose Style*, 1928) have hailed Swift as the inevitable and clear master of "pure prose" style. Swift is, without doubt, the major satirist in prose, yet he is also a first-rate light poet (in the manner of Horace and the coarser Samuel "Hudibras"

Butler), and, if anything, his reputation as a poet is rising. Furthermore, Swift wrote political pamphlets with ruthless force, and his prose in sermons, letters, and treatises is virile and direct. Finally, Swift should not be forgotten as wit and jester. He invented a child-language when corresponding with Stella, wrote mock-Latin sayings, devised wicked epigrams, created paraphrases of Vergil and Ovid, and could even toy with versifying when devising invitations to dinner. In a word, Swift is the all-around expert in English in straightforward exposition—especially when it is bent to provoke savage mockery and the *jeu d'esprit*.

Biography

Jonathan Swift was born in Dublin, Ireland, on November 30, 1667, after the death of his father, a lower-middle class Anglo-Irishman. His grandfather, the Reverend Thomas Swift, had been a vicar in Herefordshire. His father, also named Jonathan, had settled in Ireland to work as a steward of the King's Inns in Dublin. His mother was Abigail Erick, the daughter of a Leicestershire clergyman. Swift's mother entrusted her young son to a nurse, who spirited the infant Swift away from Ireland for several years; he was eventually returned, and he was peculiarly linked with Ireland throughout his life. In any case, it was his fancy to picture himself a lonely outcast amid barbarians.

Swift attended Kilkenny School in his youth and Trinity College, Dublin, obtaining a bachelor's degree in 1686. He spent most of the following decade at Moor Park, Surrey, in the household of Sir William Temple, the distinguished Whig statesman. It was at Moor Park that Swift met, in 1689, the child of Esther Johnson (whom Swift later immortalized as "Stella"), the daughter of Temple's widowed housekeeper. Swift helped in supervising her education and inaugurated a lifelong (and little understood) relationship, for Stella later immigrated to Dublin and spent her life near the Anglican Dean Swift. Naturally, under Temple's aegis, Swift hoped for introductions and advancement, but little came of promises and possibilities, and in 1694 he returned to Dublin long enough to be ordained an Anglican priest (in 1695). He subsequently was reunited with Temple until the latter's death in 1699. Thereafter, he returned to Ireland as chaplain to the Earl of Berkeley. His reputation for talent and wit was rapidly growing.

Swift's great political period took place in London from 1708 to 1714. He became the chief spokesman, apologist, and pamphleteer for the powerful Tory leaders then in power, Robert Harley and Henry St. John, first Viscount Bolingbroke. Their fall and disgrace ushered in a lengthy era of Whig dominance that permanently drove Swift back to what he must have considered exile in Ireland. Swift had been finally rewarded (although he would have perceived it as a paltry recognition) with the deanery of St. Patrick's Cathedral in Dublin, where he served for the remainder of his life. His powerful satires had earned him powerful enemies, and significant advancement in the Anglican Church or in England was never permitted to him.

In any event, Swift served with precision, justness, and rectitude as a clergyman and

Jonathan Swift
(Library of Congress)

continued throughout his career to be an admirable satirist and wit. He even elected to champion the rights of the maltreated Irish, and he came to be admired as their avatar and protector, a "Hibernian Patriot." In his last years, Swift suffered increasingly from deafness and vertigo (the results of a lifelong affliction by Ménière's syndrome, a disease of the inner ear), which resulted in senility and, most likely, a stroke. Guardians were appointed to oversee his affairs in his last years, and he died in 1745, shortly before his seventy-eighth birthday.

Swift played his last ironic jest on humankind in his will, which committed the bulk of his estate to the founding of a "hospital" for fools and madmen, just as he had pronounced the plan in his *Verses on the Death of Dr. Swift, D.S.P.D.* (1739):

> He gave the little Wealth he had,
> To build a House for Fools and Mad;
> And shew'd by one satyric Touch,
> No Nation wanted it so much

ANALYSIS

It must be noted that Jonathan Swift's "fictions" are nothing like conventional novels. They seldom detail the "adventures" of a hero or even a protagonist and never conclude with a character's romantic achievement of goals or fulfillment of desires. Indeed, Swift is the great master of fictionalizing nonfiction. His satires always purport to be something factual, humdrum, diurnal, unimaginative: a treatise, a travel diary, an annotated edition, a laborious oration, a tendentious allegory, a puffed-out "letter to a friend." Extremist Protestant sects condemned fiction, and "projectors" and would-be investigators in the dawning age of science extolled the prosaic, the plodding, the scholarly, the methodical, and the factual. At the same time, urban population growth and the rise of the middle class created a growing new audience, and printing presses multiplied in accordance with demand. Many "popular" and best-seller art forms flourished: sermons, true confessions, retellings (and second parts) of hot-selling tales and political harangues, news items, hearsay gossip, and science all became jumbled together for public consumption, much of which led to spates of yellow journalism. Throughout his life Swift rebelled against such indelicacies and depravities, and his satiric procedure included the extremist parody of tasteless forms—*reductio ad absurdum*. It was by such means that Swift secured his fame as an author.

A TALE OF A TUB

Doubtless his most dazzling prose performance of this kind was his earliest, *A Tale of a Tub*, which appeared anonymously in 1704. (Swift, in fact, published most of his satires anonymously, although his work was usually instantly recognized and acclaimed.) *A Tale of a Tub* is actually a "medley" of pieces imitating the penchant for an author's combining fiction, essays, letters, verse, fragments, or anything else to enable him to amass a book-length manuscript. It contains "The Battle of the Books," a wooden allegorical piece in the manner of *Aesop's Fables*, detailing the "quarrel of ancients versus moderns," and a fragmentary treatise titled "The Mechanical Operation of the Spirit," trussed up in the inept form of a casual letter to a friend.

The treatise mocks the new "scientific" trend of reducing all things to some species of Cartesian (or Newtonian) materialism. Rather comically, it deploys in a blasé manner the language of ancient Greek and Roman atomists—Democritus and Epicurus—as if they were contemporary modernists. Indeed, one pervasive theme throughout this volume is the ridiculousness of the modernist position of "independence"—although the moderns might be ignorant of the past, the ideas and genres of classical antiquity keep recurring in their works, a fact that belies their supposed originality (even while demonstrating that, as a result of solipsism, their form and control disintegrate into chaos).

Clearly, the titular piece, "A Tale of a Tub," is Swift's early masterpiece and one of the great (and most difficult) satires in any language. In its pages, an avowed fanatic "modern" aspires to "get off" an edition, to tout and sell himself, to make money, to demonstrate his uniqueness and, however evanescently, tyrannically to be "the latest modern." He seeks to reedit an old tale of three brothers and their adventures. Naturally, he decorates and updates such a version to give it the latest cut and fashion, the style and wit and jargon of the moment. (It is perhaps an accident that this tale of the dissensions of Peter, Martin, and Jack parallels the vicissitudes of the history of Christianity, as it splinters into differing and quarreling religious sects. The modern appears ignorant of historical sense.)

The new version of the old story, however, is fragmented: Every time the modern's imagination or his fancy supplies him with a spark, he promptly follows his rather meandering muse and travels into an elaboration, an annotation, or a digression. In fact, the opening fifty pages of the work are cluttered with the paraphernalia of "modern" publishing: dedications, publisher's comments, introductions, apologies, notes to the second edition, acknowledgments, prefaces, and forewords. Thereafter, when such a cloud of ephemeral formalities would seem to have been dispensed with, the author still manages to interject a plethora of digressions—afterthoughts, asides, cute remarks apropos of nothing, commentary, snipings at critics, obsequious snivelings for the reader, canting pseudophilosophy for the learned, and pity and adoration for himself. In no time at all, the entire tale is awash in detours, perambulations, and divagations.

This modern storyteller is nothing if not effervescent, boorish, and chronically self-indulgent. He claims that his pipe dreams and diversions are in essence planned excursions and in fact deliberately philosophical meditations, rich with allegorical meanings. The opposite is also true, and the modern's tub is like an empty cart—rattling around most furiously in its vacuity, making the most noise. Furthermore, the digressions become unwieldy. The tale is disrupted more and more frequently, and the digressions become longer and longer. The modern is his most penetrating in the trenchant section IX—a digression in praise of madness—as he coyly confesses that his reason has been overturned, his intellect rattled, and that he has been but recently confined. The continued multiplication of digressions (until they subvert sections of the tale) and the finale, when the modern loses his notes and his ramblings give out entirely, are easily understood as the wanderings of a madman—a modern who suppresses the past, memory, reason, and self-control. If Swift's warning about the growing taste for newness, modernity, and things-of-the-moment appears madcap and farcical, it is nevertheless a painfully close nightmare preview of future fashions, fantasms, and fallacies that subsequently came to be real.

A Tale of a Tub clearly demonstrates several of Swift's most common fictional ploys and motifs. Some representative of the depraved "moderns" is usually present, always crass, irreligious, ignorant, arrogant, proud, self-adulatory, concerned with the events of the moment. Indeed, Swift was fond of scrupulously celebrating every April 1 as All Fools' Day, but he also recognized April 2: All Knaves' Day. He doubtless felt that both halves of humankind deserved some token of official recognition. Swift also favored mixing the two, however: He frequently shows readers that a man who is manipulator, con man, and knave in one set of circumstances is himself conned, befooled, and gulled in another. As such, the modern reveals an unexpected complexity in his makeup; he also illustrates the era (as Swift imagines it) that he inhabits—a period overfull of bad taste and poor writing, which are the broad marks of cultural decadence.

In the work of a satirist, the world is regularly depicted as cyclic in historic periods, and usually in decline. Swift and Sir William Temple both stressed some trend toward decay in the modern era and spoke often of barbarians and invasions; it was a type of satiric myth suitable to the disruptive fictions that the satirist envisions. In section IX of *A Tale of a Tub*, the modern vacillates between viewing all humankind as "curious" or "credulous," as busy probers, analysts, and excavators or as superficial and inert: knaves versus fools. As is typical of Swift, the fool and knave personas are infused with enough familiar traits to suggest that all people partake of either. Further, Swift entraps his reader by implying that there are no other categories: One is either fool or knave or both. His irony is corrosive and inclusive, capturing the reader in its toils. In that sense, Swift is deliberately disruptive; he seeks to startle and to embroil the reader in his fictions about stupidity and depravity. To such an end, he tampers with logic to make his case appear substantial and manipulates paradox to keep his readers off balance. Such techniques lend Swift his volatile force.

These strategies are to be found in Swift's best verse; the same may be said for his two great ironic short-prose pieces: *Argument Against Abolishing Christianity* (1708) and *A Modest Proposal for Preventing the Children of Poor People of Ireland from Being a Burden to Their Parents or the Country, and for Making Them Beneficial to the Public* (1729). Both of these works seek to shock the reader and to propose the discomforting, the alarming, the untenable.

GULLIVER'S TRAVELS

Swift's undisputed masterpiece is *Gulliver's Travels*, originally titled *Travels into Several Remote Nations of the World, in Four Parts, by Lemuel Gulliver, First a Surgeon, and Then a Captain of Several Ships*. This fictional work accommodates all of Swift's perennial themes and does so effectually. First, the work is perhaps the definitive study of new middle-class values, specifically the preoccupation with slang, cash, smug self-righteousness, self-assertion, and self-congratulation. Second, it might not be considered a "novel" in the conventional sense of the term, but it is a delightfully fact-filled simulation of adventure fiction, and it stems assuredly from the satiric picaresque tradition (in Spain and France) that greatly contributed to the formulation of modern novelistic techniques and themes.

Swift's Lemuel Gulliver (a mulish gull) is a model representative of the fool and the knave: He aspires to befool others but nevertheless befuddles himself. His medium is the very popular literary genre of the travelogue, or record of a "voyage of discovery." The genre grew popular through its Cartesian emphasis on an inductive observer-self and the Romantic subject of adventures in far-off lands. Such a travelogue format allows the narrator to take his readers on a vicarious journey of adventure and concludes by suggesting that the traveler has fulfilled the pattern of the bildungsroman and has attained education, growth, experience, and Aristotelian *cognitio* (insight, maturation, the acquisition of new knowledge). As might be expected in an exemplary case manipulated by Swift, Gulliver is anything but the apt learner. He is a crass materialist for whom experiences consist of precise measurements of objects observed, a tedious cataloging of dress, diet, and customs, and an infinite variety of pains in note taking, recording, transcribing, and translating. He is superficiality and rank objectivity incarnate. Naturally, therefore, his everyday mean density prevents his acquisition of any true understanding.

Gulliver is a minor physician, the mediocre little man, anxious, like Daniel Defoe's Robinson Crusoe, to make sightseeing tours and to acquire cash. His first of four voyages carries him to the land of six-inch mites, the Lilliputians, and his second voyage to the land of gargantuan giants, the Brobdingnagians. Gulliver remains myopic in both locations, for he can hardly consider that tiny creatures can (and do) perpetuate monstrous deeds, and, once he perceives that the giants are rather tame, he leaps to the conclusion that they are infinitely superior to other human types (even though their political and social institutions are no better than they should be, given the quirks and flaws of human nature). In sum, the tour from very small to very large merely stimulates in Gulliver a sense of wondrous contrast: He expects in these different worlds wondrous differences.

Amusingly, what the reader finds is much the same—that is, the uneven and imperfect human nature. Equally amusing, Gulliver behaves much the same himself in his attempts to ingratiate himself with his "superiors": He aspires to become a successful competitor in all worlds as a "titled" nobleman, a "nardac," a "courtier" with "connections" at court. Like many middle-class people, he is a man in the middle, aspiring above all for upward mobility, mouthing the commonplaces of the day, utterly incapable of judging people and events. He is also the worst sort of traveler; he is a man who sees no further than his own predilections and preconceptions and who imitates all the manners that he sees around him. Actually, the realms of big and little are merely distortions of the real world. Here, one of the work's central ironies is found in the fact that Gulliver could have learned as much, or as little, if he had stayed at home.

The world of sizes is replaced in Gulliver's third voyage by the world of concepts: The muddled peoples he visits are victims of mathomania and abstraction-worship. At the same time, it is revealed that the world of the past, like the world of the present, has been tainted and corrupt. Even the potentially ideal Struldbruggs, who live forever, are exposed as being far from lucky. They are, rather, especially accursed by the afflictions of impotence, depression, and senility. Swift has, with cartoon facility, carted Gulliver all around the world, showing him the corrosive face of fallen humanity, even among the various robbers, cowards, pirates, and mutineers that had beset him as he traveled in European ships—but Gulliver does not see.

The stage is properly set for the fourth voyage. Utilizing his favorite ploys of reversal and entrapment, Swift puts Gulliver into a land of learned and rational horses (the

Houyhnhnms) and debauched hairy, monkeylike beasts (the Yahoos). Once again, there is no middle ground: All in this world is rational horse or wolfish (and oafish) bestiality. Obviously, Gulliver chooses the equestrian gentlemen as his leaders and masters. (Indeed, throughout all the voyages, Gulliver the conformist is in quest of a staid position and "masters" who will tell him what to do and grant him praise and sustenance for his slavish adulation.)

Slowly it is revealed, however, that the Yahoos are men: Gulliver *is* a debased, gross, and deformed member of the Yahoo tribe; as Swift sweetly and confoundingly phrases it, Gulliver is a "perfect yahoo." The horses themselves rebuff this upstart, and Gulliver, who has undergone every other sort of ignominy in the course of his travels, is finally evicted as an undesirable alien from the horsey paradise. At last, Gulliver thinks he has learned a lesson; he aspires to be a horse, and, back in Europe, he shuns the human species and favors the environs of straw and stables. He has hardly acquired the rationality of his leaders and appears quite mad. Swift's ultimate paradox seems to imply that people can "know" about reason and ideals but can never master or practice them. Even here, however, Swift cruelly twists the knife at the last moment, for Gulliver, several years later, is revealed as slowly forgetting his intense (and irrational) devotion to the Houyhnhnms and slowly beginning to be able to tolerate and accept the lowly human race that he had earlier so intransigently spurned. Gulliver cannot even stick to a lesson painfully and rudely learned during many years; he lacks the brains, drive, ambition, and consistency necessary to keep him on any course. Gulliver's travels eventually get him nowhere.

In sum, *Gulliver's Travels* makes a huge tragicomical case for the absurdity of pretentious humankind. Gulliver is fool enough to believe that he is progressing and knave enough to boast about it and to hope to gain some position and affluence from the event. At his proudest moments, however, he is little more than a driveler, a gibbering idiot who is raveningly insane. Gulliver's painful experiences and the brute instruction his readers acquire are a caustic finale to much of the heady and bold idealism of the Renaissance and a cautionary plea for restraint in an era launched on celebrating reason, science, optimism, and enlightenment. Time has shown that Swift was largely right: Blithe superconfidence in people, their sciences, and their so-called progress is very likely to come enormously to grief. *Gulliver's Travels* speaks to everyone because it addresses crucial issues about the human condition itself.

John R. Clark

OTHER MAJOR WORKS

POETRY: *Cadenus and Vanessa*, 1726; *On Poetry: A Rapsody*, 1733; *Verses on the Death of Dr. Swift, D.S.P.D.*, 1739; *The Poems of Jonathan Swift*, 1937, 1958 (3 volumes; Harold Williams, editor).

NONFICTION: *A Discourse of the Contests and Dissensions Between the Nobles and the Commons in Athens and Rome*, 1701; *The Battle of the Books*, 1704; *The Accomplishment of the First of Mr. Bickerstaff's Predictions*, 1708; *Argument Against Abolishing Christianity*, 1708 (first published as *An Argument to Prove That the Abolishing of Christianity in England May, as Things Now Stand, Be Attended with Some Inconveniences, and Perhaps Not Produce Those Many Good Effects Proposed Thereby*); *Predictions for the Year 1708*, 1708; *A Project for the Advancement of Religion, and the Reformation of Manners by a Person of Quality*, 1709; *A Vindication of Isaac Bickerstaff, Esq.*, 1709; *The Conduct of the Allies and of the Late Ministry, in Beginning and Carrying on the Present War*, 1711; *A Proposal for Correcting, Improving, and Ascertaining the English Tongue, in a Letter to the Most Honourable Robert Earl of Oxford and Mortimer, Lord High Treasurer of Great Britain*, 1712; *The Public Spirit of the Whigs, Set Forth in Their Generous Encouragement of the Author of the Crisis*, 1714; *A Letter from a Lay-Patron to a Gentleman, Designing for Holy Orders*, 1720; *A Proposal for the Universal Use of Irish Manufacture*, 1720; *A Modest Proposal for Preventing the Children of Poor People of Ireland from Being a Burden to Their Parents or the Country, and for Making Them Beneficial to the Public*, 1729; *The Drapier's Letters to the People of Ireland*, 1735; *A Complete Collection of Genteel and Ingenious Conversation, According to the Most Polite Mode and Method Now Used at Court, and in the Best Companies of England, in Three Dialogues*, 1738; *Directions to Servants in General . . .*, 1745; *The History of the Four Last Years of the Queen, by the Late Jonathan Swift DD, DSPD*, 1758; *Journal to Stella*, 1766, 1768; *Letter to a Very Young Lady on Her Marriage*, 1797; *The Correspondence of Jonathan Swift*, 1963-1965 (5 volumes; Harold Williams, editor).

MISCELLANEOUS: *Miscellanies in Prose and Verse*, 1711; *Miscellanies*, 1727-1733 (4 volumes; with Alexander Pope and other members of the Scriblerus Club); *The Prose Works of Jonathan Swift*, 1939-1968 (14 volumes; Herbert Davis, editor).

BIBLIOGRAPHY

Barnett, Louise. *Jonathan Swift in the Company of Women*. New York: Oxford University Press, 2007. Focuses on Swift's relationships with the women in his life and his attitudes toward the fictional women in his texts. Explores Swift's contradictory views and illustrates how he respected and admired individual women yet loathed the female sex in general. Offers a critical, nonjudgmental discussion of the misogynistic attitude Swift displays in his writing when he expresses contempt and disgust for the female body.

Connery, Brian A., ed. *Representations of Swift*. Newark: University of Delaware Press, 2002. Collection of essays examines, among other topics, Swift's treatments of gender, class, and Ireland. Includes an analysis of *A Tale of a Tub*.

Ehrenpreis, Irvin. *Swift: The Man, His Works, and the Age*. 3 vols. Cambridge, Mass.: Harvard University Press, 1962-1983. Monumental biography rejects long-held myths about Swift and provides much previously unavailable information about the author and his works. Relates Swift to the intellectual and political currents of his age.

Fox, Christopher, ed. *The Cambridge Companion to Jonathan Swift*. New York: Cambridge University Press, 2003. Collection of essays about Swift's life and work includes analysis of *A Tale of a Tub* and *Gulliver's Travels* and discussions of Swift's religion, the language and style of his works, and his representation of women.

Fox, Christopher, and Brenda Tooley, eds. *Walking Naboth's Vineyard: New Studies of Swift*. Notre Dame, Ind.: University of Notre Dame Press, 1995. Collection of essays opens with an introduction that discusses Swift in relation to Irish studies, and the subsequent essays all consider aspects of Swift as an Irish writer.

Glendinning, Victoria. *Jonathan Swift: A Portrait*. New York: Henry Holt, 1998. Biography serves to illuminate Swift's nature as a proud and intractable man. Investigates the main events and relationships of Swift's life, which may be viewed as a tapestry of controversy and paradox.

Hunting, Robert. *Jonathan Swift*. Boston: Twayne, 1989. Good source of biographical information as well as insightful, if general, analysis of Swift's art. Devotes one chapter to *Gulliver's Travels*. Includes chronology, notes and references, bibliography, and index.

Kelly, Ann Cline. *Jonathan Swift and Popular Culture: Myth, Media, and the Man*. New York: Palgrave, 2002. Chronicles the creation of Swift's literary legend in his own time and in succeeding generations. Swift realized that in "a print-contracted world, texts create authors, not the other way around," and Kelly demonstrates how the writer constructed a print persona that differed from the "real" individual.

Nokes, David. *Jonathan Swift, A Hypocrite Reversed: A Critical Biography*. New York: Oxford University Press, 1985. Offers a good introduction for the general reader seeking information about Swift's life and works, drawing heavily on Swift's writings. Nokes views Swift as a conservative humanist.

Palmieri, Frank, ed. *Critical Essays on Jonathan Swift*. New York: G. K. Hall, 1993. Collection of essays is divided into sections on Swift's life and writings, *Gulliver's Travels*, *A Tale of a Tub* and eighteenth century literature, and his poetry and nonfiction prose. Includes index.

Quintana, Ricardo. *The Mind and Art of Jonathan Swift*. 1936. Reprint. New York: Oxford University Press, 1953. One of the standards of Swift criticism, concentrating on the public Swift. Examines his political activities and writings, tracing the intellectual sources of his thought. Includes synopses of his major works and provides historical background.

Rawson, Claude. *The Character of Swift's Satire: A Revised Focus*. Newark: University of Delaware Press, 1983. Presents eleven essays by Swift scholars, including John Traugatt's excellent reading of *A Tale of a Tub*, Irvin Ehrenpreis on Swift as a letter writer, and F. P. Lock on Swift's role in the political affairs of Queen Anne's reign.

VOLTAIRE

François-Marie Arouet

Born: Paris, France; November 21, 1694
Died: Paris, France; May 30, 1778
Also known as: François-Marie Arouet

PRINCIPAL LONG FICTION

Zadig: Ou, La Destinée, histoire orientale, 1748 (originally published as *Memnon: Histoire orientale*, 1747; *Zadig: Or, The Book of Fate*, 1749)
Le Micromégas, 1752 (*Micromegas*, 1753)
Histoire des voyages de Scarmentado, 1756 (*The History of the Voyages of Scarmentado*, 1757; also known as *History of Scarmentado's Travels*, 1961)
Candide: Ou, L'Optimisme, 1759 (*Candide: Or, All for the Best*, 1759; also known as *Candide: Or, The Optimist*, 1762; also known as *Candide: Or, Optimism*, 1947)
L'Ingénu, 1767 (*The Pupil of Nature*, 1771; also known as *Ingenuous*, 1961)
L'Homme aux quarante écus, 1768 (*The Man of Forty Crowns*, 1768)
La Princesse de Babylone, 1768 (*The Princess of Babylon*, 1769)

OTHER LITERARY FORMS

Voltaire (vohl-TAYR) is probably the most prolific and versatile writer of any age. He wrote in all the literary forms, and he wrote in them concurrently. His numerous plays fill 6 volumes, and his correspondence 102 volumes. He was especially active toward the end of his life; living at Ferney in his eighties, he wrote pamphlets, many plays, and one of his best philosophical poems, *Épître à Horace* (1772). He went to Paris at the age of eighty-three, shortly before he died, to see a production of his latest classical tragedy, *Irène* (pr. 1778). At the time of his death, he was at work on a new play and rewriting others.

In many ways, Voltaire wished to be considered as a defender of the classical tradition. His plays are mainly classical, embodying the unities and dealing with highborn heroes. *Œdipe* (pr. 1718; *Oedipus*, 1761) was widely acclaimed in Voltaire's day, as were *Zaïre* (pr. 1732; English translation, 1736) and *Mérope* (1743; English translation, 1744, 1749). He also, however, introduced devices and techniques that ultimately led to the demise of classical theater, including local color, such as red togas for members of the Senate in *Brutus* (pr. 1730; English translation, 1761) and real cannon fire in *Adélaïde du Guesclin* (pr. 1734). Voltaire's later plays include a certain amount of tearful sensibility that was a characteristic of Denis Diderot's bourgeois dramas.

Voltaire composed many kinds of poetry. As a young man, he achieved much acclaim with his epic poem *La Ligue* (1723) and *La Henriade* (1728, a rewriting of *La Ligue; Henriade*, 1732). *Henriade*, which narrates Henry IV's successful struggle against the

Voltaire
(Library of Congress)

Catholic League, was reprinted through the beginning of the nineteenth century. Today, these poems have no appeal. Voltaire also wrote satiric and philosophical poetry, including *Le Mondain* (1736; *The Man of the World*, 1764). This poem caused a scandal with its suggestion that a pleasurable life on earth is the only positive happiness one can grasp and that one should enjoy it rather than wait for a life after death. This element of audacious irreverence is a quality that spices all of Voltaire's work and was what his admirers appreciated. Voltaire's *Épître à Horace* is one of the best of Voltaire's philosophical epistles.

Voltaire has some renown as a historian. His *Le Siècle de Louis XIV* (1751; *The Age of Louis XIV*, 1752) reveals meticulous research and a journalistic bent. Voltaire praises the reign of Louis XIV in order to criticize the reign of Louis XV. *Essai sur les mœurs* (1756, 1763; *The General History and State of Europe*, 1754, 1759) presents a philosophical review of historic events. Other nonfiction works popularize the accomplishments of Sir Isaac Newton in science and of John Locke in philosophy (*Éléments de la philosophie de Newton*, 1738; *The Elements of Sir Isaac Newton's Philosophy*, 1738). In *Lettres philosophiques* (1734; originally published in English as *Letters Concerning the English Nation*, 1733; also known as *Philosophical Letters*, 1961), Voltaire, with his powerful satire, praises English customs and institutions as a method of criticizing French society of his day. Censorship, which outlawed much of Voltaire's work, not only added to the satirist's celebrity but also increased the prices charged for his books. The articles that Voltaire wrote for *Dictionnaire philosophique portatif* (1764, enlarged 1769; *A Philosophical Dictionary for the Pocket*, 1765; also known as *Philosophical Dictionary*, 1945, enlarged 1962) were also offensive to the establishment, full of his propaganda on the subject of fanaticism, judicial corruption, and social oppression.

Achievements

Voltaire's career spanned sixty years, and during that time he achieved great fame and even greater notoriety. Voltaire's literary ambitions were revealed when he chose *Œdipe* as the subject of his first tragedy. His ambition was to rival Pierre Corneille, and at the age of twenty-four he was already hailed as a worthy successor to both Jean Racine and Corneille. In the theater, Voltaire considerably delayed the demise of classical tragedy, and he remained an extremely popular dramatist of the age. Between 1745 and 1803, his plays were staged many more times than those of Corneille and Racine. Today, however, Voltaire's plays are no longer of interest to audiences.

Voltaire also enjoyed success in the field of poetry. *La Ligue* was so highly acclaimed that it put epic poetry back in fashion. Voltaire's love of the classical tradition stemmed, no doubt, from his Jesuit education at Louis-le-Grand. His poetry also brought him prestige at court and financial rewards. After the successful production of *La Princesse de Navarre* in 1745, performed at the wedding of Louis XV, Voltaire was given the post of royal historiographer and a pension of two thousand francs a year, and later was made a gentleman of the king's chamber. The following year, 1746, Voltaire achieved another ambition when he was finally elected to the Académie Française. He had been denied this privilege several times before because of the various scandals he had caused. Madame du Châtelet tried to protect him from his own indiscretion; she once locked up his outrageous *La Pucelle d'Orléans* (1755, 1762; *The Maid of Orleans*, 1758; also as *La Pucelle: Or, The Maid of Orleans*, 1785-1786), a scurrilous writing on the subject of Joan of Arc.

Voltaire's philosophical and satiric writings, such as his tales and pamphlets, not only brought him literary fame but also endangered his liberty. For this reason, Voltaire lived much of his life in exile or on the French-Swiss border.

One of the most astonishing aspects of Voltaire is his schizophrenic outlook. He dearly wished to have access to the noble classes (which accounts for his name change), while at the same time he despised the inequality inherent in the privilege of noble birth. A champion of the classical tradition, Voltaire inadvertently eroded its hold on his century by his innovations in drama and the novel. It is surprising that a champion of French classical tragedy and epic poetry should be the prime mover in introducing the latest developments in English literature, philosophy, and science into France. Voltaire's efforts to create a climate for liberty of thought and belief did eventually ameliorate conditions in France. The Encyclopedists, with Voltaire at their head, were ultimately responsible for producing a climate of critical thinking and a desire for reform that culminated in the French Revolution. Voltaire's *Philosophical Letters* were burned in public because they did not display the respect due "authority." Voltaire nevertheless would have been horrified to see the revolutionary tide sweep away this authority, even though it was corrupt. He enjoyed the cultivated nobility and the gracious support this class gave to the arts; he would have had no faith in the judgment of unrefined and poorly educated republicans. Still, the new ideas he had promulgated traveled through France and even to North America. Like John Locke, many of whose ideas are to be found in the American Bill of Rights and the Constitution, Voltaire contributed to political philosophy as it was developing in Europe and even in the United States.

It is through his satiric and philosophical writings that Voltaire exercised that influence. Whereas his effect on literature disappeared at the beginning of the nineteenth century, his emphasis on reason and critical thinking still dominates the French mind. The ideals of liberty of thought and justice are his legacy.

Biography

Voltaire was born François-Marie Arouet in Paris in 1694. His father was a highly placed official and belonged to the upper middle class. Voltaire received an excellent classical education at the Jesuit school of Louis-le-Grand in Paris, where he displayed a talent for writing poetry. He also probably acquired his taste for theater there.

The Abbé de Châteauneuf, Voltaire's godfather, introduced the twelve-year-old boy to the Society of the Temple, which was the domain of worldly libertines. Voltaire's taste for witty irreverence and for luxurious living was definitely encouraged by this company. In 1711, Voltaire became a law student. As early as 1716, his satiric writing, aimed at the king's regent and the poet Antoine Houdar de la Motte, caused Voltaire to be exiled twice to the provinces. In 1717, after writing a second time satirizing the regent, Voltaire was imprisoned (fairly comfortably) in the Bastille for eleven months. During this stay, he completed *Oedipus* and began to write *La Ligue*. Upon leaving prison, he changed his name to de Voltaire. He became famous with the success of *Oedipus* in 1718 and *La Ligue* in 1723, and as a result he was invited to the literary and social circles of the wealthy. He even became a habitué of the court and had three of his plays, *Oedipus*, *Mariamne* (pr. 1724; English translation, 1761), and *L'Indiscret* (pr., pb. 1725) performed as part of the celebrations for Louis XV's marriage in 1725.

Late in 1725, Voltaire had a dispute with the chevalier de Rohan, who ridiculed Voltaire's use of a false aristocratic name. Angered by a beating at the hands of Rohan's men, Voltaire challenged the noble to a duel. None of Voltaire's aristocratic friends supported him in the matter, which increased Voltaire's hatred of the unfairness of privilege. A *lettre de cachet* (a letter of arbitrary arrest issued by the king) sent him to the Bastille. Soon—in May, 1726—Voltaire was allowed to go into exile in England, where he spent three years frequenting the literary circles of the day. There he wrote his *Philosophical Letters*, prepared four tragedies, and published *Henriade*. Voltaire returned to France in 1729 and once again gained access to literary circles. In 1730, his play *Brutus* was produced. The influence of William Shakespeare, acquired in England, is obvious in Voltaire's drama. *Zaïre* was presented in 1732 and *Adélaïde du Guesclin* in 1734. In the same year, Voltaire also took a great risk when he published his highly critical *Philosophical Letters* for the first time in France.

From 1734 to 1744, Voltaire lived in the du Châtelet castle at Cirey, where Madame du Châtelet, Voltaire's mistress, restrained Voltaire's volatile literary indiscretions somewhat. This period proved to be a most productive one. Voltaire wrote several plays during this time, including *Alzire* (pr., pb. 1736; English translation, 1763) and *Mérope*. He also wrote his provocative *The Man of the World* while at Cirey. Both Madame du Châtelet and Voltaire took an interest in physics, chemistry, and astronomy; it is at Cirey that Voltaire wrote *The Elements of Sir Isaac Newton's Philosophy*.

For the three years following 1744, Voltaire was involved in life at court. His protectress, Madame de Pompadour, was, like him, of a humble background. The king and queen always distrusted Voltaire. After a thoughtless remark, Voltaire was obliged to flee the court and go to the summer home of the duchesse du Maine, the Château d'Anet at Sceaux. In *Zadig*, Voltaire satirizes life at court.

In 1747, Madame de Châtelet died in childbirth. Voltaire was extremely pained by this loss. There was no longer a reason to remain in France, and Voltaire spent the years from 1750 to 1753 at the court of Frederick the Great of Prussia. He published *The Age of Louis XIV* in Berlin in 1751. There he also wrote his satiric philosophical tale *Micromegas*. Although he had hoped to discover in Frederick his ideal of the "enlightened" monarch, Voltaire was as independent as Frederick was authoritarian, and the visit soon ended. These two men still respected each other greatly, however, and continued to correspond.

In 1755, Voltaire moved to Les Délices, an estate near the Swiss border. He lived there from 1755 to 1760, and it was there that, still in a depressed frame of mind, he wrote *Candide*.

From 1760 until his death, Voltaire resided in Ferney, on French soil, although situated very close to the Swiss border. Voltaire was extremely active during this period. He wrote some six thousand letters, as well as pamphlets, plays, and tales. In closing his letters, he usually wrote "Écrasez l'infâme" (crush the vile), by which he meant that superstition and intolerance must be eliminated. He wrote philosophical tales here, waging his battle against the usual targets; *Ingenuous* appeared at this time, as did many other philosophical tales. Voltaire championed the causes of the Calas and Sirven families and also of La Barre; all three were cases of the miscarriage of justice and of religious persecution.

Voltaire, taking his own advice at the end of *Candide*, did much to improve the region of Ferney. He built a church, installed a tannery, and established a watchmaking industry. He even had his area exempted from the salt tax. In 1778, at the age of eighty-three, Voltaire went to Paris in triumph to watch a production of *Irène*. His popularity was at its highest, and the accolades and honors he received during his sojourn proved too much for him; he died shortly thereafter.

Analysis

Voltaire was the most influential writer in eighteenth century France. He epitomizes the philosopher of the *siècle des lumières*, the Age of Enlightenment; his curiosity embraces all the developments of his day, whether French or otherwise European, scientific or literary. His faith in human reason does not waver, although his optimism about human progress often does. His writings reflect the changing literary tastes of the century as he defends a waning classical tradition while himself introducing the most outrageous innovations. His theater particularly embodies both of these tendencies, whereas his tales tend to exploit traditional literary forms in order to introduce a unique type of satiric philosophical story.

Voltaire's long fiction includes many rather short stories, which have been called indiscriminately *romans philosophiques* (philosophical novels) or *contes philosophiques* (philosophical tales). According to Henri Coulet, Voltaire himself used the term *histoire* (story). Because satire such as Voltaire's depends on economy of style and the tales have no real development of plot or character, they are limited in length by the genre itself.

Candide is considered to be the most perfect example of the philosophical novel, revealing Voltaire's brilliant irony and vivacious wit. All the tales are humorous tragicomedies and include incidents that are by turns absurd, grotesque, poetic, romantic, and shocking. The unifying element is always the philosophical theme that Voltaire is stressing. Voltaire began writing his tales at the age of forty-five, when his ideas were firmly established; hence, the concerns and reforms he seeks to address remain fairly constant throughout the tales. Despite the fact that these stories are meant to appeal primarily to the intellect, they are eminently entertaining. Voltaire's writings are rooted firmly in the humanistic rationalism of the first half of his century rather than in the literature of pre-Romantic sensibility, which made its appearance in the late 1700's.

Henri Bénac's suggestion that the tales fall into four chronological groups related to the development of Voltaire's thought is widely accepted. Bénac proposes that the first two groups—of 1747 to 1752 and 1756 to 1759—reveal Voltaire's growing realization that war must be waged against evils such as intolerance, injustice, corruption, and ignorance. The first group includes such stories as *Le Monde comme il va* (1748; revised as *Babouc: Ou, Le Monde comme il va*, 1749; *Babouc: Or, The World as It Goes*, 1754; also known as *The World as It Is: Or, Babouc's Vision*, 1929), *Memnon: Or, Human Wisdom*, and *La Lettre d'un Turc* (1750); *Zadig* and *Micromegas* are the best known of the group. The second group includes *History of Scarmentado's Travels*, which is the outline of *Candide*. In the third group figure *Jeannot et Colin* (1764; *Jeannot and Colin*, 1929), *Le Blanc et le noir* (1764; *The Two Genies*, 1895), and, best known, *Ingenuous*, *The Man of Forty Crowns*, and *The Princess of Babylon*. According to Bénac, the tales in this third group are, like Voltaire's pamphlets, weapons in his war against oppression of all kinds. In the last group, Bénac sees Voltaire searching for a morality on which to base a humane and free society. Tales in this period include *L'Histoire de Jenni* (1775) and *Les Oreilles du Comte de Chesterfield* (1775; *The Ears of Lord Chesterfield and Parson Goodman*, 1826).

Zadig

The concerns of the early tales recur throughout all the stories, but Voltaire presents the different tales with a rich range of tones. *Zadig*, like other tales of this early group, is imbued with sunny humor and gaiety despite the sardonic irony that underscores the misfortunes of the hero. Voltaire sketches his hero Zadig with an unusually delicate touch, and some passages dazzle momentarily with rare poetry: "He marveled at these vast globes of light which to our eyes appear to be only feeble sparks. . . . His soul flew up into the infinite and, detached from his senses, contemplated the immutable order of the universe."

Memnon: Histoire orientale contained fifteen chapters that reappeared in *Zadig* in 1748. The story of Zadig is in the picaresque tradition, which is to say that the hero, on his travels, meets with many adventures. The plot of such a tale is of necessity episodic and highly imaginative. Zadig, a wealthy, virtuous, and handsome young Babylonian, is about to marry the beautiful young Semire, who loves him "passionately." When a jealous youth, Orcan, attempts to abduct Semire, Zadig bravely rescues his betrothed, receiving a wound that might mean the loss of an eye. Instead of expressing her gratitude, Semire protests that she hates one-eyed men, and she promptly marries Orcan. Zadig recovers quickly and marries another woman, Azora, whose faithfulness he puts to the test by pretending to have died. Unfortunately, Azora fails the test. Zadig encounters difficulties with the law when he makes scientific deductions from observing the tracks of the queen's dog and the king's horse, leading a huntsman to deduce that Zadig stole the animals. Zadig eventually becomes the king's prime minister.

His next misfortune arises through no fault of his own: Queen Astarté falls in love with him. The king, in jealousy, plots to kill them both, and Zadig has to flee. As he arrives in Egypt, he sees an Egyptian beating a woman, who asks Zadig to save her. In the ensuing fight, Zadig kills his adversary. Zadig is arrested and imprisoned for this act, then sold as a slave and taken to Arabia by his master, Sétoc, with whom he becomes close friends. Zadig dissuades a young widow from burning herself on her husband's funeral pyre, as is the religious custom. He also persuades an Egyptian, an Indian, a Chinese, a Greek, and a Celt to worship the same Supreme Being. Zadig is accused of impiety by Arabian priests and condemned to be burned. The young widow whom he saved now helps him escape.

Zadig next goes to the island of Serendib (Ceylon) on behalf of Sétoc. He makes a good impression on the king of the island and helps him to find an honest minister. On his travels, Zadig meets the brigand chief Arbogad and learns that King Moabdar has gone mad and been killed, and Astarté has disappeared. Zadig eventually discovers that Astarté is a captive of Ogul, who is sick with an imaginary illness. Zadig cures Ogul, and the two return to Babylon, where peace is restored. Zadig wins a tournament that is held to decide who shall be the new king of Babylon and marry Astarté. Zadig wins the tournament but is cheated, and his rival claims the victory. In the middle of his despair, Zadig meets a hermit who reveals to him the secret of happiness, and Zadig learns to accept the ways of Providence. Zadig guesses the correct answers to the riddles and finally marries Astarté.

Zadig the hero—whose name in Arabic means "just"—attempts to be happy in a world where goodness is frustrated by absurd and illogical interventions of fate. At one point, Zadig says: "I was sent to execution because I had written verses in praise of the King; I was on the point of being strangled because the Queen had yellow ribbons; and here I am a slave with you because a brute beat his mistress. Come, let's not lose heart; perhaps all this will end."

The absurdity of Zadig's world, which is out of control and beyond the powers of logical explanation, is not the horror evoked in Franz Kafka's fiction; unlike Kafka, Voltaire does not attempt to create a sense of dreamlike but undeniable reality in either setting or characterization. Voltaire's exotic Eastern novel is in the tradition of the fifteenth century *The Arabian Nights' Entertainments*, also known as *The Thousand and One Nights*, translated from the Arabic by Antoine Gallard and much in vogue after the success of Montesquieu's *Lettres persanes* (1721; *Persian Letters*, 1722). The events are as unreal as those of the fairy tale, and the sensibility of the reader is not touched by Zadig's dilemmas. Instead, Voltaire disturbs the comfort of the reader's reason, logic, and innate sense of order and justice; the irony of Voltaire is at work. The frustration of Zadig becomes that of his audience. The knight Itobad steals Zadig's white suit of armor during the night, leaving his green suit in its place so that Zadig cannot claim the hand of Astarté, and Zadig cannot prove that he is the victor of the tournament, because the combatants must conceal their identities until a victor is proclaimed. Zadig has often been punished unjustly for being good, and here he is once again cheated of a happiness that is almost within his grasp. The audience is robbed of an anticipated happy ending and is frustrated by this anticlimax.

Voltaire was a master of the art of satire, and he often made use of anticlimax as an effective satiric technique. Zadig, after bewailing a list of horrifying punishments he has narrowly escaped, says, "Come, let's not lose heart; perhaps all this will end." This anticlimactic statement satirizes both Zadig's naïve optimism and the ridiculous optimism of the philosophers Gottfried Wilhelm Leibniz and Friedrich August Wolf—that "this is the best of all possible worlds"—which was much in vogue in the eighteenth century.

This leitmotif, the attack on optimism, is one of the many minor satiric barbs that Voltaire uses to spice his tale. Other satiric attacks abound in *Zadig* and reappear throughout the tales. Eighteenth century readers, usually members of the nobility and upper middle class, took delight in synthesizing the apparent subject of Voltaire's narrative with the real and often audacious object of its satire. Voltaire makes a dangerous allusion to the court when the fisherman tells Zadig how archers "armed with a royal warrant were pillaging his house lawfully and in good order." The ironic effect is achieved by the surprising juxtaposition of "pillaging" and "lawfully." Voltaire's irony had its basis in reality: He had been forced to flee the court at Versailles after making disparaging remarks about the courtiers being cheats. In *Zadig*, Voltaire also frequently satirizes the judicial system and judges who are "abysses of knowledge," who "prove" Zadig looked out of a window even though Zadig has answered none of their questions.

Voltaire's anticlericalism and antireligious bent often figure in the satire of *Zadig*. Almona the Arab widow intends to burn herself on her husband's funeral pyre, as the Brahman religion demands. Zadig the philosopher reasons her out of this plan, convincing her that she is about to take a ridiculous course in order to satisfy her vanity and not her religious principles. Zadig also persuades Sétoc that it is ridiculous to worship shining lights (the stars), and he demonstrates his reasons by kneeling and appearing to worship lighted candles. The "bonzes," who represent the monks, "chanted beautiful prayers to music, and left the state a prey to the barbarians." Zadig's rationalism (and Voltaire's) is primarily concerned with people's practical problems in society.

Voltaire's primary philosophical theme, however, is people's concern with destiny. Zadig vacillates between hope and despair as fate deals him many adverse blows. Despite his ingenuity and virtue, which he displays when he acts as the prime minister of King Moabdar, Zadig is presented as the plaything of destiny. The fisherman's story and the hermit incident reinforce the supremacy of this philosophical question as the main theme. How do philosophers explain the sufferings of a good person in the hands of a malevolent destiny? Voltaire resolves this problem happily with a deus ex machina ending. The angel Jesrad, representing divine intervention, tells Zadig to stop his questioning and simply worship Providence. Most men, Jesrad explains, form opinions with limited knowledge. Zadig's virtue triumphs, and he wins his queen and rules with "justice and love. Men blessed Zadig and Zadig blessed heaven." The skies of Zadig remain free of the blackness of *Candide*.

MICROMEGAS

Micromegas, which appeared in 1752, is a philosophical tale in a more literal sense, being primarily a vehicle for ideas on relativity. It is a very short tale, with almost no action (in stark contrast to the episodic *Zadig*) and only two main protagonists. Micromegas (which is Greek for "little big one") is a very tall inhabitant of the planet Sirius who has been banned from court for writing a book about insects that the "Mufti" of his planet has found to be heretical. He goes on an interplanetary voyage, finally arriving on the planet Saturn, where he meets a dwarf. (Voltaire intended his readers to recognize in the dwarf a caricature of his own enemy, Bernard le Bovier de Fontenelle.) The two travelers arrive on Earth and finally discover minute humans in a boat. The travelers attend a banquet at which various forms of philosophical credos are represented, allowing Voltaire to launch a satiric attack on the theories of Aristotle, René Descartes, Nicolas Malebranche, and Leibniz. Voltaire approves of the philosophy of the follower of John Locke. A storm develops, and the philosophers fall into the pocket of Micromegas. Although the giant is angry that such small creatures have so much pride, he gives a book to the philosophers; its pages, however, are blank. Voltaire gives the closing line to the dwarf (his enemy, Fontenelle), who, upon receiving the blank book—supposedly a philosophical treatise revealing the final truth about things—says, "Ah . . . that's just what I suspected." This last line was extremely offensive to Fontenelle, because it implied that he agreed that all of his metaphysical speculations over the past years had been wasted effort—that such truths were impossible to discover and prove. This attack on metaphysics is the main thrust of Voltaire's satire in *Micromegas*. Voltaire ridicules the philosophers in the boat, implying that "our little pile of mud" is relatively unimportant when seen in relation to the rest of the cosmos and that the opinions of its inhabitants are hence practically worthless. The philosophers in the boat all talk at once and all have different opinions. Voltaire shows that this kind of truth is "relative" to the person uttering it, and unreliable.

Voltaire's *Micromegas* is in direct imitation of Jonathan Swift's *Gulliver's Travels* (1726), and Montesquieu had previously used this type of travel story in *Persian Letters*. Voltaire, then, used an established subgenre, the fictional travelogue, as a vehicle for social commentary: The traveler in a strange land, seeing things for the first time, has no prejudice and puts into a new perspective situations that have been seen in only a certain way for centuries. This fresh perspective opens the way for critical appraisal and reform.

In *Micromegas*, Voltaire makes little effort to convince the reader of the reality of his story; the tale must be accepted as fantasy. The satire is less complicated, less adroit, and less sparkling than it is in *Zadig*. The main purpose of the satire is to address subjects of great interest to Voltaire's contemporaries; little of the subject matter of *Micromegas* is of interest to the modern reader. These two early works, *Zadig* and *Micromegas*, do, however, share a lighthearted spirit of enjoyment as Voltaire ridicules general stupidity and personal enemies. In these works, too, Voltaire formulated what would become the constant subjects of his satiric attacks throughout his tales.

CANDIDE

Candide belongs to the second group of tales described by Bénac and is distinguished by its radical pessimism and bitter irony, in contrast to the sunny atmosphere of the previous two tales. *Candide* is considered the epitome of the philosophical tale, and it remains highly relevant today. Unlike Voltaire's other writings, *Candide* is still read everywhere. The tale's atmosphere is dark and often despairing. Voltaire was shocked by the horrors and atrocities of the Seven Years' War, which began in August, 1756, when Frederick the Great invaded Saxony. The Lisbon earthquake in 1755 also horrified Voltaire, causing him to reflect on what kind of Providence could inflict death on the innocent and guilty alike. The optimistic philosophy of Leibniz and Wolf seemed totally absurd in the midst of so much human suffering.

The satire in *Candide* is directed above all against this optimistic philosophy, epitomized in the character Pangloss. The characters in this tale are caricatures, deformed so that each represents only one characteristic or outlook. Candide, the hero, represents naïve, good, and reasonable humanity. The philosopher Martin symbolizes a cynical Manichaeanism that acknowledges the power of evil as well as of good in the world. James, who represents real human goodness and charity, is allowed to drown in stormy seas after rescuing a sailor who had attempted to murder him. Such is the bitter mood of the tale.

The form of this novel is basically picaresque, as in *Zadig*, but Voltaire also parodies the novel of adventure and the novel of sentiment. The characters continually die horrible deaths after suffering gruesome tortures in various lands, but they somehow miraculously (and ridiculously) reappear, having been saved or cured. Their tearful reunions are a parody of the sentimental literature that Samuel Richardson's *Pamela: Or, Virtue Rewarded* (1740-1741) introduced to France from England and that infiltrated the bourgeois dramas of Diderot, and indeed of Voltaire's own theater. These reappearances also reinforce the central unity of the novel. A finely orchestrated rhythm unifies the entire tale; it is not simply that the main aim of the satire holds the tale together, as in the other stories. The fates (and philosophies) of secondary characters affect the hero in a rhythmic ebb and flow of alternating hope and despair that echo across the desolate landscape of a sad humanity in the throes of war, persecution, and suffering.

A gloss of the incidents in the tale reveals that there is no development of character or plot as such, and it underlines the rapid and vertiginous pace of the tale's episodes. This brisk pace lightens the seriousness of the atrocities being described, preventing the reader from dwelling on them or taking them to heart. Hence, Voltaire employs a technique of diminution, undercutting the value and dignity of human life.

Candide lives happily in a château in Westphalia with the baron of Thunder-ten-tronckh. Pangloss, the disciple of the optimistic philosophy of Leibniz, also lives there as tutor, as does Cunegonde, the baron's beautiful daughter, whom Candide loves. Candide agrees with Pangloss that all works out for the best in this wonderful world at the château. The baron, however, discovering the two lovers embracing, chases Candide out of the château. He is carried off forcibly to join an army and fight. After deserting, he goes to Holland, where he meets Pangloss, who has become a beggar and is barely recognizable with the sores of a terrible disease. Candide learns that all the people of the château have been killed.

Candide takes Pangloss to his benefactor, James the Anabaptist, who restores the sick man. The three then set sail for Lisbon, where James has a business engagement. On the way to Lisbon, their ship is wrecked in a storm, and James is drowned, while a sailor who had tried to murder him is saved. In Lisbon, Pangloss and Candide live through an earthquake that kills thirty thousand people. As Candide and Pangloss wander through the destroyed city, Pangloss attempts to comfort the citizens with his philosophy that "all is for the best"—a philosophy that, as Voltaire makes clear in his juxtaposition of Pangloss's theories to the suffering about him, is ludicrous if not cruel. Overhearing Pangloss's remarks, an officer of the Inquisition questions Pangloss about his belief in Original Sin and Free Will. Pangloss, sputtering his rationalizations, is arrested along with Candide—"one for having spoken, the other for having listened with an air of approval." Pangloss is hanged, but Candide is saved by the timely arrival of Cunegonde, who has escaped from the massacre of her family.

As things are beginning to seem more hopeful, Candide is obliged to kill two people, and he has to flee to America. He takes refuge with some Jesuits in Paraguay, where he miraculously meets Cunegonde's brother, who has also escaped the massacre at the château and has become a priest. Although he embraces Candide as a brother, his mood suddenly shifts when Candide announces that he intends to marry Cunegonde, and in the ensuing fight, Candide kills the brother of his beloved. After similar incidents in Eldorado, Surinam, Venice, and Constantinople, Candide finally finds Cunegonde. After all of her suffering, she has become very ugly, but, true to his word, Candide marries her. He then takes the advice of a wise old Turk and installs himself and his companions in an estate. He refuses to ask any more philosophical questions about evil and suffering in favor of hard work and practical reality—thus the novel's famous closing line: ". . . we must cultivate our garden."

In 1759, the year that *Candide* was published, Voltaire bought Ferney, an estate on the French-Swiss border, which has led critics to surmise that Candide's conclusions about work and the happiness to be found in practical progress are those of Voltaire. Once Voltaire was installed at Ferney, he gained confidence and energy and bombarded his public and his enemies with pamphlets, essays, plays, and stories, waging numerous legal battles on behalf of those persecuted for religious reasons. *Ingenuous* was written during this last, very active period of Voltaire's life. Although Voltaire was seventy-three years old when he wrote this work, his incredible intellectual and creative vigor had not diminished.

INGENUOUS

Ingenuous is one of the weapons Voltaire used in his unremitting battle against intolerance and injustice and belongs to the third group of novels delineated by Bénac. Voltaire's confidence had returned, and he wrote with a sure hand; none of the tales that follow *Candide* can rival the grandeur of *Ingenuous*.

Ingenuous is the most romantic of Voltaire's stories, and its plot is narrative rather than episodic. The tone of the story is more naturalistic, as are the characters. The device of a voyage is used again; the religious and social systems of France in the time of Louis XIV are seen through the eyes of the Huron stranger, who, without prejudice and with candid reasoning, questions institutions and beliefs that have been taken for granted and must now be considered from a new perspective.

The character of the Huron is in the tradition of the "noble savage" popularized by a missionary, baron de Lahontan, who praised the uncorrupted American Indian. The unity of the tale lies in the unfolding of the story of two lovers: Hercules Kerkabon (as the Huron is later named) and Mademoiselle de St. Yves. The satire used here also unites with the central love theme, targeting the corrupt Catholic Church and its priests, monks, and practices, which are instrumental in separating the lovers and ruining their chance for happiness. Voltaire also satirizes the court officials and Jansenism.

Voltaire's wit has a somewhat subdued tone throughout *Ingenuous*; the satire resides in the calmly reasoned arguments of the Huron, who questions all the basic doctrines of Jesuit and Jansenist alike. Voltaire, using the Huron as his mouthpiece, explains very simply all of his objections to the two religions. At the time of writing this tale, Voltaire was involved in the trials of the Calas family, the Sirven family, and La Barre, and his hatred of religious persecution and his anger at the injustices meted out by a corrupt judicial system were therefore as intense as they had ever been.

The story reflects the century's taste for cosmopolitanism. The Huron has been reared by a Huron tribe in Canada and arrives on the Lower Brittany coast in 1689. It is "discovered" that he is the lost child of the Abbé Yerkabon and his sister. Their brother went to Canada as a soldier and was killed by the Iroquois. The Abbé claims Hercules as his nephew and baptizes him as a Catholic. The beautiful Mademoiselle de St. Yves acts as his godmother. Hercules later falls in love with Mademoiselle de St. Yves but cannot marry his godmother, because the Church forbids it. Mademoiselle de St. Yves is sent to a convent, and Hercules, who is by now a hero for helping to defend the French against an English attack, goes to Versailles to engage the king's help in his marriage scheme. At Versailles, he is arrested and imprisoned in the Bastille, where he meets Gordon, a Jansenist. After much study and discussion, he converts Gordon to Deism. Now Mademoiselle de St. Yves goes to Versailles to save Hercules, but she must submit to a government minister in order to obtain her lover's release. She never recovers from the shame and dies of her chagrin. Hercules is tempted to take his own life but recovers himself and becomes an excellent officer and philosopher. The tale does not end with the expected happy ending for the lovers, but Voltaire suggests that even if ambitions and ideals cannot be attained, there are compromises that can be made and one can be tolerably happy—a message similar to that of *Candide*.

THE MAN OF FORTY CROWNS

The Man of Forty Crowns, published the year after *Ingenuous*, displays a strong contrast in style. The two tales have in common the underlying interest of Voltaire in practical things. In *Ingenuous*, Voltaire has Hercules recover from his loss and become a good soldier; in *The Man of Forty Crowns*, Voltaire has his protagonist discuss tax reform with a mathematician. There is a great difference, however, between these polemics and those of *Ingenuous*. In the later tale, Voltaire writes for a clever and agile mind able to follow the mathematical bent of his arguments. There is scarcely a plot or an appealing character to enliven the discussion. Voltaire, as usual, satirizes monks (who do not pay taxes), despotic monarchs, unfair judicial systems, and ignorant people who think they know more than they do. This highly polemical tale, amusing for Voltaire's eighteenth century circle, is of little interest today; not even the odd humorous remark, such as the suggestion that smiles and songs be taxed, can redeem the lack of relevance or interest of this story for a modern reader.

Voltaire's tales do suffer a slight impoverishment in translation. The musicality of the French language offsets the dryness of the succinct, economic prose and the laconic, pointed understatement. Polemical tales such as *The Man of Forty Crowns* particularly suffer in English translation.

Of Voltaire's many tales (some two dozen in all), *Candide* remains the most popular. Perhaps it has universal appeal because the evils it portrays persist in today's world. Wars are still waged in the name of religious causes, and political prisoners continue to be tortured and cast into jail without trial. Unfortunately, Voltaire is no longer here to provoke people's consciences and fire their minds with his energetic fury. Without him, the genre of the philosophical tale lies in disuse.

Avril S. Lewis

OTHER MAJOR WORKS

SHORT FICTION: *Le Monde comme il va*, 1748 (revised as *Babouc: Ou, Le Monde comme il va*, 1749; *Babouc: Or, The World as It Goes*, 1754; also known as *The World as It Is: Or, Babouc's Vision*, 1929); *Memnon: Ou, La Sagesse humaine*, 1749 (*Memnon: Or, Human Wisdom*, 1961); *La Lettre d'un Turc*, 1750; *Le Blanc et le noir*, 1764 (*The Two Genies*, 1895); *Jeannot et Colin*, 1764 (*Jeannot and Colin*, 1929); *L'Histoire de Jenni*, 1775; *Les Oreilles du Comte de Chesterfield*, 1775 (*The Ears of Lord Chesterfield and Parson Goodman*, 1826).

PLAYS: *Œdipe*, pr. 1718 (*Oedipus*, 1761); *Artémire*, pr. 1720; *Mariamne*, pr. 1724 (English translation, 1761); *L'Indiscret*, pr., pb. 1725 (verse play); *Brutus*, pr. 1730 (English translation, 1761); *Ériphyle*, pr. 1732; *Zaïre*, pr. 1732 (English translation, 1736); *La Mort de César*, pr. 1733; *Adélaïde du Guesclin*, pr. 1734; *L'Échange*, pr. 1734; *Alzire*, pr., pb. 1736 (English translation, 1763); *L'Enfant prodigue*, pr. 1736 (verse play; prose translation, *The Prodigal*, 1750?); *Zulime*, pr. 1740; *Mahomet*, pr., pb. 1742 (*Mahomet the Prophet*, 1744); *Mérope*, pr. 1743 (English translation, 1744, 1749); *La Princesse de Navarre*, pr., pb. 1745 (verse play; music by Jean-Philippe Rameau); *La Prude: Ou, La Grandeuse de Cassette*, pr., pb. 1747 (wr. 1740; verse play; adaptation of William Wycherley's play *The Plain Dealer*); *Sémiramis*, pr. 1748 (*Semiramis*, 1760); *Nanine*, pr., pb. 1749 (English translation, 1927); *Oreste*, pr., pb. 1750; *Rome sauvée*, pr., pb. 1752; *L'Orphelin de la Chine*, pr., pb. 1755 (*The Orphan of China*, 1756); *Socrate*, pb. 1759 (*Socrates*, 1760); *L'Écossaise*, pr., pb. 1760 (*The Highland Girl*, 1760); *Tancrède*, pr. 1760; *Olympie*, pb. 1763; *Le Triumvirat*, pr. 1764; *Les Scythes*, pr., pb. 1767; *Les Guèbres: Ou, La Tolérance*, pb. 1769; *Sophonisbe*, pb. 1770 (revision of Jean Mairet's play); *Les Pélopides: Ou, Atrée et Thyeste*, pb. 1772; *Les Lois de Minos*, pb. 1773; *Don Pèdre*, pb. 1775 (wr. 1761); *Irène*, pr. 1778; *Agathocle*, pr. 1779.

poetry: *Poème sur la religion naturelle*, 1722; *La Ligue*, 1723; *La Henriade*, 1728 (a revision of *La Ligue*; *Henriade*, 1732); *Le Mondain*, 1736 (*The Man of the World*, 1764); *Discours en vers sur l'homme*, 1738 (*Discourses in Verse on Man*, 1764); *Poème de Fontenoy*, 1745; *Poème sur la loi naturelle*, 1752 (*On Natural Law*, 1764); *La Pucelle d'Orléans*, 1755, 1762 (*The Maid of Orleans*, 1758; also known as *La Pucelle: Or, The Maid of Orleans*, 1785-1786); *Poème sur la désastre de Lisbonne*, 1756 (*Poem on the Lisbon Earthquake*, 1764); *Le Pauvre Diable*, 1758; *Épître à Horace*, 1772.

nonfiction: *An Essay upon the Civil Wars of France . . . and Also upon the Epick Poetry of the European Nations from Homer Down to Milton*, 1727; *La Henriade*, 1728 (*Henriade*, 1732); *Histoire de Charles XII*, 1731 (*The History of Charles XII*, 1732); *Le Temple du goût*, 1733 (*The Temple of Taste*, 1734); *Lettres philosophiques*, 1734 (originally published in English as *Letters Concerning the English Nation*, 1733; also known as *Philosophical Letters*, 1961); *Discours de métaphysique*, 1736; *Éléments de la philosophie de Newton*, 1738 (*The Elements of Sir Isaac Newton's Philosophy*, 1738); *Discours en vers sur l'homme*, 1738-1752 (*Discourses in Verse on Man*, 1764); *Vie de Molière*, 1739; *Le Siècle de Louis XIV*, 1751 (*The Age of Louis XIV*, 1752); *Essai sur les mœurs et l'esprit des nations*, 1756, 1763 (*The General History and State of Europe*, 1754, 1759); *Traité sur la tolérance*, 1763 (*A Treatise on Religious Toleration*, 1764); *Commentaires sur le théâtre de Pierre Corneille*, 1764; *Dictionnaire philosophique portatif*, 1764 (enlarged 1769 as *La Raison par alphabet*; also known as *Dictionnaire philosophique*; *A Philosophical Dictionary for the Pocket*, 1765; also known as *Philosophical Dictionary*, 1945, enlarged 1962); *Avis au public sur les parracides imputés aux calas et aux Sirven*, 1775; *Correspondence*, 1953-1965 (102 volumes).

miscellaneous: *The Works of M. de Voltaire*, 1761-1765 (35 volumes), 1761-1781 (38 volumes); *Candide, and Other Writings*, 1945; *The Portable Voltaire*, 1949; *Candide, Zadig, and Selected Stories*, 1961; *The Complete Works of Voltaire*, 1968-1977 (135 volumes; in French).

Bibliography

Aldridge, A. Owen. *Voltaire and the Century of Light*. Princeton, N.J.: Princeton University Press, 1975. Reexamines the life and career of Voltaire within the context of European intellectual and political history, providing many useful insights. Presents information in a pleasant style equally suited to specialists and general readers. Also offers stimulating readings of *Candide* and other selected works as well as a valuable bibliography.

Bird, Stephen. *Reinventing Voltaire: The Politics of Commemoration in Nineteenth Century France*. Oxford, England: Voltaire Foundation, 2000. Focuses on the critical response to Voltaire in nineteenth century France, where his legacy was both vilified and venerated. Includes bibliography and indexes.

Cronk, Nicholas, ed. *The Cambridge Companion to Voltaire*. New York: Cambridge University Press, 2009. Collection of essays examines Voltaire's life, philosophy, and works. Includes discussions of Voltaire as a storyteller, Voltaire and authorship, and Voltaire and the myth of England as well as an analysis of *Candide* by Philip Stewart.

Davidson, Ian. *Voltaire in Exile: The Last Years*. New York: Grove Press, 2004. Chronicles Voltaire's life during his exile from France, when he actively campaigned against censorship, war, torture, capital punishment, the alliance between church and state, and other perceived injustices. Includes an analysis of much of Voltaire's personal correspondence.

Gray, John. *Voltaire*. New York: Routledge, 1999. Volume in Routledge's Great Philosophers series provides a concise overview of Voltaire's philosophy. Includes bibliography.

Havens, George R. *The Age of Ideas*. New York: Henry Holt, 1955. Often reprinted and providing a model and inspiration for many writers, Havens's witty, informed overview of the Enlightenment and its precursors remains authoritative as a guide to trends and thinkers of the period. Contains groups of chapters devoted to Voltaire, Charles de Montesquieu, Denis Diderot, and Jean-Jacques Rousseau; the four chapters devoted to Voltaire provide an excellent introduction to the man and his work, with brief but perceptive readings of such texts as *Zadig* and *Candide*.

Knapp, Bettina Liebowitz. *Voltaire Revisited*. New York: Twayne, 2000. Good introductory study describes Voltaire's life and devotes separate chapters to all of the genres of his works, including *Candide* and other philosophical tales. Includes bibliography and index.

Mason, Haydn Trevor. *"Candide": Optimism Demolished*. New York: Twayne, 1992. Examination of Voltaire's novel is divided into two parts: The first addresses the work's literary and historical context, including its critical reception, and the second provides a reading of the book's view of history, philosophy, personality, structure, and form. Includes notes and annotated bibliography.

_______. *Voltaire*. New York: St. Martin's Press, 1975. Comprehensive monograph (not to be confused with the biography Mason published six years later, cited below) is intended for the interested undergraduate or general reader. Steers clear of the traditional chronological approach in order to present Voltaire's works by genre, treating first his drama and dramatic criticism and then proceeding to historiography, short fiction, poetry, and polemics. Supplemented by a useful if brief bibliography.

_______. *Voltaire: A Biography*. Baltimore: Johns Hopkins University Press, 1981. Presents a concise but lively survey of the subject's life, clearly relating the major works to their contexts, including their inspiration or—as is especially pertinent in the case of Voltaire—provocation. Closely documented, useful both as biography and as criticism, this volume is recommended to students and general readers alike.

Pearson, Roger. *Voltaire Almighty: A Life in Pursuit of Freedom*. London: Bloomsbury, 2005. Readable, compelling account of Voltaire's life focuses on his love of liberty and how that passion informed his life and work. Includes bibliography, index, and illustrations.

Vartanian, Aram. "*Zadig:* Theme and Countertheme." In *Dilemmas du roman*, edited by Catherine Lafarge. Saratoga, Calif.: Anima Libri, 1990. Analyzes Voltaire's novel and argues that its philosophical theme of impersonal fate is counterpoised against a background theme, creating a contrapuntal movement of the narrative structure. Asserts that the story is told in such a way that its overall meaning emerges from a network of tensions felt among its various elements.

KURT VONNEGUT

Born: Indianapolis, Indiana; November 11, 1922
Died: New York, New York; April 11, 2007
Also known as: Kurt Vonnegut, Jr.

PRINCIPAL LONG FICTION

Player Piano, 1952
The Sirens of Titan, 1959
Mother Night, 1961
Cat's Cradle, 1963
God Bless You, Mr. Rosewater: Or, Pearls Before Swine, 1965
Slaughterhouse-Five: Or, The Children's Crusade, a Duty-Dance with Death, 1969
Breakfast of Champions: Or, Goodbye Blue Monday, 1973
Slapstick: Or, Lonesome No More!, 1976
Jailbird, 1979
Deadeye Dick, 1982
Galápagos, 1985
Bluebeard, 1987
Hocus Pocus, 1990
Timequake, 1997
God Bless You, Dr. Kevorkian, 1999 (novella)

OTHER LITERARY FORMS

Although known primarily for his novels, Kurt Vonnegut (VON-uh-guht) also wrote for Broadway and television and published a children's book and several books of essays.

ACHIEVEMENTS

Critical acclaim eluded Kurt Vonnegut until *Slaughterhouse-Five* was published in 1969. An immediate best seller, it earned for the author respect from critics who had previously dismissed him as a mediocre science-fiction writer. Over the course of his career, Vonnegut was honored as the Briggs-Copeland Lecturer at Harvard University, as a member of the National Institute of Arts and Letters, and as the Distinguished Professor of English Prose at the City University of New York. Through his insightful and sympathetic treatment of the psychologically and morally crippled victims of the modern world, Vonnegut earned a reputation as one of the greatest humanist writers of his time.

BIOGRAPHY

Kurt Vonnegut, Jr., was born in Indianapolis, Indiana, in 1922. Both the location and the era of his birth helped shape his distinctive worldview. Growing up in the American heartland in the calm interval between the world wars, Vonnegut had a brief vision of a middle-class world that embraced the values of honesty, decency, and human dignity. For Vonnegut, this was the world as it should be, a world unravaged by violence and war, a world untouched by technology. This period of childhood happiness was, however, merely the calm before the storm in a life that would be rocked by a series of personal and national disasters: the suicide of his mother on Mother's Day; his prisoner-of-war experience in World War II; the deaths of his sister and brother-in-law; the dissolution of his first marriage; the bombings of Dresden and Hiroshima; the assassinations of President John F. Kennedy and the Reverend Martin Luther King, Jr.; the Vietnam War; the death of his first wife, with whom he had maintained a close friendship; and the death of his brother Bernard. All the heartaches of his family and his nation reverberate through Vonnegut's work, while the artist, through his fiction, stands as advocate for a saner, calmer world.

During the years of the Great Depression, Vonnegut's family suffered emotional and financial setbacks. When Vonnegut entered Cornell University in 1940, his father forbade him to study the arts and chose instead for his son a career in science, which he believed would guarantee job security. In 1943 Vonnegut left Cornell to enlist in the U.S. Army, despite his own public opposition to the war. Less than one year later, he was captured by the Germans and, in 1945, survived one of the greatest massacres of the war, the Allied firebombing of Dresden. This horror pursued Vonnegut for twenty-three years, until he worked through the pain by writing *Slaughterhouse-Five*.

After the war, Vonnegut married and began studies in anthropology at the University of Chicago. After three years, he left college and took a job as a publicist with General Electric (GE), where his brother worked as a physicist. Vonnegut's background in science and the disillusionment he experienced at GE influenced his first two novels, *Player Piano* and *The Sirens of Titan*, both parables of dehumanization in a technological society.

Between 1952 and 1998, Vonnegut wrote more than a dozen novels, numerous essays, a Broadway play, and a musical work, *Requiem*, that was performed by the Buffalo Symphony. He and Joe Petro III had a showing of twenty-six of their silk-screen prints in Denver in 1996. Despite his varied artistic talents, however, Vonnegut has always been known primarily for his fiction. In 1978, Vonnegut remarried, and he and his wife, Jill Krementz, settled in New York City. Vonnegut lived in New York until his death in 2007 at the age of eighty-four.

ANALYSIS

In his novels, Kurt Vonnegut coaxes the reader toward greater sympathy for humanity and deeper understanding of the human condition. His genre is satire—sometimes biting, sometimes tender, always funny. His arena is as expansive as the whole universe and as tiny as a single human soul. Part philosopher, part poet, Vonnegut, in his fictive world, tackles the core problem of modern life: How can the individual maintain dignity and exercise free will in a world overrun by death and destruction, a world in which both science and religion are powerless to provide solutions? The reader will find no ready answers in Vonnegut, only a friendly guide along the questioning path.

Vonnegut himself behaved with a commendable sense of responsibility, dignity, and decency: He labored long to show humankind its ailments and to wake it to the work it has to do. He admitted to having lived comfortably while many of the world's population suffered, but in quoting the words of American socialist Eugene Debs in his dedication to *Hocus Pocus*, he seems to define the position that he himself took as human being and as author and public figure for half of the twentieth century: "While there is a lower class I am in it. While there is a criminal element I am of it. While there is a soul in prison I am not free." He spoke out in many forums for many causes and for all of humankind, and his has been a wide audience.

PLAYER PIANO

Ilium, New York, sometime in the near future, provides the setting for Vonnegut's first dystopian novel, *Player Piano*. Ilium is a divided city. On one side of the river live the important people, the engineers and managers who program and operate the computers and machines that run people's lives. On the other side of the river, Homestead, live the downtrodden inhabitants of the city, those locked into menial, dehumanizing jobs assigned to them by the central computer.

Paul Proteus, the protagonist, is the brilliant young manager of the Ilium Works, a man being groomed for even greater success. Just as Ilium is a divided city, however, so is Paul divided about his life and his future. Paul suffers a growing discontent with his job at the Ilium Works, where people have been replaced by machines and machines are supervised by computers. Outwardly, Paul has no reason for worry or doubt. He has the best job and the most beautiful wife in Ilium, he is being considered for the highest post in his company, and he is climbing the ladder of success. Nevertheless, Paul's uneasiness increases. At first he seeks escape, settling on a farm in an attempt to get back to nature and free himself from his automatic life. He finds, however, that he has become an automaton, completely out of touch with the natural world, and his attempt at escape fails.

Finally, Paul is drawn to the other side of the river. His sympathy for the dehumanized masses and his acknowledgment of complicity in their plight drive Paul to join the masses in armed revolution. The fighters take to the streets, frantically and indiscriminately destroying all machines. The revolution fails, leaving Paul disillusioned and defeated, realizing that he has been manipulated by leaders on both sides of the conflict. Now he must surrender and face execution.

Paul's manipulation, first by those who would replace people with machines and then by those who would destroy the machines, is symbolized by the "player piano" of the title. The simplest of machines, the player piano creates its music without the aid of human beings, neatly rendering the skilled musician obsolete. Paul is entranced by the music of the player piano, in his fascination manipulated by the machine just as it manipulates its ivory keys.

The most striking symbol of the story, however, is the small black cat that Paul befriends as it wanders aimlessly through the Ilium Works. The cat, symbol of all that is natural and pure, despises the monstrous factory machines. The doomed animal is helplessly sucked into an automated sweeper, which spits it down a chute and ejects it outside the factory. Miraculously, it survives, but as Paul races to its rescue, the cat is roasted on the factory's electric fence, symbolizing humanity's destruction by the forces of technology. With characteristic Vonnegut irony, however, *Player Piano* ends on an affirmative note. Although the price of escape is its life, the cat does escape the Ilium Works. Near the end of the novel, Paul sees beautiful flowers growing outside the factory—flowers rooted in cat excrement, signifying ultimate rebirth and a glimmer of hope for Paul and his world.

Mother Night

In his third novel, *Mother Night*, Vonnegut peers even more deeply into the human soul, exploring the roots of human alienation, probing an individual's search for his "real" identity, and uncovering the thin veil that separates reality from illusion. The story is told as the memoir of Howard W. Campbell, Jr., a self-proclaimed "citizen of nowhere." A successful writer and producer of medieval romance plays, Campbell sees himself as a sensitive *artiste*. Nevertheless, he allows himself to be recruited by Major Frank Wirtanen to be an American double agent posing as a Nazi radio propagandist in Germany. Secretly, Campbell sends coded American messages in his propaganda broadcasts, but he does not understand the code and never comprehends the messages he transmits. Still unaware, he even transmits the news of his beloved wife's death.

Publicly, Campbell is reviled as a traitorous Nazi hatemonger, but he does not mind because he enjoys being on the radio. Eventually, however, he begins to lose touch with his "real" self. Is he the sensitive artist, the cruel Nazi, or the American patriot? Like Paul Proteus, Campbell allows himself to be manipulated by those around him. With no will or identity of his own, Campbell is easy prey for those who would use him for their own ends.

Two of Campbell's manipulators are his postwar friend George Kraft and his sister-in-law Resi, who poses as Campbell's long-lost wife, Helga. George and Resi are actually Russian spies plotting to capture Campbell and transport him to Russia. They abandon this plan, however, when they realize their love for Campbell, and they finally attempt to escape to freedom with him. Before the three can flee together, however, the Russians are arrested by American agents. Campbell is arrested as well but is soon freed by his friend Frank Wirtanen.

Gripped by existential fear at finding himself a free man, Campbell appeals to a Jewish couple in his apartment building, a doctor and his mother, both survivors of the Nazi death camp Auschwitz. Campbell begs to be tried for his crimes against the Jews and soon finds himself awaiting trial in a Jerusalem prison. Before Campbell goes to trial, Frank Wirtanen sends a letter on his behalf, explaining how he had recruited Campbell and honoring him as an American patriot. Campbell, however, can never be a truly free man until he purges his conscience. Upon his release from prison, he is nauseated by the prospect of his freedom, knowing that he is one of the many people "who served evil too openly and good too secretly." In his failure to resist evil and his openness to manipulation by others, Campbell had given up his free will and lost his ability to choose. Coming to this realization, he finally asserts his will to choose and ironically chooses to die, vowing to hang himself "for crimes against himself."

CAT'S CRADLE

Equally dark is Vonnegut's fourth novel, *Cat's Cradle*. In addition to its broad parody of science and religion, *Cat's Cradle* expands on Vonnegut's earlier themes of the dangerous misuse of science and technology, human beings' moral responsibility in an immoral world, and the importance of distinguishing reality from illusion. The parodic tone is set in the very first line, "Call me Jonah," bringing to mind the Old Testament book of Jonah. Like that Jonah, this protagonist (really named John) faithfully pursues God's directives but never truly comprehends the order behind God's plan. Continuing the parody, John encounters the Bokononist religion, whose bible, The Books of Bokonon, proclaims in its first line, "All of the true things I am about to tell you are shameless lies," an obvious inversion of the Johannine maxim "You will know the truth, and the truth will make you free" (John 8:32). In the world John inhabits, the only real freedom is the ultimate freedom—death.

John is writing a book, "The Day the World Ended," an account of the bombing of Hiroshima. His obsession with the destruction of Hiroshima foreshadows his involvement in the eventual destruction of the world by "ice-nine," a substance that converts liquid into frozen crystals. In *Cat's Cradle*, the atomic bomb and ice-nine are both the doomsday toys of an amoral scientist, Dr. Felix Hoenikker. Hoenikker pursues his work so intensely that he has little time for his three children, who grow up to be emotionally warped and twisted Products of Science. Hoenikker's only legacy to his children is the ice-nine he was brewing in the kitchen before his sudden death on Christmas Eve. After their father's death, the three children—Angela, Frank, and Newt—divide the ice-nine among themselves, knowing that it is their ticket to a better future. Newt, a midget, barters his ice-nine for an affair with a Russian ballerina. The homely Angela uses her portion to buy herself a husband. Frank gives his to Miguel "Papa" Monzano, dictator of the Caribbean Republic of San Lorenzo, in exchange for the title of general and the hand of Monzano's beautiful adopted daughter, Mona.

Pursuing information on the Hoenikker family, John finds himself in San Lorenzo, where he is introduced to Bokononism. The people of San Lorenzo are desperately poor, for the soil of the island is as unproductive as the Sahara. The island's teeming, malnourished masses find their only comfort in Bokononism, which urges them to love and console one another. John finds that, ironically, the religion started as a game by the island's founders. Knowing no way to lift the country from its destitution, they decided to give the people hope by inventing a religion based on *foma*, or comforting lies. The religion encouraged people to find strength in their *karass*, groups of people with whom they are joined to do God's mysterious will. To strengthen the faith of the people, Bokononism was outlawed, its founder banished on pain of death. As the people's faith grew, so did their happiness and their dependence on *foma*, until all the inhabitants of the island were "employed full time as actors in a play." For the inhabitants of San Lorenzo, illusion had become reality.

Soon after his arrival on the island, John finds that Papa Monzano is critically ill; it is expected that "General" Frank Hoenikker will succeed Papa and take the beautiful Mona as his bride. Secretly, however, Frank has no desire to rule the island or to marry Mona. He is a simpering mass of insecurities, hiding behind his fake title. Frank's life, like everything around him, has been a lie: He has bought a false sense of dignity, which he wears like a military uniform, but inside he is gripped with fear, the same fear that pulses through the veins of the dying dictator. Papa and Frank become symbols for all people, running scared and grasping at false comforts as they confront brutal reality. Faced with the horror of an agonizing death, Papa clutches his vial of ice-nine, his last illusion of security and power. Uttering the desperate cry, "Now I will destroy the whole world," he swallows the poison and turns himself into an ice-blue frozen statue. Papa's power proves illusory, however, as John and the Hoenikker children clean up the mess and seal off Papa's bedroom.

John, Frank, Angela, and Newt inform the staff that Papa is "feeling much better" and go downstairs to watch a military celebration. Despite their success at covering up Papa's death and hiding their secret, John and the Hoenikker children sense impending doom. As all the islanders watch the military air show, a bomber careens out of control and bursts into flames, setting off a massive explosion and landslide. As his castle disintegrates, Papa Monzano's body is propelled from the bedroom closet and plunges into the waiting sea, infecting all with ice-nine.

As the story ends, only John, Newt, and Bokonon remain, awaiting their imminent death. John recalls Angela's heroic end, remembering how she had clutched her clarinet bravely and played in the face of death, music mocking terror. John dreams of climbing the highest mountain and planting some magnificent symbol. As his heart swells with the vision of being the last man on the highest mountain, Newt mocks him and brings him back to earth. The story concludes with the last verse of The Books of Bokonon, in which Bokonon mourns human stupidity, thumbs his nose at God, and kills himself with ice-nine.

Like many of Vonnegut's satirical writings, *Cat's Cradle* functions as a wake-up call for humanity. For Vonnegut, heroism is not a dream; dignity is not an illusion. Still, he understands all too well the fear that grips an individual on the brink of action, the torpor that invades the soul. In his frustration, all the artist can do is plod on, calling out his warnings as he goes.

SLAUGHTERHOUSE-FIVE

Vonnegut's efforts to touch the soul of humanity are most fully realized in his sixth novel, *Slaughterhouse-Five*, his most moving and brilliant work. Incorporating all of Vonnegut's common themes—the nature of reality and illusion, the question of free will and determinism, the horror of humankind's cruelty to itself, the vision of life as an ironic construct—*Slaughterhouse-Five* produces "an image of life that is beautiful and surprising and deep." This often misunderstood novel leads the reader on a time-warped journey, as popular films say, "to hell and back." Emotionally suffocated by his experience in World War II, Vonnegut waited twenty-three years to tell the story of his capture by the Germans and his survival of the Allied firebombing of Dresden, the calculated annihilation of a quarter of a million refugees and civilians in an unguarded city.

As befits a tale of such distorted experience, *Slaughterhouse-Five* breaks all novelistic conventions. The story is divided into ten sections spanning the years from 1944 to 1968. Opening with a simple, first-person narrative, Vonnegut describes his return to Dresden in 1967. He recounts his life after the war, discusses his wife and children, and relives a conversation with his old war buddy Bernard V. O'Hare, in which he reveals why *Slaughterhouse-Five* is subtitled *The Children's Crusade*. In the original Children's Crusade of 1213, Catholic monks raised a volunteer army of thirty thousand children who were intent on traveling to Palestine but instead were sent to North Africa to be sold as slaves. In the end, half the children drowned en route and the others were sold. For Vonnegut, this incident provides the perfect metaphor for all wars: hopeless ventures fought by deluded children. Thus Vonnegut prepares the reader for this personal statement about the tragedy of war. Nevertheless, the reader remains unprepared for the narrative shape of the tale.

Breaking from his reverie, Vonnegut reads from a Gideon Bible the story of Lot's wife, turned to a pillar of salt for looking back on Sodom and Gomorrah. To Vonnegut, her reaction was tender, instinctively human, looking back on all those lives that had touched hers, and he adopts Lot's wife as a metaphor for his narrative stance. *Slaughterhouse-Five* will be a tale told by a "pillar of salt." Vonnegut assumes the role of a masked narrator, a disinterested party, allowing himself the aesthetic distance he needs to continue his painful journey. When the reader turns to chapter 2, however, another surprise appears, as chapter 2 begins, "Listen: Billy Pilgrim has come unstuck in time."

To increase his emotional distance from the story, Vonnegut, the masked narrator, tells not his own story but the story of pathetic Billy Pilgrim, Vonnegut's mythical fellow soldier. Through time travel over which he has no control, Billy is forced to relive the chapters of his life in seemingly random order. For Billy, as for Vonnegut, his war chronology is too unsettling to confront head-on. Instead of assimilating his life experiences, Billy unconsciously tries to escape the memory of them by bouncing back and forth in time from one experience to another. Not until the end of the tale can he face the crucial moment, the horror of Dresden.

The reader first sees Billy as a forty-six-year-old retired optometrist living in Ilium,

New York. Billy's daughter, Barbara, thinks that he has lost his mind. Billy has given up interest in business and devotes all of his energies to telling the world about his travels to the planet Tralfamadore. Two years earlier, Billy had been captured by aliens from Tralfamadore and had spent six months on their planet. Billy's belief in Tralfamadorian philosophy is the great comfort of his life, and he is eager to share this philosophy with the world. The aliens taught Billy, the optometrist, a better way to "see." On Tralfamadore, time is not linear; all moments are structured and permanent, and death is merely one moment out of many moments in a person's life. The Tralfamadorians do not mourn the dead, for even though a person may be dead in one moment, he or she is alive and happy in many others. The Tralfamadorians respond to life's temporary bad moments with a verbal shrug, "So it goes." Their world is a world without free will, without human responsibility, without human sorrow. On an intellectual level, Billy hungrily embraces their philosophy, yet deep inside him (as inside Vonnegut) stirs the need to reconstruct his life, to reconcile his past. So, armed with Tralfamadorian detachment, Billy steps back in time to where it all began.

It is 1944, and Billy, a night student at the Ilium School of Optometry, is drafted into action in World War II. No soldier is more unsuited to war than is Billy. Timid and friendless, he is a chaplain's assistant, a hapless soul with a "meek faith in a loving Jesus which most soldiers found putrid." Billy's marching companion is Roland Weary, a savage young man even by military standards. Weary's father collects ancient instruments of torture, and Weary regales Billy with gruesome tales of cruelty, giving the gentle boy an unwanted view of a monstrous world. Weary, a callous, stupid killing machine, is the natural result of humanity's barbarity. Although physically robust, he is morally depleted, a symbol of the spiritually bankrupt world into which poor Billy has been thrust. Billy—kind, sensitive, tenderhearted—has no natural defenses against the barbarity that surrounds him, so he becomes unstuck in time.

After a brief respite of time travel, Billy returns to the war. He and Weary have been captured behind German lines, taken prisoner by two toothless old men and two young boys. The Germans are accompanied by a guard dog, a female German shepherd named Princess who had been stolen from a farmer. Princess and Billy are confused and shivering from the cold. Of the whole motley group, only the barbarous Weary belongs at war. Billy, Princess, the old men, and the young boys symbolize helpless humanity in the grip of military madness.

Billy and his fellow prisoners, including Vonnegut and Bernard V. O'Hare, are taken to a prisoner-of-war camp before their transport to Dresden. As Billy recalls these moments of his life, he is moved to time-travel many times. He flashes forward to 1948, when, emotionally shattered by his war experience, he checks himself into a veterans' hospital for mental patients. Here the reader is introduced to Valencia Merble, Billy's unlovely fiancé, and Eliot Rosewater, his fellow mental patient. In the hospital, Eliot and Billy devour the science-fiction novels of author Kilgore Trout. They are drawn to Trout's work for the same reason Billy is drawn to the philosophy of Tralfamadore: Human experience on Earth has been too disturbing; life seems meaningless. Escaping to the world of science fiction relieves the pressure, enabling Eliot and Billy to "reinvent" themselves in a kinder universe.

Before Billy returns to his war story, he again relives his adventures on the planet Tralfamadore, where he spends six months in the Tralfamadore Zoo, displayed in a glass cage. Here Billy learns of his own death in 1976. He will be murdered by Paul Lazarro, a former inmate in the prisoner-of-war camp. The maniacal Lazarro, incorrectly blaming Billy for the death of Roland Weary, has plotted revenge since 1944. Naturally, Billy's innocence makes his meaningless death doubly absurd. At this time, Billy also learns of the eventual destruction of Earth by the Tralfamadorians. While testing a new rocket fuel for their spacecraft, they accidentally blow up the universe. "So it goes."

When Billy returns to his war story, he and his fellow American soldiers are in Dresden, working in a factory producing vitamin syrup for pregnant women. Soon, however, there will be no pregnant women in Dresden. The American prisoners of war are quartered underground in a former pig butchery—slaughterhouse number five. On the night of February 13, 1945, Billy (and Vonnegut) nestles safely in the shelter while the city is flattened by British and American firebombs. The next morning, the prisoners go aboveground and find the city as lifeless as the surface of the moon. Only the one hundred American prisoners and their guards had survived. In chapter 10, Vonnegut himself returns as narrator. It is 1968. In the intervening years, Billy has survived an airplane crash in which all of his fellow passengers died. Valencia, frantically hurrying to see Billy in the hospital, has died of accidental carbon-monoxide poisoning. Robert Kennedy and Martin Luther King, Jr., have been assassinated. The Vietnam War is raging.

Finally, Vonnegut takes the reader back to Dresden. He and Billy are there, where the prisoners of war are digging for bodies, mining for corpses. Billy's digging companion dies of the dry heaves, unable to face the slaughter. Billy's friend Edgar Derby is executed for stealing a teapot. When the corpse mines are closed down, Billy, Vonnegut, and their companions are locked up in the suburbs to await the end of the war. When the war is over, the freed soldiers wander out into the street. The trees are blooming and the birds are singing; springtime has finally arrived for Kurt Vonnegut.

Looking back on the novel, the reader realizes that Billy's time travels have been more than simply a coping device; they provide a learning tool as well. The jumbled events to which Vonnegut subjects Billy are not random and meaningless. Even if Billy remains blankly ignorant of the connections between events in his life, both the reader and the author learn about emotional survival in the modern world. For Vonnegut, who called himself "the canary in the coal mine," Billy's story is a parable and a warning to all humankind: a warning that men and women must resist the temptation to abandon their free will, as Billy had, and an exhortation to keep one's dignity in the face of modern dehumanization.

That *Slaughterhouse-Five* is a story of survival may seem contradictory or ironic, but that is always Vonnegut's approach. It would be hard for the reader to imagine more death than is witnessed here—the slaughter in Dresden and the deaths of Billy, his wife, his father, and assorted soldiers, all culminating in the foretelling of the destruction of the universe by the Tralfamadorians—yet the reader comes to understand that everything about Vonnegut's tale is ironic. Edgar Derby is executed, amid the Dresden corpse mines, for stealing a teapot; Billy, sitting in a slaughterhouse, is saved from destruction. No wonder Billy sees himself as the plaything of uncontrollable forces. Vonnegut knows better, however. Billy, comfortably numbed by Tralfamadorian philosophy, never reinvents himself—but Vonnegut does. Writing this book enabled the author to face his past, his present, and his future. In fact, after writing *Slaughterhouse-Five*, Vonnegut proclaimed that he would never *need* to write another book. *Slaughterhouse-Five* embodied for Vonnegut the spirit of the phoenix: his soul, through his art, rising from the ashes.

After the spiritual and psychological rejuvenation wrought by *Slaughterhouse-Five*, Vonnegut became a totally unfettered artist in his next two books, *Breakfast of Champions* and *Slapstick*. In *Breakfast of Champions*, he sets all of his characters free, disdaining his role as puppeteer. Admitting that, in English poet John Keats's words, he had been "half in love with easeful Death," he asserts that he has rid himself of this dangerous fascination. In *Slapstick*, he becomes frankly autobiographical, abandoning his aesthetic distance, eschewing all masks, facing his uncertain future and painful past with calm equanimity.

GALÁPAGOS

In *Galápagos*, which Vonnegut himself called his best novel, the ghost of Leon Trotsky Trout, son of Kilgore Trout, calmly tells the story of humankind from 1986 to a point one million years in the future. He tells of the end of humankind as known by its "big-brained" twentieth century readers and of the new Adam and Eves and their new Eden. Satirist and atheist that he is, Vonnegut idealizes no part of or party to his story. Knowledge is still the poisoned apple, but naturalist Charles Darwin, not God, is the featured figure of this final record of human life as known to its recorder.

Leon Trout died in the construction of the luxury liner the *Bahia de Darwin*, the launching of which is advertised as "the nature cruise of the century." Worldwide crises, however, cause all but a paltry few to withdraw their names from the list of passengers and crew. The cruise itself is begun by accident, and Mary Hepburn, not the figurehead captain, Adolf von Kleist, guides it to its destination. This unaware Adam and sterile-but-godlike Eve, with six Kanka-bono girls "from the Stone Age," begin the new race according to Darwin's (and God's?) dictum: Having eaten of the rotten apple, humankind, with its big, self-destructive brain, is no longer fit to survive; it is a matter of shrink and swim or die. Humankind thus becomes small-brained fisherkind as witnessed by the curious ghost of Leon Trout—who can now, having so witnessed, travel through the blue tunnel into the Afterlife.

Satirist, moralist, and spokesperson for humankind that he is, Vonnegut, like Jonathan Swift before him, offers in *Galápagos* his modest proposal to a humankind bent on its own destruction. He also offers as epigraph to this tome the words of Anne Frank: "In spite of everything, I still believe people are really good at heart."

Hocus Pocus

Hocus Pocus is perhaps Vonnegut's grimmest and most powerful indictment of Americans and American life, indicative of why fifteen years later he would title a collection of essays *A Man Without a Country* (2005). The novel is set in 2001, enabling Vonnegut a decade earlier to project his vision of what the United States would soon become. What he sees is revealed by his first-person narrator, his typical war veteran—this time a veteran of the Vietnam War, fittingly for this novel, America's most humiliating military venture. The narrator is presented as the last person to leave by helicopter from the top of the U.S. embassy in Saigon, and the experience enables him to emerge from this personal underground a changed man, convinced that all pro-war propaganda is "hocus pocus," of which he was an admitted master as a military spokesman himself, and now dedicated to trying to tell the truth, without self-serving deception.

What the United States has become in the near future is a schizophrenic, disintegrating world, symbolized both by the college for the wealthy but learning disabled where the narrator finds postwar employment and by the prison for impoverished and uneducated minorities directly across a lake from the college. The U.S. Supreme Court has reinstituted racial segregation, at least in prisons, and while the number of learning-disabled wealthy students has remained a constant at three hundred, the prison population has grown constantly, to ten thousand. Also, the United States is basically under absentee ownership, having been sold bit by bit to foreign nations and individuals by wealthy Americans who "take the money and run," unwilling to be responsible for the country's future. Race- and class-based uprisings are prevalent, including in the South Bronx, and gasoline is so scarce and expensive that it is to be found only in semisecret locations.

In his role as teacher of physics, the narrator attempts to expose the overweening pride and abysmal ignorance that have generated much of the disintegration of America, both represented by the failed perpetual-motion machine created by the college's founder and prominently placed in the foyer of the college library, proof of blind faith in technological solutions by humans who are, in the words of the narrator's dead war buddy, "1,000 times dumber and meaner than they think they are." The narrator's efforts only get him fired as a college teacher, however, with the firing orchestrated by a college trustee who is a conservative television talk-show host and whose daughter used the technology of voice recording to take the narrator's statements out of context and thereby convict him of anti-American teaching. As the narrator notes, a history professor at the college says much worse, but only about the distant past, whereas the narrator, Eugene Debs Hartke (aptly named), talks about America's present inequalities, injustices, and delusional destructiveness.

After he is fired, Hartke is hired by the prison, the director of which is a Hiroshima survivor who was saved from incineration by mere chance when he went into a ditch to retrieve a ball at the time the explosion occurred—a reflection of Vonnegut's belief that time and chance are the prime movers of the universe. Inevitably, given the race- and class-divided world, a prison break occurs, and the nonwhite prisoners (who have had nothing to do in prison except watch television reruns) attack the college and kill the faculty and staff who are present (the students are away on vacation). The prisoners are themselves killed when enough American military forces finally arrive from the Bronx and other intracountry battlefronts to address the prison break. Hartke is then arrested, accused of being the ringleader of the prison break, because he is Caucasian and educated—it is assumed that no members of a minority group could have planned the event. He is imprisoned, from which location and viewpoint he putatively authors the novel.

Unlike in *Galápagos* and *Bluebeard*, there is very little optimism in *Hocus Pocus*, aside from the narrator's humane insight and understanding. The novel conveys Vonnegut's conviction that humans will ultimately destroy themselves, probably sooner than they think, given their arrogance and ignorance and self-deception—their hocus pocus. After *Timequake* was published, Vonnegut admitted that he had struggled mightily in writing one more novel after *Hocus Pocus*, and one reason was probably that he subconsciously realized that he said it all in *Hocus Pocus* and said it incredibly well. *Hocus Pocus* is the powerful culmination of Vonnegut's fiction.

TIMEQUAKE

In *Timequake* Vonnegut has humankind, because of a glitch in time, replay the years 1991 to 2001 "on automatic pilot." He speaks as failed author of a ten-year project, *Timequake One*. Kilgore Trout, whom he personally identifies as his alter ego and as look-alike to his father, plays a crucial role in this novel. Vonnegut reprises his authorial roles as science-fiction writer, fiction writer, autobiographer, and spokesman for humankind.

Vonnegut's fictional story shows characters living and dying, living and dying again, and then waking and reeling from the reintroduction of free will. When humanity is roused from its ten years on automatic pilot, Trout becomes its hero. Because people have had no free will for ten years, they have forgotten how to use it, and Trout shows them the path to readjustment. Trout's words, for which he is celebrated, are, "You were sick, but now you're well again, and there's work to do."

Vonnegut's epilogue honoring his "big brother Bernie," who died toward the end of *Timequake*'s composition, calls to mind his prior references to saints he has known who, in an indecent society, behave decently. His references throughout *Timequake* and this final tribute to Bernard Vonnegut seem a recommendation of that gentle man to the status of saint.

Karen Priest; Judith K. Taylor
Updated by John L. Grigsby

OTHER MAJOR WORKS

SHORT FICTION: *Canary in a Cat House*, 1961; *Welcome to the Monkey House*, 1968; *Bagombo Snuff Box: Uncollected Short Fiction*, 1999.

PLAY: *Penelope*, pr. 1960 (revised pr., pb. 1970 as *Happy Birthday, Wanda June*).

TELEPLAY: *Between Time and Timbuktu: Or, Prometheus-5, a Space Fantasy*, 1972.

NONFICTION: *Wampeters, Foma, and Granfalloons (Opinions)*, 1974; *Palm Sunday: An Autobiographical Collage*, 1981; *Conversations with Kurt Vonnegut*, 1988; *Fates Worse than Death: An Autobiographical Collage of the 1980's*, 1991; *Like Shaking Hands with God: A Conversation About Writing*, 1999 (with Lee Stringer); *A Man Without a Country*, 2005; *Armageddon in Retrospect, and Other New and Unpublished Writings on War and Peace*, 2008.

CHILDREN'S LITERATURE: *Sun Moon Star*, 1980 (with Ivan Chermayeff).

BIBLIOGRAPHY

Allen, William Rodney. *Understanding Kurt Vonnegut*. Columbia: University of South Carolina Press, 1991. Presents critical analysis of Vonnegut's fiction, emphasizing in particular the works produced during his "major phase" in the 1960's, including *Slaughterhouse-Five*. Supplemented with annotated bibliography and index.

Boon, Kevin A., ed. *At Millennium's End: New Essays on the Work of Kurt Vonnegut*. Albany: State University of New York Press, 2001. Collection of eleven essays examines Vonnegut's moral vision.

Klinkowitz, Jerome. *"Slaughterhouse-Five": Reforming the Novel and the World*. Boston: Twayne, 1990. Provides a thorough and modern treatment of *Slaughterhouse-Five* that debunks earlier, fatalistic interpretations of the novel. Includes a comprehensive chronology, a thorough bibliography, and an index.

_______. *The Vonnegut Effect*. Columbia: University of South Carolina Press, 2004. One of the most authoritative scholars of Vonnegut's work presents insightful analysis of all of his major fiction. Provides biographical information and discusses how the events of Vonnegut's life influenced his writing.

_______. *Vonnegut in Fact: The Public Spokesmanship of Personal Fiction*. Columbia: University of South Carolina Press, 1998. Makes a case for Vonnegut as a sort of redeemer of the novelistic form after writers such as Philip Roth declared it dead. Traces Vonnegut's successful integration of autobiography and fiction in his body of work.

Klinkowitz, Jerome, and John Somer, eds. *The Vonnegut Statement*. New York: Delacorte Press, 1973. Collection of essays by various authors constitutes one of the most important accountings of Vonnegut's early career. Establishes the nature and sources of Vonnegut's reputation during this important period, analyzing his career through *Slaughterhouse-Five*.

Leeds, Marc. *The Vonnegut Encyclopedia: An Authorized Compendium*. Westport, Conn.: Greenwood Press, 1995. Provides a comprehensive, descriptive listing that identifies Vonnegut's most frequently recurring images and all his characters. Indispensable for serious students of Vonnegut's work.

Morse, Donald E. *The Novels of Kurt Vonnegut: Imagining Being an American.* Westport, Conn.: Praeger, 2003. Examines Vonnegut's novels against the framework of American history and the literature of the twentieth century.

Reed, Peter J., and Marc Leeds, eds. *The Vonnegut Chronicles: Interviews and Essays.* Westport, Conn.: Greenwood Press, 1996. Collection includes three interviews with Vonnegut and eleven essays on his work by various scholars. Among the topics that Vonnegut addresses in the interviews are postmodernism and experimental fiction. Includes chronology, bibliography, and index.

Tomedi, John. *Kurk Vonnegut.* Philadelphia: Chelsea House, 2004. Presents an informative overall survey of Vonnegut's life and literary work, including his nonfiction.

Vonnegut, Kurt, Jr. Interview by Wendy Smith. *Publishers Weekly,* October 25, 1985. Vonnegut discusses his writing career and his work, with an emphasis on his opposition to book censorship.

EVELYN WAUGH

Born: London, England; October 28, 1903
Died: Combe Florey, Somerset, England; April 10, 1966

PRINCIPAL LONG FICTION

Decline and Fall, 1928
Vile Bodies, 1930
Black Mischief, 1932
A Handful of Dust, 1934
Scoop, 1938
Put Out More Flags, 1942
Brideshead Revisited: The Sacred and Profane Memories of Captain Charles Ryder, 1945 (revised 1959)
Scott-King's Modern Europe, 1947
The Loved One, 1948
Helena, 1950
Men at Arms, 1952
Love Among the Ruins: A Romance of the Near Future, 1953
Officers and Gentlemen, 1955
The Ordeal of Gilbert Pinfold: A Conversation Piece, 1957
The End of the Battle, 1961 (also known as *Unconditional Surrender*)
Basil Seal Rides Again: Or, The Rake's Regress, 1963
Sword of Honour, 1965 (includes *Men at Arms*, *Officers and Gentlemen*, and *The End of the Battle*)

OTHER LITERARY FORMS

Evelyn Waugh (waw) wrote seven travel books, three biographies, an autobiography, and numerous articles and reviews. The only completed section of Waugh's planned three-volume autobiography, *A Little Learning* (1964), discusses his life at Oxford and his employment as a schoolmaster in Wales—subjects fictionalized in *Brideshead Revisited* and *Decline and Fall*. The autobiographical background for virtually all of Waugh's novels is evident in his travel books, his diaries, and his letters. His articles and reviews for English and American periodicals include a wide range of topics—politics, religion, and art—and contribute to his reputation as a literary snob, an attitude Waugh himself affected, especially in the 1940's and 1950's.

ACHIEVEMENTS

Evelyn Waugh is esteemed primarily as a satirist, especially for his satires on the absurdly chaotic world of the 1920's and 1930's. His ability to make darkly humorous the

Evelyn Waugh
(Library of Congress)

activities of the British upper class, his comic distance, and his vivid, at times brutal, satire made his early novels very popular among British and American literary circles. His shift to a more sentimental theme in *Brideshead Revisited* gave Waugh his first real taste of broad popular approval—especially in America—to which he reacted with sometimes real, sometimes exaggerated, snobbishness. Waugh's conservative bias after the war, his preoccupation with religious themes, and his expressed distaste for the "age of the common man" suggested to a number of critics that he had lost his satiric touch. Although his postwar novels lack the anarchic spirit of his earliest works, he is still regarded, even by those who reject his political attitudes, as a first-rate craftsman of the comic novel.

Biography

Evelyn Arthur St. John Waugh was born in Hampstead, a suburb of London, in 1903 to Arthur and Catherine Waugh. He attended Lancing College from 1917 to 1924 and

Hertford College, Oxford, from 1921 to 1924, from which he left without taking a degree. Although Waugh turned to writing novels only after aborted careers as a draftsman, a schoolmaster, and a journalist, his family background was literary; his father directed Chapman and Hall publishers until 1929, and his older brother Alec published his first novel, *The Loom of Youth*, in 1917.

Waugh's years at Oxford and his restless search for employment during the 1920's brought him experiences that were later fictionalized in several of his novels. After leaving Oxford in 1924, he enrolled in the Heatherley School of Fine Art, where he aspired to be a draftsman; later in that year, he was apprenticed to a printer for a brief period. His employment as a schoolmaster in Wales in 1925 and in Buckinghamshire in 1926 formed the background for his first novel, *Decline and Fall.* His struggle to establish himself as a writer and his participation in the endless parties of London's aristocratic youth during the last years of the 1920's are fictionalized in his second novel, *Vile Bodies*.

In 1927, Waugh was engaged to Evelyn Gardner and, despite the objections of her family, married her in 1928 when his financial prospects seemed more secure after the publication of his life of Dante Gabriel Rossetti and his first novel. In 1929, while Waugh was working in seclusion on *Vile Bodies*, his wife announced that she was having an affair; the couple, temperamentally unsuited to each other, were divorced that year.

The next seven years of Waugh's life were a period of activity and travel. Two trips to Africa in 1930 and 1931 resulted in a travel book and provided Waugh with the background of *Black Mischief.* A journey through Brazil and British Guiana in 1932 resulted in another travel book and his fourth novel, *A Handful of Dust*. In addition, Waugh traveled to the Arctic and once more to Africa; he was a correspondent for the London *Times*, reviewed books for *The Spectator*, and wrote a biography of Edmund Campion, a British Catholic martyr. During this unsettled period, Waugh converted to Roman Catholicism in 1930, an event that provided much of the stability of his later life. In 1933, he met Laura Herbert, a Catholic, whom he married in 1937, after securing an annulment of his previous marriage from the Catholic Church.

Waugh's experiences during World War II are fictionalized in *Put Out More Flags* and the *Sword of Honour* trilogy. After several months unsuccessfully seeking military employment, Waugh joined the Royal Marines in 1939 and was part of an ineffectual assault on Dakar in 1940. Later in 1940, Waugh joined a commando unit with which he served in the Middle East, taking part in the battle of Crete in 1942. In 1943, after an injury in parachute training, Waugh was forced to resign from the commandos, and, in 1944, he was granted military leave to write *Brideshead Revisited*. In the last year of the war, he served as a liaison officer with the British Military Mission in Yugoslavia, where he struggled against the persecution of Roman Catholics by the partisan government.

Waugh's life from 1945 to 1954 was relatively stable. The success of *Brideshead Revisited*, a Book-of-the-Month Club selection in the United States, brought him moderate financial security and several offers from filmmakers. Although none of these film offers materialized, they resulted in the trip to Hollywood in 1947 that inspired *The Loved One*, and in several commissioned articles for *Life* magazine. During this nine-year period, Waugh published four short novels and the first volume of the World War II trilogy. In the first three months of 1954, on a voyage to Ceylon, Waugh suffered the mental breakdown that he later fictionalized in *The Ordeal of Gilbert Pinfold*.

Waugh led a relatively reclusive life during the last ten years, avoiding the public contact that had made him notorious earlier. In this period, he finished the war trilogy and published a biography of Ronald Knox, another travel book on Africa, the first volume of his autobiography, a revision of *Brideshead Revisited*, and the recension of the war trilogy into a single volume; he also began several other projects that were never completed. Waugh died on Easter Day in 1966.

ANALYSIS

Evelyn Waugh's novels are distinguished by the narrative detachment with which they survey the madness and chaos of the modern age. His characters participate in a hopeless, often brutal, struggle for stability that hardens them to the absurdities of civilization and leads them, ultimately, to an unheroic retreat from the battle of life. Ironic detachment, thus, is Waugh's principal comic technique and his principal theme as well.

Because each of Waugh's novels reflects actual experiences, the nature of this detachment changes through the course of his career. In his early works, which satirize the havoc and instability of the 1920's and 1930's, he achieves comic detachment by splicing together the savage and the settled, the careless and the care-ridden, the comic and the tragic. Victims and victimizers alike are caught in the whirlwind of madness. Waugh's satiric method changes in his postwar novels: Comically ineffectual characters still wage battle against the absurdities of life, but one is more aware of their struggle to maintain or recapture spiritual and moral values amid the absurdity. Waugh maintains comic distance in these novels by recommending a quiet sort of spiritual heroism as the only source of people's happiness in the uncertain postwar world.

DECLINE AND FALL

Waugh's first novel, *Decline and Fall*, traces the misadventures of Paul Pennyfeather, a temperate, unassuming student of theology at Scone College, Oxford. He is "sent down" for indecent behavior when drunken members of the university's most riotous (and, ironically, most aristocratic) club assault him, forcing him to run the length of the quadrangle without his trousers. Like Voltaire's Candide, Pennyfeather is an innocent victim temperamentally ill suited for the world into which he is thrust. Indeed, *Decline and Fall* owes much to *Candide: Ou, L'Optimisme* (1759; *Candide: Or, All for the Best*, 1759): its Menippean satire, its cyclical "resurrection" of secondary characters, and the hero's ultimate resignation from life.

The action itself provides a thin framework for Waugh's satire on modern life.

Pennyfeather finds employment, as Waugh himself did, as a schoolmaster in Wales—the only occupation, Pennyfeather is told, for a young man dismissed from the university for indecent behavior. At Llanabba Castle, he meets three characters with whose stories his own is interlaced: Grimes, a pederast and bigamist who pulls himself out of the continual "soup" he gets into by feigning suicide; Prendergast, a doubting cleric who becomes a "modern churchman" and is eventually murdered by a religious fanatic; and Philbrick, the school butler, a professed impostor, jewel thief, and arsonist who manages to secure a continual life of luxury by his preposterous stories about his criminal life. At Llanabba, Pennyfeather also meets Margot Beste-Chetwynde, a rich socialite to whom he becomes engaged; he is arrested the afternoon of their wedding for unknowingly transporting girls to France for her international prostitution ring. His innocent association with Margot thus leads to his conviction for another act of "indecent behavior," this time leading to a prison sentence in Blackstone Gaol—a "modern" penal institution.

What strikes one about the novel is not the injustices served Pennyfeather, but the very madness of the world with which his innocence contrasts. Characters with criminal designs—Margot, Philbrick, and Grimes—are unaffected by changes in fortune; those in charge of social institutions—Dr. Fagan of Llanabba Castle and Sir Lucas-Dockery of the experimental prison—are eccentrically out of touch with reality. Their absurdity, when contrasted with Pennyfeather's naïve struggle, defines Waugh's theme: The only sanity is to become cautiously indifferent to the chaos of modernism. At the end of the novel, when Pennyfeather returns to Oxford under a new identity and continues his study of the Early Church, he assumes the role of a spectator, not a participant, in the madness of life.

Although *Decline and Fall*'s narrative structure is more derivative and its characters less fully rounded than those of Waugh's later novels, it displays techniques typical of his fiction at its best. The callous descriptions of the tragic—little Lord Tangent's death from Grimes's racing pistol or Prendergast's decapitation at Blackstone Gaol—and their fragmented interlacement into the plot are hallmarks of Waugh's comic detachment. Tangent's slow death from gangrene is presented through a series of casual offstage reports; the report of Prendergast's murder is incongruously worked into verses of a hymn sung in the prison chapel, "O God, our Help in Ages Past." The tragic and the savage are always sifted through an ironic filter in Waugh's novels, creating a brutal sort of pathos.

A HANDFUL OF DUST

Waugh's fourth novel, *A Handful of Dust*, was his first to present a dynamically sympathetic protagonist. Pennyfeather, from *Decline and Fall*, and Adam Symes, from *Vile Bodies*, attract one's interest largely because they provide a detached perspective from which one can observe the chaos of modern civilization. Basil Seal in *Black Mischief*, although a participating rogue, is amiable largely because of his comic disregard for the mischief he makes. Tony Last of *A Handful of Dust*, however, is a fully sympathetic character as well as a pathetic victim of the modern wasteland to which the title alludes. Unlike

Paul Pennyfeather, Tony is not simply an observer of social chaos: His internal turmoil is set against the absurdity of external events, and in that respect, his quest for lost values anticipates that of Charles Ryder in *Brideshead Revisited* and of Guy Crouchback in *Sword of Honour.*

Waugh's theme is the decadence of tradition, emblematized, as it is in many of Waugh's novels, by the crumbling estates of the aristocracy. Tony's futile effort to maintain his Victorian Gothic estate, Hetton Abbey, thus symbolizes his struggle throughout the plot. He is wedded to the outmoded tradition of Victorian country gentlemen, while his wife, Brenda, embraces the social life of London. She eventually cuckolds Tony by having an affair with the parasitic John Beaver, whose mother, an interior decorator, sees in her son's affair an opportunity to "modernize" Hetton with chromium plating and sheepskin carpeting.

The pathos one feels for Tony is ultimately controlled by the absurd contexts into which Waugh sets the pathetic scenes. When his son, John Andrew, dies in a riding accident, Tony is left emotionally desolate, yet the cause of the accident is ironic; John Andrew's horse is startled by a backfiring motorcycle, a modern "horse." Later, one is made brutally aware of the irony of Tony's grief when one learns of Brenda's initial reaction to the news of her son's death: She assumes it was John Beaver, her lover, not John Andrew, her son, who died. In the same way, Tony's later divorce from Brenda empties him of values he traditionally respected. He consents to the legal convention that he should give evidence of his infidelity, even if his wife has been the unfaithful partner. His evidence incongruously turns into an uncomfortable weekend with a prostitute and her daughter at Brighton, and the absurdity of this forced and inconsummate infidelity further defines Tony's loneliness. Ironically, it provides him with a means to deny an exorbitant divorce settlement that would force him to sell Hetton Abbey.

In the end, Tony searches for his Victorian Gothic city in the jungles of South America and suffers a delirium in which his civilized life at Hetton Abbey is distorted; these scenes are made comically pathetic by interlaced scenes of Brenda in London trying to regain the civilized life she lost in her estrangement from Tony. Ultimately, she does not find in London the city she sought, nor does Tony in South America. Tony does find, instead, an aberration of his vision; he is held captive by an illiterate who forces him to read aloud from Charles Dickens's novels in perpetuity.

Perhaps Waugh's emotional reaction to his own divorce from Evelyn Gardner prior to the publication of the novel accounts for the increase of pathos in *A Handful of Dust*. Perhaps Waugh realized that thinness of characterization in his earlier novels could lead only to stylistic repetition without stylistic development. Whatever the reason, this novel depicts characters struggling for moral equilibrium in a way that no previous Waugh novel had done.

BRIDESHEAD REVISITED

Brideshead Revisited is different from Waugh's earlier novels in two important ways. First, it is the only novel Waugh finished that employs the first-person point of view. (He had attempted the first person in "Work Suspended" in 1942, but either the story itself faltered or Waugh could not achieve a sufficient narrative detachment to complete it.) Second, *Brideshead Revisited* was the first novel in which Waugh explicitly addressed a Roman Catholic theme: the mysterious workings of divine grace in a small aristocratic Catholic family. As a result, it is Waugh's most sentimental and least funny novel. Although it departed radically from his earlier satires, it was Waugh's most popular and financially successful work.

The narrative frame creates much of what is sentimental in the novel but also provides a built-in detachment. Charles Ryder's love for Sebastian Flyte during his years at Oxford in the 1920's and for Julia Mottram, Sebastian's sister, a decade later, live vividly in Ryder's memories when he revisits the Brideshead estate during a wartime bivouac. His memories tell the story of Sebastian's and Julia's search for happiness, but because they are remembered by an emotionally desolate Ryder, the novel is a study of his spiritual change as well.

Before he meets Sebastian, Ryder is a serious-minded Oxford undergraduate, not unlike Paul Pennyfeather at the end of *Decline and Fall*. Like Pennyfeather, he is drawn into a world for which he is unprepared, yet unlike Waugh's earlier protagonist, Ryder is enthralled by a make-believe world of beauty and art. The Arcadian summer Ryder spends with Sebastian at Brideshead and in Venice are the most sumptuously written passages in any of Waugh's novels, reflecting—as Waugh admitted in his 1959 revision of the novel—the dearth of sensual pleasures available at the time of its composition. The change in style also reflects a change in theme. Sebastian's eccentricities about his stuffed bear, his coterie of homosexual "aesthetes," and his refusal to take anything seriously would have been the object of satire in Waugh's earlier novels. In *Brideshead Revisited*, however, the absurdities are sifted through the perspective of a narrator aware of his own desperate search for love. When Sebastian's make-believe turns to alcoholism, the narrator himself becomes cynically indifferent.

Ryder's love for Julia ten years after he has left Brideshead is an attempt to rediscover the happiness he lost with Sebastian. One is more aware, in this second half of the narration, of Ryder's cynicism and of the discontentment that cynicism hides. When he and Julia fall in love on a transatlantic voyage back to England, they are both escaping marriages to spouses whose worldly ambitions offer no nourishment for the spiritual emptiness each feels. Julia's return to the Church after the deathbed repentance of her father causes Ryder to realize that he has fathomed as little about Julia's faith as he had about Sebastian's. The narration itself thus ends on a note of unhappiness that recalls the separation of Ryder and Sebastian. In the epilogue following Ryder's memories, however, Waugh makes it clear that the narrator himself has converted to Catholicism in the intervening years. Ryder sees in the sanctuary light of the chapel at Brideshead the permanence he sought with Sebastian and Julia and finds contentment, if not hope for the future.

It is easy to overstress the religious implications of the novel. Indeed, many critics find Julia's hysteria about sin, Lord Marchmain's return to the Church, and Ryder's conversion strained. Some, such as Edmund Wilson, see the novel as an adulation of the British upper classes. *Brideshead Revisited*, however, is less a Roman Catholic novel than it is a lament for the past and a study in spiritual and artistic awakening. It was a turning point in Waugh's fiction: His novels after *Brideshead Revisited* dealt less with the absurdity of life and more with the spiritual values that have disappeared as a result of the war.

The Loved One

Perhaps the grimmest of Waugh's satires, *The Loved One* presents a sardonic vision of American culture. Its principal satiric target is Forest Lawn Memorial Park—a place that in many ways served for Waugh as the epitome of American pretensions to civilization. In "Half in Love with Easeful Death," an essay he wrote for *Life* in 1947 after his visit to Hollywood, Waugh describes Forest Lawn as it would appear to archaeologists in the next millennium: a burlesque necropolis, like the tombs of the pharaohs in its aspirations, but, in fact, the product of a borrowed, devalued culture. His version of Forest Lawn, Whispering Glades, is a distorted wonderland in which the cosmetic and the artificial substitute for beauty and in which banality is glorified and substitutes for the poetic vision.

It is fitting that the protagonist, Dennis Barlow, be a poet—even though an unproductive one who has been seduced to Hollywood by a consultantship with Megalo Studios. Like many of Waugh's other protagonists, he is the filter through which one sees absurdities satirized. Like Basil Seal in *Black Mischief* and *Put Out More Flags*, he is an opportunist, flexible enough to engineer a profit for himself out of the chaotic world into which he is thrust. His vision is grimly sardonic, however, in a way that even Seal's is not.

When he first enters Whispering Glades, he is intrigued, as Seal would be, by its absurd glamour and by the potential of using that glamour to improve his own position at The Happier Hunting Grounds, a pet mortuary where he is employed. Whispering Glades, however, has a far deeper attraction; it would be the kind of place, if it were real, that would appeal to any poet, but Barlow is enchanted by its very fraudulence. At the human-made Lake Isle of Innisfree (complete with mechanized humming bees), Barlow falls in love with a mortuary cosmetician and enchants her by the very fact that he is a poet. The enchantment is false, just as everything is at Whispering Glades; he sends her plagiarized verses from *The Oxford Book of English Verse* and pledges his troth to her by reciting a stanza from Robert Burns's "A Red, Red Rose" at The Lover's Nook near the Wee Kirk o' Auld Lang Syne.

If plagiarism lies at the heart of Barlow's involvement at Whispering Glades, it also lies at the heart of Whispering Glades itself and the characters who work there—even though the place and the people are possessed by the utmost seriousness. The girl with whom

Barlow falls in love is named Aimee Thanatogenos. Although she professes to be named after Aimee McPherson—the American huckster of religion whom Waugh satirized in *Vile Bodies*—her given name and her surname both translate into the euphemism that embodies all of Whispering Glades's false coating: "The loved one." Her enchantment with Barlow eventually takes the form of a burlesque tragedy. She is torn between Barlow and the head mortician, Mr. Joyboy—a poet of a different sort, whose special art is preparing infant corpses.

Aimee's tragedy results from a bizarre sequence of events, comic in its effects. When she discovers Joyboy's mother fixation and Barlow's fraudulence, she seeks advice from her oracle, the Guru Brahman, an advice columnist. When the Guru, Mr. Slump—fired from his job and in an alcoholic funk—advises Aimee to jump off a roof, she kills herself in the more poetic environment of Whispering Glades. Her suicide by drinking embalming fluid gives a doubly ironic force to her name and to the title of the novel. The tragedy ends with a darkly humorous catharsis. Joyboy, fearful that Aimee's death on his table might mar his lofty position at Whispering Glades, consents to Barlow's extortion and to Barlow's plan to cremate their beloved Aimee at The Happier Hunting Grounds. The novel's conclusion, thus, strikes the grimmest note of all: Barlow sits idly by, reading a cheap novel, while the heroine—a burlesque Dido—burns in the furnace.

In some ways, *The Loved One* is atypical of Waugh's postwar novels. In *Scott-King's Modern Europe* and the *Sword of Honour* trilogy, Waugh turns his satiric eye to political issues. *The Loved One*, however much it satirizes American values, transcends topical satire. Barlow lacks the spiritual potential of Charles Ryder in *Brideshead Revisited*, even though he displays Ryder's callousness. Barlow is an artist in search of beauty, but he leaves California, ironically, with an artist's load far different from what he expected. It is the view of an ironist, like Waugh himself, who could hardly make a better travesty of Whispering Glades than it makes of itself.

SWORD OF HONOUR

The *Sword of Honour* trilogy, like *Brideshead Revisited*, is infused with a predominantly religious theme; it traces Guy Crouchback's awakening to spiritual honor—a more active form of spiritual growth than Charles Ryder experienced. Like *Brideshead Revisited, Sword of Honour* is more somber and more deliberately paced than Waugh's satires in the 1920's and 1930's, but it shares with his early works a detached satiric framework. Each volume is composed at a distance of ten or more years from its historical occurrence and, as a result, reflects a greater consciousness of the long-range implications of the absurdities presented.

MEN AT ARMS

Men at Arms concerns the chaos of Britain's first entry into the war, much like Waugh's wartime satire *Put Out More Flags*. One is immediately aware, however, of the difference in Waugh's detachment. *Put Out More Flags* was the product of a writer in his mid-thirties looking wryly at the days of peace from the middle of the war. Its protagonist, Basil Seal, is a mischief-making opportunist for whom greater chaos means greater fun and profit; the novel satirizes the madness of a world that leaves the characters trapped in the ever-changing insanity of war. *Men at Arms*, however, and, indeed, the entire trilogy, looks back from the perspective of the author's later middle age, with a sense of disappointment at the final results of the war. Appropriately enough, Guy is an innocent at the outset of the war, not a mischief maker like Basil Seal. He is a middle-aged victim who is literally and figuratively cast into a battle for which he is ill prepared.

Guy's heroic illusions are shattered in three successive stages through the separate volumes of the trilogy. *Men at Arms* concerns Guy's search for the self-esteem he lost eight years earlier after his divorce from his wife. As an officer-trainee in the Royal Corps of Halberdiers, Guy temporarily finds self-respect, but the elaborate traditions of the Halberdiers and his traineeship at commandeered preparatory schools cause Guy to revert to adolescence. His physical awkwardness, his jealousy of fellow trainees, his vanity about growing a mustache, his ineffectual attempt to seduce his former wife on Saint Valentine's Day, and the blot he receives on his military record at the end of the novel all seem more appropriate for a schoolboy than for an officer preparing to lead men into battle.

As in Waugh's earlier novels, the comedy of *Men at Arms* depends not on the protagonist, but on the events and characters that he encounters. Apthorpe, a middle-aged *miles gloriosus*, and Ben Ritchie-Hook, Guy's brigadier, represent two forms of the military insanity for which Guy trains. Apthorpe's preoccupation with boots, salutes, and his portable field latrine, the "Box," makes him an unlikely candidate for leading men into battle; Ritchie-Hook, whose only notion of military strategy is to attack, makes an elaborate game out of officer training by booby-trapping Apthorpe's "Box"—a prank that causes Apthorpe to sink deeper into his madness. The confrontation between Apthorpe and Ritchie-Hook defines an absurd pattern that recurs later in the trilogy. Seeming madmen control the positions of power, and the protagonist is unwittingly drawn into their absurd worlds.

OFFICERS AND GENTLEMEN

Officers and Gentlemen further trains Guy in the illogic of military life, this time focusing on the efforts of gentlemen soldiers to re-create the comforts of their London clubs during the war. The novel ends on a more somber note, however, than did *Men at Arms*. Guy finds temporary solace in the commando unit to which he is transferred after his disgrace as a Halberdier and believes again that he will find some honorable role to play in the war, but the British defeat at Crete at the end of this volume negates whatever notions of honor he entertained.

Even more than *Men at Arms*, *Officers and Gentlemen* relentlessly parodies esprit de corps and pretentions to heroism. Ian Kilbannock's gentlemanly service as a military journalist, for example, is to transform the ineffectual Trimmer into a propaganda hero for the common person. Julia Stitch's yacht, the *Cleopatra*, brings the comforts of the English social world to the Mediterranean war. The burrowing Grace-Groundling-Marchpole absurdly continues the secret file he began in *Men at Arms* about Guy's supposed counterintelligence activities. All of these events occur while England is suffering the first effects of German bombing and while the British disgrace at Crete looms ahead.

For a time, Guy imagines that the commandos are the "flower of England"; he even sees Ivor Claire as the ideal soldier, the kind of Englishman whom Hitler had not taken into account. The flower withers, however, in the chaotic retreat of British forces from Crete. Although Guy himself manages to maintain an even keel through most of the ordeal, the officers with whom he serves prove unheroic. His commander, "Fido" Hound, suffers a complete mental collapse in the face of the retreating troops; Ivor Claire, unable to face the prospect of surrendering, deserts his men and flees to India, where he is protected by his genteel birth. Eventually, Guy unheroically joins a boat escaping from the island and, exhausted, suffers a mental collapse. Guy initially resists Julia Stitch's efforts to cover up Claire's disgrace, but eventually he destroys his own diary recording the orders to surrender when he learns that nothing will be done about Claire's desertion and when he learns of England's alliance with Russia. Unlike the first volume, the second volume ends with Guy's realization that he is an ineffectual player in a war that has lost a sense of honor.

It is curious to note that Waugh announced in the dust-jacket blurb for *Officers and Gentlemen* that, although he had planned the series for three volumes, he wanted his readers to regard it as finished with this second volume. The grimness of Guy's disillusionment thus sheds a somber light on Waugh's personal dilemma during the mid-1950's. After completing about a third of the draft of this second volume, Waugh suffered the mental collapse he later fictionalized in *The Ordeal of Gilbert Pinfold*. Guy's hallucination at the end of *Officers and Gentlemen* probably owes some of its vividness to the madness Waugh himself endured in 1954, and perhaps the numbness that affects Guy at the end of the novel reflects Waugh's own consciousness of his failing physical and mental powers.

THE END OF THE BATTLE

Men at Arms and *Officers and Gentlemen* each deflate Guy's illusions about honor. *The End of the Battle* follows the same pattern in terms of wartime politics and in terms of Guy's military life, but in personal terms, Guy achieves a kind of unheroic, unselfish honor by the end of the novel. As a soldier, Guy accomplishes nothing heroic; even his efforts to liberate the Jewish refugees from partisan Yugoslavia is unsatisfying. Although most of the refugees are liberated, the leaders of the group—the Kanyis—are imprisoned and presumably executed. Guy's struggle with the Yugoslavian partisans and his disgust at Britain's alliance with the Communist-bloc countries further define the dishonorable end that Guy and Waugh see in the war.

Unlike the two previous volumes, however, *The End of the Battle* ends on a note of tentative personal hopefulness, effected by Guy's renewed Roman Catholic faith. In the first two novels of the trilogy, Guy's religion lay dormant—a part of his life made purposeless since his divorce from Virginia. In *The End of the Battle*, the death of Guy's piously religious father causes Guy to realize that honor lies not in the "quantitative judgments" of military strategy, but in the spiritual salvation of individual souls. Guy's efforts to rescue the Yugoslavian Jews is selflessly honorable, even if ultimately futile. His remarriage to Virginia, who is pregnant with Trimmer's baby, is directed by the same sense of honor. Guy has little to gain emotionally from his remarriage; he does it for the preservation of the child's life and, implicitly, for the salvation of its soul. It is a different sort of heroism than he sought at the beginning of the war, possible only because Virginia has died.

Sword of Honour is, in many ways, a fitting climax to Waugh's literary career. It poignantly expresses his reverence for religious values yet recognizes the anomalous existence of those values in the modern world. It burlesques the eccentric and the absurd, yet moves beyond superficial satire to a more deeply rooted criticism of postwar politics. It displays Waugh's masterful ability to capture minor characters in brisk, economical strokes while working them thematically into the emotional composition of the protagonist. Waugh's importance as a novelist lay in his ability to achieve this kind of economy in a traditional form. He kept alive, in short, a tradition of the comic novel that reaches back to the eighteenth century.

James J. Lynch

OTHER MAJOR WORKS

SHORT FICTION: *Mr. Loveday's Little Outing*, 1936; *Work Suspended, and Other Stories Written Before the Second World War*, 1948; *Tactical Exercise*, 1954; *Charles Ryder's Schooldays, and Other Stories*, 1982; *The Complete Stories of Evelyn Waugh*, 1999.

NONFICTION: *Rossetti: His Life and Works*, 1928; *Labels: A Mediterranean Journal*, 1930; *Remote People*, 1931; *Ninety-two Days*, 1934; *Edmund Campion: Jesuit and Martyr*, 1935; *Waugh in Abyssinia*, 1936; *Robbery Under the Law*, 1939; *The Holy Places*, 1952; *The Life of the Right Reverend Ronald Knox*, 1959; *Tourist in Africa*, 1960; *A Little Learning*, 1964; *The Diaries of Evelyn Waugh*, 1976 (Michael Davie, editor); *A Little Order: A Selection from His Journalism*, 1977; *The Letters of Evelyn Waugh*, 1980 (Mark Amory, editor); *The Essays, Articles, and Reviews of Evelyn Waugh*, 1984.

BIBLIOGRAPHY

Carens, James F., ed. *Critical Essays on Evelyn Waugh*. Boston: G. K. Hall, 1987. Contains twenty-six essays divided into three sections: general essays, essays on specific novels, and essays on Waugh's life and works. A lengthy editor's introduction provides a chronological overview of Waugh's literary work and a discussion of Waugh criticism. Includes index and bibliography.

Cook, William J., Jr. *Masks, Modes, and Morals: The Art of Evelyn Waugh*. Rutherford,

N.J.: Fairleigh Dickinson University Press, 1971. Considers Waugh's novels squarely in the ironic mode, tracing the author's development from satiric denunciation to comic realism to romantic optimism to ironic realism. Presents lengthy analyses of the novels and argues that they move from fantasy to reality and from satire to resignation. Includes bibliography and index.

Crabbe, Katharyn. *Evelyn Waugh*. New York: Continuum, 1988. Informative volume provides a chronology of Waugh's life, a short biography, five chapters of detailed criticism on Waugh's major novels, and a concluding chapter on Waugh's style. Includes bibliography and index.

Davis, Robert Murray. *Evelyn Waugh: Writer.* Norman, Okla.: Pilgrim Books, 1981. Drawing from previously unavailable manuscript materials, Davis examines Waugh's artistic technique, his extensive revisions, and his reworkings of his novels. Begins with a chapter on Waugh's biography of Dante Gabriel Rossetti and then focuses exclusively on the novels, *Brideshead Revisited* and *Sword of Honour* in particular. Includes index.

Hastings, Selina. *Evelyn Waugh: A Biography.* Boston: Houghton Mifflin, 1994. Excellent, lively biography is not an academic work such as that written by Stannard (cited below) but instead represents an attempt to capture Waugh's personality as it appeared to him and to his friends.

Lane, Calvin W. *Evelyn Waugh*. Boston: Twayne, 1981. Relatively brief work contains a detailed chronology, a biography stressing the factors that influenced Waugh's literary career, and lengthy treatments of his novels. Includes four interviews with Waugh and a bibliography. Indispensable for Waugh scholars.

Patey, Douglas Lane. *The Life of Evelyn Waugh: A Critical Biography.* Cambridge, Mass.: Blackwell, 1998. Discusses Waugh's life within the context of his work, providing critical assessments of his novels and other writings. Devotes one chapter to an in-depth examination of *Brideshead Revisited.*

Stannard, Martin. *Evelyn Waugh: The Early Years, 1903-1939*. New York: W. W. Norton, 1987.

_______. *Evelyn Waugh: The Later Years, 1939-1966*. New York: W. W. Norton, 1992. Scholarly, well-documented two-volume account of Waugh's life and literary career provides valuable publication details about the novels and uses Waugh's diaries and letters as resource materials. Includes many photographs and illustrations, a genealogical chart of Waugh's ancestry, a selected bibliography, a general index, and an index of Waugh's works.

Villa Flor, Carlos, and Robert Murray Davis, eds. *Waugh Without End: New Trends in Evelyn Waugh Studies*. New York: Peter Lang, 2005. Collection of essays originally presented at a 2003 symposium examines such topics as Waugh and Catholicism, Waugh's representation of the English gentleman, homosexual themes in his work, and *Brideshead Revisited.*

Waugh, Alexander. *Fathers and Sons: The Autobiography of a Family.* London: Headline, 2004. Evelyn Waugh's grandson chronicles four generations of his family, focusing on their father-son conflicts and their literary achievements. Includes illustrations, bibliography, and index.

FAY WELDON

Born: Alvechurch, Worcestershire, England; September 22, 1931
Also known as: Franklin Birkinshaw

PRINCIPAL LONG FICTION

The Fat Woman's Joke, 1967 (also known as . . . *And the Wife Ran Away*, 1968)
Down Among the Women, 1971
Female Friends, 1974
Remember Me, 1976
Words of Advice, 1977 (also known as *Little Sisters*, 1978)
Praxis, 1978
Puffball, 1980
The President's Child, 1982
The Life and Loves of a She-Devil, 1983
The Shrapnel Academy, 1986
The Heart of the Country, 1987
The Hearts and Lives of Men, 1987
The Rules of Life, 1987
Leader of the Band, 1988
The Cloning of Joanna May, 1989
Darcy's Utopia, 1990
Growing Rich, 1992
Life Force, 1992
Affliction, 1993 (also known as *Trouble*)
Splitting, 1995
Worst Fears, 1996
Big Women, 1997 (also known as *Big Girls Don't Cry*)
Rhode Island Blues, 2000
The Bulgari Connection, 2001
Mantrapped, 2004
She May Not Leave, 2005
The Spa Decameron, 2007 (also known as *The Spa*)

OTHER LITERARY FORMS

Fay Weldon began her writing career with plays for radio, television, and theater, but she soon transferred her efforts to novels, and it is her novels for which she has become best known. She has also published short stories and a good deal of nonfiction. The latter includes a biography of Rebecca West; an introduction to the work of Jane Austen in fictional form, *Letters to Alice on First Reading Jane Austen* (1984); an "advice book" for modern women, *What Makes Women Happy* (2006); an autobiography, *Auto da Fay* (2002); and a collection of her journalism, *Godless in Eden* (1999). Her collections of short fiction include *Moon over Minneapolis: Or, Why She Couldn't Stay* (1991) and *Wicked Women* (1995). She has also put her comic gifts to work in three books for children, *Wolf the Mechanical Dog* (1988), *Party Puddle* (1989), and *Nobody Likes Me* (1997).

ACHIEVEMENTS

In addition to a successful career as an advertising copywriter, Fay Weldon has enjoyed a long career as a television scriptwriter, a playwright (for television, radio, and theater), and a novelist. Her radio play *Spider* (1972) won the Writers' Guild Award for Best Radio Play in 1973, and *Polaris* (1978) won the Giles Cooper Award for Best Radio Play in 1978. Weldon has earned growing acclaim for her humorous fictional explorations of women's lives and her biting satires that expose social injustice, and her novel *Praxis* was nominated for the prestigious Booker Prize. In 1983, Weldon became the first woman chair of judges for the Booker Prize. She was recognized for her many achievements in 1997, when she received the Women in Publishing Pandora Award. In 2000, she was made a Commander of the Order of the British Empire.

BIOGRAPHY

Fay Weldon was born Franklin Birkinshaw in the village of Alvechurch, England, in 1931. Her mother, who wrote under the name Pearl Bellairs, her maternal grandfather, Edwin Jepson, and one of her uncles were all novelists. While still a child, Weldon emigrated with her family to New Zealand, where her father worked as a doctor. When she was six years old, her parents divorced, and Weldon eventually returned to England with her mother and sister to live with her grandmother. This experience of being reared by a single mother in an era that did not easily accommodate single-parent families gave Weldon early insight into the lot of women living beyond the pale of the nuclear family; she was able to observe, at first hand, both the trials women faced and the importance of family and of humor in overcoming these difficulties.

In 1949, Weldon earned a scholarship to St. Andrews University in Scotland, and in 1952 she graduated with an M.A. in economics and psychology. Her first marriage, to Ronald Bateman, a man twenty years her senior, lasted less than two years, leaving her to support her son, Nicholas, as a single mother. She drifted through a series of jobs involving writing of various sorts: writing propaganda for the Foreign Office, answering problem letters for a newspaper, and, finally, composing advertising copy. In this last career she was quite successful, producing many jingles and slogans—a few of which stuck in the memory beyond their use in specific campaigns—and honing her talent for concision, wit, and catchy, memorable phrasing.

In 1960, she married Ronald Weldon, a London antiques dealer; they settled in a North

London suburb, where they had three children: Daniel (born 1963), Thomas (born 1970), and Samuel (born 1977). Beginning in the mid-1960's, Weldon combined professional and family responsibilities with a burgeoning career as a writer. Her first efforts were directed toward writing plays. Her one-act play *Permanence* was produced in London in 1969 and was followed by many successes. For British television, Weldon wrote more than fifty screenplays, including an award-winning episode of the series *Upstairs, Downstairs*. Writing for television led to fiction: Weldon's first novel, *The Fat Woman's Joke*, in 1967, began life as a television play. Her third novel, *Female Friends*, solidified her reputation, and Weldon quit her job in advertising. She earned further acclaim for *Praxis* and *The President's Child*, but *The Life and Loves of a She-Devil* proved a breakthrough work, introducing her work to a mass audience when it was made into a motion picture, *She-Devil* (1989), starring Meryl Streep and Roseanne Barr.

Her eventual divorce from Ronald Weldon in 1994 caused a certain amount of bitterness, which she expressed in some of her subsequent fiction. She later married poet Nicholas Fox; they lived briefly in Hampstead before moving to Shaftesbury in Dorset. Weldon seemed to mellow after her marriage to Fox, and she experienced something of an existential break when she had a vision of "the gates of paradise" (or possibly Hell) during a near-death experience suffered in 2005 when an allergic reaction caused her heart to stop. Even though the gates in question seemed hideously tacky and vulgar, she subsequently had herself baptized after being a committed atheist for most of her life. She had already begun to suggest in both her fiction and her nonfiction that she had recanted some of her earlier views, although she sacrificed none of her acerbic sarcasm in making the point. Her widely quoted opinion that men had gotten a rough deal as a result of the advancement of feminism seemed to some of her former admirers a particularly painful item of moral treason. Her combative "advice book," *What Makes Women Happy*—a title that suggests, perhaps presumptuously, that she now knows the answer—argues that the apparent reply is sex, chocolate, and shopping but that slightly deeper analysis would suggest a more refined alliterative triad of family, friends, and food.

ANALYSIS

Fay Weldon's fiction explores women's lives with wit and humor in the cause of a determined opposition to the clichés of romantic fiction. Weldon is caustic in her implicit condemnation of injustice but avoids preaching by satirizing both sides of every issue and by revealing the gulf between what characters say and what they do. Despite their realistic settings, her novels blend fable, myth, and the fantastic with satire, farce, and outlandish coincidence; the combination produces highly distinctive tragicomedies of manners.

Weldon's admiration for writers such as Jane Austen (whose work she has adapted for television) is expressed openly in *Letters to Alice on First Reading Jane Austen*, but it is also evident from the parallels in Weldon's own work. In a typical early Weldon novel, a limited cast of characters interacts in a defined setting. A series of misunderstandings or trivial coincidences initiates the action, which then takes on a momentum of its own, carrying all along with it until an equally trivial series of explanations or coincidences brings closure and a resolution that restores all to their proper place. The theme is often a minor domestic drama, such as a marital crisis, rather than an epic upheaval, but such personal interactions are seen to represent in microcosm society as a whole and therefore have a universal appeal.

Over time, her novels have become more wide-ranging in their settings, narrative devices, and claims, sometimes recruiting fantastic devices in order to attempt deeper analyses of the issues at stake, but generally her works still convey the impression that Weldon is not much given to elaborate planning, preferring to allow her characters and story lines to develop their own momentum. This has sometimes taken her into unexpected narrative terrain, but she always retains a keen intelligence and a trenchant wit. Although her works focus primarily on the lives of women, Weldon comments on a wide-ranging number of issues with relevance to all. Her work reveals a deep yet unsentimental compassion for all human beings, an understanding of their weaknesses and foibles, and a celebration of their continued survival and ability to love one another in the face of adversity.

. . . AND THE WIFE RAN AWAY

This structure is present even in Weldon's early work, no doubt because it is a formula that works well for television. In her first novel, originally titled *The Fat Woman's Joke* but renamed *. . . And the Wife Ran Away* for its American publication in 1968, Weldon takes as her subject the crisis in the marriage of a middle-aged, middle-class couple, Esther and Alan Wells, when Alan decides to have an affair with his young and attractive secretary, Susan. The beginning of Alan's affair coincides with Esther and Alan's joint decision to go on a diet, a symbolic attempt, Weldon suggests, to recapture not only their lost youthful figures but also their youthful love, ambition, and optimism. Infidelity, the novel therefore subtly suggests, is related to aging and to a more deep-seated identity crisis. Weldon frequently uses hunger or the satisfaction of food as a metaphor for other, more metaphysical and intangible, needs, and this theme recurs in a number of her works (for example, in the short story "Polaris," 1985).

The influence of Weldon's background as a scriptwriter (and the novel's origin as a play) is also evident in this book's form. Esther, who has left her husband at the opening of the novel, recounts her version of events to her friend Phyllis as she gorges herself on food to compensate for the self-denial she has suffered during the diet. Esther's narrative is intercut with scenes of Susan telling her version of events to her friend Brenda. The novel is thus almost entirely conveyed through dialogue describing flashbacks seen from the perspectives of the female characters. This technique is evident elsewhere in Weldon's early work—for example, in *Female Friends*, where parts of the novel are presented in the form of a script.

THE LIFE AND LOVES OF A SHE-DEVIL

The Life and Loves of a She-Devil stands as one of Weldon's most accomplished works. It represents the themes that are the hallmark of Weldon's fiction (a concern with women's lives and the significance of human relationships such as marriage) while encompassing her use of fantasy in one of her most carefully constructed and formally satisfying novels. The plot tells the story of a middle-class, suburban housewife, Ruth, whose accountant husband leaves her for a rich and attractive writer of romance novels. Unlike the typical wife, however, Ruth does not simply bow to the inevitable. When her husband calls her a "she-devil" in a moment of anger, this becomes her new identity, and she musters a formidable array of resources to live up to it. Through a series of picaresque adventures, she makes the life of her husband, Bobbo, and his new love, Mary Fisher, impossible. She has Bobbo framed and then imprisoned for embezzlement, destroys Mary's ability and will to write, and finally undergoes massive plastic surgery so that she looks just like her now-dead rival and can assume her place in Bobbo's broken life. The configuration at the end of the novel thus mirrors the beginning, but with the variation that the power dynamics of the relationship have been inverted: Ruth is now in command, while Bobbo has been humiliated and accepts his fate like a downtrodden wife.

The tale not only presents a certain kind of symmetry reminiscent of fairy stories but also evokes a poetic magic in the telling of it. Many of the chapters begin with a variation on the opening line of the novel: "Mary Fisher lives in a High Tower, on the edge of the sea." These incantations, repeated with variations, have the hypnotic quality of a witch's spell, reinforcing both Ruth's supernatural power and her obsession with Mary Fisher (whose residence in a tower evokes a fairy-tale princess). This poetic refrain also unifies the narrative and gives a cyclical structure to the plot.

THE SHRAPNEL ACADEMY

On the surface, *The Shrapnel Academy* is a variation on the stale British motif of the "country house weekend." A group of characters, most of them unknown to one another, are seen arriving at the Shrapnel Academy, a military institute, for a weekend. Bad weather will ensure that they remain confined to the academy, cut off from the outside world and forced to confront one another and the problems that arise.

While many novelists fail to acknowledge the presence of the host of servants who make such country weekends possible, Weldon's novel takes the reader below stairs and into the lives of the hundreds of illegal immigrant servants and their extended families and camp followers—as in *Upstairs, Downstairs*, the early 1970's television series about an upper-class Edwardian family and its servants to which Weldon contributed an award-winning episode. *The Shrapnel Academy* ventures beyond realist conventions by presenting a clash between shortsighted, class-based militarism and the struggle for survival and dignity in the microcosm of the academy, eventually extending into quasi-apocalyptic allegory.

As in most of Weldon's novels, no single villain is responsible for the misfortunes that befall the characters in *The Shrapnel Academy*; all the characters bear some degree of responsibility for the accumulation of trivial choices and decisions that combine to make up the climactic "frightful tidal wave of destiny." Many continual thematic elements of Weldon's work recur in *The Shrapnel Academy*, including revenge fantasy, food symbolism, and transfigurations of myth and fable. Formally, too, the novel displays typical characteristics of Weldon's work (short narrative passages with aphoristic asides, the use of dialogue) as well as innovative and experimental qualities. The author interrupts the narrative at frequent intervals, sometimes to offer satirical summaries of military history, highlighting advances in warfare or giving accounts of famous battles. Weldon brings out the absurdity of celebrating such "progress" and uses her fine wit to draw the reader's attention to the Orwellian doublespeak and underlying assumptions of military thinking. At other times, Weldon interpellates the reader directly, apologizing for the delay in getting on with the story or inviting the reader to put him- or herself in the place of one of the characters—invitations that pointedly drive home the lesson that the reader is no better than the characters he or she is inclined to judge.

Life Force

Weldon also breaks strategically with her readers' expectations in *Life Force*, which, instead of being an indictment of male callousness and infidelity, is a lusty tribute to male sexuality. The central figure in the book is Leslie Beck, a man with no virtues except his power to please women through the skillful use of his huge genitalia and his equally outsized imagination. Structurally, *Life Force* follows the pattern established in Weldon's earlier novels: It begins with a seemingly unimportant incident that stimulates the narrator to relive and reassess complex relationships; that incident eventually becomes a crucial element in a dramatic resolution, in which a woman avenges herself upon a man who has wronged her.

When Leslie Beck turns up at the Marion Loos Gallery, carrying a large painting by his late wife Anita, it does not seem possible that this unappealing, sixty-year-old man could for so long have been the Lothario of upper-middle-class London. However, the owner of the gallery, who at this point is the first-person narrator, explains to the reader why she is so shocked when she sees the unimpressive painting that her former lover expects her to sell on his behalf. Its subject is the bedroom and the bed in which Leslie once gave Marion so much pleasure. Naturally, the painting prompts Marion to recall her involvement with Leslie and to wonder how much Anita knew about the affair.

Nothing in this novel is as straightforward as it seems, however. In the second chapter, Weldon not only changes narrators—now telling the story through the eyes of Nora, another of Beck's former lovers—but also has Nora admit that it was she, not Marion, who actually wrote the first chapter, simply imagining herself as Marion. Although the two narrators continue to alternate as the book progresses, from time to time the author reminds us that Marion's narrative is Nora's fiction, based as much on gossip and guesses as on fact. Weldon thus suggests that since the only approach to truth is through what human beings see and say, what we call reality will always include as much fiction as fact.

GROWING RICH

Growing Rich describes the harassment of three adolescent girls by a Mephistophelian figure who has promised one of them as a prize to the wealthy businessman with whom he has made a Faustian pact. Cast in the same mock-folkloristic mode as *The Life and Loves of a She-Devil*, this novel seems to be casting around for a different moral but cannot in the end discover one. The demon is incarnate as the businessman's chauffeur and is thus referred to as "the Driver," which implies that the novel's presiding proverb is "Needs must when the devil drives"—and, indeed, even the novel's primary heroine, Carmen, cannot in the end avoid his driving. Carmen withstands his subtler temptations easily enough, although her friends Annie and Laura are not nearly so fortunate, but she cannot ultimately prevail against his nastier threats. In the end, the fact that she is not required to yield everything demanded by his blackmail cannot conceal the fact that she does yield.

The Driver is an intriguing literary creation: an apt devil for the modern age, whose acid observations reveal as strong a kinship with Alain-René Lesage's Asmodeus as with Christopher Marlowe's Mephistopheles. *Growing Rich*, like most of Weldon's works, is so exuberantly good-humored that even its blackest comedy is little more than black-edged, and the same is true of the marginal gothic elements of many of its predecessors and successors among her long fiction, including the mock-Dickensian melodrama *The Hearts and Lives of Men*, the mock-science-fictional *The Cloning of Joanna May*, and the similarly fantasized *Splitting* and *Mantrapped*. Like many modern authors, Weldon simply cannot take the fantastic seriously enough to make the most of its inherent narrative energy, but the frothy frivolity with which she invests it carries its own rewards.

TROUBLE

In *Trouble*, Weldon again turns her attention to a society that permits men to victimize women. The protagonist of this novel, which was first published in England under the title *Affliction*, is Annette Horrocks, a woman who, after ten years of trying, has finally become pregnant, only to find that her once-devoted husband, Spicer, has become monstrous. Not only does he now seem to loathe Annette, but also none of his tastes, opinions, and prejudices are what they were just a few months before.

Eventually, Annette discovers the source of the problem: Spicer has been seduced by a pair of unscrupulous, sadistic New Age psychiatrists. Before she is finally cured of what she comes to recognize as her addiction to Spicer, Annette loses her home, her baby, and very nearly her mind. If in *Life Force* Weldon shows the battle of the sexes as essentially comic, in *Trouble* she tells a story with tragic overtones. Again she points out how vulnerable women are in a society that believes men have a monopoly on the truth, but in this case she shows what can happen when the male version of reality is reinforced by the self-seeking therapy industry, the primary target of satire in this novel.

WORST FEARS

Worst Fears is one of Weldon's novels most clearly marked by the scars of her 1994 divorce. Its protagonist, Alexandra, an actor, is suddenly precipitated into crisis by the unexpected death of her husband, Ned, and is required, as conventional parlance has it, to "put his affairs in order." This involves her in a disquieting sequence of discoveries about the "true identity" Ned had succeeded in hiding from her for many years, which eventually extend to nightmarish extremes. Members of all of the professions that Weldon learned to hate in the course of her own divorce—especially therapists and lawyers—become targets for her bile here, although the burden of the role of primary traitor within the plot falls on a child-care provider: a dangerous cuckoo in the domestic nest.

RHODE ISLAND BLUES

In *Rhode Island Blues*, Weldon presents an elaborate examination of female family ties, dominated by the character of eighty-five-year-old Felicity, whose granddaughter Sophie, a film editor—the novel's primary protagonist—undertakes a quixotic quest to find the old woman's "lost" granddaughter. In the process, Sophie uncovers a great deal of family history extended over the generations and begins to reassess her relationship with her own mother. The novel's transatlantic movements, occasioned by the fact that Felicity was a war bride, add an extra dimension of cultural comparison, while a fantastic edge is added by Felicity's consolatory delusions.

THE BULGARI CONNECTION

The Bulgari Connection is an interesting experiment in novelistic product placement, as the writing of the work was financed by the Italian jewelry company. This connection is, however, incidental to the network of the plot, which develops a version of the eternal triangle. Businessman Barney Salt deserts his wife, Grace, for television personality Doris Dubois, thus inviting a she-devil-like revenge. The revenge in question is duly visited after Grace takes up with artist Walter Wells and receives a new lease on life that is quite literal—an aspect of the plot explicitly modeled on Oscar Wilde's *The Picture of Dorian Gray* (1890).

As on several previous occasions, Weldon picked up themes from this novel for further extrapolation in her next work, the identity-exchange comedy *Mantrapped*, whose heroine awakes one morning to find herself in a man's body. There, as in *The Bulgari Connection*, elements of Weldon's own autobiography are clearly recycled, but the fantastic embellishments in both books serve as useful distancing devices for putting "reality" into a broader and more comfortable perspective.

SHE MAY NOT LEAVE

She May Not Leave is an elaborate expansion of the child-care-worker subplot from *Worst Fears*, complicated by intergenerational issues echoing those in *Rhode Island Blues*, both elements being carefully ameliorated by a conscientious attempt to strike an evenhanded balance. The protagonist, Hattie, is busily employed in a literary agency and has trouble juggling her relationships with her partner, Martin, a political journalist; her grandmother, Frances, who is busy tracing the family history; and her daughter, Kitty. Polish au pair Agnieszka is an extremely dubious godsend, but she might well be indispensable no matter how problematic she eventually proves to be. As in many Weldon novels, the eventual "resolution" of *She May Not Leave* is unashamedly artificial and rather tokenistic, but the breezy tone illustrates the author's recovered sense of well-being and the essential irrepressibility of her character.

THE SPA DECAMERON

In a plot that echoes *The Shrapnel Academy* but lacks that novel's male/militaristic component, *The Spa Decameron* features wealthy female guests who are snowed in for ten days at a Cumbrian health spa over the Christmas/New Year holidays. As the facilities gradually begin to fail and the staff who maintain the guests' comforts and privileges begin to desert or rebel, the women pass the time by telling one another their instructive life stories, somewhat after the fashion of the plague-beleaguered characters in Giovanni Boccaccio's classic *Decameron: O, Prencipe Galeotto* (1349-1351; *The Decameron*, 1620). *The Spa Decameron* is, however, much more tightly organized around a thematic core than is its model; it really is a novel in spite of its discursive structure.

The characters' experiences gradually add up to a grotesque survey of the possibilities open to modern women and the threats facing them, including adultery, gender reassignment surgery, incest, abortion, husband murder, lesbian sexuality, and child abuse—to name but a few. The principal viewpoint character, Phoebe, is able to supplement the tales she hears further by virtue of her (possibly imaginary) ability to hear other people's thoughts; she does not tell her own story, partly—the reader suspects—because it cannot withstand melodramatic comparison with the stories the other characters tell, but also, and more appropriately, because it still remains to be equipped with a satisfactory sense of closure.

Melanie Hawthorne;
Rosemary M. Canfield Reisman
Updated by Brian Stableford

OTHER MAJOR WORKS

SHORT FICTION: *Watching Me, Watching You*, 1981; *Polaris, and Other Stories*, 1985; *Moon over Minneapolis: Or, Why She Couldn't Stay*, 1991; *Angel, All Innocence, and Other Stories*, 1995; *Wicked Women: A Collection of Short Stories*, 1995; *A Hard Time to Be a Father*, 1998.

PLAYS: *Permanence*, pr. 1969; *Time Hurries On*, pb. 1972; *Words of Advice*, pr., pb. 1974; *Friends*, pr. 1975; *Moving House*, pr. 1976; *Mr. Director*, pr. 1978; *Action Replay*, pr. 1979 (also known as *Love Among the Women*); *After the Prize*, pr. 1981 (also known as *Woodworm*); *I Love My Love*, pr. 1981; *Tess of the D'Urbervilles*, pr. 1992 (adaptation of Thomas Hardy's novel); *The Four Alice Bakers*, pr. 1999; *The Reading Group*, pb. 1999.

TELEPLAYS: *The Fat Woman's Tale*, 1966; *Wife in a Blonde Wig*, 1966; *Dr. De Waldon's Therapy*, 1967; *Fall of the Goat*, 1967; *The Forty-fifth Unmarried Mother*, 1967; *Goodnight Mrs. Dill*, 1967; *What About Me*, 1967; *Hippy Hippy Who Cares*, 1968; *Ruined Houses*, 1968; *£13083*, 1968; *The Three Wives of Felix Hull*, 1968; *Venus Rising*, 1968; *Smokescreen*, 1969; *The Loophole*, 1969; *Office Party*, 1970; *Poor Mother*, 1970; "On Trial," 1971 (episode of television series *Upstairs, Downstairs*); *Hands*, 1972; *The Lament of an Unmarried Father*, 1972; *A Nice Rest*, 1972; *Old Man's Hat*, 1972; *A Splinter of Ice*, 1972; *Comfortable Words*, 1973; *Desirous of Change*, 1973; *In Memoriam*, 1974; *Aunt Tatty*, 1975 (adaptation of Elizabeth Bowen's story); *Poor Baby*, 1975; *The Terrible Tale of Timothy Bagshott*, 1975; *Act of Rape*, 1977; "Married Love," 1977 (episode of television series *Six Women*); *Honey Ann*, 1980; *Life for Christine*, 1980; *Pride and Prejudice*, 1980 (adaptation of Jane Austen's novel); "Watching Me, Watching You," 1980 (episode of television series *Leap in the Dark*); *Little Miss Perkins*, 1982; *Loving Women*, 1983; *Redundant! Or, The Wife's Revenge*, 1983.

RADIO PLAYS: *Spider*, 1972; *Housebreaker*, 1973; *Mr. Fox and Mr. First*, 1974; *The Doctor's Wife*, 1975; *Polaris*, 1978; *All the Bells of Paradise*, 1979; "Weekend," 1979 (episode in radio series *Just Before Midnight*); *I Love My Love*, 1981.

NONFICTION: *Letters to Alice on First Reading Jane Austen*, 1984; *Rebecca West*, 1985; *Sacred Cows: A Portrait of Britain, Post-Rushdie, Pre-Utopia*, 1989; *Godless in Eden: A Book of Essays*, 1999; *Auto da Fay*, 2002; *What Makes Women Happy*, 2006.

CHILDREN'S LITERATURE: *Wolf the Mechanical Dog*, 1988; *Party Puddle*, 1989; *Nobody Likes Me*, 1997.

EDITED TEXT: *New Stories Four: An Arts Council Anthology*, 1979 (with Elaine Feinstein).

BIBLIOGRAPHY

Barreca, Regina, ed. *Fay Weldon's Wicked Fictions*. Hanover, N.H.: University Press of New England, 1994. Collection of eighteen essays, five by Weldon herself, deals with leading themes and techniques in Weldon's fiction and various issues raised by her work, such as her relation to feminism and her politics and moral stance.

Cane, Aleta F. "Demythifying Motherhood in Three Novels by Fay Weldon." In *Family Matters in the British and American Novel*, edited by Andrea O'Reilly Herrera, Elizabeth Mahn Nollen, and Sheila Reitzel Foor. Bowling Green, Ohio: Bowling Green State University Popular Press, 1997. Points out that in *Puffball, The Life and Loves of a She-Devil*, and *Life Force*, dysfunctional mothers produce daughters who are also dysfunctional mothers. Argues that Weldon agrees with the feminist position that mothering cannot be improved until women cease to be marginalized.

Dowling, Finuala. *Fay Weldon's Fiction.* Rutherford, N.J.: Fairleigh Dickinson University Press, 1998. Examines the themes and techniques in Weldon's fiction, with the principal emphasis on the novels.

Faulks, Lana. *Fay Weldon.* New York: Twayne, 1998. Provides a good introduction to Weldon's life and work, with a focus on the novels. Describes Weldon's fiction as "feminist comedy," contrasting with feminist writing that depicts women as oppressed. Also examines Weldon's experiments with narrative techniques.

Ferreira, Maria Aline Salgueiro Seabra. "Cloning and Biopower: Joanna Russ and Fay Weldon." In *I Am the Other: Literary Negotiations of Human Cloning.* Westport: Conn.: Greenwood Press, 2005. Presents a critical discussion of the role of cloning in Weldon's novel *The Cloning of Joanna May.*

Mitchell, Margaret E. "Fay Weldon." In *British Writers*, Supplement 4 in *Contemporary British Writers*, edited by George Stade and Carol Howard. New York: Charles Scribner's Sons, 1997. Presents detailed information on Weldon's life and work, divided into sections titled "Weldon's Feminism," "The Personal as Political," "Nature, Fate, and Magic," "Self and Solidarity," and "Fictions."

Paloge, Helen. *The Silent Echo: The Middle-Aged Female Body in Contemporary Women's Fiction.* Lanham, Md.: Lexington Books, 2007. Discusses the depiction of middle-aged women in the novels of Weldon, Margaret Atwood, Joan Barfoot, Joyce Carol Oates, and others.

Weldon, Fay. "Nature, Science, and Witchcraft: An Interview with Fay Weldon." Interview by Joanna Zylinska. *Critical Survey* 12, no. 3 (2000): 108-122. Weldon discusses her writing, particularly her novels and their inspirations.

Wilde, Alan. "'Bold, But Not Too Bold': Fay Weldon and the Limits of Poststructuralist Criticism." *Contemporary Literature* 29, no. 3 (1988): 403-419. Focuses primarily on literary theory, using *The Life and Loves of a She-Devil* as an arena to pit poststructuralism against New Criticism, offering some useful comments regarding moderation versus extremism in this novel.

H. G. WELLS

Born: Bromley, Kent, England; September 21, 1866
Died: London, England; August 13, 1946
Also known as: Herbert George Wells

PRINCIPAL LONG FICTION

The Time Machine: An Invention, 1895
The Wonderful Visit, 1895
The Island of Dr. Moreau, 1896
The Wheels of Chance: A Holiday Adventure, 1896
The Invisible Man: A Grotesque Romance, 1897
The War of the Worlds, 1898
When the Sleeper Wakes: A Story of the Years to Come, 1899
Love and Mr. Lewisham, 1900
The First Men in the Moon, 1901
The Sea Lady, 1902
The Food of the Gods, and How It Came to Earth, 1904
Kipps: The Story of a Simple Soul, 1905
In the Days of the Comet, 1906
Tono-Bungay, 1908
The War in the Air, and Particularly How Mr. Bert Smallways Fared While It Lasted, 1908
Ann Veronica: A Modern Love Story, 1909
The History of Mr. Polly, 1910
The New Machiavelli, 1910
Marriage, 1912
The Passionate Friends, 1913
The Wife of Sir Isaac Harman, 1914
The World Set Free: A Story of Mankind, 1914
Bealby: A Holiday, 1915
The Research Magnificent, 1915
Mr. Britling Sees It Through, 1916
The Soul of a Bishop: A Novel—with Just a Little Love in It—About Conscience and Religion and the Real Troubles of Life, 1917
Joan and Peter: The Story of an Education, 1918
The Undying Fire: A Contemporary Novel, 1919
The Secret Places of the Heart, 1922
Men Like Gods, 1923
The Dream, 1924

Christina Alberta's Father, 1925
The World of William Clissold: A Novel at a New Age, 1926 (3 volumes)
Meanwhile: The Picture of a Lady, 1927
Mr. Blettsworthy on Rampole Island, 1928
The King Who Was a King: The Book of a Film, 1929
The Autocracy of Mr. Parham: His Remarkable Adventure in This Changing World, 1930
The Buplington of Blup, 1933
The Shape of Things to Come: The Ultimate Resolution, 1933
The Croquet Player, 1936
Byrnhild, 1937
The Camford Visitation, 1937
Star Begotten: A Biological Fantasia, 1937
Apropos of Dolores, 1938
The Brothers, 1938
The Holy Terror, 1939
All Aboard for Ararat, 1940
Babes in the Darkling Wood, 1940
You Can't Be Too Careful: A Sample of Life, 1901-1951, 1941

Other literary forms

H. G. Wells's short stories appear in several collections, including *The Stolen Bacillus, and Other Incidents* (1895), *Tales of Space and Time* (1899), *The Country of the Blind, and Other Stories* (1911), and *A Door in the Wall, and Other Stories* (1911). In *The Outline of History: Being a Plain History of Life and Mankind* (1920) and *Experiment in Autobiography: Discoveries and Conclusions of a Very Ordinary Brain Since 1866* (1934), Wells extended his literary range. His sociological essays include *A Modern Utopia* (1905) and *Mind at the End of Its Tether* (1945).

Achievements

H. G. Wells is best known for his science-fiction novels, several of which have been adapted as popular films. A socialist and Fabian, he was a spokesman for women's rights and international peace movements, for which he wrote books of advocacy in essay and fictional form. Wells was also an effective novelist of social satire and comedy.

Biography

Herbert George Wells was born in 1866 at Bromley in Kent, England, to Joseph and Sarah Neal Wells. He attended a commercial academy from 1874 to 1880. Having run away from his apprenticeship in a drapery shop, he taught in a preparatory school. Then he attended the London Normal School of Science from 1884 to 1887, studying biology un-

H. G. Wells
(Library of Congress)

der T. H. Huxley. In 1891 he was married to Isabel Mary Wells, and he published "The Rediscovery of the Unique." *The Time Machine* brought him fame in 1895, the same year that he divorced Isabel to marry Amy Catherine Robbins.

In 1914, having visited Russia, Wells published a prophecy, *The War That Will End War*; that year his son Anthony West was born to Rebecca West.Wells supported a "League of Free Nations" and entered the propaganda effort against Germany. In 1920 he made another trip to Russia, to meet Vladimir Ilich Lenin, and published *Russia in the Shadows*. Wells was defeated as a Labour candidate for Parliament in 1922, and Amy Catherine died in 1927. He coauthored a book on biology before visiting Russia and the United States in 1934 to meet Joseph Stalin and President Franklin D. Roosevelt. In 1935 he wrote film scenarios for *Things to Come* and *The Man Who Could Work Miracles*. In 1938, Orson Welles's radio broadcast of an adaptation of Wells's novel *The War of the Worlds* frightened many people in the United States, paving the way for Wells's successful lecture tour there in 1940. Wells died in London on August 13, 1946.

Analysis

H. G. Wells's early scientific romances begin with *The Time Machine* and conclude with *The First Men in the Moon*. His social satires and comic romances commence with

Kipps and end with *The History of Mr. Polly*. Didactic fiction dominated his last decades, from *Ann Veronica* to *You Can't Be Too Careful*. Throughout is a struggle between science and socialism. Visions of doom alternate with calls for reform and renewal; individuals acquire knowledge of science but lose control of their destinies.

THE TIME MACHINE

Wells's early novels are journeys of ironic discovery. The enduring point of *The Time Machine* is in the Time-Traveller's frightening discovery in the year 802701. He encounters the Eloi, who have been terrorized by the Morlocks, molelike creatures who prey on the flesh of the Upper-worlders. They are the fruits of an evolutionary process of separating capitalists from workers. Before he returns to his own time, the Time-Traveller accidentally moves even further into the future, to an Earth about to fall into a dying Sun.

THE ISLAND OF DR. MOREAU

Edward Prendick, narrator of *The Island of Dr. Moreau*, is a castaway, grateful to reach Moreau's island—until he realizes its horrors. He thinks that Moreau is turning people into animals, but when he finds the Beast-people, he realizes his mistake. Moreau explains that pain is animality, and he excises pain to humanize animals, but they kill him as they revert to their animal natures. Prendick barely escapes becoming an animal before he returns to civilization, where he has anxiety attacks about people's animality.

Pessimism is never far from the surface of Wells's writing. Losing faith in reason, he turned to prophetic satire, as in *The Invisible Man*. In this story, Griffin, having failed to anticipate the awful effects of losing visibility, has lapsed in ethical responsibility because he had no training or economic opportunity to make better use of his knowledge. Lacking love, he lacks constructive purpose for his power. His invisibility represents knowledge itself, as either destructive or constructive. Knowledge and power combine without sympathy in *The War of the Worlds* to result in catastrophe. The narrator is a frightened man struggling to compete for survival of the fittest. He believes that the Martians are little more than brains, dispassionate reason threatening annihilation. All brain with no sympathy threatens civilization, but so does instinct with no brain. The Martians are near success when suddenly they begin to die, ironically having succumbed to some of Earth's tiniest life-forms, bacteria.

THE FIRST MEN IN THE MOON

Wells reverses the cosmic journey in *The First Men in the Moon*, as Bedford accompanies eccentric scientist Cavor to mine the Moon, adding private enterprise to science. The heroes find an intoxicating mushroom, which prompts Bedford to speculate that his private motive for profit will produce public benefits—even for the Moon itself. This madly grandiose notion is subverted when Bedford and Cavor are captured by the antlike Selenites, who live under the surface of the Moon. When Bedford escapes alone to Earth, Cavor sends messages that he is to be executed to prevent Earth inhabitants from returning with their violent ways, to do to the Moon what Wells had envisioned in *The War of the Worlds*, where Earth was invaded by Martians.

THE FOOD OF THE GODS, AND HOW IT CAME TO EARTH

The Food of the Gods, and How It Came to Earth edges beyond science and humor into socialism and satire. Experiments with Boomfood on a chicken farm cause mass destruction through the creation of giant chickens, rats, and wasps; human babies become giants, and ordinary mortals grow terrified. Wells is on the giants' side, because they can make a new world by destroying the faults of the old. People accommodate to preserve old ways, but they shut their eyes to truth, eventually causing a crisis of choice between old and new. The story ends as the giants prepare for a war with the little people.

IN THE DAYS OF THE COMET

With *In the Days of the Comet* Wells presents a more optimistic view of changes that can be made in the world. Willie Leadford describes life before the great "change," when a comet turned Earth into paradise. The power of the novel, however, is in the rhythm of rage and hate that accelerates as Willie pursues the woman he loved, to kill her and her new lover. This momentum is accented by other accelerating events, including economic crisis and war with Germany. The comet changes all, including Willie and his beloved, Nettie, who offers to live with both lovers. In a new world, people learn to accept polygamy as natural and right.

KIPPS

Kipps: The Story of a Simple Soul is a story like Charles Dickens's *Great Expectations* (1860-1861, serial; 1861, book). The aunt and uncle who reared Kipps expected him to become a store clerk; Kipps has not been very skilled at anything he has undertaken, and he proves no better at handling an unexpected inheritance. Kipps has a dreary existence: He gains no real pleasure from life, not even from reading. Life in lower-middle-class commercial and shopkeeping society is without substance, imagination, or purpose. Kipps's first thought is to buy a banjo, though he cannot play it. Thinking more seriously of his prospects, he asks his art teacher to marry him, and she proceeds to teach him to speak and dress properly. Kipps tries and hopes, until he encounters an old love, Ann Pornick, working as a maid. He snubs her and in his guilt asks her forgiveness; she not only forgives him but also marries him. Thus, Kipps has stumbled through mistake after mistake, from education to apprenticeship to courtship and marriage. Finally, when he loses most of his fortune, he and his wife resign themselves to a restricted life and open a bookshop.

Wells's satire is directed at Kipps for trying to be more than he can be, for misplacing values in a system of manners; indeed, Wells intensely scorns the social superficialities. The protagonist of *Tono-Bungay*, George Ponderevo, has much in common with Kipps, but George is less simple and more reflective. His early life is like Kipps's (and Wells's) in that he resists training for trade, shows a talent for science, marries above his class, divorces, and rediscovers a childhood romance, through scenes of satiric analysis of the social snobs, religious bigots, and capitalist cutthroats of England. More sympathetic is ambitious Uncle Teddy, who makes a fortune with Tono-Bungay, a bogus medicine, and launches a disastrous career in the "romance of modern commerce." George Ponderevo is more a master of his destiny than is Kipps. After the collapse of his uncle's financial empire, George turns to engineering as a means of commitment to scientific objectivity. He is beyond society and governments, as he is alone in the world of love.

Science triumphs over socialism and capitalism in *Tono-Bungay*, while individual vitality triumphs over all ideas in *The History of Mr. Polly*, another of Wells's best comic novels from his middle period. This story begins with a discontented middle-aged shopkeeper, Mr. Polly, contemplating his boredom, indigestion, and proud misuse of English. He decides to burn his shop and cut his throat. Having succeeded in his arson but having forgotten to cut his throat, he deserts his wife for happy obscurity as a fat woman's handyman, forgetting the life he detested. Although Mr. Polly is an absurd creature, surrounded by stupid, unambitious people, he is sympathetic because he rebels against that absurdity and stupidity. Wells rewards Mr. Polly well for his rebellion.

ANN VERONICA

Wells also rewards the heroine of his infamous novel *Ann Veronica*, which takes up more fully the themes of free love and women's rights. Ann Veronica Stanley rebels against her father's authority and flees to London, where she attends university lectures in biology. Having thrown herself into the cause of women's suffrage, she is arrested and imprisoned. Then she elopes with her biology instructor, a married man, to Switzerland. This unconventional woman, however, receives a very conventional reward: She marries her lover, has children, and becomes reconciled with her father.

Having put new ideas into old literary forms with *Ann Veronica*, Wells set the direction of his writing for the rest of his life. In his later novels, ideas, argument, debate, and intellectual analysis become prominent, often at the expense of literary form. Feminist causes give way to issues of world peace in books dealing with the world wars, the one that was and the one to come. *Mr. Britling Sees It Through* is one of the best, though it is a troubling confusion of political despair and comic resignation. Touches of good humor keep the book going with scenes of absurdity, as when Mr. Britling tries to drive his car or Mr. Direck tries to understand British manners. This good humor erodes, however, under the pressure of the events of World War I. Mr. Britling's son is killed, his children's German tutor also is killed, and his private secretary is terribly wounded. The war nearly destroys Mr. Britling, but he sees it through, clinging to a religious hope of divine struggle through human suffering. He commits himself to the cause of world peace, but in the course of writing a letter to the German parents of his children's tutor, he gradually gives way to outrage against Germany and finally collapses in grief. The novel ends when Mr. Britling gets up from his writing to look out his window at the sunrise.

Such an ending hints of an uncertainty in Wells's own commitment to hope. His novels analyze the dead end of civilization and call for redirection through peaceful applications of scientific discoveries. Wells's bitterness at the barbarism of World War I emerges again in *Mr. Blettsworthy on Rampole Island*, whose hero, driven by an unhappy love affair and a failing business, travels to forget. This is one of Wells's most interesting later works, combining anthropology and psychology with experimentation in form. Mr. Blettsworthy's experience with cannibals on Rampole Island may be a fantasy of his madness or an insight into reality, but his experience on the battlefield of World War I is a plunge into an all-too-real madness. Blettsworthy's romantic life of optimism finally yields to a cynical discontent with reality. His perspective is not, however, Wells's final word, since Blettsworthy's business partner, Lyulph Graves, speaks at the end for a philosophy of "creative stoicism," like the attitude that is assumed by Mr. Britling and, perhaps, by Wells himself. Certainly there were differing points of view in Wells's imagination. These differences may express intellectual confusion, but they gave substance to his fiction and saved it from succumbing utterly to his tendency to preach.

THE AUTOCRACY OF MR. PARHAM

The opposition of Blettsworthy and Graves is repeated in the relationship of Mr. Parham with Sir Bussy Woodcock in *The Autocracy of Mr. Parham*, which envisions a time when humankind might destroy itself through another barbarous world war. Mr. Parham voices the Fascist call (by Benito Mussolini) to traditional discipline and order as a way to prevent self-destruction; Sir Bussy expresses suspicion of dictatorship, social discipline, and intellectual utopias. Wells employs an entertaining device for exposing the differences between his protagonists: He brings them into a fantasy of the future as the result of a séance.

Possessed by a Nietzschean force calling itself the "Master Spirit," Mr. Parham's ego is loosed upon the world as the British dictator Lord Paramount. He goes to war with the United States and Germany, aiming for Russia, but he cannot command the obedience of Sir Bussy, who refuses to use a powerful new gas to destroy the opposition. After the séance, Mr. Parham discovers that Sir Bussy has had a dream very much like his own fantasy. Wells's use of comic irony is very strong in the conclusion, as Mr. Parham is deflated by Sir Bussy's plans to preach peace through the very means by which Mr. Parham had hoped to reach the world himself: journalism. Mr. Parham is a smug intellectual who knows where the world ought to go, if it would only follow his instructions; Sir Bussy is a muddled businessman, limited by the contingencies of immediate events and satisfied with the disorganized vitality that distresses Mr. Parham. This difference between creative capitalism and intellectual autocracy is imaged as a difference in personalities caught in a play of life's ironies.

Wells's scientific romances display an optimistic hope for a future made better by scientific discoveries, countered by the pessimistic doubt that humankind could make the necessary choices for social and political progress. Wells shows sympathy and scorn for the stunted characters of his middle novels, for Kipps, George Ponderevo, and Mr. Polly; he exposes their inadequacies, largely as products of a narrow, stultifying environment, but he also rescues them in life-affirming conclusions. Finally, between the great wars, H. G. Wells, like his Mr. Britling, "saw it through," exercised the "creative stoicism" of Lyulph Graves, and occasionally managed to rise above his pamphleteering style to produce entertaining novels of lives muddled by uncertainty, conflict, and contradiction.

Richard D. McGhee

Other major works

SHORT FICTION: *The Stolen Bacillus, and Other Incidents*, 1895; *The Plattner Story, and Others*, 1897; *Thirty Strange Stories*, 1897; *Tales of Space and Time*, 1899; *The Vacant Country*, 1899; *Twelve Stories and a Dream*, 1903; *The Country of the Blind, and Other Stories*, 1911; *A Door in the Wall, and Other Stories*, 1911; *The Short Stories of H. G. Wells*, 1927 (also known as *The Complete Stories of H. G. Wells*, 1966); *The Favorite Short Stories of H. G. Wells*, 1937 (also known as *The Famous Short Stories of H. G. Wells*, 1937).

NONFICTION: *Honours Physiography*, 1893 (with Sir Richard A. Gregory); *Text-Book of Biology*, 1893 (2 volumes); *Certain Personal Matters*, 1897; *A Text-Book of Zoology*, 1898 (with A. M. Davis); *Anticipations of the Reaction of Mechanical and Scientific Progress upon Human Life and Thought*, 1902 (also known as *Anticipations*); *The Discovery of the Future*, 1902; *Mankind in the Making*, 1903; *A Modern Utopia*, 1905; *The Future in America: A Search After Realities*, 1906; *Socialism and the Family*, 1906; *This Misery of Boots*, 1907; *First and Last Things: A Confession of Faith and Rule of Life*, 1908; *New Worlds for Old*, 1908; *The Great State: Essays in Construction*, 1912 (also known as *Socialism and the Great State*); *An Englishman Looks at the World: Being a Series of Unrestrained Remarks upon Contemporary Matters*, 1914 (also known as *Social Forces in England and America*); *The War That Will End War*, 1914; *God, the Invisible King*, 1917; *The Outline of History: Being a Plain History of Life and Mankind*, 1920; *Russia in the Shadows*, 1920; *The Salvaging of Civilization*, 1921; *A Short History of the World*, 1922; *Socialism and the Scientific Motive*, 1923; *The Open Conspiracy: Blue Prints for a World Revolution*, 1928; *Imperialism and the Open Conspiracy*, 1929; *The Science of Life: A Summary of Contemporary Knowledge About Life and Its Possibilities*, 1929-1930 (with Julian S. Huxley and G. P. Wells); *The Way to World Peace*, 1930; *What Are We to Do with Our Lives?*, 1931 (revised edition of *The Open Conspiracy*); *The Work, Wealth, and Happiness of Mankind*, 1931 (2 volumes); *After Democracy: Addresses and Papers on the Present World Situation*, 1932; *Evolution: Fact and Theory*, 1932 (with Huxley and G. P. Wells); *Experiment in Autobiography: Discoveries and Conclusions of a*

Very Ordinary Brain Since 1866, 1934 (2 volumes); *The New America: The New World*, 1935; *The Anatomy of Frustration: A Modern Synthesis*, 1936; *World Brain*, 1938; *The Fate of Homo Sapiens: An Unemotional Statement of the Things That Are Happening to Him Now and of the Immediate Possibilities Confronting Him*, 1939; *The Common Sense of War and Peace: World Revolution or War Unending?*, 1940; *The New World Order: Whether It Is Obtainable, How It Can Be Attained, and What Sort of World a World at Peace Will Have to Be*, 1940; *The Conquest of Time*, 1942; *Phoenix: A Summary of the Inescapable Conditions of World Reorganization*, 1942; *Science and the World Mind*, 1942; *Crux Ansata: An Indictment of the Roman Catholic Church*, 1943; *'42 to '44: A Contemporary Memoir upon Human Behaviour During the Crisis of the World Revolution*, 1944; *Mind at the End of Its Tether*, 1945.

CHILDREN'S LITERATURE: *The Adventures of Tommy*, 1929.

BIBLIOGRAPHY

Batchelor, John. *H. G. Wells*. New York: Cambridge University Press, 1985. Important work, intended as an introduction to Wells as both writer and thinker, examines the entire body of his writings. Includes bibliography and index.

Bergonzi, Bernard. *The Early H. G. Wells: A Study of the Scientific Romances*. Toronto, Ont.: University of Toronto Press, 1961. Classic study is still among the most knowledgeable accounts available of Wells's early fantasies. Focuses on the remarkable affinity of the content of these novels and short stories with the search for new worlds and behavior that characterized the period around the beginning of the twentieth century.

Coren, Michael. *The Invisible Man: The Life and Liberties of H. G. Wells*. London: Bloomsbury, 1992. Biography contradicts other authors' flattering portraits of Wells. Argues that Wells was often on the "wrong side" of literary and political debates, as evidenced by his anti-Semitic comments, belief in racial eugenics, and advocacy of concentration camps.

Costa, Richard Hauer. *H. G. Wells*. Rev. ed. Boston: Twayne, 1985. Provides a sympathetic survey of Wells's career and influence, with an emphasis on the major novels in the context of literary traditions before and after Wells. Includes a chronology, a review of trends in Wells criticism, notes, an annotated bibliography, and an index.

Hammond, J. R. *An H. G. Wells Chronology*. New York: St. Martin's Press, 1999. Presents detailed information on the events of Wells's life and his literary works. Includes bibliographical references and index.

_______. *An H. G. Wells Companion*. New York: Barnes & Noble Books, 1979. An indispensable tool for the Wells scholar. Part 1 describes Wells's background and his literary reputation, part 2 is an alphabetical listing and annotation of every title Wells published, part 3 provides succinct discussions of his short stories, part 4 contains a brief discussion of his book-length romances, part 5 addresses individual novels, and part 6 is a key to characters and locations. Includes an appendix on film versions of Wells's fiction and a bibliography.

_______. *A Preface to H. G. Wells*. New York: Longman, 2001. Concise volume presents an overview of Wells's work as well as biographical information; critical commentary on Wells's fiction, particularly *The Time Machine* and *Tono-Bungay*; and a discussion of his literary reputation.

Haynes, Roslynn D. *H. G. Wells, Discoverer of the Future: The Influence of Science on His Thought*. London: Macmillan, 1980. Presents a thorough discussion of the influence of science on Wells's fiction and sociological tracts. Shows how science helped Wells to achieve an analytical perspective on the problems of his time, from art to philosophy. Includes bibliography and index.

Huntington, John, ed. *Critical Essays on H. G. Wells*. Boston: G. K. Hall, 1991. Collection of essays includes contributions that address Wells's major writings, including *Tono-Bungay* and *The History of Mr. Polly*, as well as discussions of his science fiction and his treatments of social change, utopia, and women.

MacKenzie, Norman, and Jeanne MacKenzie. *The Life of H. G. Wells: The Time Traveller*. Rev. ed. London: Hogarth, 1987. Excellent, comprehensive work is one of the most detailed scholarly biographies of Wells available.

Rinkel, Gene K., and Margaret E. Rinkel. *The Picshuas of H. G. Wells: A Burlesque Diary*. Urbana: University of Illinois Press, 2006. "Picshuas" is the term Wells used for the sketches and cartoons he drew for his second wife, Jane. The sketches reproduced in this book convey the dynamics of their relationship and provide readers with fascinating insights into Wells's psyche and personal life. This work serves as an excellent addition to Wells biographies and as a complement to his own writing.

Wagar, W. Warren. *H. G. Wells: Traversing Time*. Middletown, Conn.: Wesleyan University Press, 2004. Analyzes all of Wells's work, focusing on the author's preoccupation with the unfolding of public time and the history and future of humankind. Demonstrates how Wells's writings remain relevant in the twenty-first century.

COLSON WHITEHEAD

Born: New York, New York; 1969
Also known as: Arch Colson Chipp Whitehead

PRINCIPAL LONG FICTION

The Intuitionist, 1999
John Henry Days, 2001
Apex Hides the Hurt, 2006
Sag Harbor, 2009

OTHER LITERARY FORMS

Although Colson Whitehead is primarily a novelist, he has also published the collection of essays *The Colossus of New York: A City in Thirteen Parts* (2003), a work that makes clear the importance of place and surroundings for him. Working as a journalist and as a critic of books, music, and television has enabled Whitehead to develop the keen sense of language and its nuances that plays a significant role in his fiction. He has published articles in a wide variety of publications, including *The New York Times*, *Salon*, *Spin*, *New York Magazine*, *Harper's*, and *Granta*.

ACHIEVEMENTS

Colson Whitehead was heralded as a talented writer from the publication of his first novel. *The Intuitionist* received the New Voices Award presented by the Quality Paperback Book Club and was a finalist in the competition for the Hemingway Foundation/PEN Award. Whitehead was from this first endeavor opening the way for a new type of novel that defies classification. *The Intuitionist* can be read as an allegory, as a detective novel, or even as a comedic tale. His next novel, *John Henry Days*, further broke the boundaries of the traditional novel with its multilevel structure, its satire, and its probing look at historical and contemporary racism. The work received the Young Lions Award and was a finalist for both the National Book Critics Circle Award and the Pulitzer Prize. Whitehead's ability to create fiction that goes beyond the traditional norms of the genre earned him a MacArthur Fellowship in 2002. His work continues the tradition of the intellectual black novel, which is part of the canon of African American literature.

BIOGRAPHY

Arch Colson Chipp Whitehead was born in Manhattan in New York City in 1969; he grew up in the Fort Greene neighborhood in Brooklyn. He attended Trinity School and Harvard University, and after graduating from Harvard in 1991, he began a career in journalism as a pop-culture critic for *The Village Voice*. At first he wrote about books and music; later, he became the newspaper's television columnist.

Whitehead first decided he wanted to be a writer of fiction when he was a child and began reading Stephen King's books. While in college, he discovered the works of more authors who increased his desire to write, including the fiction of Thomas Pynchon and Ishmael Reed. In 1999, Whitehead published his first novel, *The Intuitionist*. His second novel, *John Henry Days*, followed in 2001. His next publication was the collection of essays *The Colossus of New York*, which appeared in 2003. In this nonfiction work composed of personal memories, vignettes, and meditations, Whitehead captures all of the varied and often contradictory qualities of New York City. In 2006, he returned to fiction with the publication of another novel, *Apex Hides the Hurt*. His fourth novel, *Sag Harbor*, published in 2009, is a semiautobiographical story. Whitehead is a fellow at the Cullman Center for Scholars and Writers.

ANALYSIS

Colson Whitehead writes novels that break the traditional rules of fiction writing. His works defy classification into the standard categories. In *The Intuitionist*, the inclusion of features of the detective story add to the intrigue of the novel, but at the same time the work satirizes the detective story. The novel is really neither satire nor detective fiction per se. The setting of *The Intuitionist* is anachronistic: The city in which the fiction takes place is futuristic in the technology depicted and in the focus of the inhabitants on verticality; in this world, elevators are the cornerstone of society. Ethically and morally, however, the inhabitants of the city resemble people living in a city in the United States in the mid-twentieth century.

In *John Henry Days*, Whitehead experiments even more with the novel form. He exercises his privilege as author to take the narrative where he wishes, ignoring any traditional formula. The work includes many digressions and interpolated stories as Whitehead presents events without regard for chronological order. There is a shooting in the novel that Whitehead recounts very early in the work and then again near the end—and neither time does he reveal who was killed. The novel ends without closure; rather, the reader is left to finish the story.

THE INTUITIONIST

The Intuitionist is a combination of allegory, detective novel, futuristic novel, and social satire that addresses prejudice and racial discrimination. The story is set in a large metropolitan city in the middle of the twentieth century. The society is highly advanced technologically and totally devoted to a cult of elevators. Progress is linked to verticality and its improvement, and modernization and success are equated with upward mobility. Everyone reads *Lift*, a weekly magazine that informs the public about what is happening in the elevator industry. Other aspects of the society contrast sharply with its technologically advanced status, however. Political corruption, exploitation, and racial prejudice govern everyday life. Technologically the society is futuristic, but morally it remains locked in a

1940's or 1950's mentality. Using elements of the detective story of the mid-twentieth century—such as mobsters, abandoned warehouses, and late-night assignations—Whitehead gives the story an ambiance of believability.

The Intuitionist recounts the trials of Lila Mae Watson, an African American elevator inspector. She works for the Department of Elevator Inspectors, which, in this verticality obsessed society, is one of the most powerful departments, possibly the most powerful, in the metropolis. All elevator inspectors adhere to one of two different approaches to elevator inspection: An elevator inspector is either an Empiricist or an Intuitionist. An Empiricist inspects an elevator by getting into the elevator shaft and checking the mechanism to see if it meets the specifications. An Intuitionist, in contrast, evaluates the condition of an elevator by listening and by feeling the mechanism's vibrations, becoming one with the elevator. The department is heavily staffed by Empiricists, and Lila Mae is an Intuitionist. Lila Mae's life is a constant ordeal, as she is marginalized by her race, her sex, and her adherence to Intuitionist theory.

In spite of her exclusion, Lila Mae has an impressive record as an inspector and is assigned to inspect the elevators in the Fanny Briggs Memorial Building. A short time after she has inspected the elevators there, one of the elevators crashes. This is a catastrophe for her, given that it could mean the end of her career, and she becomes determined to find out what happened. The Elevator Guild is in the process of electing a new guild chair; the two candidates are Frank Chancre, an Empiricist, and Orville Lever, an Intuitionist. Lila Mae becomes convinced that Chancre, who is known to have connections to a mob boss, has had the elevator sabotaged.

Whitehead complicates his narrative by adding another intrigue: Suddenly papers from the research of the late James Fulton, father of Intuitionism, start showing up with Lila Mae's name on them. Fulton had been researching a black box, the perfect next-generation elevator. Lila Mae decides that she must find the blueprints for the black box and at the same time exonerate herself in regard to the crash. Whitehead turns his narrative into a detective novel as he relates Lila Mae's search, which involves deceptions, false leads, and mob enforcers, and an ambiance of danger invades the narrative. After he has led the reader as well as Lila Mae down a number of false trails, Whitehead concludes the story in a totally unexpected way. The elevator was not sabotaged, it just did a free fall, as elevators sometimes do. Arbo Elevators believed that Lila Mae had Fulton's papers on the black box, and the company wanted them to avoid bankruptcy. Whitehead then adds a section on Fulton's thoughts during his last working days and concludes the novel with Lila Mae, who has become obsessed with completing Fulton's research, alone in a small room working to create the perfect elevator.

In *The Intuitionist* Whitehead uses the metaphor of verticality to delineate African Americans' difficulty in being upwardly mobile in a racially prejudiced society. He develops this theme through the characters of Lila Mae and James Fulton. Lila Mae's father was an elevator operator in a department store where no African Americans were allowed, with the exception of those who worked there. Lila Mae is determined to achieve upward mobility through her own efforts. She puts up with living in a converted janitor's closet at the elevator inspectors' academy, and nothing—not the ransacking of her apartment, her kidnapping by Chancre's thugs, or her deception by Fulton's false nephew—deters her from her goal. Lila Mae is determined to succeed in spite of a system that puts every obstacle in her way.

James Fulton, a light-skinned African American, had been able to achieve upward mobility because of his ability to pass for white. He had become a respected researcher in verticality, in upward mobility in elevators, but throughout his life he knew that the discovery of his true racial identity would have destroyed his career and denied him acceptance in society. Consequently, infuriated and seeking revenge, he played a joke on everyone by creating the concept of the black box. The perfect elevator that was to transform the city's landscape was not real—it was simply a trick that the clever Fulton played to get back at the prejudiced closed society in which he lived.

JOHN HENRY DAYS

John Henry Days incorporates allegory, comedy, pathos, satire, and social realism while at the same time elucidating the dilemma of keeping history and myth alive in a mechanized, materialistic world of consumerism. The novel is set in 1996 during John Henry Days—a festival honoring the American folk legend—in Talcott, West Virginia. At the same time, the post office in Talcott is issuing a new commemorative stamp featuring John Henry—part of a series honoring other American folk legends as well, such as Paul Bunyan and Pecos Pete. J. Sutter, an African American who is very aware of being a member of a racial minority group, is a junketeer who is trying to set a record for having attended the most consecutive events. Pamela, an African American whose deceased father left a large collection of John Henry memorabilia, is at the Talcott festivities because the town wants to buy her father's collection. Other characters include Albert Miggs, a stamp collector; Lucien Joyce, the owner of a publicity agency that has a list of reporters (including Sutter) ready to cover such events; and Sutter's cronies Dave, Frenchie, Tiny, and One Eye.

The apparent narrative is a sprawling account of the days of the John Henry celebration, which are typical of such small-town festivals. Sutter's motel is just adequate; the food, except for the prime rib, is scarcely exciting; the talent is local. The actor Ben Vereen was scheduled to attend the celebration, but he was taken ill at the last minute. Neither Pamela nor the junketeers are really pleased to be there. Pamela has a purpose beyond the town's interest in her father's collection—she has actually come to bury her father's ashes in the neglected cemetery where John Henry is buried. The junketeers are there for the free food and drink and whatever else they can get for free and because they are on the list—and, of course, Sutter is there because he is going for the record. Miggs is there because he collects railroad stamps, and he wants the new John Henry stamp for his collection.

The real narrative of this novel is found in the digressions, however—in the interpolated stories and the long conversations of the junketeers. In these parts of the book, Whitehead examines a number of concepts and issues. One of the major themes of the novel is consumerism, with a focus on how advertising controls people's lives. Sutter and the other junketeers make their living by going from one publicity event to another and writing about the events for various publications. Lucien Joyce, whose agency employs them, has a reputation for being willing to publicize any event, no matter how trivial, for the right amount of money. The junketeers glory in all the free things they get: food, liquor, motel rooms, and sometimes articles that are being publicized. Receipts are everything; turned in, they produce reimbursement. The John Henry Days celebration is cluttered with John Henry merchandise. Whitehead depicts an America obsessed with material things and the desire to get as much as possible for free.

The legend of John Henry—the railroad steel-driving man who died with a hammer in his hand, competing against a steel-driving machine—as well as a chapter on Pamela's temporary job for an Internet company and the junketeers' lifestyle, especially Sutter's, elucidate the enslavement and dehumanization of people, first by the forces of industrialization and then by those of the digital information age. In chapters about John Henry, Whitehead depicts how John Henry trades his enslavement in the cotton fields for a comparable slavery, driving steel, laying track for the railroad, and buying at the company store.

Sutter and the other junketeer journalists go where the events are. Just as John Henry exists to drive steel, Sutter and the others exist to follow the event circuit. When Sutter enters the Big Bend Tunnel with Pamela, he is enticed but also frightened by the fact that the tunnel cuts him off from the digital information world. Whitehead emphasizes the total lack of interaction among the temporary workers at Pamela's workplace as well as their lack of individuality: All have exactly the same items with which to work, and all make no attempt to personalize their workstations. Whitehead portrays these characters as functions of their work environment. The characters are closed, hiding their inner selves, hiding what Sutter is afraid might be released in the Big Bend Tunnel.

In both the main narrative of *John Henry Days* and in the digressions, Whitehead illustrates the difficulty of being a dark-skinned individual in a racially prejudiced society. John Henry was a black man, yet he is the folk hero of a prejudiced white population. Pamela and Sutter are the only two African Americans at the John Henry Days opening banquet. Sutter is there because he is a journalist who will publicize the event; Pamela is there because she has her father's collection—both characters have something the town wants. The novel ends with Sutter trying to decide if he will leave early with Pamela or stay for the banquet. A shooting takes place, but the outcome is unclear: Has Sutter been killed? Whitehead gives clues, but the reader must decide whether the clues are false.

Shawncey Webb

OTHER MAJOR WORK

NONFICTION: *The Colossus of New York: A City in Thirteen Parts*, 2003.

BIBLIOGRAPHY

Bell, Bernard W. *The Contemporary African American Novel: Its Roots and Modern Literary Branches*. Amherst: University of Massachusetts Press, 2004. Discusses Whitehead's work and the work of other African American writers as seeking experimentation in the novel and abandoning the traditions and roots of the African American novel.

Liggins, Saundra. "The Urban Gothic Vision of Colson Whitehead's *The Intuitionist* (1999)." *African American Review* 40, no. 2 (2006): 359-370. Places the novel in the gothic tradition based on its setting and the "horror" created by the allegorical treatment of the black struggle for upward mobility.

Porter, Everette. "Writing Home." *Black Issues Book Review*, May/June, 2002. Offers discussion of Whitehead's obsession with place and its influence on his novels.

Russell, Alison. "Recalibrating the Past: *The Intuitionist*." *Critique* 49, no. 1 (2007): 46-60. Describes *The Intuitionist* as an anti-detective novel and discusses textual authority in regard to race, identity, and history.

Whitehead, Colson, and Walter Mosley. "Eavesdropping." Interview. *Book*, May, 2001. In conversation with author Mosley, Whitehead discusses his goals in writing, the difficulties he encountered in publishing *The Intuitionist*, and his sense of himself as a black writer.

TOM WOLFE

Born: Richmond, Virginia; March 2, 1931
Also known as: Thomas Kennerly Wolfe, Jr.

PRINCIPAL LONG FICTION

The Bonfire of the Vanities, 1987
A Man in Full, 1998
I Am Charlotte Simmons, 2004

OTHER LITERARY FORMS

Tom Wolfe is known as one of the most original and influential of the New Journalists to come to popular attention during the mid-1960's. His collections of essays and original drawings on contemporary American lifestyle include *The Pump House Gang* (1968), *Radical Chic and Mau-Mauing the Flak Catchers* (1970), and *Mauve Gloves and Madmen, Clutter and Vine, and Other Stories, Sketches, and Essays* (1976). In these and other works, Wolfe skewered the foibles of a period he named the me decade. In *The Painted Word* (1975), he addressed what he saw as the false pretensions and theory-driven impulses of modern art, and he took on the similar hoaxing of the general public by architects in *From Bauhaus to Our House* (1981).

Prior to his venture into long fiction, Wolfe's most extensive and successful work was *The Right Stuff* (1979), a lengthy, well-researched, and engrossing study of the manned spaceflight efforts of the United States from their beginnings through the end of the original Mercury program. The book has been widely recognized for its incisive and penetrating exploration of the unique worldview of test pilots and astronauts and for its explanation of the almost inexpressible concept of "the right stuff."

ACHIEVEMENTS

During his career, although often attacked by cultural critics, Tom Wolfe has become one of the most recognized and honored of American writers. In 1973, he received the Frank Luther Mott Award for research in journalism, and in 1977 he was named Virginia Laureate for Literature. After the publication of *The Right Stuff*, he was widely recognized, winning the Award in Excellence in Literature from the American Institute of Arts and Letters, the Columbia Journalism Award, and the American Book Award. In 1986 he was given the Washington Irving Medal for Literary Excellence.

An even more important mark of Wolfe's achievement, however, is the fact that he is largely credited with launching an entire literary movement, that of New Journalism, which emerged during the 1960's and 1970's and influenced not only nonfiction writing but also fiction itself.

BIOGRAPHY

Born and raised in Richmond, Virginia, Thomas Kennerly Wolfe, Jr., enjoyed a childhood that exposed him to the world of the arts, especially literature. After graduating from Washington and Lee University, he enrolled at Yale University, where he majored in American studies. Before completing his dissertation but after finishing his course work, he left Yale to work at the *Springfield Union* newspaper, where he began as a city hall reporter. He received his doctorate from Yale in 1957.

In 1959 Wolfe took a position with *The Washington Post*, and then, in 1962, joined one of the most literate and well-written newspapers in the nation, the *New York Herald-Tribune*, as a staff writer for its Sunday magazine supplement. Wolfe quickly established a reputation as one of the paper's finest reporters, with a style that was innovative, energetic, and unique. In 1965 Wolfe angered the literary establishment with a scathing, accurate, and enormously funny dissection of the sacrosanct *New Yorker* magazine.

During these years Wolfe, along with such writers as Norman Mailer, Truman Capote, and Hunter S. Thompson, was establishing what would become known as New Journalism, a genre that blurred or even erased the boundaries between the reporter and the story, and that reveled in subjective and highly idiosyncratic styles. Wolfe's *The Kandy-Kolored Tangerine-Flake Streamline Baby* (1965), a collection of articles chronicling the youth culture of the mid-1960's, was followed by *The Electric Kool-Aid Acid Test* (1968), his in-depth study of author Ken Kesey and his drug-indulging band of Merry Pranksters. In 1979 Wolfe published the quintessential volume of New Journalism, *The Right Stuff*, a history of the formative years of the U.S. space program.

In 1984 Wolfe embarked on a daring and risky adventure, writing a novel to be published in successive issues of *Rolling Stone* magazine. Much as English writers Charles Dickens and William Makepeace Thackeray had done, Wolfe committed himself to producing chapters on a tight deadline. The first installment of *The Bonfire of the Vanities* first appeared in *Rolling Stone* in July, 1984; the twenty-seventh and final installment appeared almost exactly one year later. Wolfe subsequently revised the work substantially, and it was published in hardcover in 1987. The novel became a best seller that also won great critical acclaim. An unsuccessful and much-criticized motion-picture adaptation of the novel was released in 1990. For almost a decade following *The Bonfire of the Vanities*, Wolfe returned to journalism. It was not until 1998 that he again turned to fiction, publishing *A Man in Full*, about Atlanta real estate entrepreneur Charlie Croker. Like *The Bonfire of the Vanities*, the novel was embraced by critics and the reading public; it too became a best seller and further confirmed Wolfe's ability to write successfully, even brilliantly, in both nonfictional and fictional genres.

ANALYSIS

Tom Wolfe's novels are grounded in the social realism and satire of writers such as Dickens, Thackeray, and Honoré de Balzac, and they are filled with the sharp observations of class and caste characteristic of his nonfiction pieces. Wolfe has stated that he admires Balzac's assessment of himself as "society's secretary" and that he wants his own writing to reflect reality.

The Bonfire of the Vanities

The Bonfire of the Vanities is satire in its clearest and most uncompromising sense, an expression of moral nausea made bearable only by the presence of sharp, mordant humor. The novel's title and much of its theme come from two major sources. The first is the career of the Italian reforming cleric Girolamo Savonarola (1452-1498), who for a brief time convinced the citizens of Florence to destroy their luxury goods in a literal bonfire of the vanities. After their initial exuberance wore off, the Florentines decided to burn Savonarola instead. The second source is Thackeray's novel *Vanity Fair* (1847-1848, serial; 1848, book), which satirizes the excesses of society in early nineteenth century England.

The plot of the novel is relatively simple: Sherman McCoy, a bond trader on Wall Street and self-proclaimed "master of the universe" for his financial dealings, is indulging in an adulterous affair with Maria Ruskin, wife of a wealthy financier. One evening, as Sherman is returning Maria from the airport in his Mercedes, he goes astray and ends up in the unfamiliar and frightening confines of the Bronx. Fleeing what appears to be a bungled highway robbery attempt, Maria, who is driving, accidentally hits a young black man, Henry Lamb, with the car.

When Henry Lamb ends up with a concussion in the hospital, activist Reverend Bacon mobilizes the black community to force Bronx district attorney Abraham Weiss and his assistant Larry Kramer into action. The police find evidence that might link Sherman to the crime, and British tabloid journalist Peter Fallow writes a series of articles about the incident that further inflame tensions in the city. Sherman is indicted, and during the trial he and Maria turn against each other. Her crucial evidence is disallowed on a technicality, and Sherman's indictment is dismissed, resulting in a near riot. In a brief, ironic epilogue cast a year later, many of the major characters have fallen, through divorce, disgrace, or defeat in reelection campaigns. Only Sherman remains, still a defendant, as well as Reverend Bacon, the manipulator of protests and protesters.

The characters in *The Bonfire of the Vanities* are defined by their possessions. The book is a lovingly precise catalog of clothes, shoes, furniture, and accessories, all of fine craftsmanship and artistry, but valued, sometimes worshiped, because of their cost. Additionally, the vanities are appropriately relative: Sherman McCoy's $1.6 million apartment is juxtaposed with the $750 rent-controlled love nest that assistant district attorney Kramer takes over from Maria for his own mistress. The antics of Sherman's supposed friends as they try to make their way in the hive of society are no less ridiculous than the efforts of Abraham Weiss to remain district attorney.

The Bonfire of the Vanities falters when it approaches the terrain and the people alien to its hero, Sherman McCoy—the Bronx and its African American population, most of them poor, many of them victimized by crime, some of them criminals themselves. Although Wolfe's ear for speech and nuance is unrivaled, he is less certain about the other aspects of the lives of these characters, more cautious and ambivalent about entering into their minds and psyches. The Reverend Bacon is given minimal treatment, pictured as an accomplished, even sophisticated, shakedown artist skilled at piercing the armor of the white establishment, whether through guilt, fear, or power politics. It is a portrait accurate enough to be satirically truthful but so broad as to be uncomfortably close to stereotype. Roland Auburn, a black youth involved in the aborted robbery attempt, is a man who can arrange for endless deliveries of new white sneakers while imprisoned in the New York City criminal justice system. Beyond Auburn and Bacon, the black characters in *The Bonfire of the Vanities* are "extras" in the crowds during Reverend Bacon's demonstrations.

Still, the novel pulsates with the energy, vigor, and vulgarisms of New York City in the latter half of the twentieth century. Sherman McCoy and his fellow characters may not be up to anything essentially worthwhile in the long-range scheme of things (always a consideration of the satirist), and they are certainly deeply flawed human beings, but they are as destructive as the followers of Savonarola and as active as the puppets Thackeray created.

A MAN IN FULL

An acidly etched survey of the influences of race and wealth, caste, and class on life in the new South, *A Man in Full* is set in the South's unofficial capital, Atlanta, Georgia. This is the city of Charlie Croker, who came roaring out of southwestern Georgia to achieve fame playing both offense and defense as Georgia Tech's "Sixty Minute Man" to become one of Atlanta's most successful and well-known real estate developers. His latest creation, Croker Concourse, gleams proudly northeast of the central city, a symbol of his triumph, but already bank loan officers are demanding that Charlie restructure his company and sell off executive toys such as his jets, and they even cast coldly calculating eyes on his beloved plantation, Turpmtine.

Atlanta lawyer Roger White II (dubbed Roger Too White by his fraternity brother Wes Jordan, now Atlanta's mayor) is asked to secure Charlie Croker's public support of Fareek "The Cannon" Fanon, a star football player at Georgia Tech accused (although neither officially nor publicly) of date rape by the daughter of one of Atlanta's most influential businessmen. In exchange, Roger White can help Charlie by having the banks ease their demands.

In the meantime, Conrad Hensley, a warehouse worker in California for Croker Global Foods, is laid off as part of a drive to cut costs for Charlie's far-flung companies. Before long, in a series of misadventures, Conrad sits in a prison cell, his only diversion a volume of Epictetus, the Stoic philosopher. He begins to read and then to understand. Delivered from prison by an earthquake, Conrad makes his way to Atlanta, where he meets and befriends Charlie Croker and imparts the teachings of Epictetus. At the news conference during which he is expected to support Fanon, Charlie turns away from the banks, the black politicians, and the white power structure to reclaim his own integrity. It is when he renounces those who had a claim on his soul that Charlie Croker truly becomes "a man in full."

As Wolfe glaringly exposes New York City in *The Bonfire of the Vanities*, he goes after Atlanta in *A Man in Full*. The city's acclaimed economic strength, like Charlie Croker's own empire, is an illusion. The towers downtown are deserted when work ends as their inhabitants begin the longest and worst commute in the United States, leaving the inner city 75 percent African American, creating a division that is as fatal as it is fatally ignored. Within the two communities, black and white, there are further divisions, highlighted by degrees of color, levels of wealth, and shades of accents and dialect—all of which, once again, Wolfe captures with a mix of confidence and exuberance.

I Am Charlotte Simmons

In a preface to *I Am Charlotte Simmons*, Wolfe details a scientific study of two groups of cats, those in one group having small portions of their brains removed, those in the other remaining intact. The altered cats begin displaying aberrant behavior, engaging in doglike sexual movements but without stimulus and responding passively to terrifying situations, seemingly unable to sense danger. More intriguing is the reaction of the unaltered cats kept caged in full view of the show: They copy what they see. At first this scenario seems to bear little relationship to what promises to be a typical Wolfe study, this time of campus life at a fictional elite university modeled on several schools he visited in preparing to write the novel. The reader soon sees what he has in mind, however, in his tale of an innocent girl sent into a collegiate den of wolves.

Charlotte Simmons is a star in her backwoods North Carolina town. She has earned a perfect 1600 on her SATs and is enrolled at Dupont University. Her high intelligence and wide reading have not prepared her for the real world, however, where people drink, swear, and have casual sex. She is an outcast, scorned and ridiculed, yet three distinctly stereotypical college types seek her attention. Hoyt Thorpe is the best-looking boy in the best fraternity; he also has a running competition with his fraternity brothers to bed "fresh meat" (freshman girls) within seven hours. Jojo Johansen is the only white starter on the university's basketball team. He appears intellectually challenged, though he eventually manages to earn an inflated C+ on a paper without the writing talent of Charlotte's third pursuer, Adam Gellin, a college tutor. Adam works for the newspaper and sees himself as intellectually superior, belonging to a group of leftist thinkers who have labeled themselves the Millennial Mutants.

These renderings of the worst in any student body are not made easier to bear by the presence of a sympathetic protagonist. Charlotte is at first too rigid, smug, and clueless to be perceived of as intellectually gifted or as one who has any understanding of a world beyond the hills of her home. Then she plunges into the new reality of campus life, however, and begins to assume all the values of the group, viewing intellectual activity as less important than looking good by hanging around with the right people. In other words, in Wolfe's view, Charlotte is the typical college student on a modern-day campus where athletes are adored, fraternities pump out future leaders, and nerds lurk in the shadows thinking deep thoughts. She has observed and then joined in, clearly influenced, as were the intact cats described in the preface.

To a disturbing extent, Wolfe's view may ring true, but he has been faulted for creating caricatures rather than developing characters in *I Am Charlotte Simmons*. His people, as well as their motivations and morals, lack depth. He may want to show the university as a microcosm of the larger society, but he fails to provide the reader with a hint of reality. Somewhere among the status-seeking, morally loose coeds and the slacker, self-important, womanizing frat boys, somewhere among the athletes granted degrees for athletic rather than intellectual prowess and the countercultural types with puffed-up visions of their importance and the lack of worth of others, there are serious students. Do not look for them here.

Michael Witkoski
Updated by Gay Pitman Zieger

OTHER MAJOR WORKS

NONFICTION: *The Kandy-Kolored Tangerine-Flake Streamline Baby*, 1965; *The Electric Kool-Aid Acid Test*, 1968; *The Pump House Gang*, 1968; *Radical Chic and Mau-Mauing the Flak Catchers*, 1970; *The New Journalism*, 1973; *The Painted Word*, 1975; *Mauve Gloves and Madmen, Clutter and Vine, and Other Stories, Sketches, and Essays*, 1976; *The Right Stuff*, 1979; *In Our Time*, 1980; *From Bauhaus to Our House*, 1981; *The Purple Decades: A Reader*, 1982; *Hooking Up*, 2000.

BIBLIOGRAPHY

Bloom, Harold, ed. *Tom Wolfe*. New York: Chelsea House, 2001. Collection of important critical responses to Wolfe's work also provides a thorough introduction by Bloom.

Leith, Sam. "Muscular Prose, Soft Centre." Review of *I Am Charlotte Simmons*, by Tom Wolfe. *Spectator*, November 13, 2004. Presents a detailed analysis of the novel, concluding that it is flawed work.

McEneaney, Kevin T. *Tom Wolfe's America: Heroes, Pranksters, and Fools*. Westport, Conn.: Praeger, 2009. Discusses Wolfe's life and writings, both fiction and nonfiction, with a focus on the author's themes, his use of irony, and his interest in pranks.

McKeen, William. *Tom Wolfe*. New York: Twayne, 1995. Provides students and general readers with an introduction to Wolfe's life and career. Especially good in discussing Wolfe's career as a practicing journalist, including his articles, such as his piece on *The New Yorker* that so outraged traditionalists.

Ragan, Brian Abel. *Tom Wolfe: A Critical Companion*. Westport, Conn.: Greenwood

Press, 2002. Intended as a guide for students, this book contains a biographical chapter, a contextual chapter introducing the concept of "new journalism" and Wolfe's role in it, and analyses of all of his major works.

Salamon, Julie. *The Devil's Candy: "The Bonfire of the Vanities" Goes to Hollywood.* Boston: Houghton Mifflin, 1991. Focuses on the making of the film version of Wolfe's novel, but useful for helping readers better understand and appreciate the many artistic nuances and insights in Wolfe's carefully layered work that were lost in its translation to the big screen.

Schulman, Sam. "Body and Soul." *Commentary* 119, no. 1 (January, 2005): 67. Presents a thoroughly entertaining critique of *I Am Charlotte Simmons*.

Scura, Dorothy, ed. *Conversations with Tom Wolfe.* Jackson: University Press of Mississippi, 1990. Collection of interviews with Wolfe presents the author's views on numerous topics, including writers he admires, his politics, his use of satire, and his approach to the discipline of writing.

Shomette, Doug, ed. *The Critical Response to Tom Wolfe.* Westport, Conn.: Greenwood Press, 1992. Collection of critical responses to Wolfe's writings over the years addresses primarily his journalistic works, but a section is devoted to the early responses to and criticisms of *The Bonfire of the Vanities*.

Bibliography

Every effort has been made to include studies published in 2000 and later. Most items in this bibliography contain a listing of secondary sources, making it easier to identify other critical commentary on novelists, movements, and themes.

THEORETICAL, THEMATIC, AND HISTORICAL STUDIES

Altman, Janet Gurkin. *Epistolarity: Approaches to a Form*. Columbus: Ohio State University Press, 1982. Examines the epistolary novel, explaining how novelists use the letter form to develop characterization, further their plots, and develop meaning.

Beaumont, Matthew, ed. *Adventures in Realism*. Malden, Mass.: Blackwell, 2007. Fifteen essays explore facets of realism, which was critical to the development of the novel. Provides a theoretical framework for understanding how novelists attempt to represent the real and the common in fiction.

Brink, André. *The Novel: Language and Narrative from Cervantes to Calvino*. New York: New York University Press, 1998. Uses contemporary theories of semiotics and narratology to establish a continuum between early novelists and those of the postmodern era in their conscious use of language to achieve certain effects. Ranges across national boundaries to illustrate the theory of the development of the novel since the seventeenth century.

Brownstein, Rachel. *Becoming a Heroine: Reading About Women in Novels*. New York: Viking Press, 1982. Feminist survey of novels from the eighteenth century through the latter half of the twentieth century. Examines how "becoming a heroine" defines for women a sense of value in their lives. Considers novels by both men and women, and discusses the importance of the traditional marriage plot.

Bruzelius, Margaret. *Romancing the Novel: Adventure from Scott to Sebald*. Lewisburg, Pa.: Bucknell University Press, 2007. Examines the development of the adventure novel, linking it with the medieval romance tradition and exploring readers' continuing fascination with the genre.

Cavallaro, Dani. *The Gothic Vision: Three Centuries of Horror, Terror, and Fear*. New York: Continuum, 2005. Study of the gothic novel from its earliest manifestations in the eighteenth century to the early twenty-first century. Through the lenses of contemporary cultural theories, examines readers' fascination with novels that invoke horror, terror, and fright.

Doody, Margaret Anne. *The True Story of the Novel*. New Brunswick, N.J.: Rutgers University Press, 1996. Traces the roots of the novel, traditionally thought to have been developed in the seventeenth century, to classical Greek and Latin texts that exhibit characteristics of modern fiction.

Hale, Dorothy J., ed. *The Novel: An Anthology of Criticism and Theory, 1900-2000*. Malden, Mass.: Blackwell, 2006. Collection of essays by theorists and novelists. Includes commentary on the novel form from the perspective of formalism, structuralism, poststructuralism, Marxism, and reader response theory. Essays also address the novel through the lenses of sociology, gender studies, and feminist theory.

_______. *Social Formalism: The Novel in Theory from Henry James to the Present*. Stanford, Calif.: Stanford University Press, 1998. Emphasizes the novel's special ability to define a social world for readers. Relies heavily on the works of contemporary literary and cultural theorists. Provides a summary of twentieth century efforts to identify a theory of fiction that encompasses novels of many kinds.

Hart, Stephen M., and Wen-chin Ouyang, eds. *A Companion to Magical Realism*. London: Tamesis, 2005. Essays outlining the development of Magical Realism, tracing its roots from Europe through Latin America to other regions of the world. Explores the political dimensions of the genre.

Hoffman, Michael J., and Patrick D. Murphy, eds. *Essentials of the Theory of Fiction*. 2d ed. Durham, N.C.: Duke University Press, 1996. Collection of essays by influential critics from the late nineteenth century through the twentieth century. Focuses on the essential elements of fiction and the novel's relationship to the world it depicts.

Lodge, David. *The Art of Fiction: Illustrated from Classic and Modern Texts*. New York: Viking Press, 1993. Short commentaries on the technical aspects of fiction. Examples from important and minor novelists illustrate literary principles and techniques such as point of view, suspense, character introduction, irony, motivation, and ending.

Lynch, Deirdre, and William B. Walker, eds. *Cultural Institutions of the Novel*. Durham, N.C.: Duke University Press, 1996. Fifteen essays examine aspects of long fiction produced around the world. Encourages a redefinition of the genre and argues for inclusion of texts not historically considered novels.

Moretti, Franco, ed. *The Novel*. 2 vols. Princeton, N.J.: Princeton University Press, 2006. Compendium exploring the novel from multiple perspectives, including as an anthropological, historical, and sociological document; a function of the national tradition from which it emerges; and a work of art subject to examination using various critical approaches.

Priestman, Martin, ed. *The Cambridge Companion to Crime Fiction*. New York: Cambridge University Press, 2003. Essays examine the nature and development of the genre, explore works by writers (including women and ethnic minorities) from several countries, and establish links between crime fiction and other literary genres. Includes a chronology.

Scaggs, John. *Crime Fiction*. New York: Routledge, 2005. Provides a history of crime fiction, explores key subgenres, and identifies recurring themes that suggest the wider social and historical context in which these works are written. Suggests critical approaches that open crime fiction to serious study.

Shiach, Morag, ed. *The Cambridge Companion to the Modernist Novel*. New York: Cambridge University Press, 2007. Essays explaining the concept of modernism and its influence on the novel. Detailed examination of works by writers from various countries, all influenced by the modernist movement. Includes a detailed chronology.

Vice, Sue. *Holocaust Fiction*. New York: Routledge, 2000. Examines controversies generated by novels about the Holocaust. Focuses on eight important works, but also offers observations on the polemics surrounding publication of books on this topic.

Zunshine, Lisa. *Why We Read Fiction: Theory of Mind and the Novel*. Columbus: Ohio State University Press, 2006. Applies theories of cognitive psychology to novel reading, explaining how experience and human nature lead readers to constrain their interpretations of a given text. Provides numerous examples from well-known novels to illustrate how and why readers find pleasure in fiction.

Laurence W. Mazzeno

Glossary of Literary Terms

absurdism: A philosophical attitude, pervading much of modern drama and fiction, that underlines the isolation and alienation that humans experience, having been thrown into what absurdists see as a godless universe devoid of religious, spiritual, or metaphysical meaning. Conspicuous in its lack of logic, consistency, coherence, intelligibility, and realism, the literature of the absurd depicts the anguish, forlornness, and despair inherent in the human condition. Counter to the rationalist assumptions of traditional humanism, absurdism denies the existence of universal truth or value.

allegory: A literary mode in which a second level of meaning, wherein characters, events, and settings represent abstractions, is encoded within the surface narrative. The allegorical mode may dominate an entire work, in which case the encoded message is the work's primary reason for being, or it may be an element in a work otherwise interesting and meaningful for its surface story alone. Elements of allegory may be found in Jonathan Swift's *Gulliver's Travels* (1726) and Thomas Mann's *Der Zauberberg* (1924; *The Magic Mountain*, 1927).

anatomy: Literally the term means the "cutting up" or "dissection" of a subject into its constituent parts for closer examination. Northrop Frye, in his *Anatomy of Criticism* (1957), uses the term to refer to a narrative that deals with mental attitudes rather than people. As opposed to the novel, the anatomy features stylized figures who are mouthpieces for the ideas they represent.

antagonist: The character in fiction who stands as a rival or opponent to the *protagonist*.

antihero: Defined by Seán O'Faoláin as a fictional figure who, deprived of social sanctions and definitions, is always trying to define himself and to establish his own codes. Ahab may be seen as the antihero of Herman Melville's *Moby Dick* (1851).

archetype: The term "archetype" entered literary criticism from the psychology of Carl Jung, who defined archetypes as "primordial images" from the "collective unconscious" of humankind. Jung believed that works of art derive much of their power from the unconscious appeal of these images to ancestral memories. In his extremely influential *Anatomy of Criticism* (1957), Northrop Frye gave another sense of the term wide currency, defining the archetype as "a symbol, usually an image, which recurs often enough in literature to be recognizable as an element of one's literary experience as a whole."

atmosphere: The general mood or tone of a work; atmosphere is often associated with setting but can also be established by action or dialogue. A classic example of atmosphere is the primitive, fatalistic tone created in the opening description of Egdon Heath in Thomas Hardy's *The Return of the Native* (1878).

bildungsroman: Sometimes called the "novel of education," the bildungsroman focuses on the growth of a young *protagonist* who is learning about the world and finding his or her place in life; typical examples are James Joyce's *A Portrait of the Artist as a*

Young Man (1914-1915, serial; 1916, book) and Thomas Wolfe's *Look Homeward, Angel* (1929).

biographical criticism: Criticism that attempts to determine how the events and experiences of an author's life influence his or her work.

bourgeois novel: A novel in which the values, preoccupations, and accoutrements of middle-class or bourgeois life are given particular prominence. The heyday of the bourgeois novel was the nineteenth century, when novelists as varied as Jane Austen, Honoré de Balzac, and Anthony Trollope both criticized and unreflectingly transmitted the assumptions of the rising middle class.

canon: An authorized or accepted list of books. In modern parlance, the literary canon comprehends the privileged texts, classics, or great books that are thought to belong permanently on university reading lists. Recent theory—especially feminist, Marxist, and poststructuralist—critically examines the process of canon formation and questions the hegemony of white male writers. Such theory sees canon formation as the ideological act of a dominant institution and seeks to undermine the notion of canonicity itself, thereby preventing the exclusion of works by women, minorities, and oppressed peoples.

character: Characters in fiction can be presented as if they were real people or as stylized functions of the plot. Usually characters are a combination of both factors.

classicism: A literary stance or value system consciously based on the example of classical Greek and Roman literature. While the term is applied to an enormous diversity of artists in many different periods and in many different national literatures, "classicism" generally denotes a cluster of values including formal discipline, restrained expression, reverence for tradition, and an objective rather than a subjective orientation. As a literary tendency, classicism is often opposed to *Romanticism*, although many writers combine classical and romantic elements.

climax/crisis: The term "climax" refers to the moment of the reader's highest emotional response, whereas "crisis" refers to a structural element of plot, a turning point at which a resolution must take place.

complication: The point in a novel when the *conflict* is developed or when the already existing conflict is further intensified.

conflict: The struggle that develops as a result of the opposition between the *protagonist* and another person, the natural world, society, or some force within the self.

contextualist criticism: A further extension of *formalist criticism*, which assumes that the language of art is constitutive. Rather than referring to preexistent values, the artwork creates values only inchoately realized before. The most important advocates of this position are Eliseo Vivas (*The Artistic Transaction*, 1963) and Murray Krieger (*The Play and Place of Criticism*, 1967).

conventions: All those devices of stylization, compression, and selection that constitute the necessary differences between art and life. According to the Russian Formalists, these conventions constitute the "literariness" of literature and are the only proper concern of the literary critic.

deconstruction: An extremely influential contemporary school of criticism based on the works of the French philosopher Jacques Derrida. Deconstruction treats literary works as unconscious reflections of the reigning myths of Western culture. The primary myth is that there is a meaningful world that language signifies or represents. The deconstructionist critic is most often concerned with showing how a literary text tacitly subverts the very assumptions or myths on which it ostensibly rests.

defamiliarization: Coined by Viktor Shklovsky in 1917, this term denotes a basic principle of Russian Formalism. Poetic language (by which the Formalists meant artful language, in prose as well as in poetry) defamiliarizes or "makes strange" familiar experiences. The technique of art, says Shklovsky, is to "make objects unfamiliar, to make forms difficult, to increase the difficulty and length of perception. . . . Art is a way of experiencing the artfulness of an object; the object is not important."

detective story: The so-called classic detective story (or mystery) is a highly formalized and logically structured mode of fiction in which the focus is on a crime solved by a detective through interpretation of evidence and ratiocination; the most famous detective in this mode is Arthur Conan Doyle's Sherlock Holmes. Many modern practitioners of the genre, however, such as Dashiell Hammett, Raymond Chandler, and Ross Macdonald, have de-emphasized the puzzlelike qualities of the detective story, stressing instead characterization, theme, and other elements of mainstream fiction.

determinism: The belief that an individual's actions are essentially determined by biological and environmental factors, with free will playing a negligible role. (See *naturalism.*)

dialogue: The similitude of conversation in fiction, dialogue serves to characterize, to further the *plot*, to establish *conflict*, and to express thematic ideas.

displacement: Popularized in criticism by Northrop Frye, this term refers to the author's attempt to make his or her story psychologically motivated and realistic, even as the latent structure of the mythical motivation moves relentlessly forward.

dominant: A term coined by Roman Jakobson to refer to that which "rules, determines, and transforms the remaining components in the work of a single artist, in a poetic canon, or in the work of an epoch." The shifting of the dominant in a *genre* accounts for the creation of new generic forms and new poetic epochs. For example, the rise of *realism* in the mid-nineteenth century indicates realistic conventions becoming dominant and *romance* or fantasy conventions becoming secondary.

doppelgänger: A double or counterpart of a person, sometimes endowed with ghostly qualities. A fictional character's doppelgänger often reflects a suppressed side of his or her personality. One of the classic examples of the doppelgänger motif is found in

Fyodor Dostoevski's novella *Dvoynik* (1846; *The Double*, 1917); Isaac Bashevis Singer and Jorge Luis Borges, among others, offer striking modern treatments of the doppelgänger.

epic: Although this term usually refers to a long narrative poem that presents the exploits of a central figure of high position, the term is also used to designate a long novel that has the style or structure usually associated with an epic. In this sense, for example, Herman Melville's *Moby Dick* (1851) and James Joyce's *Ulysses* (1922) may be called epics.

episodic narrative: A work that is held together primarily by a loose connection of self-sufficient episodes. *Picaresque novels* often have episodic structure.

epistolary novel: A novel made up of letters by one or more fictional characters. Samuel Richardson's *Pamela: Or, Virtue Rewarded* (1740-1741) is a well-known eighteenth century example. In the nineteenth century, Bram Stoker's *Dracula* (1897) is largely epistolary. The technique allows for several different points of view to be presented.

euphuism: A style of writing characterized by ornate language that is highly contrived, alliterative, and repetitious. Euphuism was developed by John Lyly in his *Euphues, the Anatomy of Wit* (1578) and was emulated frequently by writers of the Elizabethan Age.

existentialism: A philosophical, religious, and literary term, emerging from World War II, for a group of attitudes surrounding the pivotal notion that existence precedes essence. According to Jean-Paul Sartre, "Man is nothing else but what he makes himself." Forlornness arises from the death of God and the concomitant death of universal values, of any source of ultimate or a priori standards. Despair arises from the fact that an individual can reckon only with what depends on his or her will, and the sphere of that will is severely limited; the number of things on which he or she can have an impact is pathetically small. Existentialist literature is antideterministic in the extreme and rejects the idea that heredity and environment shape and determine human motivation and behavior.

exposition: The part or parts of a fiction that provide necessary background information. Exposition not only provides the time and place of the action but also introduces readers to the fictive world of the story, acquainting them with the ground rules of the work.

fantastic: In his study *The Fantastic* (1970), Tzvetan Todorov defines the fantastic as a *genre* that lies between the "uncanny" and the "marvelous." All three genres embody the familiar world but present an event that cannot be explained by the laws of the familiar world. Todorov says that the fantastic occupies a twilight zone between the uncanny (when the reader knows that the peculiar event is merely the result of an illusion) and the marvelous (when the reader understands that the event is supposed to take place in a realm controlled by laws unknown to humankind). The fantastic is thus essentially unsettling, provocative, even subversive.

feminist criticism: A criticism advocating equal rights for women in political, economic, social, psychological, personal, and aesthetic senses. On the thematic level, the feminist reader should identify with female characters and their concerns. The object is to provide a critique of phallocentric assumptions and an analysis of patriarchal ideologies inscribed in a literature that is male-centered and male-dominated. On the ideological level, feminist critics see gender, as well as the stereotypes that go along with it, as a cultural construct. They strive to define a particularly feminine content and to extend the *canon* so that it might include works by lesbians, feminists, and women writers in general.

flashback: A scene in a fiction that depicts an earlier event; it may be presented as a reminiscence by a character in the story or may simply be inserted into the narrative.

foreshadowing: A device to create suspense or dramatic irony in fiction by indicating through suggestion what will take place in the future.

formalist criticism: Two particularly influential formalist schools of criticism arose in the twentieth century: the Russian Formalists and the American New Critics. The Russian Formalists were concerned with the conventional devices used in literature to defamiliarize that which habit has made familiar. The New Critics believed that literary criticism is a description and evaluation of its object and that the primary concern of the critic is with the work's unity. Both schools of criticism, at their most extreme, treated literary works as artifacts or constructs divorced from their biographical and social contexts.

genre: In its most general sense, this term refers to a group of literary works defined by a common form, style, or purpose. In practice, the term is used in a wide variety of overlapping and, to a degree, contradictory senses. Tragedy and comedy are thus described as distinct genres; the novel (a form that includes both tragic and comic works) is a genre; and various subspecies of the novel, such as the *gothic* and the *picaresque*, are themselves frequently treated as distinct genres. Finally, the term "genre fiction" refers to forms of popular fiction in which the writer is bound by more or less rigid conventions. Indeed, all these diverse usages have in common an emphasis on the manner in which individual literary works are shaped by particular expectations and conventions; this is the subject of genre criticism.

genre fiction: Categories of popular fiction in which the writers are bound by more or less rigid conventions, such as in the *detective story*, the *romance*, and the *Western*. Although the term can be used in a neutral sense, it is often used dismissively.

gothic novel: A form of fiction developed in the eighteenth century that focuses on horror and the supernatural. In his preface to *The Castle of Otranto* (1765), the first gothic novel in English, Horace Walpole claimed that he was trying to combine two kinds of fiction, with events and story typical of the medieval romance and character delineation typical of the realistic novel. Other examples of the form are Matthew Gregory

Lewis's *The Monk: A Romance* (1796; also known as *Ambrosio: Or, The Monk*) and Mary Wollstonecraft Shelley's *Frankenstein: Or, The Modern Prometheus* (1818).

grotesque: According to Wolfgang Kayser (*The Grotesque in Art and Literature*, 1963), the grotesque is an embodiment in literature of the estranged world. Characterized by a breakup of the everyday world by mysterious forces, the form differs from fantasy in that the reader is not sure whether to react with humor or with horror and in that the exaggeration manifested exists in the familiar world rather than in a purely imaginative world.

Hebraic/Homeric styles: Terms coined by Erich Auerbach in *Mimesis: The Representation of Reality in Western Literature* (1953) to designate two basic fictional styles. The Hebraic style focuses only on the decisive points of narrative and leaves all else obscure, mysterious, and "fraught with background"; the Homeric style places the narrative in a definite time and place and externalizes everything in a perpetual foreground.

historical criticism: In contrast to *formalist criticism*, which treats literary works to a great extent as self-contained artifacts, historical criticism emphasizes the historical context of literature; the two approaches, however, need not be mutually exclusive. Ernst Robert Curtius's *European Literature and the Latin Middle Ages* (1940) is a prominent example of historical criticism.

historical novel: A novel that depicts past historical events, usually public in nature, and features real as well as fictional people. Sir Walter Scott's Waverley novels established the basic type, but the relationship between fiction and history in the form varies greatly depending on the practitioner.

implied author: According to Wayne Booth (*The Rhetoric of Fiction*, 1961), the novel often creates a kind of second self who tells the story—a self who is wiser, more sensitive, and more perceptive than any real person could be.

interior monologue: Defined by Édouard Dujardin as the speech of a character designed to introduce the reader directly to the character's internal life, the form differs from other kinds of monologue in that it attempts to reproduce thought before any logical organization is imposed on it. See, for example, Molly Bloom's long interior monologue at the conclusion of James Joyce's *Ulysses* (1922).

irrealism: A term often used to refer to modern or postmodern fiction that is presented self-consciously as a fiction or a fabulation rather than a mimesis of external reality. The best-known practitioners of irrealism are John Barth, Robert Coover, and Donald Barthelme.

local colorists: A loose movement of late nineteenth century American writers whose fiction emphasizes the distinctive folkways, landscapes, and dialects of various regions. Important local colorists include Bret Harte, Mark Twain, George Washington Cable, Kate Chopin, and Sarah Orne Jewett. (See *regional novel.*)

Marxist criticism: Based on the nineteenth century writings of Karl Marx and Friedrich Engels, Marxist criticism views literature as a product of ideological forces determined by the dominant class. However, many Marxists believe that literature operates according to its own autonomous standards of production and reception: It is both a product of ideology and able to determine ideology. As such, literature may overcome the dominant paradigms of its age and play a revolutionary role in society.

metafiction: This term refers to fiction that manifests a reflexive tendency, such as Vladimir Nabokov's *Pale Fire* (1962) and John Fowles's *The French Lieutenant's Woman* (1969). The emphasis is on the loosening of the work's illusion of reality to expose the reality of its illusion. Other terms used to refer to this type of fiction include "irrealism," "postmodernist fiction," "antifiction," and "surfiction."

modernism: An international movement in the arts that began in the early years of the twentieth century. Although the term is used to describe artists of widely varying persuasions, modernism in general was characterized by its international idiom, by its interest in cultures distant in space or time, by its emphasis on formal experimentation, and by its sense of dislocation and radical change.

motif: A conventional incident or situation in a fiction that may serve as the basis for the structure of the narrative itself. The Russian Formalist critic Boris Tomashevsky uses the term to refer to the smallest particle of thematic material in a work.

motivation: Although this term is usually used in reference to the convention of justifying the action of a character from his or her psychological makeup, the Russian Formalists use the term to refer to the network of devices that justify the introduction of individual *motifs* or groups of motifs in a work. For example, "compositional motivation" refers to the principle that every single property in a work contributes to its overall effect; "realistic motivation" refers to the realistic devices used to make a work plausible and lifelike.

multiculturalism: The tendency to recognize the perspectives of those traditionally excluded from the canon of Western art and literature. In order to promote multiculturalism, publishers and educators have revised textbooks and school curricula to incorporate material by and about women, members of minority groups, persons from non-Western cultures, and homosexuals.

myth: Anonymous traditional stories dealing with basic human concepts and antinomies. According to Claude Lévi-Strauss, myth is that part of language where the "formula *tradutore, tradittore* reaches its lowest truth value. . . . Its substance does not lie in its style, its original music, or its syntax, but in the story which it tells."

myth criticism: Northrop Frye says that in myth "we see the structural principles of literature isolated." Myth criticism is concerned with these basic principles of literature; it is not to be confused with mythological criticism, which is primarily concerned with finding mythological parallels in the surface action of the *narrative.*

narrative: Robert Scholes and Robert Kellogg, in *The Nature of Narrative* (1966), say that by "narrative" they mean literary works that include both a story and a storyteller. The term "narrative" usually implies a contrast to "enacted" fiction such as drama.

narratology: The study of the form and functioning of *narratives*; it attempts to examine what all narratives have in common and what makes individual narratives different from one another.

narrator: The *character* who recounts the *narrative*, or story. Wayne Booth describes various dramatized narrators in *The Rhetoric of Fiction* (1961): unacknowledged centers of consciousness, observers, narrator-agents, and self-conscious narrators. Booth suggests that the important elements to consider in narration are the relationships among the narrator, the author, the characters, and the reader.

naturalism: As developed by Émile Zola in the late nineteenth century, naturalism is the application of the principles of scientific *determinism* to fiction. Although it usually refers more to the choice of subject matter than to technical conventions, those conventions associated with the movement center on the author's attempt to be precise and scientifically objective in description and detail, regardless of whether the events described are sordid or shocking.

New Criticism: See *formalist criticism.*

novel: Perhaps the most difficult of all fictional forms to define because of its multiplicity of modes. Edouard, in André Gide's *Les Faux-monnayeurs* (1925; *The Counterfeiters*, 1927), says the novel is the freest and most lawless of all *genres*; he wonders if fear of that liberty is the reason the novel has so timidly clung to reality. Most critics seem to agree that the novel's primary area of concern is the social world. Ian Watt (*The Rise of the Novel*, 2001) says that the novel can be distinguished from other fictional forms by the attention it pays to individual characterization and detailed presentation of the environment. Moreover, says Watt, the novel, more than any other fictional form, is interested in the "development of its characters in the course of time."

novel of manners: The classic examples of this form might be the novels of Jane Austen, wherein the customs and conventions of a social group of a particular time and place are realistically, and often satirically, portrayed.

novella, novelle, nouvelle, novelette, novela: Although these terms often refer to the short European tale, especially the Renaissance form employed by Giovanni Boccaccio, the terms often refer to that form of fiction that is said to be longer than a short story and shorter than a novel. "Novelette" is the term usually preferred by the British, whereas "novella" is the term usually used to refer to American works in this *genre*. Henry James claimed that the main merit of the form is the "effort to do the complicated thing with a strong brevity and lucidity."

phenomenological criticism: Although best known as a European school of criticism practiced by Georges Poulet and others, this so-called criticism of consciousness is also propounded in the United States by such critics as J. Hillis Miller. The focus is less on individual works and *genres* than it is on literature as an act; the work is not seen as an object but rather as part of a strand of latent impulses in the work of a single author or an epoch.

picaresque novel: A form of fiction that centers on a central rogue figure, or picaro, who usually tells his or her own story. The plot structure is normally *episodic*, and the episodes usually focus on how the picaro lives by his or her wits. Classic examples of the mode are Henry Fielding's *The History of Tom Jones, a Foundling* (1749; commonly known as *Tom Jones*) and Mark Twain's *Adventures of Huckleberry Finn* (1884).

plot/story: "Story" refers to the full *narrative* of *character* and action, whereas "plot" generally refers to action with little reference to character. A more precise and helpful distinction is made by the Russian Formalists, who suggest that "plot" refers to the events of a narrative as they have been artfully arranged in the literary work, subject to chronological displacement, ellipses, and other devices, while "story" refers to the sum of the same events arranged in simple, causal-chronological order. Thus story is the raw material for plot. By comparing the two in a given work, the reader is encouraged to see the narrative as an artifact.

point of view: The means by which the story is presented to the reader, or, as Percy Lubbock says in *The Craft of Fiction* (1921), "the relation in which the narrator stands to the story"—a relation that Lubbock claims governs the craft of fiction. Some of the questions the critical reader should ask concerning point of view are the following: Who talks to the reader? From what position does the narrator tell the story? At what distance does he or she place the reader from the story? What kind of person is he or she? How fully is he or she characterized? How reliable is he or she? For further discussion, see Wayne Booth, *The Rhetoric of Fiction* (1961).

postcolonialism: Postcolonial literature emerged in the mid-twentieth century when colonies in Asia, Africa, and the Caribbean began gaining their independence from the European nations that had long controlled them. Postcolonial authors, such as Salman Rushdie and V. S. Naipaul, tend to focus on both the freedom and the conflict inherent in living in a postcolonial state.

postmodernism: A ubiquitous but elusive term in contemporary criticism, "postmodernism" is loosely applied to the various artistic movements that followed the era of so-called high modernism, represented by such giants as James Joyce and Pablo Picasso. In critical discussions of contemporary fiction, the term "postmodernism" is frequently applied to the works of writers such as Thomas Pynchon, John Barth, and Donald Barthelme, who exhibit a self-conscious awareness of their modernist predecessors as well as a reflexive treatment of fictional form.

protagonist: The central *character* in a fiction, the character whose fortunes most concern the reader.

psychological criticism: While much modern literary criticism reflects to some degree the impacts of Sigmund Freud, Carl Jung, Jacques Lacan, and other psychological theorists, the term "psychological criticism" suggests a strong emphasis on a causal relation between the writer's psychological state, variously interpreted, and his or her works. A notable example of psychological criticism is Norman Fruman's *Coleridge, the Damaged Archangel* (1971).

psychological novel: A form of fiction in which *character*, especially the inner lives of characters, is the primary focus. This form, which has been of primary importance at least since Henry James, characterizes much of the work of James Joyce, Virginia Woolf, and William Faulkner. For a detailed discussion, see *The Modern Psychological Novel* (1955) by Leon Edel.

realism: A literary technique in which the primary convention is to render an illusion of fidelity to external reality. Realism is often identified as the primary method of the novel form: It focuses on surface details, maintains a fidelity to the everyday experiences of middle-class society, and strives for a one-to-one relationship between the fiction and the action imitated. The realist movement in the late nineteenth century coincides with the full development of the novel form.

reception aesthetics: The best-known American practitioner of reception aesthetics is Stanley Fish. For the reception critic, meaning is an event or process; rather than being embedded in the work, it is created through particular acts of reading. The best-known European practitioner of this criticism, Wolfgang Iser, argues that indeterminacy is the basic characteristic of literary texts; the reader must "normalize" the text either by projecting his or her standards into it or by revising his or her standards to "fit" the text.

regional novel: Any novel in which the character of a given geographical region plays a decisive role. Although regional differences persist across the United States, a considerable leveling in speech and customs has taken place, so that the sharp regional distinctions evident in nineteenth century American fiction have all but disappeared. Only in the South has a strong regional tradition persisted to the present. (See *local colorists*.)

rhetorical criticism: The rhetorical critic is concerned with the literary work as a means of communicating ideas and the means by which the work affects or controls the reader. Such criticism seems best suited to didactic works such as satire.

roman à clef: A fiction wherein actual people, often celebrities of some sort, are thinly disguised.

romance: The romance usually differs from the novel form in that the focus is on symbolic events and representational characters rather than on "as-if-real" characters and events. Richard Chase says that in the romance, character is depicted as highly stylized, a function of the plot rather than as someone complexly related to society. The romancer is more likely to be concerned with dreamworlds than with the familiar world, believing that reality cannot be grasped by the traditional novel.

Romanticism: A widespread cultural movement in the late eighteenth and early nineteenth centuries, the influence of which is still felt. As a general literary tendency, Romanticism is frequently contrasted with *classicism.* Although many varieties of Romanticism are indigenous to various national literatures, the term generally suggests an assertion of the preeminence of the imagination. Other values associated with various schools of Romanticism include primitivism, an interest in folklore, a reverence for nature, and a fascination with the demoniac and the macabre.

scene: The central element of *narration*; specific actions are narrated or depicted that make the reader feel he or she is participating directly in the action.

science fiction: Fiction in which certain givens (physical laws, psychological principles, social conditions—any one or all of these) form the basis of an imaginative projection into the future or, less commonly, an extrapolation in the present or even into the past.

semiotics: The science of signs and sign systems in communication. According to Roman Jakobson, semiotics deals with the principles that underlie the structure of signs, their use in language of all kinds, and the specific nature of various sign systems.

sentimental novel: A form of fiction popular in the eighteenth century in which emotionalism and optimism are the primary characteristics. The best-known examples are Samuel Richardson's *Pamela: Or, Virtue Rewarded* (1740-1741) and Oliver Goldsmith's *The Vicar of Wakefield* (1766).

setting: The circumstances and environment, both temporal and spatial, of a *narrative.*

spatial form: An author's attempt to make the reader apprehend a work spatially in a moment of time rather than sequentially. To achieve this effect, the author breaks up the *narrative* into interspersed fragments. Beginning with James Joyce, Marcel Proust, and Djuna Barnes, the movement toward spatial form is concomitant with the *modernist* effort to supplant historical time in fiction with mythic time. For the seminal discussion of this technique, see Joseph Frank, *The Widening Gyre* (1963).

stream of consciousness: The depiction of the thought processes of a *character*, insofar as this is possible, without any mediating structures. The metaphor of consciousness as a "stream" suggests a rush of thoughts and images governed by free association rather than by strictly rational development. The term "stream of consciousness" is often used loosely as a synonym for *interior monologue.* The most celebrated example of stream of consciousness in fiction is the monologue of Molly Bloom in James Joyce's *Ulysses* (1922); other notable practitioners of the stream-of-consciousness technique include Dorothy Richardson, Virginia Woolf, and William Faulkner.

structuralism: As a movement of thought, structuralism is based on the idea of intrinsic, self-sufficient structures that do not require reference to external elements. A structure is a system of transformations that involves the interplay of laws inherent in the system itself. The study of language is the primary model for contemporary structuralism. The structuralist literary critic attempts to define structural principles that operate intertextually throughout the whole of literature as well as principles that operate in *genres* and in individual works. One of the most accessible surveys of structuralism and literature available is Jonathan Culler's *Structuralist Poetics* (1975).

summary: Those parts of a fiction that do not need to be detailed. In *Tom Jones* (1749), Henry Fielding says, "If whole years should pass without producing anything worthy of . . . notice . . . we shall hasten on to matters of consequence."

thematics: According to Northrop Frye, when a work of fiction is written or interpreted thematically, it becomes an illustrative fable. Murray Krieger defines thematics as "the study of the experiential tensions which, dramatically entangled in the literary work, become an existential reflection of that work's aesthetic complexity."

tone: The dominant mood of a work of fiction. (See *atmosphere.*)

unreliable narrator: A narrator whose account of the events of the story cannot be trusted, obliging readers to reconstruct—if possible—the true state of affairs themselves. Once an innovative technique, the use of the unreliable narrator has become commonplace among contemporary writers who wish to suggest the impossibility of a truly "reliable" account of any event. Notable examples of the unreliable narrator can be found in Ford Madox Ford's *The Good Soldier* (1915) and Vladimir Nabokov's *Lolita* (1955).

Victorian novel: Although the Victorian period extended from 1837 to 1901, the term "Victorian novel" does not include the later decades of Queen Victoria's reign. The term loosely refers to the sprawling works of novelists such as Charles Dickens and William Makepeace Thackeray—works that frequently appeared first in serial form and are characterized by a broad social canvas.

vraisemblance/verisimilitude: Tzvetan Todorov defines vraisemblance as "the mask which conceals the text's own laws, but which we are supposed to take for a relation to reality." Verisimilitude refers to a work's attempts to make the reader believe that it conforms to reality rather than to its own laws.

Western novel: Like all varieties of *genre fiction*, the Western novel—generally known simply as the Western—is defined by a relatively predictable combination of *conventions*, *motifs*, and recurring themes. These predictable elements, familiar from many Western films and television series, differentiate the Western from *historical novels* and idiosyncratic works such as Thomas Berger's *Little Big Man* (1964) that are also set in the Old West. Conversely, some novels set in the contemporary West are regarded as Westerns because they deal with modern cowboys and with the land itself in the manner characteristic of the *genre*.

Charles E. May

GUIDE TO ONLINE RESOURCES

WEB SITES

The following sites were visited by the editors of Salem Press in 2009. Because URLs frequently change, the accuracy of these addresses cannot be guaranteed; however, long-standing sites, such as those of colleges and universities, national organizations, and government agencies, generally maintain links when sites are moved or updated.

American Literature on the Web

http://www.nagasaki-gaigo.ac.jp/ishikawa/amlit

Among this site's features are several pages providing links to Web sites about specific genres and literary movements, southern and southwestern American literature, minority literature, literary theory, and women writers, as well as an extensive index of links to electronic text collections and archives. Users also can access information for five specific time periods: 1620-1820, 1820-1865, 1865-1914, 1914-1945, and since 1945. A range of information is available for each period, including alphabetical lists of authors that link to more specific information about each writer, time lines of historical and literary events, and links to related additional Web sites.

Books and Writers

http://www.kirjasto.sci.fi/indeksi.htm

This broad, comprehensive, and easy-to-use resource provides access to information about hundreds of authors throughout the world, extending from 70 B.C.E to the twenty-first century. Links take users from an alphabetical list of authors to pages featuring biographical material, lists of works, and recommendations for further reading about individual authors; each writer's page also includes links to related pages on the site. Although brief, the biographical essays provide solid overviews of the authors' careers, their contributions to literature, and their literary influences.

The Canadian Literature Archive

http://www.umanitoba.ca/canlit

Created and maintained by the English Department at the University of Manitoba, this site is a comprehensive collection of materials for and about Canadian writers. It includes an alphabetical listing of authors with links to additional Web-based information. Users also can retrieve electronic texts, announcements of literary events, and videocasts of author interviews and readings.

A Celebration of Women Writers

http://digital.library.upenn.edu/women

This site presents an extensive compendium of information about the contributions of women writers throughout history. The "Local Editions by Authors" and "Local Editions by Category" pages include access to electronic texts of the works of numerous writers, including Louisa May Alcott, Djuna Barnes, Grazia Deledda, Edith Wharton, and Virginia Woolf. Users can also access biographical and bibliographical information by browsing lists arranged by writers' names, countries of origin, ethnicities, and the centuries in which they lived.

Contemporary Writers

http://www.contemporarywriters.com/authors

Created by the British Council, this site offers "up-to-date profiles of some of the U.K. and Commonwealth's most important living writers (plus writers from the Republic of Ireland that we've worked with)." The available information includes biographies, bibliographies, critical reviews, news about literary prizes, and photographs. Users can search the site by author, genre, nationality, gender, publisher, book title, date of publication, and prize name and date.

Internet Public Library: Native American Authors

http://www.ipl.org/div/natam

Internet Public Library, a Web-based collection of materials, includes this index to resources about writers of Native American heritage. An alphabetical list of authors enables users to link to biographies, lists of works, electronic texts, tribal Web sites, and other online resources. The majority of the writers covered are contemporary Indian authors, but some historical authors also are featured. Users also can retrieve information by browsing lists of titles and tribes. In addition, the site contains a bibliography of print and online materials about Native American literature.

LiteraryHistory.com

http://www.literaryhistory.com

This site is an excellent source of academic, scholarly, and critical literature about eighteenth, nineteenth, and twentieth century American and English writers. It provides numerous pages about specific eras and genres, including individual pages for eighteenth, nineteenth, and twentieth century literature and for African American and postcolonial literature. These pages contain alphabetical lists of authors that link to articles, reviews, overviews, excerpts of works, teaching guides, podcast interviews, and other materials. The eighteenth century literature page also provides access to information about the eighteenth century novel.

Literary Resources on the Net

http://andromeda.rutgers.edu/~jlynch/Lit

Jack Lynch of Rutgers University maintains this extensive collection of links to Internet sites that are useful to academics, including numerous Web sites about American and English literature. This collection is a good place to begin online research about the novel, as it links to hundreds of other sites with broad ranges of literary topics. The site is organized chronically, with separate pages for information about the Middle Ages, the Renaissance, the eighteenth century, the Romantic and Victorian eras, and twentieth century British and Irish literature. It also has separate pages providing links to Web sites about American literature and to women's literature and feminism.

LitWeb

http://litweb.net

LitWeb provides biographies of more than five hundred world authors throughout history that can be accessed through an alphabetical listing. The pages about each writer contain a list of his or her works, suggestions for further reading, and illustrations. The site also offers information about past and present winners of major literary prizes.

The Modern Word: Authors of the Libyrinth

http://www.themodernword.com/authors.html

The Modern Word site, although somewhat haphazard in its organization, provides a great deal of critical information about writers. The "Authors of the Libyrinth" page is very useful, linking author names to essays about them and other resources. The section of the page headed "The Scriptorium" presents "an index of pages featuring writers who have pushed the edges of their medium, combining literary talent with a sense of experimentation to produce some remarkable works of modern literature." The site also includes sections devoted to Samuel Beckett, Umberto Eco, Gabriel García Márquez, James Joyce, Franz Kafka, and Thomas Pynchon.

Novels

http://www.nvcc.edu/home/ataormina/novels/default.htm

This overview of American and English novels was prepared by Agatha Taormina, a professor at Northern Virginia Community College. It contains three sections: "History" provides a definition of the novel genre, a discussion of its origins in eighteenth century England, and separate pages with information about genres and authors of nineteenth century, twentieth century, and postmodern novels. "Approaches" suggests how to read a novel critically for greater appreciation, and "Resources" provides a list of books about the novel.

Outline of American Literature
http://www.america.gov/publications/books/outline-of-american-literature.html

This page of the America.gov site provides access to an electronic version of the ten-chapter volume *Outline of American Literature*, a historical overview of prose and poetry from colonial times to the present published by the U.S. Department of State. The work's author is Kathryn VanSpanckeren, professor of English at the University of Tampa. The site offers links to abbreviated versions of each chapter as well as access to the entire publication in PDF format.

Voice of the Shuttle
http://vos.ucsb.edu

One of the most complete and authoritative places for online information about literature, Voice of the Shuttle is maintained by professors and students in the English Department at the University of California, Santa Barbara. The site provides thousands of links to electronic books, academic journals, association Web sites, sites created by university professors, and many, many other resources about the humanities. Its "Literature in English" page provides links to separate pages about the literature of the Anglo-Saxon era, the Middle Ages, the Renaissance and seventeenth century, the Restoration and eighteenth century, the Romantic age, the Victorian age, and modern and contemporary periods in Britain and the United States, as well as a page focused on minority literature. Another page on the site, "Literatures Other than English," offers a gateway to information about the literature of numerous countries and world regions.

ELECTRONIC DATABASES

Electronic databases usually do not have their own URLs. Instead, public, college, and university libraries subscribe to these databases, provide links to them on their Web sites, and make them available to library card holders or other specified patrons. Readers can visit library Web sites or ask reference librarians to check on availability.

Canadian Literary Centre

Produced by EBSCO, the Canadian Literary Centre database contains full-text content from ECW Press, a Toronto-based publisher, including the titles in the publisher's Canadian fiction studies, Canadian biography, and Canadian writers and their works series, *ECW's Biographical Guide to Canadian Novelists*, and *George Woodcock's Introduction to Canadian Fiction*. Author biographies, essays and literary criticism, and book reviews are among the database's offerings.

Literary Reference Center

EBSCO's Literary Reference Center (LRC) is a comprehensive full-text database designed primarily to help high school and undergraduate students in English and the humanities with homework and research assignments about literature. The database contains massive amounts of information from reference works, books, literary journals, and other materials, including more than 31,000 plot summaries, synopses, and overviews of literary works; almost 100,000 essays and articles of literary criticism; about 140,000 author biographies; more than 605,000 book reviews; and more than 5,200 author interviews. It also contains the entire contents of Salem Press's MagillOnLiterature Plus. Users can retrieve information by browsing a list of authors' names or titles of literary works; they can also use an advanced search engine to access information by numerous categories, including author name, gender, cultural identity, national identity, and the years in which he or she lived, or by literary title, character, locale, genre, and publication date. The Literary Reference Center also features a literary-historical time line, an encyclopedia of literature, and a glossary of literary terms.

MagillOnLiterature Plus

MagillOnLiterature Plus is a comprehensive, integrated literature database produced by Salem Press and available on the EBSCO*host* platform. The database contains the full text of essays in Salem's many literature-related reference works, including *Masterplots*, *Cyclopedia of World Authors*, *Cyclopedia of Literary Characters*, *Cyclopedia of Literary Places*, *Critical Survey of Long Fiction*, *Critical Survey of Short Fiction*, *World Philosophers and Their Works*, *Magill's Literary Annual*, and *Magill's Book Reviews.* Among its contents are articles on more than 35,000 literary works and more than 8,500 writers, poets, dramatists, essays, and philosophers, more than 1,000 images, and a glossary of more than 1,300 literary terms. The biographical essays include lists of authors' works and secondary bibliographies, and almost four hundred overview essays offer information about literary genres, time periods, and national literatures.

NoveList

NoveList is a readers' advisory service produced by EBSCO. The database provides access to 155,000 titles of both adult and juvenile fiction as well information about literary awards, book discussion guides, feature articles about a range of literary genres, and "recommended reads." Users can search by author name, book title, or series title or can describe the plot to retrieve the name of a book, information about the author, and book reviews; another search engine enables users to find titles similar to books they have enjoyed reading.

Rebecca Kuzins

GEOGRAPHICAL INDEX

SUBJECT INDEX